GETTING BETTER

Television & Moral Progress

GETTING
BETTER

Henry J. Perkinson

WITH A NEW EPILOGUE
BY THE AUTHOR

Transaction Publishers
New Brunswick (U.S.A.) and London (U.K.)

First paperback edition 1996
New material this edition copyright © 1996 by Transaction Publishers, New Brunswick, New Jersey 08903. Copyright © 1991 by Transaction Publishers.

This book is printed on acid-free paper that meets the American National Standard for Permanence of Paper for Printed Library Materials.

Library of Congress Catalog Number: 95-22872
ISBN: 1-56000-864-4
Printed in the United States of America

Library of Congress Cataloging-in-Publication Data

Perkinson, Henry J.
  Getting better : television and moral progress / Henry J. Perkinson ; with a new epilogue by the author.
      p. cm.
  Includes bibliographical references (p.   ) and index.
  ISBN 1-56000-864-4 (pbk. : alk. paper)
  1. Television broadcasting—United States—Moral and ethical aspects. 2. United States—Civilization—1945- I. Title.
HE8700.8.P47 1995
302.23'45—dc20   95-22872
                                                                    CIP

For Audrey

The greatest events ... are comprehended last: The generations which are their contemporaries do not experience such events—they live past them.

—Friedrick Nietzsche, August 1886

I believe television is going to be the test of the modern world, and that in this new opportunity to see beyond the range of our vision we shall discover either a new and unbearable disturbance of the general peace or a saving radiance in the sky. We shall stand or fall by television—of that I am quite sure.

—E. B. White, July 1938

Contents

1

How Television Made Civilization Moral

We continually hear much about the "bad" effects of television and little or nothing about its "good" effects. This book is about how television has made things better ... or, more precisely, how television has made our culture more moral.

The facts about television are well known:

- In 1948 there were fewer than one hundred thousand television sets in the United States; one year later, Americans possessed 1 million sets. By 1954, more than 40 million sets were around, and the next year—1960— 150 million Americans claimed to have television sets. Presently, there are one and a half television sets for every household in the United States.[1]
- Over 90 million people watch television every day. (At the high point of movies, in 1945, 90 million people went to the movies once a week.)[2]
- The average home has its TV set on for more than seven hours per day.[3]
- The average U.S. citizen watches about twelve hundred hours of TV each year, and Americans spend about half of their leisure time viewing TV.[4]
- From age five to eighteen, an American child watches approximately fifteen thousand hours of TV—30 percent more than the number of hours spent in school.[5]

Given these facts, it seems reasonable to conclude that television must have a significant impact on U.S. culture. Strangely enough, few scholars have studied this matter. Instead, they have conducted

1

extensive research on the impact of television on people. These investigators have specially worried about the impact of television on young people. The advent of television obviously reduced the amount of time children spend playing; it decreased the amount of time children spend on cooking, cleaning, and other household chores; moreover, children now spend less time reading, listening to the radio, and going to the movies. Television, in short, has cut into all the activities of daily life. But researchers have worried most about children's values, attitudes, and behavior—has television changed them?

The first major study of the effects of television on people appeared in 1961 in a book written by Professors Wilbur Schram, Jack Lyle, and Edwin Parker and called *Television in the Lives of our Children*. Based on eleven separate investigations in ten different communities, the project examined how children used television. Not unexpectedly, they found that children selected material on television that best fit their interests and needs. As to effects on children, the researchers found that these were minimal. TV provided a great deal of children's incidental learning: It improved the vocabulary and played a role in children's fantasy life. But the research identified no dramatic or threatening influence, as was evident from the widely quoted conclusion: "For *some* children, under *some* conditions, *some* television is harmful. For *other* children, under the same conditions, or for the same children under other conditions, it may be beneficial. For *most* children, under *most* conditions, *most* television is probably neither harmful nor particularly beneficial."[6]

As the 1960s wore on, however, more and more Americans expressed the opinion that—in spite of the research findings—TV was responsible for the rising crime rates (according to the FBI, violent crime increased 100 percent between 1958 and 1968), the urban riots (between 1964 and 1968, riots broke out in over 100 cities), and the political assassinations (between 1963 and 1968 four major political figures were assassinated). The problem of increased civic unrest brought President Johnson in June 1968 to create a National Commission on the Causes and Prevention of Violence (NCCPV). In addition to its final report submitted in December 1969, the commission issued a fifteen-volume series of reports, one of which was *Violence and the Media*, edited by Robert Baker and Sandra Ball.[7]

Part of this report contained a content analysis of portrayals of violence in prime-time television programs. Overall, this analysis revealed that TV presented the United States as a violent country, filled with many violent people. On television, people not only used violence as the main means to reach their goals, violence also served as the primary method of conflict resolution. The task force went beyond analysis to try to find out if the norms of television modified or changed the actual norms of the viewing audience. It concluded that watching TV violence could both reenforce violent behavior and cause it. The investigators made no claim that exposure alone changed people. Rather such change as occurred, they explained, was a matter of social learning, which takes place largely through the process of identification.

Following the report of the NCCPV, Congress funded a large-scale research program to probe the issues of televised violence more thoroughly. This major research project produced five volumes collectively referred to as the "Surgeon General's Report." Adopting the social learning theory employed by the NCCPV, the research project went further insofar as the investigators tried to ascertain under what condition people did accept TV models as guides to behavior. They found that the condition of continual exposure to violence did lead to an increase in aggressive behavior.[8]

Form Over Content

All the studies I have mentioned so far assumed that it is the content of television that effects human conduct. During the 1950s and 1960s, another, more controversial, approach appeared—an approach that regarded the *form* of television as the cause of changes in human behavior. As Marshal McLuhan, the most famous proponent of this approach put it: "The medium is the message." (The "content" of a medium, he quipped, is like the juicy piece of meat carried by the burglar to distract the watchdog of the mind.)[9]

For McLuhan, all media—in and of themselves—exert a compelling influence on people. Prehistoric, or tribal man, McLuhan maintained, existed in a harmonious balance of the senses, perceiving the world equally through hearing, smell, touch, sight, and taste. Technological innovations, however, extend human abilities and senses, thereby altering their balance, changing man and what he perceives, and modifying his conduct and behavior. McLuhan maintained that the wheel was simply an extension of the foot, clothing an extension of the skin, and the phonetic alphabet an extension of the eye. But his main focus of interest was on what he claimed were the basic technological innovations in the history of human culture: the invention of the phonetic alphabet, which jolted tribal man out of his sensory balance and gave dominance to the eye; the introduction of moveable type, which accelerated this process; and the invention of the telegraph in 1844, which heralded an electronic revolution that will ultimately retribalize man by restoring his sensory balance. The electronic media are the telegraph, radio, film, telephone, computer, and television—all of which have not only extended a single sense or function, as the older media did, but have enhanced and extended our entire central nervous system, "thus transforming all aspects of our social and psychic existence."[10]

In spite of what one might assume, television, according to McLuhan, does not simply, or even primarily, extend our visual sense. Unlike film or photography, television is primarily an extension of the sense of touch. This follows, McLuhan argues, from the fact that the television image is one of low intensity or definition that, unlike the photograph or film, induces the active participation of the viewer. In McLuhan's jargon, television is a "cool" medium where the viewer "continually fills in vague and blurry images, bringing himself into in-depth involvement with the screen and acting out a constant creative dialogue with the iconoscope.[11] So, the primary effect of TV on people is that it makes them seek involvement and participation. McLuhan traced these effects in the "new sensitivity to the dance, plastic arts and artifacts, as well as the demand for the small car, the paperback, sculptured hairdos, and molded dress effects—to say nothing of a new concern for complex efforts in cuisine and in the use of wines." The preference for depth participation has also prompted in the young a strong desire for religious experience. Moreover, it has destroyed the lineality fostered by printing: Since TV, "the assembly line has disappeared from industry. Staff and line structures have dissolved in management. Gone are the stag line, the part line, the receiving line, and the pencil line from the back of nylons." And TV, McLuhan tells us, caused the abrupt decline of baseball(!).[12]

Although some of McLuhan's proclamations ("probes," he called them) sound like madcap poetry of free association, there does seem to be some credibility to the claim that the medium is the message. Harold Innis for example, McLuhan's lesser known and less flamboyant mentor, argued that all media have a bias toward space and time; when people wrote on stone tablets, the messages lasted a long time, but they couldn't be carried very far—such writing was biased in favor of time and against space. But when people began to write on paper, this medium was biased in favor of space (it could be easily carried great distances) and against time (its longevity was limited). From such characteristics of media, Innis drew some startling conclusions, such as that with the advent of writing on paper (or papyrus) it became possible to maintain a complex political identity over wide geographical areas with far-flung bureaucratic controls.

Neil Postman, another believer in the primacy of form, believes, like Innis, that different media of communication have different biases. He suggests that each medium—speech, print, or television, for example—changes the structure of discourse by encouraging certain uses of the intellect, by forming certain definitions of intelligence and wisdom, and by demanding a certain kind of content.[13] He has argued, for example, that television has caused the disappearance of childhood: In a print culture, he says, many adult "secrets" were kept hidden from (innocent) children; but television has disclosed those secrets to all, hence the disappearance of childhood. He has also argued that television has become the first curriculum for all young people, relegating the curriculum of the schools to second place and causing, in its wake, attempts by schools to become more and more places of entertainment and teachers to be more and more like television performers.[14] In his most recent book, *Amusing Ourselves to Death*, Postman argues that television has converted politics and religion into entertainment.

The Viewer as Agent

All these scholars and researchers, both those who study the content of TV and those who analyze its form, have focused on the impact of television on human beings, on how television has changed how people think, feel, believe, and behave. Now, television probably does effect people, and it is likely that both the content as well as the form of the medium affects them. But there are no uniform effects, nor are all people affected equally. So, generalizations about the effects of television on people are hard to come by. Indeed, the effects of television on people are, in great part, a product of what the viewer brings to television, and this varies as the viewer is young or old, male or female, black or white, experienced or inexperienced, etc. So, any generalizations about television must be highly qualified.

My own objections to this approach to understanding the effects of television focus on the epistemological assumptions inherent in it. First, although many of its supporters deny it, this approach construes human beings as passive receptors whose conduct is determined by what they receive. Look at the verbs used by those who adopt this approach. They say that television "causes," "influences," "activates," "cultivates," "models," "shapes,"and "reenforces" what people think, feel, believe, and do.

The odor of determinism is here, although many try to ignore it. This approach assumes that people, in one way or another, become what they behold. If television is nonlinear, violent, sexist, racist, present-centered, or nonanalytical, then, the argument goes, people who watch television will become nonlinear, violent, sexist, racist, present-centered, and nonanalytical. In addition, there is usually an unwitting acceptance of the notion that human beings learn through induction: The more one watches television, the more instances one experiences, the stronger will be its impact on one's thoughts, feelings, and behavior. Yet, no one has ever explained *how* television causes these changes in people. This is probably because most people believe that we learn inductively, through association.

The notion that human beings are passive receptors who learn inductively through repeated experiences or exposures is an epistemological belief so widely accepted that most people regard this as common sense. Yet, as Karl Popper has shown, this "common sense" epistemology cannot be true because it is logically false.[15] Popper has introduced an alternative epistemology that construes human beings as creators, not receptors. We create our knowledge—our ideas, theories, and understandings. We create our beliefs and attitudes. We create our acts and operations—our conduct. We also create our political, social, and economic arrangements—our culture. Human beings create, he says, whenever they discover inadequacies in what they have previously created. The process is one of trial and error elimination. What this Popperian epistemology does is to shift attention away from people and on to what people create: their theories and their political and social and economic arrangements—their culture.

Television Displays Relationships

Throughout this book, I have adopted this Popperian epistemology and have tried to argue that television has facilitated this procedure of trial and error elimination through which human beings have improved their culture. My argument is that television, when it first emerged, encoded the existing culture, thereby distancing it in a new way. This facilitated critical scrutiny of that culture so that people uncovered the inadequacies and contradictions inherent in it. This led to error elimination: the modification of the culture in light of the newly uncovered inadequacies.

Moreover, television focuses on a specific kind of problem or inadequacy: moral inadequacy. Television focuses on moral inadequacies because it has a bias toward encoding relationships. That is, whether we are watching a drama, a situation comedy, a game show, or the news, our attention is drawn primarily to the relationships among the people presented on the screen. We pay less attention to the content of the programs we watch than to the patterns of relationships expressed in how people interact with one another. What we remember is not what they say or even what they did, but rather the pattern and structure of the relationships that exist between Archie and Edith and Ralph and Alice, or between Furillo and Henry Goldblum, Spencer and Hawk, John Boy and his mother, Cagney and Lacey, and Crockett and Tubbs, or between Roger Mudd and Connie Chung, and Hugh Downs and Barbara Walters.

There is nothing arcane or mysterious about this bias of television to encoding relationships; it follows from the fact that television communicates analogically. Analogic communication is different from the other form of communication humans use, which is called digital communication. In digital communication, we use names to refer to things, acts, events. Thus, we say or write: "The cat caught a mouse." Speech, writing, print are all media for digital communication. The other kind of communication, analogic communication, emerged much earlier in the history of evolution, so animals, as wells as humans, share it. Analogic communication is carried out largely by means of body movements: tension of voluntary muscles, changes in facial expression, hesitation, shifts in tempo of speech or movement, or overtones of the voice and irregularities of respiration. When a dog barks, for example, it is the expressive part of his body—his tail, lips, hairs on the back of his neck, and so on—that tell us at what object of the environment he is barking, and what patterns of relationship to that object he is likely to follow in the next few seconds.[16]

Humans usually translate analogic communications into digital. So, when the cat rubs up against our legs, we interpret this as a request for milk: The cat, we think, is saying: "Give me some milk." Actually, however, the cat is invoking a relationship: "Be my mother." The cat cannot speak; it has no words. What it does is make movements and sounds that are characteristically those that kittens make to a mother cat. The cat's analogic communication proposes or invokes a relationship of dependency.

Since the time when speech emerged, the primary mode of communication for humans has been digital. Nevertheless, as Bateson notes, our mammalian ancestry is "very near the surface, despite recently acquired linguistic tricks." He goes on: "If A says to B, 'The plane is scheduled to leave at 6:30,' B rarely accepts this remark as simply and solely a statement of fact about the plane. More often, he devotes a few neurons to the question: 'What does A's telling me this indicate for my relationship to A?' "[17]

Television is primarily a medium for analogic communication. It is true that it provides digital communication, too. After all, people on television do speak, and printed words often appear on the screen. But when people speak, it is the way they speak—the tone, the intensity, the inflections, the rhythm, the tempo as well as the facial expressions, gestures, and posture—that communicates a more elemental message: a message about relationships, about the roles and contingencies of relationships, the patterns of relationships. We all know the pattern of relationships that exists between Archie and Edith, Crockett & Tubbs, Dr. Craig and Ehrlich, and Cagney and Lacey. And we know all this through analogic communication.

With analogic communication, however, there is no argumentative function since there is nothing comparable to the logical syntax of digital communication: Analogic communication is nondiscursive. Nor does it contain any tense or mood—there is no past or future, or any conditional mood in analogic communication. It is presentational. One is involved with, or ensnared by, analogical communication.

Because television, as a medium of analogic communication, is primarily presentational and nondiscursive, we respond to it differently from how we respond to writing and print. We respond affectively rather than cognitively. Questions of truth and validity give way to questions of liking or not liking what we view. Television provokes feelings more than thought. Our criticisms, therefore, take the form of "this is good" or "this is bad," rather than "this is true" or "this is false." Television therefore educes moral criticism, and that criticism focuses primarily on the relationships encoded on the screen—relationships among people and relationships between people and nature. Note that I do not claim that television makes people more moral; only that it evokes moral criticism. So I say only that television makes people more morally sensitive to their culture—more conscious of the evils it contains, or causes. And when this criticism leads, as it has, to the removal or reduction of these evils, the culture gets better. So, although television has not made people more moral, it has facilitated the moral improvement of our culture.

In the chapters that follow, I will show how this took place in the social, political, economic, and intellectual realms of U.S. culture. My focus is on the 1960s and 1970s: on the 1960s because it was during this decade that most U.S. homes first owned a television set; on the 1970s because by the end of that decade the impact of television on U.S. culture had diminished due to the great increase in the number of television channels as well as the emergence of the VCR. Cable television, satellite dishes and the birth of new networks gave viewers a much wider choice than had existed before. Now, instead of the fare provided by the three networks, many watched sports, reruns, or quiz shows, while others watched old movies on cable or the VCR. Only in the matter of politics, particularly the presidential campaigns, could one find great numbers of Americans viewing the same shows—the same speeches, advertisements and debates.

Notes

1   Lowery, *Milestones in Mass Communications Research*, 171.
2   Mankiewicz and Swerdlow, *Remote Control*, 17.
3   *Nielson Report, on Television 1989.*
4   Newcomb, ed., *Television: The Critical View*, 335.
5   Postman, *Teaching as a Conserving Activity*, 60.
6   Schram et al., *Television in the Lives of Our Children*, 1.
7   Baker and Ball, eds., *Violence and the Media.*
8   Surgeon General's Scientific Advisory Committee on Television and Social Behavior, *Television and Growing Up: The Impact of Televised Violence.*

9   McLuhan, *Understanding Media*, 18.
10   McLuhan, "Interview," 60.
11   Ibid., 61
12   McLuhan, *Understanding Media*, 280, 284.
13   Postman, *Amusing Ourselves to Death*, 27.
14   Postman, *Teaching as a Conserving Activity*, especially chapters 3 and 4.
15   Popper, *Objective Knowledge*, 32-105.
16   Bateson, *Steps to an Ecology of Mind*, 370.
17   Ibid., 367.

2

Television and Society

By the 1960s, a mass audience—made up of all those who watched television—could readily recognize that modern society did not live up to its professed value of individualism. The social relationships now visible on the TV screen revealed that many people were not treated as individuals but as members of groups: racial groups, sex groups, age groups, or ethnic groups. Moreover, members of these groups were excluded from competition. In sports, scholarship, business, and the arts, blacks did not compete with whites, nor females with males. Blacks and women had their own athletic leagues, their own schools, their own businesses, their own separate art worlds. Nor were women and blacks equal to white males: In some cases they were not even equal before the law, and in most areas of endeavor, they did not have the same equal opportunity to succeed as did white males. Moreover, the reasons for excluding, segregating, and discriminating against blacks and women were not based on objective, empirical differences between the races and between the sexes but rather on subjective beliefs tenaciously held by white males—racist and sexist beliefs that blacks and women are inferior. So, these relationships that existed in the society violated the principal values of modern civilization: the values of individualism, competition, equality, and objectivity. Some people were deprived of life chances simply because they were homosexuals, or because they were old, or

11

young or because they didn't speak English. It is, of course, true that women, blacks, gays, old people, and the young, had *always* known that they were treated differently from others in the population, but what was new in the 1960s was the moral indignation—in some cases, moral outrage—about these relationships.

No one who has lived through it will deny that the 1960s and 1970s marked a time of dramatic and far-reaching social change. Suddenly, blacks, women, gays, and the youth in the United States and in other Western societies were protesting against how they were treated and were beginning to agitate for change. This happened not because social conditions had changed. No, it happened because at that point people suddenly recognized that the existing, long-standing social arrangements were morally inadequate.

The youth movement, women's liberation, the civil rights movement, and the gay movement were the most talked about, but these two decades also produced dramatic changes in how society treated the sick, the elderly, the handicapped, the mentally ill, and the poor. And there were abrupt changes in the prevailing social arrangements for unwed mothers, for divorced couples, for criminals, for addicts, and for ex-nuns. Other social relationships changed, too: between husbands and wives, teachers and students, employers and employees, and parents and children.

I do not say that people become more moral in the 1960s and 1970s, but only that at this time they began to view the existing social arrangements from a moral point of view. Television created this new moral sensitivity. It did this because television, like all media, encodes the culture and thereby distances it from people, which allows them to criticize it. But, unlike print, television is a participatory medium; it involves people in what is happening on the screen. Reading about a football game, a funeral, or a political convention is not like watching these events on television. When reading, one can be more detached, more objective. But television, unlike print, is a nondiscursive medium, so that it educes an affective response from viewers. People like or dislike what the medium presents; they are emotionally involved. And because television is also an analogic medium as well, it has a bias toward focusing on relationships among and between people. The social relationships presented on their television screens distressed many people. Women, blacks, the young, the old, the homosexuals—all saw themselves depicted in relationships that were unfair, discriminatory, unjust. These relationships were the stereotypical relationships common in society, but now that they were encoded on the TV screen, people could see with greater facility how those relationships interdicted the life chances of those who were oppressed.

The Amos and Andy Show, for example, which had presented black stereotypes over the radio for twenty years, found that its popularity plummeted once the show was presented on television in the early 1950s. The television show raised the consciousness of blacks (and of some whites) whose protests led to its cancellation in less than two years. Or, take women on television: Although some women had long complained about it, now everyone could see on television that girls were treated simply as sex objects—in commercials, in situation comedies, in westerns, in dramas. And, if they appeared there at all, the television "news shows" presented females as "weather girls" subject to chauvinistic put-downs from the male announcers. Older women saw themselves limited to the roles of housewife and mother, usually silly, scatterbrained, or melodramatic. Commercials depicted women as stupid and incompetent, unable to select a laundry soap or dog food without a man (or a male "voiceover") telling her what to do.

Television and the Women's Movement

Back in 1848, some three hundred women assembled at Seneca Falls, New York, to hold the first women's rights convention in the United States. Led by middle-class women operating through a network maintained by the medium of print—newsletters, newspapers, books, pamphlets, and magazines—the early feminist movement focused on women's rights: the right to hold property in their own name, the right to sue for divorce, the right to an education on a par with men and, above all else, the right to vote. The struggle for women's suffrage was a long one, culminating in 1920 with the passage of the nineteenth amendment to the Constitution. At that point, most female activists in the United States, as well as the public at large, assumed that women now had equality—or at least as much as they wanted. Over the next quarter of a century, the suffrage movement became a vague, historical memory, and by midcentury the word feminist had become an epithet. The coming of television caused a rebirth of feminism. But this time women demanded not only equal rights but complete liberation from the domination of males. The struggle now became more than a demand for rights: It grew into a protest against sexism.

The contemporary women's movement, in the words of Betty Freidan, one of its first spokespersons, is "dedicated to the proposition that women first and foremost are human beings who, like all other people in society, must have a chance to develop to their fullest human potential." As she and others pointed out, existing relationships between men and women interdicted the development of women: These relationships restricted women's opportunities for careers, for career advancement, and for education. They restricted women socially and psychologically.

The contemporary women's liberation movement aims at the total destruction of unfair relationships between men and women wherever they exist: in the family (between husband and wife, brother and sister, father and mother), and in schools, at work, in church. The movement seeks to root out discriminating relationships in real life as well as those portrayed in novels, plays, movies, art, and advertising. The protests extend to the use of sexist language in print and speech. Many women reject long-standing practices, customs, and mores— like men opening doors for women or giving them their seat on a crowded bus—because these are symbolic of the unfair relationship that prevails between men and women.

In 1966 in Washington, D.C., thirty-two women from twelve states and the capitol organized the National Organization of Women (NOW) with the stated purpose: "to take action to bring women into full participation in the mainstream of U.S. society now, exercising all the privileges thereof in truly equal partnership with men." Between 1967 and 1974, NOW went from fourteen chapters to over seven hundred; from one thousand members to forty thousand. NOW works locally and nationally on court cases and legislation lobbying, on matters of discrimination against women in hiring and promotion, on matters of reproduction and child care. It opposes abortion laws; it advocates birth control clinics and day care centers for children. It insists that 51 percent of the positions of leadership in government, industry, and the professions should be held by women since women comprise more than 51 percent of the population.

In 1967, the more radical Red Stocking group was founded with the proclamation: "After centuries of individual and preliminary political struggle, women are uniting to achieve their final liberation from male supremacy." Simultaneously, other groups began to form all over the country: Loosely organized, they were sometimes completely independent of other groups. By late 1970, there were women's liberation groups ranging from NOW to Older Women's Liberation (OWL) in every major city in the nation and in many smaller cities, with up to two hundred different groups operating in both New York and Los Angeles. In 1973, *Women Today*, an independent national newsletter, published a directory of several thousand groups. These groups conduct "rap" sessions to help raise the consciousness of women about feminist issues. They also mount protests against discriminating policies and practices: male-only clubs, bars, restaurants, sex-segregated newspaper want ads, sexist movies and lectures, employers who discriminate against women, and laws that oppress women. They participate in women's liberation conferences, women's liberation days, and women's marches.[1]

The contemporary women's liberation movement is quite different from the earlier women's rights movement. For, while the earlier movement focused on the legal, educational, and political rights of women, it actually enhanced the traditional roles of wife and mother, worker in the home, protector of children, and helpmate of husband. The contemporary women's movement still insists on women's rights but goes far beyond this to challenge the existing relationships prevalent between men and women: It challenges the license of men to have advantages, and it tries to alter the existing status and role relationships. Secondly, the contemporary women's movement is a mass movement involving all classes, not just the middle class. Thirdly, unlike the well-known leaders of the earlier women's rights movement, there are today no recognized national leaders who can speak for the women's liberation movement. And, finally, there are no networks of communication. The movement expanded, in Gloria Steinem's phrase, "not by organization, but by contagion"; women's groups, as Jo Freeman put it,"grew like mushrooms."[2]

What needs explaining, therefore, is how the contemporary women's liberation movement grew so rapidly into a mass movement without the aid of national leaders or a network of communication. Television, I think, provides an explanation.

Television Documents Male-Female Stereotypes

Although some analysts have attempted to explain why the female revolt came about when it did, few have mentioned the influence of television. (Meyerwitz did offer an ingenious explanation of the role television played in the women's liberation movement.[3] While his explanation complements mine, it suffers, like most other television analyses, from reliance on an inductive epistemology.) Most analysts of the women's liberation movement have pointed to the fact that the increased industrialization and urbanization of society brought more women into the work force, especially more married women who, having a more permanent stake in their jobs, resented not being paid as much as men. But the social strain this caused merely created the potential for the movement, not the feminist movement itself.[4]

The earlier women's rights movement was generated by print. It began, according to most historians, in 1848, when Lucretia Mott and Elizabeth Cady Stanton printed a notice of a women's rights convention in the *Seneca County Courier*. No such similar event marked the beginning of the contemporary women's liberation movement: Neither the publication of Betty Friedan's *The Feminine Mystique* nor the formation of NOW created the movement; indeed, both the book and the organization appeared at a moment when women were already receptive to the ideology of women's liberation. Through the medium of television, all women, in all walks of life, had come to share the same perceptions and the same aversions to the male-female relationships in the existing social arrangements.

The medium of print can and did effectively disclose all violations of women's rights—whether it be a matter of unequal pay, voting rights, employment opportunities, or educational discrimination. With television, however, the problem is exposed as not simply a legal matter but as a problem of the culture itself: The social arrangements—the gender role definitions, the stratification of the sexes—categorically disadvantage women.

Moreover, with television, communication is instantaneous and exposure nationwide. In the age of television, there is no longer a need for a communication network through the medium of print. Nor is it necessary that there be national leaders, for now the medium of television serves the role that leaders played as agents of change in the age of print. Indeed, television, with its omnivorous, insatiable appetite for new and different images, relentlessly exposes the activities of any so-called leaders or spokespersons, making them predictable, hence not worthy of future "media exposure." Television uses up leaders.

How did television raise the consciousness of women? How did it make them aware of their victimization? Television, as everyone knows, presents stereotypes—at least it did in the 1960s when women were never presented as individuals or persons but only as part of a relationship: a mother ("Mama"), a wife ("My Favorite Husband"), or a sex object ("The Milton Berle Show"). In the formulaic situation comedies of the 1950s and 1960s, women always displayed the same predictable characteristics in each week's new situation—revenge, control, manipulation—in the continual battle between the sexes that was the stuff of these domestic farces ("I Love Lucy," "The Life of Riley"). Week after week, the woman would demonstrate her superiority over the men. But she was still patronized, still inferior, still requiring validation by males. Even though he may have been a stupid boob, he always knew better or thought he knew better than the "little woman."

On the dramatic shows of this time, women were for the most part excluded. One study found that as late as the early 1970s only 28 percent of the characters in prime-time programming were female.[5] Women were never seen caring for the sick (except as nurses) or coping with social problems as lawyers, detectives, teachers, or newspaper people. Women were housewives, girl friends, or maybe secretaries.

The early game shows ("Strike It Rich!" "Break the Bank!" "Queen for a Day!" "The Price is Right!") clearly displayed women as stupid, silly, and grasping—as creatures whose highest aim in life was to win a dishwasher or a television set.

The commercials portrayed a woman as incapable of cleaning a sink, washing the clothes, or taking care of children and pets without a man telling her how. The woman's job—the message was clear—was to be beautiful: smooth hands, clean complexion, shining hair, fresh breath, all so that she could ensnare a man. For, a woman is worthless without a man. Even more than this: The commercials revealed that an ugly woman has no credibility in society; no one wants to look at her, much less listen to what she has to say.

The relationships women had with men when encoded on television exposed to all the fact that women were in the world but not of it. They were not involved in politics, art, or science; they didn't even understand those fields. Their only interest in life was in attracting men. Although some television analysts have argued that television stereotypes perpetuate the existing social arrangements, I think they do the opposite: I think they help to *destroy* existing social arrangements. By encoding the stereotypical relationships of women in this society, television revealed women to themselves. Television became *the* reference source for women. Through the medium of television, women came to recognize their own lack of autonomy and freedom of choice. They saw that women for the most part lived in residential ghettos, shut off from the life of the world. And they came to realize that those women who were engaged in any activity outside the home were not taken seriously. Through television, they found out what they had been allowed to do and what not; they saw what doors were shut and how sanctions were applied against the violators of assigned roles. And through the critical analysis of the relationships encoded on television, women began to trace the consequences of subscribing to the notion that the traditional role of women is to live for others and to find their identities in personal relationships—as mother and wife. They began to see that to live in response to others is to live a life that is necessarily fragmented and ephemeral.

In serving as the reference source, television did more than reveal women to themselves; it also revealed comparative information about men: the rewards, advantages, and privileges they enjoyed. Men initiate, lead, advise, and dominate; women follow. Television exposed men at work: as doctors, lawyers, detectives, firemen, etc. And, as situation after situation unfolded, the message was that women had no place in the man's world. Moreover, "You don't belong here" clearly meant "We don't want you here." So television also became the reference source for what men thought of women and what behaviors men deemed were proper for women. It showed that males think women are innately inferior and regard females who think otherwise as sick, bad, crazy, stupid, ugly, or incompetent. It showed that males believe that they know and understand everything because they, unlike females, are logical, rational, and objective. This is why it is said that women are not capable of knowing what's good for them, why women are a bundle of contradictions, and why they are not worth arguing with. This is also, of course, why women are not good at arithmetic or science. The message women received from male-dominated television was that she is weak and cannot cope with the world by herself. But she can be dependent on *him*; *he* will do it for her; *he* is indispensable.

Women responded to all these exposures with moral outrage. The limitations these male-female relationships placed on them were unfair and unjust. The designated roles imposed by the culture curtailed their growth and weakened their sense of identity. In this culture, women were childlike cripples.

Now, many women had long known and resented this; they did not need television to tell them how unsatisfactory their condition was. But, prior to television, most women were inclined to view this as a "personal failure"; their own personal inadequacies, they thought, prevented them from accepting and adapting to the existing male-female relationships present in the culture. Television diminished this self-blame by providing normative references that enabled women to see that other women, *all* women, were victims of male discrimination. Instead of blaming themselves, women now began to blame the system, the culture. Their feelings of deprivation were not due to personal inadequacies but to the inadequacies of the system.

Blaming the system, however, is not enough to start a protest movement. For, it is possible to blame the system and merely acquiesce to it as lamentable but inevitable. That's the way it is, as the long-suffering wives and mothers in the situation comedies pointed out on television week after week. For a protest movement to emerge, there has to be a perception that the system is illegitimate and therefore must be destroyed or changed. Television helped to engender widespread feelings of system illegitimacy precisely because it is an analogic medium, a medium that triggers an affective response. Women, therefore, did not merely lament the male-female relationships encoded on television, they actively disliked them. They perceived them as morally wrong. Men do not have a license or a right to oppress women. There was no justification for these relationships, nor could there ever be a justification for them. For the first time, people realized they were living in a sexist society. Once women became conscious that these relationship were illegitimate (here, TV talk shows helped raise the consciousness of women by presenting early feminists like Betty Friedan, Gloria Steinem, Germaine Greer, and others), they began to refuse to accept the culture's definition of a woman's place, woman's role, woman's identity. More and more now, women sought to define themselves, to find and use their own capabilities, to fail or succeed on their own, to claim rank and status by dint of their own actions.

Thus, television not only served as the reference source that provoked the contemporary women's liberation movement, it also served as the agency that mobilized that movement. By 1960, most U.S. homes owned at least one television set, so everyone across the nation could witness the unfair male-female relationships encoded on the screen hour after hour. By raising the consciousness of women to the reality of their situation while simultaneously provoking moral outrage, feminism spread like "contagion" as everywhere protests burst forth against the sexist, male chauvinist, culture.

Television Mobilizes the Women's Movement

Television further mobilized support for the movement through news interviews, talk shows, documentaries, and the like, where celebrities sensitive to the danger of being labelled sexists announced their subscription to the goals of the women's liberation movement. The juxtaposition of dramatic shows, commercials, and situation comedies with news events about women's protests brought the message home to those who had not understood it before. Many of these commercials and shows dramatically illustrated just what women on the news were protesting.

Another way television furthered mobilization was by showing women that collective action had a chance of succeeding. On news broadcasts, documentaries, and interview shows—some dramatic shows, too—television revealed that the system could be changed. Television's insatiable appetite for visual, newsworthy stories guaranteed that protesters' actions and rhetoric were grist for local and national television cameras.

From what they saw on television, then, women concluded not only that their cause was just but that the system was not efficacious enough, or immoral enough, to refuse to change. These perceptions of system inefficiency and deep-down moral sensitivity furthered mobilization of the movement.

The responsiveness of television to its audience also helped to mobilize the movement. Commercial television, which is necessarily extremely sensitive to viewers' likes and dislikes, responded quickly to feminist criticisms of the programming. During the 1960s, network and local stations hired female newscasters and reporters for news shows, female interviewers for talk shows, and, by the mid-1970s, had many shows where females played the leading roles: "The Mary Tyler Moore Show," "Rhoda," "Maude," "Phyllis." And viewers could watch Angie Dickinson as "Police Woman," or Lindsay Wagner as "Bionic Woman" or "Charlie's Angels." Most of the women on these shows worked in what heretofore had been a man's world. No longer were women on TV simply wives and mothers. And if they were, they were a new breed, like the heroine of "One Day at a Time": an attractive, divorced mother with a boyfriend and two teenage daughters. In these expanded TV roles, women faced a host of new problems in creating new and viable relationships with men. These status/role dilemmas all served as plots and subplots or even as running themes for these new kinds of programs.

These new shows helped mobilize the contemporary women's movement in several ways. First, the role expansion helped people to conclude that women could function in a "man's" world. Second, by confronting and probing the changed social relationships entailed by such role expansion, these shows helped provide awareness and guidance to those who would follow. These shows also encouraged great numbers of "free riders": women who would never actively protest, never join NOW, never participate in a women's march, never picket, but who did welcome and passively support the role expansion, the diminution of gender discrimination, the reduction of male domination. Finally, these shows helped to weaken male opposition to the women's liberation movement, making it less threatening.

How Things Got Better for Women

During the congressional debates on the 1964 Civil Rights Bill, Congressman Howard V. Smith of Virginia, hoping to make the bill look sufficiently silly as to divide the liberals and thereby prevent its passage, added "sex" to the section prohibiting discrimination in employment. As expected, many of the House liberals opposed the provision, arguing it would weaken the bill. Most men thought the "sex" provision was a joke. But most of the female members of the house took it very seriously. It passed—amid derisive laughter—and became the basis for forging the legal and administrative tools women used to work toward equal opportunity. By the 1970s, a federal policy of equal opportunity if not total equality had emerged in a piecemeal fashion. The Equal Employment Opportunity Act of 1972 expanded the prohibition against discrimination in hiring women to apply it to just about all jobs and positions. Jobs once closed to women were now open to them in the professions, in academia, in government, as well as in the trades and industry, manufacturing and service, both private and public sectors. Concurrently, the "Help Wanted" columns of most newspapers no longer listed jobs under separate "male" and "female" headings. The federal government also adopted policies to recompense women for past discrimination. The 1972 equal pay amendment to the Fair Labor Standards Act allowed some one hundred seventy thousand women in the following two years to recover over $80 million in back pay. At the state level, laws protecting women were also passed. Illinois, for example, passed a law making marital rape a crime. Moreover, sixteen states added equal rights amendments to their own constitutions. And most states revised their legal codes, recasting them in "gender neutral" form.[6]

The most far-reaching change in women's relationships came in 1968 when President Johnson signed an executive order directing all employers holding federal contracts—covering one-third of the labor force—to go beyond nondiscrimination, undertake "affirmative action" programs, and rectify the effects of past discrimination. The original affirmative action order did not include women, but it was later amended to do so.

Affirmative action has had the greatest impact on institutions of higher education, especially on matters of hiring, promotion, tenure, and salary. Moreover, most institutions of higher learning have women's groups who sponsor courses and programs on women's studies, and who oversee admissions policies and practices and the awarding of scholarships on a nondiscriminatory basis. Women's groups have also actively pursued the review of textbooks used at all levels of schooling in order to expunge all sexist language and illustrations. In the secondary schools, athletic programs, counseling services, courses of study, and extracurricular activities have all been revealed as sexist, and revised and refined in various ways to diminish or eliminate discrimination against girls.

Since the 1960s, then, male-female relationships in U.S. society have changed dramatically. The stereotype role relationships have been shattered: Dating, courting and marriage customs are no longer what they were. Husbands and wives, mothers and fathers, brothers and sisters now act differently. Females are no longer expected to be passive and weak, nor boys active and strong. Females, not just males, now initiate, lead, and direct the goings-on in the world. There are more working mothers then ever before, many at jobs never open to women in the past, and they are earning salaries comparable to those earned by men. Divorces have increased in number and become no-fault. Pregnancy is optional and abortion has been legalized.

By the mid-1970s, things had gotten better for women—their life chances had improved. But, as suddenly as it happened, the women's liberation movement just as suddenly collapsed. Once again, television helps explain why this happened. Just as it had set the movement going, now TV applied the brakes.

Passage and Failure of the ERA

In 1972, Congress passed the Equal Rights Amendment: "Equality of rights under the law shall not be denied or abridged by the United States or by any state on account of 'sex'." The House of Representatives passed it 354 to 231; in the Senate the vote was eighty-four to eight. Majority leader Tip O'Neil announced that the ERA had generated more mail than the Vietnam War—almost all of it favorable. The amendment was then sent to the states for ratification. To the amazement of many, this amendment to the Constitution failed to win support from a sufficient number of states. By 1982—the deadline for the amendment—only thirty-five of the required thirty-eight states had ratified it.

Why did it fail? Analysts have cited a number of possible causes. One was the resentment against the growing influence of the federal government over the lives of people. Another was the opposition of religious fundamentalists, who claimed that the Bible proscribed such an amendment. Finally, some pointed out that insurance companies, who profited from treating women differently from men on the actuarial tables, had lobbied vigorously against the amendment. Jane Mansbridge, who has made the most thoroughgoing analysis of the matter, claims that the women's liberation movement had become a collection of sects by the mid-1970s as concern over doctrinal purity led to a turning inward and a polarization of "us" and "them." These factious, warring sects were no match for the disciplined, well-organized, anti-ERA forces, led primarily by Phyllis Schlafly. STOP ERA convinced the state legislators in Florida, North Carolina, Oklahoma, and Illinois to vote down the amendment.[7]

All these explanations are mechanistic. They assume that power, force, and numbers determine the course of political events. I think that the ERA did not win ratification because by the time the deadline rolled around most people no longer believed that such an amendment was necessary. By the late 1970s, a nationwide reaction had set in against the women's liberation movement. Not that people wanted to go back to the old male-female relationships, but simply that they thought the female revolt had gone far enough. Women had won their rights; they had more equality of opportunity for schooling and for jobs. They were well on the way to equal pay for equal work. The female stereotypes had been shattered and the categorical discrimination inherent in the social arrangements had disappeared. This, of course, was not the full truth, but it was what most people believed. And they believed it because this was what they saw on television.

On their television screens, people now saw women prominently displayed as anchorwomen on news shows, as talk show hostesses, as reporters—even as sports commentators. On dramatic shows, they saw female lawyers, female physicians, female business executives, female detectives, female judges, female legislators, female firepersons, female plumbers, and female carpenters. In numerous programs and most commercials, they saw men and women, boys and girls, interacting more openly and freely than ever before. Women on television were strong, independent, assertive, and free.

At the same time, viewers now saw news broadcasts and talk show discussions about feminism and women's liberation that threatened to carry the movement to extremes that frightened them: complete sexual liberation (i.e. promiscuity), girls playing contact sports (with boys), common public toilets, homosexual marriages, a female draft, and so on. (The STOP ERA movement paraded all these threats in its TV commercials against ratification of the amendment.) Moreover, through newscasts and special documentaries as well as TV movies on social issues, viewers now became conscious of alarming social problems, which the television programs implied (or viewers inferred) were the consequences of the women's liberation movement: teenage pregnancy, unwed mothers, single-parent families, welfare dependency, wife abuse, and rape.

TV Moves from Stereotype to Myth

During the 1970s, television moved from stereotype to myth. Instead of encoding the relationships actually existing in the culture, television now encoded mythical relationships that portrayed little or no male domination and less female discrimination than actually existed in the social arrangements of the culture. Ironically, these myths now found on television came about because women had complained about the stereotypical portraits of women that television had presented in the past. But, once these stereotypes disappeared from the screen, television no longer provoked moral criticism of the male-female relationships current in society. As an analogic medium, television did still evoke a moral response, but the outrage now shifted away from the (mythic) relationships encoded on the screen to focus on the further social changes feminists demanded when they appeared on the screen. The outrage also zeroed in on the serious social problems—increased teenage pregnancy, a rising divorce rate, more wife abuse, and rape—that many saw as consequences of the already transformed relationships between men and women.

Once television had switched from stereotype to myth, it applied the brakes to the women's liberation movement. Understandably, then, most television viewers now regarded the Equal Rights Amendment as both unnecessary and dangerous: unnecessary because women clearly had as much equality or equality of opportunity as they wanted, and dangerous because demands for further changes, for more "liberation," could only create more serious social evils. Although it had now applied the brakes to the women's movement, television had made things better for women—and men. Not perfect, but better. The present social arrangements now offer both men and women more life chances than had existed before.

Television and the Black Revolution

The history of blacks in the United States is quite different from that of other U.S. ethnic groups. Slavery dominates more than half of that history, and after slavery came Jim Crow, which lasted until the 1950s in the South—where most of the blacks lived. According to Jim Crow doctrine, racial separation is natural and instinctive; hence, it is desired by both races and is beneficial to both. Secondly, since whites were thought to possess superior intelligence and had more wealth, Jim Crow doctrine insisted that political power belonged in the hands of white people—blacks must not have the suffrage since they were considered incapable of intelligently exercising that right. Thirdly, Jim Crow doctrine had it that blacks are inherently inferior beings who must be controlled by segregation in order to constrain their inherent criminality and inordinate sexual passions. Finally, segregation also guards against racial amalgamation or intermarriage, which is sinful, unnatural, and begets hybrid monstrosities.[8]

Following the reconstruction period after the Civil War, all states throughout the South imposed this Jim Crow doctrine by means of laws that mandated segregation in schools, parks, theaters, boarding houses, public toilets, trains, buses, trolleys, and water fountains. The city of Atlanta went so far as to require separate Jim Crow Bibles for blacks to swear on in court. There were Jim Crow schools, Jim Crow restaurants, Jim Crow laundries, and Jim Crow customs: Blacks were expected to tip their hats when they walked past whites, but whites did not have to remove their hats—even when they entered a black family's home; blacks called whites "sir," or "ma'am" while whites called blacks by their first names; blacks had to step aside meekly to give whites a wide berth on sidewalks and streets.

Although they did not confront Jim Crow laws outside the South, American blacks across the nation lived in a state of constant humiliation up until the 1950s. Everywhere, they encountered residential segregation, job discrimination, educational deprivation, and lower wages than whites. They were subject to police brutality, economic exploitation, and social exclusion. With almost complete impunity, the police everywhere could, and did, intimidate, harass, assault, and even kill blacks. Bankers refused to provide them loans for houses or for business ventures. Realtors would not rent offices and stores to them. Merchants refused them credit. And shopkeepers in the ghetto areas charged them higher prices for all goods and commodities. White people, not blacks, controlled the banks, the businesses, and the realty offices. Moreover, within the ghetto, whites controlled the drug traffic, prostitution, and the numbers racket.

At the midpoint of the twentieth century, black people in the United States still lived in a condition of almost complete subordination to white people. The culture of the United States categorically discriminated against them, refusing to admit their dignity as human beings. The nightly television shows of the early 1950s put Negroes in their place: They appeared as maids (in "Beulah") or as elevator operators or porters ("My Little Margie" and "The Stu Erwin Show"), or they were pictured as fools ("Amos and Andy"). The black people on these television shows did not live in the same neighborhoods as the white people, nor did any of the white families have a black friend—not the Rileys ("The Life of Riley"), not the Goldbergs ("Molly Goldberg"), not the Hansens ("Mama"), not the Bascos ("Life with Luigi"), and not the Andersons ("Father Knows Best").

But television news helped change all this.

A Paper Victory: Brown vs. Board of Education

Many analysts of American society have assumed that the Supreme Court set the Black Revolution afoot on 17 May 1954, when it announced (in *Brown vs. Board of Education of Topeka, Kansas*) that segregated schools were unconstitutional. This, supposedly, was the day the Jim Crow doctrine was eliminated, the day the walls of segregation came tumbling down. Few outside the South anticipated the massive resistance that would rise up against this Supreme Court decision, although, at that time, Mississippi Senator James Eastland had warned: "The people of the South will never accept this monstrous decision. I predict this century will bring on a century of litigation."[9] And well might this resistance have lasted a hundred years were it not for television.

There can be no doubt that the *Brown* decision was a victory for civil rights. Yet, it is important to note that this victory was a product of the medium of print.

It came about as the result of a carefully crafted campaign by the NAACP lawyers to reveal the contradictions inherent in the (printed) doctrine of "separate but equal" that the Supreme Court itself had put forth in 1896. At that time, the court had declared that segregated facilities for blacks were constitutional—provided that such separate facilities were equal.

In the *Brown* case, the Supreme Court based its decision—as it always does—on printed documents. These materials contained descriptions and arguments that purported to show that the separate educational facilities provided for black children were not equal in fact, and, furthermore, could never be equal, since segregated education is inherently unequal.

Yet, although the court had spoken, black parents who tried to enroll their children in white schools the following September discovered that the *Brown* decision had no impact on the segregated schools in the South. The Supreme Court ruling, as Herman Talmadge, then governor of Georgia, pointed out—perhaps with more prescience than he realized—was "a mere scrap of paper." The white school boards throughout the South rejected all black applicants, and sometimes those black parents who tried to register their children suffered reprisals: the loss of a job, denials of credit, even physical beatings. It is true that some eight hundred school districts did desegregate their schools over the next six years, but almost all of these were located in border states. Moreover, the so-called desegregation was merely token—one or two black students admitted to each school. So, by 1960, less than 7 percent of the black school children in the South were attending schools with whites. Senator Eastland's prediction of a hundred years of litigation was right on schedule: Only 1 percent of black children had gained entry to white schools each year since the *Brown* decision. That court decision had clearly been a turning point in black and white relations in the United States. But it did not launch the black revolt; it merely set the stage for that revolt.[10]

The Montgomery Bus Strike: Television Takes Over

The black revolt began, as Louis Lomax insisted, with the Montgomery bus strike that started in December 1955. As with all bus lines in the South, the buses of Montgomery, Alabama, were regulated by Jim Crow laws. Although Montgomery's black riders accounted for more than 75 percent of all passengers, they were regularly forced to surrender their seats to whites. In accordance with printed rules, drivers were to designate the front part of the bus for whites and the rear section for blacks in proportion to the number of blacks and whites on the bus at any given moment. As more whites came on to the bus, the driver moved an imaginary color line further back. Blacks sitting directly behind the "white-only" section would be told to get up and move further to the back of the bus.[11]

On 1 December 1955, Rosa Parks, a black seamstress, said "no" to the bus driver's demand that she get up and let a white man have her seat. Mrs. Parks was arrested. This brought on the revolt of blacks in Montgomery who, for the next thirteen months, boycotted the public bus system.

This was not the first black boycott of bus lines; blacks in Baton Rouge, Louisiana, had conducted one earlier. Nor was Mrs. Parks the first black to refuse to give up a seat on the Montgomery Bus Lines. But, as Louis Lomax recognized, the Montgomery strike did signal a change of goals as well as a change in methods to combat segregation. Moreover, it brought on a change in leadership insofar as it hurled twenty-seven-year-old Rev. Martin Luther King into the national spotlight.

Lomax did not explain how or why the revolt began in Montgomery, but Martin Luther King did. As King's book on the Montgomery story makes patently clear, television brought about the revolt. In that book, *Stride Toward Freedom*, he relates in great detail the events of 5 December, the first day of the black boycott of all Montgomery buses (that "Day of Days," he called it). After discovering that the boycott was almost 100 percent successful, the group of ministers directing it coined the name The Montgomery Improvement Association and elected Martin Luther King its president. He was to give the major address at the public meeting scheduled for that evening at the Holt Street Baptist Church. When he arrived there, King discovered that the church, which held about four thousand people, had been packed since 5:00 P.M. and that, by now, three thousand additional people were standing outside, listening over hastily installed loudspeakers. King reports that when the chairman introduced him, the packed church applauded. "I rose and stood before the pulpit. *Television cameras began to shoot from all sides*"(my emphasis).[12]

Because of the hectic events of that day, King had had only twenty minutes to prepare his speech—a speech that he knew was to be "the most decisive speech of my life." And he knew, he reports, "that reporters and television men would be there with their pencils and sound cameras, poised to record my words and send them across the nation."[13]

Here is what the television audience heard:

"There comes a time when people get tired."

"Yes, Lord."

"We are here this evening to say to those who have mistrusted us for so long that we are tired."

"Help him, Jesus."

"We are tired of being segregated and humiliated."

"Amen."

"Tired! Did you hear me when I said *tired?*"

"Yes, Lord!

"Tired of being kicked about by the brutal feet of oppression. Now we have no alternatives but to protest. For many years, we have shown amazing patience. We have sometimes given our white brothers the feeling that we liked the way were being treated. But we came here tonight to be saved from this patience that makes us patient with anything less than freedom and justice."[14]

Here was no legal argument for civil rights, no rational argument against the contradictions of segregation. No, this was an expose of how blacks felt: tired and running out of patience. Blacks were no longer fighting for civil rights. Now it had become a matter of justice, of moral justice: Racism is immoral; it is morally wrong for whites to humiliate blacks. Television, with its bias toward encoding feelings and emotions, helped people to recast America's racial problems as a moral problem. For, those who watched and listened to Martin Luther King deliver his address on television were not like you, gentle reader, decoding marks on a printed page. They *heard* him say those words; they heard the sonorous voice, the measured cadences, the deep intensity and sincere conviction carried in his voice. And the television audience heard people assembled in that church on Holt Street. They heard the heartfelt cries of subscription and support for every word that young minister spoke. More than this, they *saw* the Reverend Martin Luther King; they saw his serious, calm, dignified demeanor; they saw the gentleness, the sincerity, the power of the man. They witnessed his charisma. And they saw the dignity, determination, and commitment of the followers assembled in that church in Montgomery, Alabama.

For the first time, people across the nation, television viewers, recognized that segregation is morally wrong. Moreover, they *liked* Martin Luther King. He advocated persuasion, not coercion. Over television, to the nation at large, he emphasized the Christian doctrine of love: "Our actions must be guided by the deepest principles of our Christian faith. Love must be our regulating ideal. Once again, we must hear the words of Jesus echoing across the centuries: 'Love your enemies, bless them that curse you, and pray for them that despitefully use you.' If we fail to do this, our protest will end up as a meaningless drama on the stage of history, and its meaning will be shrouded with the ugly garments of shame."[15]

The message broadcast on television that night was one that all blacks—and most whites outside the South—could live with. As Louis Lomax noted, Martin Luther King was the first minister to "resolve the Negro problem to a spiritual matter and yet inspire the people to seek a solution on this side of the Jordan, not in the life beyond death."[16] King had united the militant and the moderate: He urged people to protest, but to do it with love. This came to be called "nonviolent protest" and, for the next ten years, was the most salient characteristic of the black revolt. Understandably so, since nonviolent protest produced the kind of spectacles made for television. Throughout the following decade, television cameras captured the dramatic confrontations provoked by the nonviolent marches, boycotts, demonstrations, sit-ins, pray-ins, and freedom rides that spread like contagion throughout the South. Here's how Julius Lester, one-time leader in the Student Non-Violent Coordinating Committee, described these goings-on:

> In those days, the Student Non-Violent Coordinating Committee (SNCC) would not allow anyone to go on a demonstration if that person so much as confessed that he would entertain a thought about hitting a white person

who had stuck him. You had to put your body in the struggle and that meant entering the church in Albany, Danville, Greenwood, Nashville, or wherever you were, entering the church and listening to prayers, short sermons on your courage and the cause you were fighting for, singing freedom songs—"Ain't Gon' Let Nobody Turn Me Round"—and you would name names—the sheriff's, the mayor's, the governor's, and whoever else you held responsible for the conditions, and, always at the end, "We Shall Overcome" with arms crossed, holding the hands of the person next to you and swaying gently from side to side, "We Shall Overcome Someday," someday, but not today because you knew as you walked out of the church, two abreast, and started marching toward town, that no matter how many times you sang about not letting anybody turn you around, rednecks and po' white trash from four counties and some from across the state line were waiting with guns, tire chains, baseball bats, rocks, sticks, clubs, and bottles, waiting as you turned the corner singing about "This Little Light of Mine" and how you were going to let it shine as the cop's billy club went up 'side your head shine shine shining as you fell to the pavement with someone's knee crashing into your stomach and someone's foot into your back until a cop dragged you away, threw you into the paddy wagon and off to the jail you and the others went, singing "I Ain't Scared of Your Jail 'Cause I Want My Freedom." ... If it was summer, the jailer would turn the heat on, and if it was winter he'd turn if off and take the mattresses, and you'd sing freedom songs (your brother sent you a note and said you looked real good on the six o'clock news on TV walking down the street singing) until the guard came and said, "Shut up all that damn noise," and you'd sing louder, and he'd take one of you out at a time, and everybody'd get quiet and listen to the screams and cries from the floor above, and then that one would come back, bleeding, and you'd sing again because if one went to jail, all went; if one got a beating, all got beatings. And then that night or the next day or the day after, the people would've got up enough money to bail you out, and you'd go back to the church and march again, and your brother would see you on the six o'clock news for thirty seconds between the stock market report and Jackie Kennedy flying to Switzerland with her children for skiing lessons.[17]

By the time he wrote this account, Lester had moved on to the next stage of the black revolt and now viewed nonviolent protest with derision and disdain. But his testimony does bear witness to the importance of television coverage of nonviolent protest. Television kept alive and fanned the moral outrage of people over the unmerited suffering blacks were enduring. Television encoded, and thus exposed, the relationships between blacks and whites in the South, and people responded critically: They felt disgust and outrage.[18]

How TV Created the Black Revolution

Initially, the black protesters did not realize how important television was to their movement. For, although the black revolt started in Montgomery when the television cameras began rolling on that evening of 5 December in the Baptist Church on Holt Street, the bus strike itself began as a print-mediated event. The initial call for the boycott, for example, came through the distribution of thirty-five thousand mimeographed leaflets to the black people of Montgomery. Jo Ann Robinson, a faculty member at Alabama State College, stayed up all night the day Rosa Parks was arrested, cutting the stencils and mimeographing the handbills that she and some of her students distributed the next day in stores, schools, bars, and churches throughout Montgomery's black neighborhoods. Moreover, the almost 100 percent effectiveness of the boycott on the first day owed nothing to television; it was, instead, the result of a network—a network held together by the telephone. This network produced more printed materials.

At the center of the network was E. D. Nixon, a pullman car porter who had formerly headed the local branch of the National Association for the Advancement of Colored People (NAACP)—during the time when Rosa Parks had served as secretary. When he heard about Mrs. Parks's arrest, Nixon telephoned her to suggest that they use her case to "break down segregation on the bus."[19] Mrs. Parks agreed. Nixon then called Fred Grey, one of the city's two black lawyers, who, in turn, called Jo Ann Robinson, president of the Women's Political Council, an organization begun in 1946 to "do something about" the arrests, humiliations, court trials and fines paid by people who just sat down on empty seats on Montgomery buses. Jo Ann Robinson called the offices of each chapter of the organization to set in operation the already-prepared plan for a bus boycott. This arm of the network produced thirty-five thousand printed leaflets calling for the boycott.

In the meantime, E.D. Nixon called a white reporter, Joe Azbell, at *The Montgomery Advertiser*. They met, and Nixon gave him one of the handbills, urging him to print it and the story on the first page of the Sunday morning edition of his newspaper. This printed message spread the news to blacks who might have missed the leaflets.

Nixon also called Ralph Abernathy, whom he knew through past work with the NAACP. Together, they identified eighteen other ministers who could mobilize the community. Nixon then called these eighteen and arranged a meeting for Friday evening—the day after Mrs. Parks's arrest. Out of that meeting there came another printed document, another leaflet announcing the boycott and inviting people to a mass meeting on Monday evening. These were distributed on Saturday and Sunday through the churches.

At that Monday night meeting, as we saw, the medium of television took over and the black revolt was born. Television made the dramatic speech of the charismatic Martin Luther King the centerpiece of that meeting. But for those who were there in the church that evening, the main item on the agenda was Rev. Ralph Abernathy's (nontelevised) reading (from a typewritten sheet) of the list of demands: (1) courteous treatment by bus drivers; (2) passengers seated on a first-come, first-served basis, with Negroes seated from the back of the bus toward the front, whites from the front toward the back; and (3) the employment of Negro bus drivers on predominantly Negro routes. Those assembled enthusiastically endorsed these timid demands, never dreaming how television would escalate them and abolish Jim Crow altogether.

Television maintained the Montgomery bus boycott for thirteen months by making it a nationally supported moral crusade. After broadcasting King's speech on that Monday evening, television cameras were again on the scene three days later when King and his delegation met with the mayor, his council, and the bus officials. Here, the cameras exposed the depth of the white racist attitude: "If we granted the Negroes these demands," the white lawyer announced, "they would go about boasting of a victory that they had won over the white people, and this we will not stand for." Later, when the boycott seemed to be lagging, television reports of the bombing of Martin Luther King's home helped to revive the feelings of moral outrage and to keep the crusade before the public. Again, when the city arrested King for conducting an illegal strike, television cameras were there. And they were there when he walked out of the courthouse and his followers spontaneously burst out singing, "We ain't gonna ride the bus no more." Finally, television cameras accompanied him when at 6:00 A.M. on 21 December 1956 he marked the end of the successful boycott by boarding a bus and taking a seat in the formerly white-only section.[20]

The black revolt began with the Montgomery bus strike because at that point television became *the* reference source for the nation for black and white relationships. Television made blacks confront the fact that they were oppressed by whites. Prior to the black revolt, most blacks had unaggressively accommodated to the existing racially segregated arrangements in the South. Psychiatric studies of southern blacks have revealed that they harbored considerable latent aggressive feelings toward whites. One psychiatrist wrote: "I have yet to see a Negro who did not unconsciously have a deep fear of and hostility toward white people."[21] The televised "Montgomery Story" helped blacks acknowledge these unconscious feelings and enabled them to condemn openly the social arrangements that oppressed them. Sitting in the back of the bus simply because one was black *was* ignominious. Giving up one's seat to a white person *was* humiliating. Being told to move to the rear of the bus *was* insulting. The dramatic presentations of their subordinate position on the television screen helped blacks become critical of the culture in which they lived. They concluded that segregation was not simply a fact of life—*it was morally wrong*. More than this, they began to declare that the entire Jim Crow doctrine was immoral and should be dismantled.

From television, too, blacks found out how whites really felt about blacks. Once the almost universal reaction of southern whites to the bus boycott was revealed on television, it became difficult for blacks to maintain the distinction between "good white folks" and "white trash." Almost all southern whites, it seems, were racist. This disheartening information, however, was accompanied by good news. For once, television became *the* reference source during the Montgomery bus strike; blacks saw that they could stand up and face the white man as an equal. Of course, many individual blacks had stood up to the white man before, but once this appeared on television, it enabled millions of blacks to become critical of their belief that they must accommodate to Jim Crow doctrine. Moreover, because television helped them see that their cause was just, they knew they could win, could defeat the unfair and immoral social arrangements. And, as the televised exploits of Martin Luther King demonstrated, blacks could do this peacefully, and with dignity—through the almost miraculous way of nonviolent resistance.

So, television not only created the black revolt, it also mobilized blacks to support it by showing that protest was possible and that freedom was within their grasp—now. Another way television mobilized blacks was through the presentation on newscasts of black protesters in juxtaposition with the stereotype blacks portrayed on television shows. Although they rarely appeared in dramas, and never as news reporters or on "talk" shows, blacks did appear in variety shows as happy and contented singers (Billy Daniels, Nat King Cole, Pearl Bailey), musicians (Hazel Scott, Lionel Hampton, Louis Armstrong), and dancers (Bill "Bojangles" Robinson). Some of these entertainers (Hazel Scott, Billy Daniels, Nat King Cole) had their own fifteen-minute musical variety shows during the 1950s. Blacks also appeared on television as stock comic characters: Eddie Anderson as Jack Benny's valet, Rochester; Louise Beavers as Beulah—a "maid with a heart of gold"; and the syndicated "Amos and Andy" show, starring Tim Moore as George "Kingfish" Stevens, a scheming con man and president of the Mystic Knights of the Sea, a fraternal order, and Spencer Williams as Andy, a cab driver for the Fresh Air Cab Company. The stark contrast between the real lives of the blacks in Montgomery, Alabama, presented on the newscasts, and the versions of blacks depicted on the variety and comedy shows led many blacks to begin to criticize and protest the stereotype blacks portrayed on television shows.

TV Mobilized White Support for the Revolution

Television not only mobilized the blacks, it also mobilized many whites in support of the black revolt. One way it did this was by presenting celebrated leaders, especially political leaders, as supporters of blacks in their struggle. The most significant political leader, of course, was the president of the United States. The first president to appear on television in support of the black revolt was Dwight Eisenhower. Yet, Eisenhower's support did not come willingly. Television extorted it from him.

Although he had appointed Earl Warren to be chief justice of the Supreme Court, President Eisenhower had distanced himself from the *Brown* decision that Warren had written. "It made no difference whether or not I endorsed it," he said. "The Constitution is as the Supreme Court interprets it and I must conform to that and do my very best to see that it is carried out in this country." Later, in a televised news conference in July of 1957, the president said he could not "imagine any set of circumstances that would ever induce me to send federal troops ... to enforce the orders of a federal court, because I believe the common sense of Americans will never require it."[22] But television forced him to do just that.

Little Rock Puts Eisenhower on the Screen

Governor Orval Faubus of Arkansas made the initial television assault. After failing to halt the federal order to integrate Central High in Little Rock, the governor appeared on statewide television the day before school was to open and announced that he intended to surround Central High with National Guardsmen because of "evidence of disorder and threats of violence." The school, he stated, must remain segregated because "it will not be possible to restore or to maintain order and protect the citizens if forcible integration is carried out tomorrow in the schools of this community." His last words were: "Blood will run in the streets if Negro people should attempt to enter Central High School." The next day, the television cameras were there to film the incredible spectacle of a school surrounded by 250 National Guardsmen. The following day, television viewers saw those National Guardsmen prevent the designated nine black children from entering the high school. Even more dramatic, the television cameras followed the path of one of these children, fifteen-year-old Elizabeth Eckford, as a jeering, angry mob yelled and spat on her, some even calling for her to be lynched.

Television reduced this classic conflict between a state and the federal government to a battle of personalities: Governor Faubus versus President Eisenhower. The next move came from Eisenhower, when he invited Faubus to meet with him at the president's summer house in Newport, Rhode Island. Television reports confirmed that a satisfactory settlement had been reached. Not that anyone heard what the parties had said to each other, but both men had appeared on the TV screen smiling and shaking hands in a friendly fashion. Obviously, the president had convinced the governor to allow the nine black children into Central High.

The following Friday, Governor Faubus appeared on television to announce that he was withdrawing the National Guard, and he asked blacks to stay away from the high school until he could arrange for peaceful segregation. He then announced that he was leaving to attend a conference of Southern governors in Georgia. Many interpreted the message from the governor as a call to whites to make peaceful desegregation impossible. When the nine children entered the school on Monday morning, the television cameras showed the angry crowd of screaming, cursing, weeping, white people around the school, many of whom turned on the journalists—black and white—beating them and breaking their equipment. By now, the crowd had swelled to such a size that the police chief removed the black children from the school to quell the rioting.

When television crews interviewed him at the conference in Georgia, Governor Faubus piously declared: "The trouble in Little Rock vindicates my good judgment in sending in the National Guard." When TV reporters interviewed *him* in Newport, President Eisenhower termed the rioting a "disgraceful occurrence." After another day of rioting, Eisenhower went on national television to tell the U.S. public he was sending the 101st Airborne Division to Little Rock. In this speech, the president revealed a sophisticated understanding of the medium of television· "To make this talk," he began, "I have come to the president's office in the White House. I could have spoken from Rhode Island, where I have been staying recently, but I felt that in speaking from the house of Lincoln, of Jackson, and of Wilson, my words could convey both the sadness I feel in the action I was compelled today to take and the firmness with which I intend to pursue this course until the orders at Little Rock can be executed without unlawful interference."

The next day, the television spectacular continued as viewers watched the lines of paratroopers in the street in front of the school drive away the protesters with bayonets poised at the ready while helicopters circled above the school. They next saw a parade of jeeps with mounted machine guns and soldiers armed with rifles convoy the nine black children to school, where each received his or her own personal military bodyguard.

On 22 September, Governor Faubus took his last shot on television, but his performance revealed how little he understood the medium. Holding up a newspaper with photographs of the troops "in action," he declared: "Evidence of the naked force of the federal government is here apparent in these unsheathed bayonets in the backs of schoolgirls." He next showed a newspaper picture of a citizen with blood streaming down his face and claimed that a federal soldier had struck the man with a gun belt. Staring into the camera, he asked:

"Does the will of the people—that basic precept of democracy—no longer matter?"

If Governor Faubus had hoped to stir up an insurrection against the federal government, he failed; and he failed, in part, because still photos on a TV screen can never have the emotional and moral impact of the sound and motion of actual television film coverage of an event. (Ten years later, the protesting students at the Democratic convention in Chicago showed everyone how to use television to mobilize the citizenry against the government.)

Instead of provoking an insurrection against the federal government, the television cameras in Little Rock now evoked moral support for the nine black children attending Central High. Television reporters dogged the steps of these very attractive, dignified, polite, students, interviewing them and photographing them as they went about the school. Television reporters also put white students on camera who, if they did not openly support the black students, did complain that it was adults and "outsiders" who had caused all the trouble. Yet, life was not easy for the nine. They were subject to harassment and threats from a minority of students throughout the school year. In February, one of the nine was expelled for fighting back. She left Little Rock to enroll in a high school in New York City. There, the television cameras recorded her arrival and reception by supportive New York City officials.

The televised Little Rock story ended in May when Ernest Green became the first black student to graduate from Central high. Later, he said, "I figured I was making a statement and helping black people's existence in Little Rock ... I kept telling myself 'I just can't trip with all these cameras watching me.' But I knew that once I got as far as that principal and received that diploma, I had cracked the wall."[23]

But it truly was no more than a crack: In a Gallup Poll taken in late 1958, Americans selected Orval Fabuus as one of their "ten most admired men." Television had mobilized the moral support of an unwilling president, but had not yet mobilized the population at large. It is, of course, true that at the time television had broadcast the Little Rock story on the nightly news, not everyone owned their own television set. Many still watched television only in bars or when they visited friends. Most people still got their "news" from newspapers and other print media. By 1960, however, television sets were less expensive and there was a set in most every home. Moreover, by the

1960s, a new generation of young black protesters had come on the scene, a generation that instinctively had a better understanding of how to use television to mobilize support for the black revolt.

TV Sit-In Spawns More Sit-Ins

In February 1960, the first sit-in took place in Greensboro, North Carolina. The television crews came to film what was happening, but sit-ins did not seem to be suitable TV fare: just some polite, nonviolent black students sitting at a lunch counter in F.W. Woolworth's waiting to be served, and some equally polite white waitresses behind the counter ignoring them. Yet, the sit-in tactics captured the imagination of young blacks—and whites, too—who spontaneously set up wildcat sit-ins throughout the South and picket lines at Woolworth stores in northern cities. In New York City, where college students picketed Woolworth's, the white Columbia student who led the demonstration told a television reporter that "injustice is everybody's concern."

By the end of the month, the sit-ins became more TV-ready when white teenagers began to physically attack the demonstrators as they sat at lunch counters. Shortly thereafter, NBC devoted one of its hour-long "White Paper" reports to the sit-ins. Television viewers across the nation watched with surprise and increased moral outrage as the always nonviolent college students—white as well as black—were struck, spit upon, burned by cigarettes ground out on their backs, soiled from catsup and coffee spilled over their heads, and physically yanked off their seats. When the police arrived, they arrested not the white teens, but the protesters.

In Nashville, the sit-in protesters had the most sophisticated organization. These protesters formed teams so that as soon as one group was arrested another filed in to take its place on the lunch counter stools. And the student organizers always told the television reporters when a sit-in was scheduled. By late March, the police had orders not to arrest the demonstrators because this only contributed to the national publicity the sit-ins were getting. "The sit-ins are instigated and planned by and staged for the convenience of the Columbia Broadcasting System" (CBS), declared Buford Ellington, governor of Tennessee.[24]

The Nashville students continued the sit-ins through February,

March, and April. Then, on 19 April dynamite destroyed the home of the black lawyer who had defended the arrested sit-in students. The next day, twenty-five hundred students and community members marched on City Hall. There, on the steps, with television cameras grinding away, Diane Nash, the student leader, confronted the mayor and asked him: "Mayor West, do you feel it is wrong to discriminate against a person solely on the basis of their race or color?" Without hesitation, West nodded and said, yes, he believed that it was wrong. Later, the mayor explained: "It was a moral question—one that a *man* had to answer, not a politician."[25] The city's store owners, whose sales had slumped because whites had feared to come downtown and blacks had boycotted them, began, within weeks, to integrate their lunch counters, pointing to the mayor as the man who was responsible.

During Easter weekend of that year, students—black and white, from North and South—attended a conference at Shaw University in Raleigh, North Carolina, that led to the formation of the Student Non-Violent Coordinating Committee (SNCC). Over the next three years, the SNCC coordinated nonviolent sit-ins, sleep-ins, and kneel-ins at segregated restaurants, waiting rooms, and theaters throughout the South.

TV Shows Violence on Freedom Ride

The most dramatic nonviolent demonstration was the Freedom Ride of 1961 sponsored by both SNCC and CORE (Congress of Racial Equality). Here, the target was segregated public transportation. Starting from Washington, D.C., the freedom riders planned to ride a Greyhound bus to New Orleans, arriving there on 17 May, the anniversary of the 1954 *Brown* decision. The strategy was for the whites in the group to sit in the back of the bus while blacks sat in the front and refuse to move when ordered. At every rest stop, blacks would go into the white-only waiting rooms and try to use all the facilities.

When the Freedom Riders reached Birmingham on Sunday, 14 May, their journey became a media event. After only occasional minor scuffles up until this time, the Freedom Riders here ran into a mob of whites who assaulted them ferociously. The next day, a television reporter interviewed Jim Peck, a white Freedom Rider, whose head was heavily bandaged. "I was beaten twice by hoodlums," he told the television audience, admitting that his head wounds had required fifty stitches. The following Saturday, the Freedom Riders left Birmingham for Montgomery, where once again a white mob of two or three hundred attacked them with fists, baseball bats, and pipes. The next day, a freedom rider who had been knocked unconscious spoke to a television reporter from his hospital bed: "Those of us who are on the Freedom Rides will continue. I'm not sure I'll be able to, but we are going on to New Orleans no matter what happens. We are dedicated to this. We will take hitting. We'll take beatings. We're willing to accept death. But we are going to keep coming until we can ride [from] anywhere in the South to anyplace else in the South as Americans, without anyone making any comment."[26]

In response to the nationwide moral outrage these televised reports provoked, the attorney general, Robert Kennedy, sent six hundred federal Marshals to accompany the Freedom Riders on the remainder of their journey. But they never reached New Orleans. For, when they arrived in Jackson, Mississippi, they were arrested for trespassing in the white-only waiting room, convicted, and put in jail for sixty days. When more Freedom Riders arrived in Jackson, they too were jailed.

By this point, many of the younger leaders of the black revolt no longer looked at nonviolence as a means for changing the hearts of white people in the South. Rather, they viewed it as a tactic to obtain national television attention. The televised reports of the violence inflicted on the nonviolent protesters produced public outrage that forced the federal government to act on behalf of the black protesters. This tactic was most successful when whites participated in the nonviolent demonstrations. Not only did televised accounts of physical attacks on white protesters intensify pressure on the federal government, but the scenes of integrated protest demonstrations showed that racial relations between black and white did not have to be antagonistic.

Made-For TV Black Protests

As nonviolence became a tactic to secure media coverage, the protests became more dramatic and specifically staged for television. This became evident in the spring of 1962, when the leader of the black revolt launched Project C (for Confrontation), which called for the televised arrest of Martin Luther King in Birmingham, Alabama, on Good Friday. The arrest elicited a phone call from President Kennedy to Coretta King, assuring her that her husband was safe and explaining that "we are doing everything we can."[27] The next phase of Project C called for using Birmingham's black children in a protest march. On 2 May, the children began their march. On the evening news, viewers watched the shocking spectacle of children as young as six years of age being herded into paddy wagons and hauled away. The first day, 959 children were taken to Birmingham jails. The next day, a thousand more children prepared to march. To prevent the march from taking place, Police Commissioner "Bull" Connor brought police dogs and fire fighters to the park where the children had assembled. That evening, watchers of the televised news witnessed an even more shocking display of violent racism: police dogs attacking children, and then water hoses blasting them, knocking them down, slamming them into curbs, and over parked cars. Some children were rolled over and over on the ground by the power of the water. These pictures from Birmingham travelled throughout the world, intensifying the federal government's worries about America's image abroad. "It was a masterpiece in the use of media to explain a cause to the general public," a Birmingham lawyer later observed. "In those days, we had fifteen minutes of national news and fifteen minutes of global news, and in marching only one block they could get enough news film to fill all of the newscasts of all the television stations in the United States."[28]

The Southern Christian Leadership Conference (SCLC) conducted the demonstrations in Birmingham fully conscious of the power of television. "In essence," explained Andrew Young, one of the black leaders, "we were consciously using the mass media to get across to the nation what our message was": that southern segregation was far more vicious than most Americans had ever realized. "The movement was really about getting publicity for injustice.... The injustice was there under the surface and as long as it stayed below the surface nobody was concerned about it. You had to bring it out in the open."[29]

The shocking attack on the black children of Birmingham prompted President Kennedy to dispatch Burke Marshall, head of the Justice Department's Civil Rights Division, who negotiated a settlement between the SCLC leaders and the businessmen of the city. Two nights later, however, rioting broke out. The televised reports of violence were followed by a television appearance by President

Kennedy, who announced that he was sending in federal troops. "This government will do whatever must be done to preserve order, protect the lives of its citizens, and uphold the law of the land.... Those who labored so hard to achieve the peaceful, constructive settlement of last week can feel nothing but dismay at the efforts of those who would replace conciliation and good will with violence and hate."[30]

The following month, television viewers watched a different kind of confrontation as Governor Wallace literally stood in the doorway of a building at the University of Alabama to block the entry of two black students trying to register. Deliberately playing to the television cameras, Wallace declared: "It is important that the people of this state and nation understand that this action is in violation of rights reserved for the state by the Constitution of the United States and the Constitution of the state of Alabama."[31] But the federal government won that televised confrontation when Nicholas Katzenbach, deputy attorney general, stared the governor in the eye and told him that the federal government intended to integrate the school. Wallace stepped aside and the black students walked through the door. The color barrier at the University of Alabama was broken. Capitalizing on the victory, President Kennedy went on television that evening and, after declaring that the nation faced a moral crisis, announced that he was sending Congress a new Civil Rights Bill.

Later that summer, the leaders of the black revolt staged a television spectacular, the largest demonstration the nation had ever witnessed: the march on Washington of some two hundred fifty thousand demonstrators assembled from all over the nation. As the rest of the country watched, these quarter of a million people—black and white—linked hands, sang "We Shall Overcome," and listened to speeches urging quick passage of the Civil Rights Bill. The highlight of the day came when Martin Luther King delivered his electrifying "I have a dream" oration.

The bombing of a black church, killing four girls, just eighteen days after the march, further mobilized support for the Civil Rights Bill. Between the spring and summer of 1963, the percentage of people regarding civil rights as "the most important problem facing America" increased from 4 percent to 52 percent—a shift in perceived public priorities never achieved before or since in so short a time.[32] The assassination of President Kennedy, coming as it did in Dallas the following November, was thought by many initially to be the work of southern whites retaliating against Kennedy for his stand on civil rights. The new president, Lyndon Johnson, in his first televised speech to a joint session of Congress a few days after the assassination, declared that "no memorial or eulogy could more eloquently honor President Kennedy's memory than the earliest possible passage of the Civil Rights Bill for which he fought."

President Johnson secured passage of this bill and signed it in July 1964. This act outlawed racial segregation and discrimination in all publicly or privately owned facilities that were open to the general public. But it ignored the issue many black leaders regarded as crucial: the right to vote. So that summer, SNCC planned a voter registration project in Mississippi. Recognizing the media value of white supporters, SNCC invited over six hundred white college students, almost half of whom were women, to join the Mississippi Freedom Summer. The volunteers were to help set up freedom schools, health clinics, and theaters; but mainly they were there to urge and prepare black Mississippians to register to vote. National television coverage of Freedom Summer intensified after three of the volunteers—two white, one black—disappeared on 21 June. On 4 August, just eighteen days before the start of the Democratic National Convention, the bodies of Goodman, Schwerner, and Chaney were found in Mississippi. They had been murdered.

At this point, television took command of the course of events. Some people thought that they could manipulate and control it, but the medium had become more powerful than any one person or group. At the Democratic National Convention in Atlantic City, a group of Mississippi blacks, called the Mississippi Freedom Democratic party, challenged the right of the all-white Mississippi delegation to represent the state. Before television cameras that were filming the hearings of the Democratic party's Credential Committee, the volatile, outspoken Fannie Lou Hamer was the star witness: "If the Freedom Democratic party is not seated now, I question America," she said. "Is this America? The land of the free and the home of the brave? When we have to sleep with our telephones off the hook because our lives be threatened daily?" Ms. Hamer went on to describe the beatings she had received in Mississippi for attending a civil rights meeting, at which point she broke down and wept.

President Johnson, who was watching the televised coverage of the convention, became alarmed that such goings-on might cause discord at the convention. He promptly called a press conference in an attempt to preempt TV coverage of the hearings. But he merely succeeded in interrupting the live coverage of Fannie Lou Hamer's testimony, for that evening her testimony dominated the network news shows. What Fannie Lou Hamer said and did was much more engaging TV fare than the avuncular pontification of Lyndon Baines Johnson. The next day, she again dominated TV coverage of the convention when she led a contingent of the Democratic Freedom party into the convention hall and tried to take the seats of the Mississippi delegation. When guards repulsed and attempted to remove them, Fannie Lou Hamer led the group in a rousing rendition of freedom songs right on the convention floor. Johnson's forces then engineered a compromise to seat two of the black Mississippi delegates, but the Democratic Freedom party rejected it—on live television. "I will have nothing to do with the political system any longer," one of the black delegates announced. The seating of the black delegates had become a moral matter, not a political issue to be worked out through negotiation. Fannie Lou Hamer told TV reporters that two seats were simply "token seats, in the back row, the same as we got in Mississippi. We didn't come all this way for that mess again."[33] That night, she again led black delegates onto the convention floor, where television cameramen filmed the fracas as guards led them away.

The following January, television cameras showed up at Selma, Alabama, for one of the most prolonged and dramatic confrontations of the black movement. Demonstrations, sponsored by the Southern Christian Leadership Conference (SCLC), went on from January until March. As all parties vied for media attention, television viewers were treated to lots of irrelevant posturing and entertainment in place of serious political protest. At one of the televised demonstrations staged by the Concerned White Citizens of Alabama, a group of segregationists began to sing "Dixie." The protesters countered by singing "America the Beautiful," while some black supporters chimed in with "We Shall Overcome."

The omnipresent TV cameramen escalated the rhetoric and the violence—on both sides. The sheriff of Selma, James Clark, was a made-for-television heavy. Like Bull Connor of Birmingham, Clark was a loud-mouthed bully who wore a helmet liner like General Patton, an Eisenhower jacket, and a swagger stick. At one point, Clark delighted TV cameramen by leaping on the back of one of the black leaders, a woman, and throwing her to the ground. At another point, C.T. Vivian, an executive staff member of SCLC, harangued Sheriff Clark and a group of armed deputies who were blocking a doorway to prevent blacks from registering to vote: "There are those who followed Hitler like you follow this Sheriff Clark. They didn't think their day would come. But they also were pulled into the courtroom and they were also given the death sentence.... You're racists in the same way Hitler was a racist." Here, Sheriff Clark ordered the television cameramen to turn off their lights. When they did, he knocked Vivian to the ground. The evening news carried the entire encounter.

Because television selected the most spectacular goings-on, the participants—on both sides—vied to be more spectacular than the other. During one march, a fifty-three-year-old demonstrator, Annie Lee Cooper, punched Sheriff Clark in the face after he jabbed her with his elbow. She slugged him two more times before deputies subdued her. Sheriff Clark then whacked her in the head with his swagger stick. Under the continual scrutiny of television, the demonstration marchers became more specialized: The black teachers marched as a group, then the undertakers, then the beauticians, and, finally, the school children. The city jails were getting crowded.

In February, the militant Black Muslim minister Malcolm X came to speak at Selma at the invitation of SNCC. He told a large crowd that "the white people should thank Dr. King for holding people in check, for there are other (black leaders) who do not believe in these (nonviolent) measures."[34]

Later that month, a policeman shot and killed Jimmy Lee Jackson, a black taking part in a protest march. Dozens of other people, including a television reporter, were badly beaten during this march. The next day, the reporter, Richard Valeriani, appeared on television from his hospital bed, his speech slurred, his head in bandages.

To protest the death of Jimmy Lee Jackson, the SCLC proposed a fifty-mile march to the state capital in Montgomery. The officials of the SNCC said the march was too dangerous, but SCLC remained undeterred. On the Sunday morning of the march, six hundred people trekked through Selma, but when they reached the Edmund Pettus bridge, they met a contingent of Alabama State Troopers. The troopers charged, knocking the marchers to the ground, firing tear gas at them, and riding horses over the fallen bodies. The networks all interrupted their regular programming to show the police assault in Selma. It looked like a war, the mayor of Selma later recalled, "that went out all over the country. And the people, the wrath of the nation, came down on us."[35]

In response to "Bloody Sunday," Martin Luther King invited prominent clergymen across the nation to participate in a "minister's march" in Selma. On 9 April, King led some fifteen hundred people to the Pettus bridge—where state troopers were waiting. After singing "We Shall Overcome" and reciting a prayer, the marchers returned to Brown's Chapel. That evening, one of the white clergymen, James Reeb, was struck on the head with a club. He died two days later.

The moral pressure exerted on President Johnson grew intense. The following Monday evening, 70 million people watched him on television as he introduced to Congress a Voting Rights Bill. He asked all his fellow Americans to support the blacks' quest for suffrage. "This cause," the president said, "must be our cause, too. Because it's not just Negroes, it's really all of us who must overcome the crippling legacy of bigotry and injustice. And *we shall* overcome."

On Sunday, 21 March, four thousand people set off once again in a march from Selma to Montgomery. Belligerent racists lined the route, shouting at the demonstrators and holding up signs for the television cameras. But there were no attacks. By Thursday, the marchers, who now had swelled to twenty-five thousand, reached Montgomery, where the national networks provided live coverage as Martin Luther King strode up the capital steps with many of the movement's heroes alongside. From the top of the steps, King delivered a stunning address to the nation:

> The road ahead is not altogether a smooth one. There are no broad highways to lead us easily and inevitably to quick solutions. We are still in for a season of suffering.... However difficult the moment, however frustrating the hour, it will not be long, because truth crushed to the earth will rise again. How long? Not long. Because you shall reap what you sow. How long? Not long ... because the arc of the moral universe is long, but it bends toward justice. How long? Not long. Because mine eyes have seen the glory of the coming of the Lord.

That evening, four Ku Klux Klan members shot and killed one of the marchers, Viola Liuzzo, a white woman from Detroit. By noon the next day, President Johnson appeared on television to announce that the FBI had arrested the four. He took time to condemn the Klan: "My father fought them many long years ago in Texas, and I have fought them all my life." Governor Wallace of Alabama further fueled public moral outrage when he appeared on the *Today* show and justified the killing: "Of course I regret the incident," he said, "but I would like to point out that people are assaulted in every state in the union.... With twenty-five thousand people marching in the streets and chanting and maligning and slandering and libeling the people of this state as they did for several hours on this network and the other networks, I think the people of our state were greatly restrained."[36]

Passage of the Civil Rights Bill

The Senate passed the Voting Rights Bill in May, the House approved it in July, and President Johnson—under the glare of television cameras—signed it into law on 9 August.

With the passage of the Voting Rights Bill, blacks, for the first time in three hundred years, gained a new sense of power and dignity, a sense of true citizenship. And whites, too, now accepted civil rights as human rights to be shared by all. The relationship between the races had changed. Things had gotten better. Televised coverage of the violent massive resistance of white southerners to the blacks who had nonviolently protested the arrangements in the South had mobilized the moral outrage of the rest of the nation and pressured all branches of the federal government to act: court orders prohibiting segregation, legislation in the form of the Civil Rights Act and the Voting Rights Act, and vigorous support from the executive in the form of federal marshals and federal voting registrars dispatched from the attorney general's office.

Television had helped Americans destroy Jim Crow. Through the medium of television, the life chances for blacks had improved. The social arrangements had gotten better—especially in the South. Segregation of races had been abolished legally and factually—in schools, restaurants, hotels, and on vehicles of public transportation. There were no longer separate toilet facilities for blacks, nor separate water fountains, laundromats, or stores. Blacks played together with whites on sports teams, they worked beside them at the same jobs, they received the same salaries for the same work. Blacks could vote and could no longer be deprived of their civil rights. Schools now taught about the role of blacks in history. Even the language itself changed: The terms "boy" and "nigger" disappeared from common parlance, as did dialect jokes. Through the medium of television, Americans had brought about dramatic improvements in the life chances of black people in the United States.

Phase Two: Black Power

Although things had gotten better, there were other consequences of television coverage of the movement that were bad. Most important, perhaps, television had escalated the violence inflicted on blacks. Sympathetic network coverage of the black protest demonstrations and critical accounts of black progress served both to heighten white resistance in the South and to intensify physical attacks on blacks. Through this dialectic with television, the logic of nonviolent protest began to reach the saturation point. How many beatings could one take? How many times could one go to jail? And were the beatings and the jailings worth the prize? Did this suffering win freedom now—as the protesters demanded? Increasing numbers of protesters grew weary of nonviolence. "I'm not going to let somebody hit up the side of my head for the rest of my life and die," one of the SNCC protesters complained. "You got to fight back. We don't demonstrate to get beat up. We demonstrate to show people what has to be done."[37] By escalating the violence against blacks, television had lowered the commitment of many blacks to the philosophy of nonviolence.

Television also clearly revealed that nonviolence was a tactic of the powerless. It did work—most of the time—but it left blacks still beholden to white people: *They* determined what rights and what freedoms blacks could enjoy. Blacks still lacked autonomy; they lacked control over their own lives. Because television faithfully encoded the relationship between the races, blacks could more clearly see how dependent on, thus inferior to, white people they really were in this culture. These encoded relationships also revealed in a way never before possible that being black in this culture was a curse. Being black was a condition to lament; it was never a source of pride. Whatever self-esteem a black person had came only from being like a white person, or being the kind of black that the man esteemed.

Perhaps most important of all, television made the battle against racism a moral crusade, and moral crusades are rarely content with gradual, slow, piecemeal change. The black protesters, especially the young ones, had less and less patience with the snail-like pace of political action that always required compromise, negotiation, and bargaining. This antipolitical attitude had surfaced on national television at the 1964 Democratic National Convention when the Mississippi Freedom Democratic party had refused to accept two seats as convention delegates. To these blacks, combating racism was not a political matter; it was a moral one. This TV-cultivated moral righteousness came to a head in the Meredith March in the summer of 1966, giving birth to the second stage of the black revolt.

James Meredith, who—through the medium of television—had become a national celebrity in 1962 when he became the first black student at the University of Mississippi, announced in the spring of 1966 that he would undertake a sixteen-day, 220-mile "walk against fear" throughout the state of Mississippi. He wanted to encourage black voter turnout in the state's 7 June primary election, but his main purpose was to demonstrate that the other Mississippi blacks could overcome the fear of white violence. On 6 June, the second day of his walk, Meredith was shot from ambush.

Within twenty-four hours, every national black leader was in Mississippi, determined to continue Meredith's march. Martin Luther King came, representing SCLC; Floyd McKissick, director of CORE came; and Stokley Carmichael, the newly elected chairman of SNCC came. Roy Wilkins, head of the NAACP, and Whitney Young, of the Urban League, came too, as did hundreds of other blacks and whites—all ready to continue the "walk against fear."

Almost immediately, dissension broke out among the leaders. McKissick and Carmichael had already gained television coverage as more radical militants than any of the others. The preceding summer, at a televised rally in Atlanta protesting the shooting of two voter registration volunteers by a white sheriff, Carmichael had announced: "We're going to tear this country down. Then we're going to build it back, brick by brick, until it's a fit place for human beings."[38] Here in Mississippi, the older leaders resisted plans to make the march more militant. As the debate grew more intense, Carmichael told both Wilkins and Young—in colorful language—that they were out of date. As a consequence, Wilkins and Young withdrew from the march, and

Carmichael and McKissick issued a manifesto that declared that "this march will be a massive public indictment and protest of the failure of American society, the government of the United States, and the state of Mississippi." Martin Luther King did not want to put President Johnson on the spot, but he remained as part of the march and tried to keep it nonviolent.[39]

On 16 June, the police in Greenwood, Mississippi, arrested Stokley Carmichael and some other marchers. He was released in time to address the rally the protest marchers held that evening. Infuriated by his arrest, Carmichael told the audience of six hundred and the television cameras covering the rally: "This is the twenty-seventh time I have been arrested. I ain't going to jail no more." He pointed out that blacks had been demanding freedom for six years and had gotten nothing. "What we gonna start saying now is 'black power.' He shouted the slogan repeatedly. Each time, the audience shouted back, "black power." Another member of SNCC leaped to the platform and asked, "What do you want?" Again and again, the audience shouted in unison what had suddenly galvanized them into a new consciousness.[40]

In a number of ways, television had prepared blacks for this new consciousness, this new awareness of the need for black power. From television, blacks had learned how their brothers lived elsewhere in the society—how they lived in the rural South, how they lived in the urban ghettos of the North. More than this, from television blacks had also learned how whites lived in American society. Through the medium of television—the reference source for black-white relations—blacks had become increasingly aware how their people were being deprived relative to white people. And they had come to recognize that blacks would always remain deprived unless they gained power.

Television also engendered receptivity to the need for black power by exposing to blacks the increasing precariousness of their lives in this culture. So long as blacks had accommodated to the existing social arrangements, they had been relatively safe. And so long as they had accepted the existing arrangements, they had believed—especially in the South—that they could count on "decent white folks" to protect them against arbitrary and wanton attacks from cruel whites. But now, blacks no longer accepted the social arrangements whites had imposed on them, and so now blacks *were* more vulnerable to victimization than ever before. At any moment, they might be attacked, or even killed. Television continually fed them information about bombings, beatings, and killings of their people. There was no one to protect them. They had to protect themselves. To do this, they needed power.

Television had also made blacks ready for the demand for black power by raising their expectations. The medium, as we saw, had ensnared President Eisenhower into the Little Rock struggle, and both presidents Kennedy and Johnson had often appeared on television, declaring support for the black movement. Had not President Johnson himself used the words "we shall overcome" on television? And hadn't he denounced all forms of racial discrimination when he signed the Civil Rights Act in 1964?

> It cannot continue. It must not continue. Our Constitution, the foundation of our republic forbids it. The principles of our freedom forbid it. Morality forbids it. And the law I will sign tonight forbids it.[41]

But the continued bombings, the beatings, and killings of blacks in the South revealed that the U.S. government *could* not, or *would* not, protect black people. Nor could the franchise really change matters. After all, northern blacks had the franchise and they still remained victims—deprived and discriminated against socially, politically, and economically.

Finally, television had prepared American blacks for the demand for black power by the widespread coverage it had given Malcolm X. In the late 1940s, Malcolm had become a protégé of the leader of the Lost-Found Nation of Islam in North America, commonly known as the Black Muslims. Like most Muslims, Malcolm had repudiated his Christian name and substituted for it the symbol of an unknown quantity. By the mid-1950s, Malcolm had become the fiery, forceful leader of the New York branch of Black Muslims. Here, in the media capital of the world, television soon "discovered" him and made him a celebrity. His first TV appearance came on the Mike Wallace show on a program entitled "The Hate that Hate Produced." Here, the national audience had its first glimpse of the Muslim leader, Elijah Mohammed, preaching in his Chicago mosque to the serious, determined-looking, black men dressed in suits and ties and their white-scarved, white-gowned Muslim sisters. They saw the restaurants and businesses the Muslims owned and operated. And they heard about the Fruit of Islam—a quasi-military security force. Television watchers learned about the puritanical ethical rules the Muslims followed, how they protected their women, abstained from alcohol and tobacco, and gave generously to the church. But what viewers remembered was Malcolm X preaching what they took to be black supremacy: The white man, Malcolm claimed, has robbed the black man of his name, his language, his culture, and his religion. By treacherously stripping the so-called "American Negro" of his history, the white man had succeeded in subjugating the black man. The white slave master and his evil system must be eliminated and replaced by an all-black nation within a nation.

According to Malcolm X, the show was edited to increase its shock value so that it was made to seem that he was preaching hatred of white people—"white devils," he called them.[42] At any rate, the uproar the show produced led to widespread coverage of the Muslims in newspapers and magazines. This led to more television appearances for the "fiery and angry" Malcolm X. By studying the medium and its format, Malcolm developed techniques and tactics through which he could control the panel discussions and debates he appeared on. One tactic was to interrupt the introductory comments of the program host in order to introduce himself, thus establishing that he, not the host, was in control of the show. Then having set *his* tone, he would sit back and allow "the white devils," and "their trained black parrots," to insist that integration, not separation, was the answer to the American Negro's problem. Malcolm would then rip that notion to pieces:

> No sane black man really wants integration! No sane white man really wants integration! No sane black man really believes that the white man ever will give the black man anything more than token integration.... For the black man in the United States the only solution is complete separation from the white man.[43]

His most powerful tactic was to go nonstop until he had said what he wanted to get said. Then, having set traps for others on the panel, he could shoot them down: He did not advocate segregation, he wanted separation. He did not incite blacks to violence; the white oppressor did that. Then, taking a swipe at the white man's religion, he would say:

The greatest miracle Christianity has achieved in the United States is that the black man in white Christian hands has not grown violent.... *It is* a miracle that the American black people have remained a peaceful people while catching all the centuries of hell that they have caught here in the white man's heaven![44]

Though he made few converts, Malcolm X did crystalize the feelings among the ghetto youth where King had left them indifferent. What most of the young resonated to was Malcolm's oft-repeated refrain on black self-hatred. "The worst crime of the white man," he said many times,

has been to teach us to hate ourselves. We hated our head, we hated the shape of our noses—we wanted one of those doglike noses, you know. Yeah, we hated the color of our skin.... And when we fell victim to this feeling of inadequacy, or infirmity, or helplessness, we turned to somebody to show us the way.

So, in various ways, television had prepared blacks throughout the nation for the black power phase of the black revolt. First, television had elicited strong support from political leaders, which had raised black people's expectations that the government would, and could, wipe out the injustice of racial discrimination. Then television had dashed those hopes through the relentless exposure of how relatively deprived and increasingly victimized blacks were in American culture. Television, therefore, intensified moral criticism of society and its institutions—the more black people watched television, the more critical they became. So, when Malcolm X appeared on their TV screens as the embodiment of black pride, black independence, and black militancy, many were ready. Perhaps, as Malcolm had been saying for a long time, and as Stokley Carmichael and Floyd McKissick and others were saying now, perhaps black power was the answer. Blacks had to become proud of being black; they had to stop seeing their blackness as a curse, as a badge of infirmity. Blacks had to identify and accept what was quintessentially their culture; they had to take pride in "soul."[45] They had to find solidarity with their black brothers and sisters. "The most important thing that black people have to do is to begin to come together, and to be able to do that, we must stop being ashamed of being black," Stokley Carmichael said in many of his speeches. "We are black and beautiful."[46] Through racial pride and racial solidarity, black people now believed they could move on to self-determination as a group. No longer dependent upon or beholden to whites, black people would finally be in control of their own destiny.

But what did this mean programmatically? Did black power mean that whites had to be expelled from the movement? Stokley Carmichael and Floyd McKissick thought so: Through their efforts, all whites were drummed out of both SNCC and CORE. Did black power mean isolation from all whites, no longer entering into coalitions with any white group? This would undermine all political action, which is why the NAACP rejected it. Black power is black death, Roy Wilkins told those attending the 1966 NAACP convention.[47]

Did black power mean the end of integration? Black advocates of community control of the schools in New York City thought so.[48] To seek integration, they argued, is to admit tacitly that white schools, white social groups, white neighborhoods are better. Integration, some even argued, was actually a subterfuge for the maintenance of white supremacy.

What then did black power mean?

Since 12 percent of the population could not ever hope to gain power over the other 88 percent, some thought that black power was a prescription for terrorism. This is why Martin Luther King never embraced the slogan. He recognized the need for greater militancy and racial pride, but he continued to reject violence. Up until his death, he tried to redefine the meaning of black power as a kind of militant nonviolence. But, once again, it was the medium of television that largely determined the course of events.

TV Defines "Black Power"

When this second phase of the black protest movement first began, television reporters persistently sought out black leaders in order to display their reactions to the ever-escalating rhetoric and acts of the advocates of black power. Those black leaders who rejected or questioned black power soon realized that public disclosure on TV of such sentiments weakened the entire black protest movement. This, they believed, was morally wrong. In the interests of solidarity, they now refused to comment or made guarded endorsements of what the more militant blacks were saying and doing. So television discouraged self-criticism within the black protest movement and coerced black leaders into accepting black power and its consequences. And, as the reactions of the black leaders became predictable, the television people turned more and more to Stokley Carmichael, recording his more intemperate remarks (the more intemperate they were, the better television they created). One remark that particularly incensed and frightened people came in a speech he gave in Cleveland in the summer of 1966: "When you talk about black power, you talk of building a movement that will smash everything Western civilization has created." Other bright, articulate blacks in SNCC vied for media coverage by upping the ante—like Julius Lester, who in his popular tract, *Look Out, Whitey! Black Power's Gon' Get Your Mama!* suggested that a race war might be on the horizon. "You can't do what has been done to blacks and not expect retribution. The very act of retribution is liberating."[49] SNCC workers in Chicago published a leaflet telling blacks: "We must fill ourselves with hate for all white things."[50]

The rhetoric of black power—continuously displayed on television—dramatically increased the visibility of SNCC. But it also made SNCC workers a target for police repression, including extraordinary surveillance and arbitrary arrests. To take off some of the heat it now experienced, the central committee of SNCC tried to restrain Carmichael. At one point, it forbade him to appear on television. It also decided that he should always be accompanied by another staff member at his engagements. Finally, the committee deposed Carmichael and replaced him with a new chairman, H. "Rap" Brown. But the bias of television soon selected Brown's most incendiary statements and escalated his rhetoric: "If America chooses to play Nazis, black folks ain't going to play Jesus," was one of his pronouncements at his first televised press conference. In Cambridge, Maryland, he made a forty-minute speech where he went farther than Carmichael ever had—urging blacks to take up arms against white society. Television carried the most inflammatory parts: "If America don't come around, we going to burn it down, brother. We are going to burn it down if we don't get our share of it." At another point, Brown said, "We are at war and we are behind enemy lines, so you better get yourself some guns."[51]

Inspired by the nationally televised doings and sayings of SNCC leaders, other militant black organizations appeared: the Black Panther

Party of Oakland, the Revolutionary Action Movement (RAM), and Ron Jarenga's US (opposed to THEM). The members of these organizations carried weapons and appeared on television as paramilitary groups intent on establishing "revolutionary law, order and justice."

Another way television now mobilized black support for black power was through its increased coverage of life in the ghettoes of U.S. cities. The passage of the Voting Rights Act and the emergence of black power had shifted the focus of protest from the rural South to the urban North. As a result, the issues now changed from civil rights to the evils of poverty and cultural discrimination. Almost daily, television reported on the extent and depth of black deprivation in the United States. The local newscasts, the network news, and shows like "CBS Reports" and "ABC SCOPE" exposed the poverty, the inadequate housing, the ineffectual and insufficient public services, the crime, and the police brutality in black ghettoes of U.S. cities. Often, these reports included coverage of demonstrations that were protesting the conditions of life in the ghetto. Sometimes, these demonstrations were deliberately staged for television. Here is an account by Charles R. Morris:

> I was the New York City welfare director at the turn of the decade when welfare demonstrations were still common, although without the flair and drama of the massive welfare rights marches of 1966 and 1967. The demonstrations followed a ritual dictated by the availability of the cameras. The demonstrators would arrive at a welfare center, often with considerable advance notice. There would be a period of aimless milling. Then someone would shout, "The TV is here." The demonstration would immediately take shape, the radical workers would march off their work stations, the leaders of the demonstration and the center director would engage in an apparently heated but highly conventionalized shouting match, perhaps some files would be strewn about, and perhaps an arrest or two would be made. People would wave their fists for the cameras and be interviewed. Everyone would hurry home to watch themselves on the early news. Welfare demonstrations hardly ever made the late news anymore.[52]

Seeing and hearing about how bad their conditions were, most blacks got angry. At times, their anger against the "immoral system" burst forth in violence. And this, too, was taken to be support for black power.

In the summer of 1965, the first major riot took place in Watts, the black quarter of Los Angeles. The arrest of a twenty-one-year-old black for drunk driving set off a five-day fiery mayhem that required over two thousand National Guard troops to quell. Thirty-four people died, over a thousand were injured, two hundred businesses were totally destroyed, and property damage was estimated at $40 million. The following summer, riots took place in Chicago, Cleveland, and some forty other smaller cities. As happened in Watts, these riots were unplanned, usually ignited by a minor incident and fueled by antagonism between the black population and the police.[53] In the summer of 1967, even more riots broke out, the major ones taking place in Tampa, Cincinnati, and, worst of all, Newark and Detroit. From Newark, the riots spread to most of the cities of northern New Jersey: Jersey City, Plainfield, New Brunswick, Elizabeth, Englewood. In Detroit, television cameras photographed what looked like a war: fire bombings, snipers, and looting, along with National Guard troops using machine guns and tanks. The pitched battles destroyed homes and businesses and killed thirty-six people, making it the most deadly riot in modern U.S. history.

In July of 1967, President Johnson appointed a National Advisory Commission on Civil Disorder to investigate the riots. The commission produced its final report of two hundred fifty thousand words on 2 March 1968. It described a deeply disturbing picture of relations between the races in the United States. It saw the nation "moving toward two separate societies, one white, one black— separate, but equal." This, the commission warned, created the risk of more major disorders. And large-scale violence, if it came, would lead to "white retaliation." "This spiral," the commission said,

> could quite conceivably lead to a kind of urban apartheid with semimartial law in many cities, enforced residence of Negroes in segregated areas, and a drastic reduction in personal freedom for all Americans, particularly Negroes.[54]

The commission blamed the riots on the white majority: "White racism is essentially responsible for the explosive mixture which has been accumulating in our cities since the end of World War II." But this was not an adequate explanation. Racism has been endemic in the United States for a long time. The question that needed answering was

Why did the riots occur when and where they did? The president's original charge to the commission had asked specifically what effect the news media had on the riots.[55] This became a central part of the commission's final report.

Like almost all research into the effects of television, the commission's study focused on the effects television had on people, accepting, as does most such research, the "common sense" epistemology that holds that we become what we behold. According to this epistemology, television exposure inductively (through continuous exposure over time) influences people's conduct. Thus, the commission asked: "Did those who rioted do so because they saw others rioting on television?" Given their epistemological assumptions, the conclusion was predictable: The commission found insufficient evidence to establish that television did cause the riots. "In some cities, people who watched television reports and read newspaper accounts of riots in other cities later rioted themselves. But the causal chain weakens," the commission report continues, "when we recall that in other cities people in very much the same circumstances watched the same programs and read the same newspaper stories but did not riot themselves."[56] Nevertheless, in spite of the insufficient evidence they found, the commission did use the traditional, common-sense, epistemological words like "shape" ("television reporting helped to *shape* people's attitudes toward the riots") and "condition" ("the news reports have *conditioned* the response of officials and police to disturbances in their own cities"). So, the commission did recognize that television had a role in the riots. It thought that television "sensationalized" what happened by exaggerating the scale and character of the riots and the mood of the people, giving viewers the impression that these were black and white confrontations. In addition, the commission faulted television for failing to analyze the riots by bringing out the causes, the underlying grievances, and conditions.[57]

Here we can see that the commission ignored both the analogic and the nondiscursive character of television. Because it is nondiscursive, television is simply not an appropriate medium for analyzing what it presents. And because it is analogic, television focuses on relationships—in this case, the relationships were between whites and blacks. Television certainly did not cause the riots. Yet, it was the most relied-on medium for information about the riots. What television presented were the relationships, the violent relationships.

This facilitated a critical appraisal of these goings-on. Both blacks and whites responded to the riots with strong moral criticisms. Some viewers became critical of the blacks who had created the conditions that had caused the rioting, and some became critical of the police who had tried to control the rioting. Thus, television coverage of the riots, like television coverage of the entire black revolt since the Montgomery bus strike, helped people become moral critics of the existing culture. And this now intensified critical outlook led people to try to change the culture by eliminating the bad policies, practices, and arrangements that this critical outlook had uncovered.

The commission issued a long list of recommendations to cities: Open up more channels of communication to the ghetto, reduce police brutality, reform the existing criminal justice system. It also made recommendations to the federal government: an employment program (create 2 million new jobs over the next three years), an education program (integrated schools, extended opportunities for both early childhood education and higher education, more vocational education), uniform national welfare programs, and a housing program (open housing laws, more low- and moderate-income housing, rent supplements, expanded public housing).

The black leaders were not impressed by these recommendations. Martin Luther King, Whitney Young, Floyd McKissick, H. Rap Brown—all gave essentially the same assessment: These were the same recommendations that they themselves had been making for years. Martin Luther King put it succinctly: These recommendations "have been made before almost to the last detail—and have been ignored before almost to the last detail.[58]

Five weeks after the national commission issued its report, Martin Luther King was assassinated. Following the television reports of his death and the televised funeral, rioting broke out in fifteen U.S. cities while students demonstrated and rioted on over one hundred college campuses. Nearly seventy thousand troops were called up to restore peace; fifty-six people were killed, thirty-five hundred were injured, twenty thousand were arrested, and damages totaled $45 million.

In the aftermath of the criticism from the National Commission on Violence and the rioting following Dr. King's death, Congress passed the 1968 Civil Rights Bill. The heart of the bill was a federal fair housing law prohibiting discrimination in the sale and rental of most housing. But it is worthy of note that the Civil Rights Act of 1968 also contained a section making it a federal crime to cross a state line to participate in an assembly that turned violent. This so-called "Rap Brown Law" became the basis for the prosecution of the Chicago Eight in the wake of the riots at the 1968 Democratic National Convention.[59]

Criticism from students in the wake of the riots also brought changes to many U.S. universities: black student centers, Afro-American clubs, and, in some cases, separate black dormitories. Curricula were reconstructed to offer black studies programs, while courses in history, sociology and anthropology were hastily revamped, as were literature, philosophy and political science courses. Universities hired more black faculty and recruited more black students, providing increased student scholarships, loans, and jobs, as well as relaxing educational standards for entry and performance.

A few months after Martin Luther King's death, Americans witnessed another assassination. On television, they saw—played over and over—the killing of Robert Kennedy. Kennedy's assassination strongly affected black Americans, who had seen him as the only presidential candidate who understood and cared about them. When asked what he would do if he were president, Kennedy had said he would have the major television networks show in prime time a two-hour documentary about ghetto life—maybe that would shock white Americans out of their apathy.[60]

After the deaths of King and Kennedy, many blacks expressed increasing pessimism and despair. Calls for violence became more strident, but a note of fatalism appeared too. Writing in *Ramparts* on the demise of nonviolence, Eldridge Cleaver said: "Now there is only the gun and the bomb, dynamite and the knife, and they will be used liberally.... America will bleed. America will suffer."[61] Stokley Carmichael asked black people to "stand up on our feet and die like men. If that's our only act of manhood, then goddam it we're going to die."[62] As the rhetoric escalated and the threats of violence grew louder, violent confrontations between police and black groups were played out on U.S. television: The Black Panthers, the Black Liberation Army, the Symbianese Liberation Army—each had its violent, but unsuccessful, conflict with the police televised on the nightly news.

Television Becomes an Obstacle to Social Change

By 1968, the black protest movement had become unfocused. Television had much to do with it. First, television had revealed the limitations of protest—both violent protest and nonviolent protest. Second, television had eaten up the black leaders of the movement and destroyed their networks. Relentless exposure of the leaders and their doings had made all of them predictable, thus not newsworthy. Indeed, there seemed no longer to be a need for leaders: The consciousness of blacks had been raised—by television—and blacks now took their cues from television. New and different spokesmen appeared on television—often leaders of local groups never heard of before—who increased and broadened the number and kinds of issues and demands: Community control of schools, reparation, group identity, black consciousness, and hiring quotas were only some of the causes they promoted. What the television screen now primarily conveyed was the frustration, anger, and hatred many blacks felt toward whites.

In the face of these diffused, unfocused, yet violent and hate-filled protests, many white people now became critical of the black protest movement. All the more so, since the world they saw displayed on television revealed that blacks had attained tremendous cultural progress: Black people now appeared regularly in many commercials, black actors now starred in prime-time shows ("Sanford and Son," "Julia," "Shaft," "Good Time," "The Jeffersons") and appeared in bit parts as lawyers, judges, physicians, teachers, professors, business executives, policemen, clergymen, and political leaders. There were critically acclaimed "specials" that celebrated the character and intelligence of black people ("Roots," "The Autobiography of Miss Jane Pittman," "A Woman called Moses"). In television ads, blacks were found playing and working together with whites. And the news shows and network special reports frequently contained accounts of blacks in the arts, in the professions, and in politics. Television—as also happened with women—had moved from stereotype to myth: Blacks had made progress in American culture, their life chances had improved, but not nearly so much as now appeared on the television screen. But since television had become the reference source for what was happening in the culture, many whites believed that the black protesters were wrong—wrong abut their facts, wrong in their methods.

Yet, when blacks looked at television, what they saw was something entirely different. For, although television had begun to present a mythical account of black people's position in the society, it still continued to encode many of the practices, procedures, and policies of the existing political, social, and economic arrangements. Television disclosed what was going on in the courts, in the schools, in business, and in industry, as well as what was going on in families, clubs, churches, hospitals, and other institutions. Through television, blacks could see that all blacks were always treated as members of a group, a group that was inevitably judged by white standards and, therefore, marked as inferior. So, when blacks looked at television— often at the same shows whites watched—they saw a racist culture encoded on the video screen. What enraged blacks even more was that whites thought that such subordination was normal and justified.

Television had helped blacks become conscious of their actual situation; it had forced them to confront their actual relations with whites. Television had exposed the culture, exposed that it was a culture that did not treat them in accordance with its own professed values—the values of individualism, equality, objectivity, and competition. In the United States, as in all of the modern Western world, people were supposed to be treated as individuals. Yet, every black who watched television could plainly see that blacks were not treated as individuals but as members of a group ("a credit to his race" or "a disgrace to his race"). In the modern world, everyone expected equal treatment. But, as television clearly revealed to them, blacks were not treated equally in this culture: In spite of more frequent appearances on TV, blacks were almost always cast in socially, politically, or economically inferior positions and roles. In the modern world, people were supposed to be judged objectively, according to fair standards and criteria. But television disclosed that the so-called objective standards used to measure them—their beauty, their speech, their art, their clothes, their styles, their skills—were all *subjective* white standards. As a consequence, blacks did not (because they could not) compete successfully with whites in the social, economic, and political arenas.

Blacks and whites agreed on the facts: Black people were more economically deprived, politically impotent, poorly educated, lacking in decent medical care, and unfairly treated by the police and the courts. But blacks and whites differed on what the facts meant. Blacks took these facts as evidence of racism. Whites took the same facts as justification for the subordination of black people. Blacks now became furious about the obtuseness of white people and at the same time angry with themselves for having accepted the roles and expectations imposed by whites, for having been patient and submissive. Television had helped blacks recognize how racist the society was.

Postmodern Justice

Initially, as we saw, the black protest movement emerged as an attempt to secure equal rights for blacks. Television helped to launch the movement and mobilize support for it from the time it began in Montgomery, Alabama. By disclosing the unfair, discriminating policies and practices of Jim Crow, television raised moral support for the struggle for equal rights. But this "color blind" solution the protest movement secured did not eliminate racism in the culture. A "color blind" society asks the black person to abnegate himself, to forget that he is black; it further asks him to view his own culture as pathological; it asks him, in effect, to become a white person with an invisible black skin. This is racism. Television helped blacks become conscious of the extent and depth of racism, and it helped them realize that white people must be brought to see black people as black—see them, and accept them ... and accept their culture. In doing this, television launched and mobilized black support for the second phase of the protest movement: the struggle for black power, the attempt to create a racially pluralist society. Blacks also now realized that most whites, although they, too, watched television, did not yet see that the existing relationships between blacks and whites contradicted the central values of modern civilization. So, if they were not going to be treated equally, as individuals, and held to truly objective standards so that they could compete fairly, then the only course of action open to them, many blacks concluded, was to demand special, preferential treatment. This became the programmatic meaning of black power. If white people refused to recognize blacks as individuals, or as equals, if they discouraged blacks from competing by unjustly applying "white" standards, then blacks would no longer compete. Instead, they would demand to be treated as a collective and insist upon unequal treatment. They would be black employees, black students, black politicians. They would insist upon quotas for blacks and demand that blacks be given preference in employment, in school admissions, and in public office appointments. Moreover, whites had to understand that when they took over positions and jobs formerly held only by white people, blacks would not carry them out in the same manner or mode as whites had. Blacks would introduce new norms, new practices, new procedures, new styles in social, political, and economic institutions. The old, supposedly objective, but actually subjective, white standards of performance would no longer apply.

Now, all this is very abstract and hard to articulate, let alone understand and accept. Needless to say, it could not be explained by the nondiscursive medium of television. But television did report the changes now taking place in the culture: the demands for and the results of affirmative action, preferential treatment, and quotas. Newscasts made the public aware of court decisions, legislation, and executive actions that supported and furthered these changes.

If this is what black power meant, many whites concluded it was immoral. It was a return to the tribalism that Western civilization had laboriously climbed out of over the past five centuries. It is true that there is more than a whiff of tribal morality here. The morality of the tribe has it that justice is what is good for the well-being of the tribe— good for one's brothers and sisters. In tribal morality preferential treatment is therefore just if it benefits the tribe. Western civilization, however, had supposedly moved beyond such a limited conception of morality to formulate the abstract morality of the open society. Based primarily on the existence of printed rules and regulations known and accepted by all, modern justice consists of treatment that is in accordance with those accepted rules of conduct. From this, it follows that each person is to be treated equally and as an individual. It further follows that the same objective rules of conduct apply to all in their competition for the prizes available in the culture. But now, black people seemed to be asking for a return to tribalism, demanding preferential treatment as a group (not equal treatment as individuals), with no regard for the objective standards that bound everyone else.

What had happened, of course, is that television had exposed the moral inadequacy of the modern values: Strict adherence to the values of individualism, equality, competition, and objectivity had intensified and legitimized racism. These values of the modern world had to be supplemented or joined to the earlier, tribal values of collectivism, cooperation, hierarchy, and subjectivity. This joining of these two sets of values created a postmodern morality. So, the demand for quotas and for affirmative action can be construed as an effort by blacks to make white people recognize that the existing rules for justice in this culture did not—never could—apply to blacks, simply because it was a racist culture. As Supreme Court Justice Powell wrote in the *Bakke* case on affirmative action: "In order to get beyond racism, we must first take account of race." Black people could never be treated as individuals or as equals until they were actually admitted to schools they had never attended, actually hired for jobs they had never performed, actually occupied political positions they had never held. Only then could white people interact with them as real people, as individuals, rather than as abstractions or as members of a group. And this would not have happened so long as blacks had to compete against whites for the available positions, since the so-called "objective" standards were white standards. Instead of competing with blacks, white people now had to cooperate with them, establishing quotas and giving them preferential treatment.

The black protest movement, like the women's movement, made things better. It improved the life chances of blacks just as the women's movement improved life chances for women. Television helped people become conscious of the limiting and discriminatory arrangements in the society, and television provoked and sustained the moral criticism that diminished those evils.

But television, in time, became a conservative force. Instead of continuing to facilitate improved relations between men and women, between white people and black people, television became an obstacle to social change. This happened when television programmers, in response to charges that the video screen presented stereotypical images of women and blacks, began to create mythical relations that no longer reflected the actual relations between the races or between the sexes. This undermined the moral criticism that had produced the dramatic social changes of the 1960s and 1970s. But as an analogic medium, television cannot help but encode the actual relationships extant in the culture. So, even as it presents mythical relationships in sit-coms and in commercials, these images reveal the still limited life chances blacks and women have in American culture: in politics, in business, in sports, and in the academic world.

Television will continue to reveal us to ourselves, continue to disclose the relations we have created in our culture. The important thing to remember is that we fallible human beings have created these relationships, so they cannot be perfect. But the good news is that they can always be improved, they can always get better. What we need are institutionalized arrangements that will encourage and regularize critical discussion of the relationships we have created so that we can modify and renew them, so that we can diminish the unhappiness they cause. Television will facilitate social criticism. It is up to us to see that such criticism leads to critical dialogue and peaceful change—not violence.

Notes

1   Yates, *What Women Want*, 11.
2   Greer, *The Female Eunuch*, 309; Freeman, *The Politics of Women's Liberation*, 147.
3   Meyerwitz, *No Sense of Place*, ch. 12.
4   Chavetz and Dworkin, *Female Revolt: Women's Movements in World and Historical Perspective*, ch. 2; Freeman, *The Politics of Women's Liberation*, ch. 1.
5   Tedesco, "Patterns of Prime Time," 119-124.
6   Mansbridge, *Why We Lost the ERA*, 190.
7   Ibid., ch. 13.
8   Turner et al., *Oppression: A Socio-History of Black-White Relations in America*, 27.
9   Lomax, *The Negro Revolt*, 85.
10   Kluger, *Simple Justice: The History of Brown v. Board of Education and Black America's Struggle for Equality*, 754.
11   Lomax, *The Negro Revolt*, 16-17.
12   King, *Stride Toward Freedom*, 47.
13   Ibid., 45
14   Lomax, *The Negro Revolt*, 101-2.
15   King, *Stride Toward Freedom*, 48.
16   Lomax, *The Negro Revolt*, 112.
17   Lester, *Look Out Whitey! Black Power's Gon' Get Your Mama!* 4-6.
18   Compare the moral outrage generated by television coverage of the physical abuse suffered by the nonviolent protesters with the limited moral outrage expressed over the brutal slaying in Mississippi of fourteen-year-old Emmet Till in the summer of 1955. The black weekly magazine *Jet*, published a shocking picture of the boy's mutilated body. But a still picture (in a black magazine) could never have the widespread and deep emotional (moral) impact of a televised sequence that presents the actual sight and sound of physical violence inflicted on innocent victims.
19   Williams, *Eyes on the Prize*, 67.
20   King, *Stride Toward Freedom*, 93, 150.
21   Zanden, James W., "The Non-Violent Resistance Movement Against Segregation, in Geschwender, ed.,*The Black Revolt: The Civil Rights Movement, Ghetto Uprisings, and Separatism*, 138.

22   Williams, *Eyes on the Prize: America's Civil Rights Years, 1954-65*, 138.
23   Ibid., 118.
24   Ibid., 135.
25   Ibid., 139.
26   Ibid., 155.
27   Ibid., 142.
28   Ibid., 191.
29   Garrow, *Bearing the Cross: Martin Luther King, Jr., and the Southern Christian Leadership Conference, 1955-1968*, 264.
30   Williams, *Eyes on the Prize: America's Civil Rights Years*, 1954-65, 194.
31   Ibid., 95.
32   Robinson, "Television and American Politics: 1956-1976," 12-13.
33   Williams, *Eyes on the Prize: America's Civil Rights Years, 1954-65*, 243.
34   Ibid., 262.
35   Ibid., 273.
36   Ibid., 285.
37   Viorst, *Fire in the Street*, 353.
38   Ibid., 363.
39   Garrow, *Bearing the Cross: Martin Luther King, Jr., and the Southern Christian Leadership Conference, 1955-1968*, 477-8.
40   Carson, *In Struggle: SNCC and the Black Awakening of the 1960s*, 209-10.
41   Wilhoit, *The Politics of Massive Resistance*, 213.
42   Malcolm X, *The Autobiography*, 238.
43   Ibid., 245-6.
44   Ibid., 245-7
45   Bonnerz, "Group Identity: The Rhetoric of Soul," in Endo and Strawbridge, eds., *Perspectives on Black America*, 5-17.
46   Carson, *In Struggle: SNCC and the Black Awakening of the 1960s*, 217.
47   Ibid., 220.
48   Ravitch, *The Troubled Crusade: American Education, 1945-1980*, 293-4.
49   Lester, *Look Out Whitey! Black Power's Gon' Get Your Mama!* 137.
50   Meier and Rudwick, eds., *Black Protest in the Sixties*, 484-90.
51   Carson, *In Struggle: SNCC and the Black Awakening of the 1960s*, 230.
52   Morris, *A Time of Passion: America 1960-1980*, 127.
53   Cirnot, "A Crowd Becomes a Riot: Watts 1965," in Endo and Strawbridge, eds., *Perspectives on Black America*, 73-87.
54   National Advisory Commission on Civil Disorders, *Report*, 1.
55   Ibid., 203, 362.
56   Ibid., 366-7.
57   Ibid., 363, 369-73.
58   Muse, *The American Negro Revolution*, 323.
59   Wilhoit, *The Politics of Massive Resistance*, 211.
60   Oates, *Let the Trumpet Sound: The Life of Martin Luther King, Jr.*, 468.
61   Blair, *Retreat to the Ghetto*, 96.
62   Carson, *In Struggle: SNCC and the Black Awakening of the 1960s*, 288.

3

Television and the Polity

With the coming of television, the modern nation-state became a more moral community. Not a moral community like those ideal states proposed by the theorists of antiquity, but rather more moral in these three ways: First, citizens were better able to select their political leaders on the basis of virtue or moral character; second, citizens were better able to monitor the moral probity of their political leaders; and third, the procedures and operations of the modern state were infused with more moral spirit. This process of moral improvement can best be followed by looking at the government of the United States since the coming of television.

How TV Improved the Selection of Political Leaders

The notions most people have about the effects of television on the selection of political leaders came from journalists like Joe McGinniss and Robert MacNeil, who popularized the belief that television "sells" candidates to the public, just like soap. I reject this belief because it rests on the associationist theory of knowledge discussed earlier: "We become what we behold," or "we believe what we see," or "we act as we are persuaded to act by the image-makers." As I noted earlier, such a theory of knowledge denies agency to those who watch television while granting agency to those who produce television. As I see it, all human beings are initiators of their own actions, creators of their own ideas, makers of their own decisions. Human conduct is not shaped, molded, or determined by forces or influences internal or external. Human conduct is the manifestation of intelligent choices; it is the act of an agent, not the effect of some cause.

In the matter of politics, citizens in the modern state make judgments about candidates for political office. Prior to television, people made such decisions largely on the basis of the party to which they belonged or were attracted to. The party always selected the candidates, thus limiting the participation of the public. The party always selected political figures who had worked their way up through the party ranks—those who were loyal and dedicated to the interests of the party. After selecting the nominee, the party then financed and ran the campaign for election. At election time, citizens voted for those candidates of the party they belonged to or identified with. Television changed all this.

In presidential politics, which we will consider here, the salient relationship is that between the citizen and the candidate. What the citizen wants to know of each candidate is: "Is he a good leader?" Before television, citizens could only ascertain this secondhand from the accounts of journalists or writers, or from the endorsements supplied by partisan supporters. And the evidence they could consult for purposes of assessing the leadership potential of the various candidates was limited to what the candidate had done (his record) and what he promised to do (his platform). But this information provides little basis for predicting how someone will conduct himself when elected. What is significant in the selection of political leaders, as other have noted, is not where the candidate stands on the issues— since these are transitory and ephemeral—nor what he promises to do—since candidates really do not know what they will do.[1] What is important is the character of the candidate. By character I mean the judgment to know what is right and the courage to do what is good. Until the coming of television, citizens had no way of personally ascertaining the character of candidates. Television presented the candidate to the citizen as no other medium could ever do. As an analogic medium, television provides a more intimate, more candid, more complete, and more immediate and unmediated understanding of political candidates than any other medium. Television eliminates all mediators between the candidate and the voters. Through television, each voter can personally judge and appraise the character of each candidate. Now citizens can see and hear the candidate in a constantly changing, real world of issues and problems. As he interacts with others and as he presents himself individually, each candidate continually enacts and discloses his own moral character. To put it negatively, as Frank O'Connor, former city council president of New York, did: "If a man is on TV long enough, no matter how phony he is, sooner or later they're going to catch up with him."[2]

Note that I am talking about the political candidate's character, not his or her personality, charm, charisma, looks, style, or image. Many commentators on the influence of television on voters have confused all of these with character and, as a result, see television as a manipulative instrument candidates can "use." Moreover, although voters frequently tell pollsters that they like one candidate more than another, such expressions of feeling are not an affirmation of the candidate's personality or good looks but rather an assessment of the candidate's character. We realize this when we look at those who have been elected since the advent of television. The roster of presidents and other elected officials demonstrates that the electorate did not select them because they had better looks, style, or image than their opponents. Think of Johnson over Goldwater, or Nixon over Humphrey. What citizens look for in candidates are evidence of good character, as surveys of voters taken the last twenty years attest. From an analysis of these surveys, Doris Graber has concluded that the top most frequently mentioned qualities citizens seek in a president are that the candidate be trustworthy, principled, compassionate, inspirational, forthright, and strong.[3]

By presenting the candidates in person in press conferences, debates, news stories, documentations, interview programs, panel discussions, and advertisements, television enables voters to see how the candidates relate to others, how they conduct themselves under stress, and how they behave when they are tired or caught off guard. And always it is how the candidate says what he says, or how he does what he does that is more important than *what* he says or does, for it is how one behaves that reveals one's character. Print best captures and encodes *what* someone says; televisions pictures capture *how* someone says it. As numerous studies of voters have revealed, people are more attentive to the picture than the spoken word.[4] Interviews have revealed that people soon forget what is said on television, but they remember the demeanor of the speaker, how he looked, sounded, and appeared—the aspects of his character that he revealed.

It is important to make clear that I am not saying that television has enabled voters to select men of virtue as their presidents. Rather, I am claiming that, since the coming of television, voters have selected what they considered to be the "better man"—the man "better" in character than his opponents. But, as the record of the last twenty-five years has made clear, those selected as the "better" men were not good enough. So, television offers no guarantee that voters will select virtuous leaders; television merely allows each voter, for the first time in the modern world, to select his leaders on the basis of his own personal assessment of the moral character of the candidate.[5]

Once voters, through the medium of television, could personally judge the character of candidates for elective office, they became more independent voters. As a result, more people forswore registering as a member of a political party. Since 1964, the number of voters registered as Independents has increased. From the earliest Gallup polls in the mid-1930s until the early 1960s, surveys indicated that 80 percent or more of the adult public identified with either the Republican or Democratic party. But by 1980, only 22 percent of the voters strongly identified themselves with a party.[6] The emergence of independent voters who now could, and did, demand to select their own candidates has led to the increase in number of presidential state primary elections.

From 1916 to 1968, only about 30 percent of national convention delegates were selected through direct primaries, the rest being chosen in state conventions dominated by party leaders and "bosses." In 1968, there were seventeen state primaries; four years later, this had increased to twenty-three, choosing 50 percent of convention delegates. In 1976, roughly 70 percent were chosen in thirty state primaries, and, by 1980, thirty-five states held state primaries that chose 74 percent of the delegates.[7]

Prior to television, delegates to the national convention actually chose the party nominee—often only after repeated balloting (the record for balloting was set in 1924, when the Democratic convention went through 103 ballots before settling on its candidate). But with the increased number of state primaries, delegates to the national convention no longer make decisions on their own; they simply register decisions made by persons voting in primaries weeks and months before. Moreover, the convention itself—where the nominee has, since 1960, been selected on the first ballot—has become a television spectacular—a show hosted, directed, and controlled by the television networks.

The rise in the number of independent voters made possible by television not only led to more participants in the candidate selection process, it also led to an increase in the number of candidates for office. Prior to television, unknowns and politically unconnected candidates, like Jimmy Carter, would have had no chance to be nominated. Nor could candidates, like Barry Goldwater, who hailed from a politically weak state like Arizona, ever get nominated. But, since the coming of television, men and women with no previous electoral experience run for political office in the federal government. They come from business (Frank Lautenberg, Lew Lehrmann), from universities (Daniel Moynihan, S.I. Hayakawa), from space programs (Harrison Schmitt, John Glenn), from sports (Bill Bradley, Jack Kemp), and from Hollywood (Shirley Temple Black, George Murphy, Ronald Reagan). Television not only removed geography and party indenture as obstacles to becoming a candidate, it also helped to eliminate age and religion as barriers.

The First Television President: John F. Kennedy

Here, the case of John Kennedy is instructive. John Kennedy was the first television president. Before him, Presidents Truman and Eisenhower had appeared on the screen: Truman to deliver his State of the Union Message in 1949, Eisenhower to use television forty-nine times in eight years in office. But neither Truman nor Eisenhower ever credited television for winning an election, while Kennedy admitted: "We wouldn't have had a prayer without that gadget."[8] By 1960, the year Kennedy was elected, some 46 million homes (88 percent of all households) had at least one TV set, and a twenty-one inch RCA black and white model cost a mere $209. Television had become a mass medium. Only the very poor and the very intellectual didn't own a set.

John Kennedy had first appeared on national television at the 1956 Democratic National Convention when he gave a nominating speech for Adlai Stevenson. In the course of the convention, he was seriously considered for nomination as vice-president but lost out to Estes Kefauver, who had achieved national celebrity status through televised coverage of the Senate crime investigation committee he had chaired.

In running for the presidency in 1960, Kennedy had two recognized liabilities: his religion and his age. He was a Catholic and therefore suspected of having allegiances to the pope that would subvert his role as president of the United States. And he was only forty-three years old and lacking in administrative experience, especially when compared to his opponent, Richard Nixon, who had already served eight years as vice-president of the country. Through the medium of television, Kennedy not only overcame these barriers to his own election but shattered forever the notion that the office of the president was to be denied to anyone because of age or religion.

The turning point in the campaign, as all commentators have noted, was the TV debate between Kennedy and Nixon. Actually, there were four debates, watched by an estimated 100 million people. The first debate turned out to be the most crucial, the one from which Nixon never recovered. In that debate, Kennedy demonstrated that, while younger and less experienced, he was in every way equal to Nixon in ability and knowledge. He displayed the character of a leader, confidently asserting that he could move the country forward. Nixon failed to offer an inspiring view of the future, content instead to score debate points against his opponent. Perhaps more important, Nixon did not look like a leader to the millions watching. He was recovering from a serious illness and looked wan and haggard. Having lost a lot of weight, his shirt collar was too large. His wrinkled gray suit (against a gray background) made him look even more washed out. He needed a shave and had what looked like theatrical make-up on his face, which dripped as he sweated profusely under the hot lights. In contrast, John Kennedy, cool and poised in a neat dark suit, appeared not only a match for the vice-president but a more forceful leader. That night, television truly presented different images of the two presidential candidates.

Most people who watched the debate on television believed that Kennedy had "won." But, of course, it was not a debate: There were no arguments, no confrontations, and no clarifications of the issues. It was, the political commentators complained, simply a media event.

Exactly. Television is not and can never be a medium suitable for the discussion of ideas. But it is more than a medium that simply presents images. These "television debates" presented more than the poise, demeanor, and style of these two men. Television disclosed their characters. As Theodore White recognized, these television debates enabled the citizens of the modern state to "recapture the tribal sense of participation in the choice of a leader."[9] Television debates allow each viewer-citizen personally and subjectively to appraise the character of those who seek to be their leaders. John Kennedy, himself, noted this in his remarks to a reporter:

> Television gives people a chance to look at their candidates close up and close to the bone. For the first time since the Greek city-states practiced their form of democracy, it brings us within reach of that ideal where every voter has a chance to measure the candidate himself.[10]

Television also broadcast nationwide the interviews Kennedy held with those concerned about his religion. One took place in West Virginia, where he was questioned by Franklin Roosevelt, Jr.; the other took place in Houston, where he responded to questions from the Greater Houston Ministerial Association. In these television interviews, Kennedy demonstrated that he did not need to clear his statements with either his cardinal or his pope, and showed that he could withstand the scrutiny of skeptics and attackers. The most memorable part of both interviews was Kennedy's swearing on an imaginary Bible to "faithfully execute the office of president of the United States and ... to the best of my ability, preserve, protect, and defend the Constitution, so help me God." Everyone in the audience, and everyone who saw the TV film bore witness to the demonstrated relationship between the candidate and God. "And if he breaks his oath," Kennedy concluded, "he is not only committing a crime against the Constitution, for which Congress can impeach him—and should impeach him—but he is committing a sin against God." Here, Kennedy raised his hand from the imaginary Bible and repeated softly, "a sin against God, for he has sworn on the Bible." By drawing the issue of religion into the campaign and exposing its dark underside, television helped voters become more critical of religious intolerance, their own included.

So far, I have argued that, in both nominating and electing

candidates, voters now can and do select them by personally and subjectively appraising their character. I have also argued that television has further improved the selection process and has made it more moral by removing those sociological and psychological barriers that prevented some from ever obtaining, or even seeking, political office.

The First Intentional Use of TV for Politicking: Johnson vs. Goldwater

There is yet another way in which television improved the selection of political leaders: It made the selection process more rigorous. The selection process became more rigorous because political candidates began to use television to expose the character inadequacies of one another. This is how Lyndon Johnson and his media consultants (the Madison Avenue agency of Doyle, Dane, Bernback) used television in the 1964 presidential campaign. Of course, candidates have always attacked the character of their opponents, but with television it became possible to corroborate such attacks, or better: It became possible to get the attacked candidate to corroborate the accusations himself—by his on-camera behavior.

Here's how it works. Television, like most media of communication, is self-reflexive: It can reflect on its own activities. That is, there can be television shows about previously shown television shows, or television stories or interviews about previously shown stories or interviews. Because it is an analogic medium that focuses on relationships, the self-reflexivity of television is primarily affective—i.e., the stories, or shows, or interviews about previously shown stories, interviews or shows are primarily displays of approval or disapproval, as in: "I like or I don't like what was previously shown on television." So, whenever someone appears on television in a reflexive mode, the camera will disclose his affective reactions. Most television reporters realize that television best conveys affective behavior, so they often guide the person being interviewed with affective questions such as: "How do you feel about [some previously televised report about you]?"

In the 1964 election, Lyndon Johnson, who had been president since the assassination of Kennedy in November 1963, avoided all the state primaries, staying in Washington, where he acted presidential and tended to the nation's business. In fact, he had decided to conduct his campaign almost completely through television. As president, he could exercise considerable control over the medium, to which end he had a fully equipped TV studio installed in the White House where a camera was kept "warm" at all times, with a director and a camera crew constantly on duty, on a five-minute alert.[11]

Johnson would engage in no debates; indeed, he saw to it that Congress did *not* pass a bill suspending the "equal time" provision of the Federal Communications Act of 1934, which had allowed the Kennedy-Nixon debates to take place in 1960. Johnson's Republican opponent, Barry Goldwater, was a personally charming, open, friendly, and engaging person; a man of principle who believed in natural law, God, the Golden Rule and the Ten Commandments. In a debate with the proud, devious, domineering, insecure, egotistical, coarse, sentimental, vindictive, and highly sensitive Lyndon Johnson, the media consultants feared that Goldwater would appear to have the better character. The Johnson television strategy therefore was to produce commercials that described the character flaws of Goldwater: He was impulsive, loose-talking, irresponsible, reckless, someone who shoots from the hip, and a thoroughly dangerous man who lacked the character necessary for assuming the office of the president of the United States.

In his acceptance speech at the Republican convention in San Francisco, Goldwater corroborated the charges when he delivered the ill-fated line to the largest nationwide television audience of his career: "Extremism in the defense of liberty is no vice, and moderation in the pursuit of justice is no virtue." This statement, in the words of Dean Burch, the national chairman of the Republican party, "gave the people who were determined to beat Goldwater over the head a handle to beat him with."[12]

Goldwater's incessant production of provocative and shocking statements provided Johnson's advisors with continuous copy. On matters of foreign policy, he had advocated: dropping "a low-yield nuclear bomb on Chinese supply lines in North Vietnam," defoliating the Vietnam forests with "low-yield atomic weapons," giving "the NATO command the right to use nuclear weapons—tactical weapons—when they are attacked," getting the United States out of the UN, stopping foreign economic aid, blockading Cuba, working to "train and equip the Cuban refugees and help put them ashore with adequate air cover," "withdrawing recognition from Russia," and unilaterally renewing nuclear testing. As to what foreigners might think, he said, "Frankly, I do not care what the rest of the world thinks of us.... I don't give a tinker's damn what the rest of the world thinks about the United States, as long as we keep strong militarily."[13]

On the domestic front, Goldwater claimed to fear Washington and centralized government more than Moscow. On unions, he said that Walter Reuther and the United Auto Workers were "a more dangerous menace than the Sputnik or anything else Russia might do." He wanted to make Social Security payments "voluntary," and advocated letting welfare be a private concern. He claimed "we have no right to tell the southern states what they must do about school integration and segregation." He was against "any form of federal grant-in-aid programs to the states for education." And the Tennessee Valley Authority "should be turned over to private enterprise, even if they only get one dollar for it." As to what other Americans might think of his views, Goldwater said such opposition was largely centered in the East, and he thought it might be wise to saw off the eastern seaboard states and let them drift out into the Atlantic Ocean.[14]

Johnson's ad men prepared a number of regional spot commercials that centered on Goldwater's dictums. One spot announcement broadcast frequently in the East depicted that area of the country being sawed off the rest of the nation and drifting out to sea. Another shown extensively throughout the Tennessee Valley area exposed the sale of the TVA to private enterprise. One presentation aimed at the elderly showed a social security card being torn up. A highly effective ad directed at dissident Republican voters contained quotes from Governor Rockefeller, Governor Scranton, Governor Romney, and Henry Cabot Lodge—Republicans all—highly uncomplimentary to Barry Goldwater. As these attacks came on the set, the viewer saw the campaign posters of all these one-time Republican candidates being trampled on during the highly emotional Republican convention. This ad served to remind the public of the virulent hostility the Goldwater supporters had unleashed on Governor Rockefeller during the convention.

The most controversial ad of the campaign—perhaps the most controversial ad in the history of political broadcasting—never mentions Goldwater's name or any statement he made about anything. It opens on a little girl standing in an open field, plucking the petals from a daisy as she counts: "1, 2, 3, 4, 5, 6, 6 [*sic*], 8, 9." When she reaches "9," a Cape Canaveral voice begins another countdown: "10, 9, 8, 7, 6, 5, 4, 3, 2, 1, zero." At zero, the camera, which throughout the second countdown had been closing in on the child's face, dissolves from her eye to a mushroom cloud that expands until it covers the screen. Then, one heard Lyndon Johnson's voice: "These are the stakes. To make a world in which all can live, or to go into the dark. We must either love each other or we must die."[15]

The self-reflexivity of television gave the dramatic commercial wide distribution. It appeared only once. But it was news, or newsworthy, since people reacted strongly to it. So newscasts reported the reactions—and showed the ad again, as part of the news story. When the Republican National Committee chairman filed a complaint with the Fair Campaign Practices Committee, this too was news and was duly reported in television news broadcasts—once again showing the commercial to explain what the fuss was about.

The reflexivity of television gave Johnson's media consultants the opportunity to carry out the next step in their strategy. Barry Goldwater, frustrated in his attempts to secure a television debate with Lyndon Johnson, denied as much access to television as the president had, found himself reduced to appearances on television newscasts and interview shows like "Face the Nation" and "Meet the Press" and paid-for television speeches. Here, he fulminated against the television commercials the Johnson forces had broadcast: "The homes of America are horrified, and the intelligence of Americans insulted by the weird television advertising by which this administration threatens the end of the world unless all-wise Lyndon is given the nation for his very own." Goldwater's candid, spontaneous reactions corroborated the very kind of character traits the commercials had accused him of. He was—on camera, for all to see—intemperate, impulsive, and reckless. He did shoot from the hip. Moreover, these short, hurried, multiple appearances on network news shows exposed the contradictory positions Goldwater held and further revealed that his explanations did not explain, that his clarifications did not clarify. His typical position, according to James David Barber was to make some shocking statement, stand amazed that it shocked people, and then explain that he only meant part of what he had said.[16]

The reactions, or overreactions, of Barry Goldwater set in motion the next stage of the strategy: a series of Democratic commercials designed to encourage Republicans to vote for Johnson. These Republicans-for-Johnson ads all had actual Republicans (or actors who said they were Republicans)—some well-known, some not—explaining why they were voting for Johnson: "As loyal Republicans, we can see no reason to support a man who rejects every tradition of our party.... Sorry, Mr. Goldwater."

Not even the long-sought-after televised endorsement of Dwight Eisenhower could save Goldwater from the election night debacle television had helped to engineer. Broadcast in late September as "Conversation at Gettysburg," the show was important for what Eisenhower did not say. Ike did not explicitly deny that Goldwater was a warmonger, but simply said that "no man who knows anything about war is going to be reckless about it." He did *not* say that he recognized Goldwater as a man of integrity and dedication, but only that the country "certainly" recognized these virtues in him. He did *not* say that he knew Goldwater would give careful thought to his responsibilities as commander-in-chief, but only that "he couldn't imagine anything Goldwater would give more thought to." These ambiguous, vague testimonials to Goldwater's character were not the assurances the public—or Goldwater—had looked for. "The most charitable thing I can say about the film," wrote Goldwater later, "is that it wasn't effective."[17]

Johnson's landslide victory on election day revealed how strongly voters felt about Barry Goldwater's character.

Learning from One's Mistakes: Richard M. Nixon

By the time Richard Nixon entered the 1968 presidential race, it was perfectly clear that he had learned the lessons taught by his two Democratic predecessors in the White House. Kennedy had used television to disclose his own character as a leader. Johnson had used it to expose the character deficiencies of his opponent. Nixon followed the lead of Kennedy in 1968, and then in 1972, when he was the incumbent, as Johnson had been in 1964, Nixon followed the pattern set by Johnson. Actually, Nixon had first learned about the power of television back in 1952 when he was running as the vice-presidential candidate. It was then that he had had to defend himself against the demand that he be removed from the Republican ticket because he had accepted special, "secret" funds from California businessmen while a senator. In a specially broadcast speech, Nixon bared his soul: "My fellow Americans, I come before you tonight as a candidate for the vice-presidency and as a man whose honesty and integrity have been questioned." In swift and measured terms, he explained that none of the $15,000 in question had gone for "personal use." Then he proceeded to catalogue "how little we (Pat and I) have and how much we owe," revealing that they had a big mortgage on their house and that Pat wore a cloth (not a fur) coat. He did admit that he had received one gift he was not giving back: a little black and white, spotted dog that his daughter Tricia, "the six-year-old," had named "Checkers." At the end of his speech, Nixon made an unprecedented appeal to the public to wire and write to the Republican National Committee as to whether or not he should be dropped from the ticket.

The "Checkers" speech was carried by 150 stations and seen by 25 million people.[18] Maudlin, pathetic and vulgar as it was, this television appearance did allow the public to judge for itself the character of the man before it on the television screen. And it judged him to be acceptable. The avalanche of letters, telegrams, and telephone calls the national committee received was overwhelmingly in favor of Nixon—by three hundred fifty to one. Later, Eisenhower publicly embraced him with the words, "You're my boy!"

The lesson of the Checkers speech was brought home to Nixon by the humiliating defeat he suffered in his 1960 campaign for the presidency. The 1952 television speech had worked because the medium had clearly and fully disclosed his character and his leadership abilities. But in the campaign of 1960 this did not happen. During that campaign for the presidency—and then again during his equally unsuccessful campaign for governor of California in 1962 the print media people interfered and distorted his message, i.e., his character. Nixon made all of this perfectly clear at a remarkable 1962 press conference he held the day after his defeat in the campaign for governor:

Good morning, gentlemen. Now that Mr. Klein has made his statement, and now that all members of the press are so delighted that I have lost, I'd like to make a statement of my own.

I appreciate the press coverage of this campaign. I think each of you covered it the way you saw it. You had to write it in the way according to your belief on how it would go. I don't believe publishers should tell reporters to write one way or another. I want them all to be free. I don't believe the FCC (Federal Communications Commission) or anybody else should silence (them).

I am proud of the fact that I defended my opponent's patriotism. You gentlemen didn't report it, but I am proud that I did that. I am proud also that I defended the fact that he was a man of good motives, a man that I disagreed with very strongly, but a man of good motives. I want that—for once, gentlemen—I would appreciate it if you would write what I say in that respect. I think it's very important that you write it. In the lead. In the lead.

I say these things about the press because I understand that that was one of the things you were particularly interested in.... And my philosophy with regard to the press has never gotten through. And I want it to get through. This cannot be said for any other U.S. figure today, I guess. Never in my sixteen years of campaigning have I complained to a publisher, to an editor, about the coverage of a reporter. I believe a reporter has got a right to write it as he feels it. I believe if a reporter believes that one man ought to win rather than the other, whether it's on television or radio or the like, he ought to say so. I will say to the reporter sometimes that I think, "Well, look, I wish you'd give my opponent the same going over that you give me."

And as I leave the press, all I can say is this: For sixteen years, ever since the Hiss case, you've had a lot of fun—a lot of fun—that you've had an opportunity to attack me and I think I've given as good as I've taken. It was carried right up to the last day. I made a talk on television, a talk in which I made a flub—one of the few that I make, not because I'm so good on television but because I've been doing it a long time. I made a flub in which I said I was running for governor of the United States. The *Los Angeles Times* dutifully reported that. Mr. Brown the last day made a flub—a flub, incidentally, to the great credit of television, that was reported—I don't say this bitterly—in which he said, "I hope everybody wins. You vote the straight Democratic ticket, including Senator Kuchel." I was glad to hear him say it, because I was for Kuchel (a Republican) all the way. The *Los Angeles Times* did not report it. I think that it's time that our great newspapers have at least the same objectivity, the same fullness of coverage, that television has. And I can only say thank God for television and radio for keeping the newspapers a little more honest."[19]

At the end of his rambling tirade to a stunned press corps, Nixon made his famous remark: "You won't have Nixon to kick around anymore, because, gentlemen, this is my last press conference." Yet, within a year he made an (admittedly half-hearted) attempt to secure the 1964 Republican nomination. But during that campaign, his most memorable public performance was his appearance in support of Barry Goldwater on a special half-hour telecast where his concluding remark was: "With all the power that a president has, the most important thing to bear in mind is this: You must not give that power to a man unless, above everything else, he has character. Character is the most important qualification the president can have.[20]

In the campaign for president in 1968, Nixon and his media consultants were determined to use television to expose those facts of his character they thought the public did not know or believe existed. As a memorandum from Ray Price, one of Nixon's media advisors, put it: "We do not want to close the gap between old myths and present realities. We want to remind supporters of the candidate's strengths, and demonstrate to nonsupporters that the Herblock[21] images are fiction. The way to do this is to let more people see the candidate as we see him, remembering that the important thing is not to win debates but to win the audience; not to persuade them to [Richard Nixon's] point of view but to win their faith in his leadership."[22]

The strategy was to produce one- and five-minute television commercials and hour-long interview shows with "citizen panelists" interviewing Nixon. There were to be no debates, no appearances on "Meet the Press," "Face the Nation," or "Issues and Answers." The strategy did call for a telethon on election eve when Nixon fielded questions called in from voters throughout the nation. Richard Nixon himself was the primary director of the television commercials, as Joe McGinniss dramatically revealed in *The Selling of the President*, when he described the filming of one of them:

Richard Nixon entered the studio at 10:50. He went straight to an enclosed dressing room called the Green Room, where Ray Voege, the quiet, blond make-up man, was waiting with his powder and cloths.

Nixon came out of the Green Room at eleven o'clock. There was a drop of three or four inches from the doorway to the floor of the stage. He did not see it and stumbled as he stepped out the door. He grinned, reflexively, and Frank Shakespeare led him to the set.

He took his position on the front of the heavy brown desk. He liked to lean against a desk, or sit on the edge of one, while he taped commercials, because he felt this made him seem informal. There were about twenty people, technicians and advisers, gathered in a semicircle around the cameras.

Richard Nixon looked at them and frowned.

"Now when we start," he said, "don't have anybody who is not directly involved in this in my range of vision. So I don't go shifting my eyes."

"Yes, sir. All right, clear the stage. Everybody who's not actually doing something get off the stage, please. Get off the stage."

"Now when you give me the fifteen-second cue, give it to me right under the camera. So I don't shift my eyes."

"Right, sir."[23]

The "citizen panel" shows were filmed live in ten different regions of the country. They were taped for repeat showings and sometimes cut up for commercials. In each show, Nixon stood alone without podium or mike, surrounded by five to seven panelists selected by his media advisors. The panelists were local citizens—both Republicans and Democrats, sometimes including local reporters. In this arena-like setting, the candidate spontaneously responded to their questions for an hour. Each panelist had prepared his or her own questions. Consequently, some of the questions were rambling, some were vague, many were general, and most of them were soft—although Nixon's staff always advised the panelists to ask tough questions. For instance, on WAVE-TV in Louisville:

Mr. Nixon, at this point in the campaign, what do you find as the greatest concerns of the people?

Have you encountered any surprises at all? I suppose not?

The polls that we have seen show you ahead nationally. Is there any hazard in being a leader?

Here are some of the questions asked on WFAA-TV in Dallas, Texas, on 13 October:

Mr. Nixon, in your acceptance speech in Miami Beach, you said that the Republican party has the leadership, the platform, and the purpose that the United States needs. What is there about your leadership that America needs?

Mr. Nixon, do you believe, sir, that under your leadership the Republican party today has more to offer black Americans than at any time in its past history?[24]

But, there were some tough questions, too. For example, panelists asked if Nixon was using panel shows to avoid professional interviewers; if civil disobedience could ever be justified; what he meant by an "honorable end" to the war in Vietnam; whether "law-and-order" were code words for racism; and whether he favored including the Viet Cong in a coalition government.[25]

TV and the Democrats' Debacle

The Democratic candidate of 1968, Hubert Humphrey, did not understand the medium of television. Instead of allowing television to disclose his character to the public, Humphrey made commercials describing his legislative record and recounting what the Democratic party had done for people. He failed to use the medium to answer the one question about his character that everyone wondered about: Was he strong enough to unite a party—and a country—now divided into hostile factions?

The Democratic party first began to come apart when Senator Eugene McCarthy challenged the incumbent Democratic president Johnson in the 1963 primary election in New Hampshire—and won. Next, Robert Kennedy, who had been attorney general during his brother's administration and now was a Democratic senator from the state of New York, entered the race and began winning every primary he entered—except for Oregon, where he lost to McCarthy. Then, on the night he won the California primary, he was shot and killed by an assassin. His tragic death left a host of saddened, confused, and even embittered delegates.

Before this, Lyndon Johnson had announced that he would not seek a second term and withdrew from contention. The growing opposition to his Vietnam policies had convinced Johnson that he could not win reelection. According to David Halberstam, what finally made up Johnson's mind was Walter Cronkite's declaration made on a special broadcast on Vietnam that the war could not be won. "It was the first time in U.S. history a war had been declared over by an anchorman,"

Halberstam wrote.[26] Johnson's withdrawal cleared the way for Hubert Humphrey, Johnson's vice-president, to declare his candidacy. Humphrey had no money, no organization, no media consultants. He was completely dependent on Lyndon Johnson's support, which he received in return for a pledge of loyalty to Johnson's policies— including his Vietnam war policies. Humphrey entered no primaries, but he came to the convention as the favorite, the favored legatee of the delegates pledged to Robert Kennedy, and the recipient of the vote controlled by party stalwarts loyal to Lyndon Johnson.

Yet, the Democrats were far from united. Kennedy's assassination in June revived the dissident groups within the party who had been quiescent since Johnson's earlier withdrawal. The dissidents opposed the war in Vietnam, as had Kennedy and as did McCarthy. But many of the Kennedy people were unsympathetic to McCarthy and rejected Humphrey for his allegiance to Johnson. Understandably then, still another voice against the war entered the struggle for nomination: Senator George McGovern of South Dakota. Finally, one other candidate, Governor Lester Maddox of Georgia, entered the race in opposition to the civil rights legislation passed by Lyndon Johnson.

When television cameras began filming the Democratic National Convention in Chicago in August 1968, the whole world watched in fascination as hostile factions among the Democratic delegates waged bitter battles on the convention floor. The convention delegates were divided into the presidential loyalists, the peace groups, and the anti- civil rights delegates (most of the last ultimately abandoned the Democratic party to support the third party candidacy of George Wallace, helping him to carry Georgia, Alabama, Mississippi, Louisiana, and Arkansas in the November election). The peace groups were divided into McCarthy supporters, McGovern supporters, and Kennedy supporters who refused to support either McGovern or McCarthy and some of whom tried to encourage Robert's brother, Teddy, to enter the fracas.

From its opening on Monday evening to its close on Thursday, the Democratic National Convention consisted of acrimonious debates, strident speeches, and frequent role calls about credentials, rules, the platform, and the nominees. A rapt public watched as the delegates struggled vociferously with the problems of racial balance, unit rule voting, Vietnam war policy, and the selection of the best man. At the same time, viewers were treated from time to time with scenes from the streets outside, where the "siege of Chicago" raged between Chicago police and "dissidents," who were not delegates but people—mostly young—who had come to Chicago to protest. They were made up of those who were antiwar, those who were draft resisters, those who were members of the new left, and those who were black nationalists. They grouped themselves under various labels: yippies, Students for a Democratic Society (SDS), the National Mobilization Committee to End the War in Vietnam, the Black Panthers, and so on. There were anywhere from two to ten thousand dissident demonstrators, confronted by Chicago's twelve thousand-man police force. Television viewers watched the bloody mayhem as police squads attacked the unarmed but provocative peace demonstrators, male and female, flailing them with clubs, spraying them with mace, and dragging bleeding prisoners across the pavement, as the crowds chanted: "The whole world is watching!"

While Governor Abraham Ribicoff was nominating George McGovern, he declared, "With George McGovern, we wouldn't have Gestapo tactics on the streets of Chicago." As the convention crowd roared, the television cameras cut to Mayor Daly of Chicago, who was shaking his fist at Ribicoff in rage "and mouthing an expletive that looked to millions of viewers like an expression he was said never to use."[27] Later, just as Mayor Joseph Alioto of San Francisco had finished nominating Hubert Humphrey, the television cameras cut away to the mayhem on the street. The images ran together, giving alternating views of the convention. In his hotel room, Humphrey raged at "that instrument," the television set, for "playing up to the kooks and rioters."[28]

The television anchormen—some of whose camera crews and reporters were attacked and arrested—publicly declared their disquiet with the goings-on. Chet Huntley, NBC news anchorman, announced that "Chicago police are going out of their way to injure newsmen and prevent them from gathering information on what's going on. The news profession in the city is now under attack by the Chicago police."[29] When Dan Rather was slugged by one of the convention guards, Walter Cronkite of CBS said—on camera: "It looks like we've got a bunch of thugs in here." And later: "If this sort of thing continues, it makes us in our anger want to just turn off our cameras and pack up our microphones and get the devil out of town and leave the Democrats to their agony."

But the public, the viewers, did not agree with the reporters. The public reaction was overwhelmingly antidemonstrators and propolice, as manifest in poll after poll and in a great outpouring of wires and letters. Here two points emerge: The first is that television viewers, as I have maintained, are agents who make their own judgments, their own interpretations of what television presents. The second point is that most people, in public matters, have a procedural conception of morality. That is, they judge an action good or bad not on substantive grounds but rather with regard to the procedures followed. Thus, most people condemned the demonstrations in Chicago not because they thought the Vietnam war was good but because of the procedures, the means, the demonstrators used to protest the war. The procedures were morally unacceptable. The demonstrators—who, of course, believed that they were acting morally—had adopted a substantive morality (actually a premodern, tribal morality). To them, the war was morally wrong. Therefore, any action that opposed the war was morally good.

The conflict between procedural morality and substantive morality plagued the Democratic campaign of 1968. Could Hubert Humphrey—nominated, as predicted, on the first ballot—bring unity to the party? Could he heal the wounds and bring the hostile factions together? Television viewers found little assurance in his acceptance speech, where he took on the personna of St. Francis of Assisi and intoned a sort of political prayer intended to bring the hostile factions together. "Listen to this immortal saint," he intoned.

> Where there is hatred, let me know love. Where there is injury, pardon. Where there is doubt, faith. Where there is despair, hope. Where there is darkness, light.
>
> We do not want a police state, but we need a state of law and order, and neither mob violence nor police brutality have any place in America.
>
> I take my stand—we are and must be one nation under God, with liberty and justice for all. This is our America.
>
> I say to America: Put aside recrimination and dissension. Turn away from violence and hatred.[30]

Humphrey then went on to thank his patron, Lyndon Johnson. This brought roaring cheers and thundering boos from the assembled delegates. Over the din, Humphrey shouted, "I truly believe that history will surely record the greatness of his contributions to the people of this land, and tonight to you, Mr. President, I say thank you. Thank you, Mr. President."[31]

Watching Humphrey give his acceptance speech led many to question his character. Humphrey seemed weak. Even if he was against the war, he wouldn't come out and say it; he lacked the strength to back away from Johnson. Moreover, he was irresolute: The following week, he one day criticized the Chicago police; the next, he defended the Chicago mayor. How could a weak, irresolute character unite the party?

Further evidence that Hubert Humphrey could not unite the party, or the nation, came a few weeks later when television reported a speech he attempted to give in Boston. Student hecklers in the audience chanted "Sell-out, sell-out, sell-out," interspersed with "Shame, shame, shame, shame," and finally "Bull shit, bull shit, bull shit." Hecklers continued to taunt and victimize him until the end of September when he made a nationally televised speech on Vietnam where he said that, if elected, he would call for a complete halt in bombing. After he did this, Humphrey began to gain on Nixon in the polls. But he was unable to convince enough voters that he had the strong character needed to unite a deeply divided nation. He lost to Nixon by five hundred seventeen thousand votes.

Nixon vs. McGovern: The Use and Misuse of Television

During his campaign for the presidency, Richard Nixon had pledged to end the bitter Vietnam war—"an honorable peace." But after the election, the conflict continued. The peace talks dragged, U.S. casualties mounted, and the protests continued on college campuses around the nation. In November 1969, the president gave a televised progress report on U.S. involvement in the Vietnam war. Immediately following the speech, news reporters analyzed it on television, most of them taking a critical tone. As Nixon, and those around him saw it, the reporters had, once again, interfered with the television message the president had presented to the citizenry. That message was: Trust me; we are making progress; I am your leader. But the news analysts wanted more than a disclosure of presidential character. They pointed out that the president's message contained nothing new, no mention of any initiatives toward a settlement.

Ten days later, Vice-President Spiro Agnew delivered a speech on television about the sins of television. He complained that the president had spent weeks in preparation of his recent speech only to have it subjected to "instant analysis" by a

> small band of network commentators and self-appointed analysts, the majority of whom expressed in one way or another their hostility to what he had to say.... The expressions on their face, the tone of the questions, and the sarcasm of their responses made clear their sharp disapproval.

Because the views of this "fraternity" did not represent the views of the United States, Agnew pointed out, there was a great gulf "between how the nation received the president's address and how the networks received it." Repeating the president's position, Agnew declared that

> the president of the United States has a right to communicate directly with the people who elected him, and the people of this country have the right to make up their own minds and form their own opinions about a presidential address without having the president's words and thoughts characterized through the prejudices of hostile critics before they can ever be digested.

This is a serious matter, he went on, because 40 million Americans watch the network news every night and, for millions of them, the networks are the sole source of national and world news. The networks, therefore, represent "a concentration of power over U.S. public opinion unknown in history." He ended by declaring that the people "are entitled to a full accounting of the stewardship of the national networks."[32]

At his press conference a few weeks later, reporters asked President Nixon for his reactions to Agnew's speech. He replied that the vice-president was his own man: "He does not clear his speeches with me just as I did not clear my speeches with President Eisenhower." He praised Agnew for talking "in a very dignified and courageous way" about the problem of unfair coverage. And later he suggested that "television stations might well follow the practice of newspapers of separating news from opinion. When opinion is expressed, label it so, but don't mix the opinion in with the reporting of the news."[33]

By the time of the 1972 campaign, Nixon and his media consultants had worked out their television strategy. Like Johnson, who had been the incumbent president in 1964, Nixon was to campaign as the president—engaging in no debates, giving few interviews or press conferences, but using his office and presidential acts to dominate, even control, network television. On the domestic side, the networks gave widespread coverage to his tax reductions and to his efforts to curb inflation through a wage and price freeze. As to Vietnam, they dutifully reported his efforts to "wind down" the war by reducing the number of U.S. troops there. At the same time, they reported his acts designed to maintain "American credibility" as a nation ready and willing to launch sudden and unpredicted military attacks: the invasion of Cambodia in 1970, the invasion of Laos in 1971, the mining of the ports of North Vietnam in 1972. Television also recorded his dramatic "breakthroughs" in international relations. When he made his journey to China, television, for the first time in history, broadcast a summit meeting live, by satellite, not only to the United States but to the entire world. And when Nixon went to Moscow for a summit meeting, television carried live his address to the Russian people. All these "presidential" acts were later used in television commercials to graphically demonstrate the president's vision, courage, and decisiveness.

Nixon went Johnson one better by using surrogates—members of his administration, including cabinet secretaries—to respond to charges and comments made by his Democratic opponent, George McGovern. Much to the chagrin of McGovern, these surrogates received equal television coverage on the network news. "But I'm running against Nixon," the frustrated man complained, not Melvin Laird (the secretary of defense) or Earl Butz (the secretary of agriculture).[34]

And just as Johnson did against Goldwater in 1964, the Nixon group produced commercials that impugned the character of the opponent. And, as had happened in 1964 with Goldwater, television exposed a frustrated, angry, and often desperate McGovern who, on camera, corroborated the Republican charge about the flaws in his character: He was reckless, irresponsible, profligate, and, unlike President Nixon, lacking in vision and steadfastness.

In one Nixon ad, a construction worker in a hard hat settles down on a scaffold to eat his lunch. He is addressed by an authoritative-sounding announcer who tells him why he should vote for Nixon:

Senator George McGovern recently submitted a welfare bill to the Congress. According to an analysis by the Senate Finance Committee, the McGovern bill would make 47 percent of the people in the United States eligible for welfare—47 percent. Almost every other person in the country would be on welfare. The finance committee estimated the cost of this incredible proposal at $64 billion the first year. That's six times what we're spending now. And who's going to pay for this? Well, if you're not the one out of two people on welfare, you do.

As the astonished worker, sandwich in mouth, stares in disbelief directly into the camera, his image is frozen on the screen.[35]

In another TV commercial, a hand sweeps toy soldiers, ships, and planes from a table as the announcer says:

The McGovern Defense Plan: He would cut the Marines by one-third, the Air Force by one-third; he would cut Navy personnel by one-fourth; he would cut interceptor planes by one-half, the Navy fleet by one-half, and carriers from sixteen to six. Senator Hubert Humphrey had this to say about the McGovern proposal: "It isn't just cutting into the fat, it isn't just cutting into manpower, it's cutting into the very security of this country."[36]

As Johnson had done in the 1964 campaign, the Nixon group used quotes from leading figures of the opposition party attacking their own nominee. The Republicans could do this because, once again, the Democratic primary campaign had created huge rifts and divisions among the contenders. During the primaries, they had attacked one another viciously—all of which had been recorded on film.

George McGovern won the Democratic nomination in large part because television had exposed serious character flaws in Edward Kennedy and Edmund Muskie, the only other serious contenders for the nomination. Television had given widespread coverage to Kennedy's bizarre behavior in the death of Mary Jo Kopechne in a car accident on Chappaquidick Island. Later, televised reports of Edmund Muskie's tearful rejoinder to a newspaper attack raised questions about his strength of character.

One source of dissension among the Democrats was the "new politics" of George McGovern. The "new politics" sprang from the Democratic party's response to the fractious 1968 convention when Hubert Humphrey captured the nomination even though Robert Kennedy and Eugene McCarthy had gathered 80 percent of the preconvention primary votes. In 1969, the Democrats created a reform commission to make the selection process more open and democratic. The commission recommended that delegations from the primary states be composed to represent the actual primary vote count, rather than giving all the votes to the winning candidates, as was traditional. The commission also discouraged the practice of electing uncommitted delegates. One of its most fateful recommendations was that "minorities," women, and youth be represented in reasonable relationship to the groups' presence in the population of the state. Since George McGovern had been chairman of the reform commission, he seemed to be the only Democratic candidate to understand that to be nominated one had to enter all of the state primaries and woo women, minorities, and the young. He did and so secured enough delegates to win the nomination on the first ballot at the national convention in Miami.

Both the new procedures and the new delegates angered and threatened the regular party members, who found themselves being replaced by delegates who "looked like the cast of *Hair*."[37] On television, some 50 million people across the United States saw the disputacious McGovernites espouse busing, abortion, and amnesty. Congressman James O'Hara, who chaired the rules committee, said later, "I think we lost the election at Miami.... The American people made an association between McGovern and gay lib, welfare rights, pot smoking, black militants, women's lib, and wise college kids."[38] Whether this was true or not, it was the case that the "new politics" destroyed the old Democratic party coalitions. Thus, the AFL-CIO executive council voted to remain neutral in the election, refusing to endorse the Democratic presidential candidate, as had been its usual practice. The union's decision released more voters to make a personal judgment of the character of the presidential candidates.

Everyone recognized that George McGovern was compassionate. He listened with sympathy and empathy to those who suffered in Richard Nixon's America: the poor, the sick, the old, the young. But many voters decided that compassion alone was inadequate for a national leader when McGovern declared—on television—that, if necessary, he would "beg" the North Vietnamese to return American prisoners. Another worry about McGovern's character emerged from the so-called Eagleton crisis. After discovering that his personal choice for vice-president, Senator Thomas Eagleton, had been hospitalized for a long time for mental illness, McGovern at first said he backed him "1,000 percent." Then, when the flow of funds to the campaign began to diminish, McGovern persuaded Eagleton to resign. This raised questions about McGovern's steadfastness, honesty, and courage, and branded him as an opportunist in the eyes of many. McGovern himself later said that this "incident convicted me of incompetence, vacillation, dishonesty, and cold calculation."[39] The judgment of the Democratic nominee for president was further questioned when he told television reporters that Sargent Shriver had accepted his invitation to serve as vice-presidential candidate—after Florida Governor Askew and Senators Kennedy, Humphrey, Muskie, and Mansfield had all refused.

In his campaign, McGovern made five televised speeches, participated in a dozen half-hour telethons, and appeared in numerous commercials where he was seen in factories, school yards, and shopping malls, answering questions put to him by the voters. Although he outspent Nixon on television appearances, McGovern failed to convince voters that he was the better-qualified candidate. He could not get people to believe that Nixon headed up "the most corrupt administration in history." Nor could he refute the charges that his welfare programs were wasteful and his Vietnam policies irresponsible. The public decided that George McGovern did not have the character to lead the nation. On election day, he lost every state except Massachusetts.

Shortly after his landslide victory in 1972, the public found out that Nixon did not have the character they had judged him to posses. He used the power of his office first to sponsor the Watergate crimes and then to try to cover them up and to harass those who sought to investigate the matter. He betrayed the public's trust. Under threat of impeachment, he resigned on 8 August 1974, passing the presidency on to Gerald Ford, who had replaced Spiro Agnew earlier that year after Agnew had resigned the vice-presidency in disgrace for taking a bribe. In the wake of such sordid goings-on, public trust in political leaders precipitously declined. Back in 1964, poll takers had found that 76 percent of the public believed that officials in Washington could be trusted "to do what is right most of the time."[40] By 1976, that proportion dropped to a mere 33 percent.

Gerald Ford: Television Exposure

In the election year of 1976, the print media "discovered" that the electorate was primarily interested in the character of the candidates for president. Magazines like *Time, Newsweek, Harpers,* and *The New Republic* all carried articles probing the character of the candidates. If I am correct, however, the electorate had always been primarily concerned with the moral character of the candidates but has only since the 1960s been able to use television to make its personal assessment of the character of those who would be its leaders. Moreover, the successful presidential candidates since 1960 had all understood this and had each tried to use the media to display their own moral character. Gerald Ford's media consultant certainly understood this, as is evident in a memo he wrote in 1975:

> People want a more honest government and a far higher morality in every walk of life. In their leaders, they look for moral leadership, strength of character, religious conviction, love of family, and great personal integrity above all else. They also look for compassion in their leaders.... They want a conservative government, but one tempered with compassion for all the people.
>
> It is particularly important to note that the people are far more influenced by their own feelings about the candidates' personal traits than by the candidates' positions on the issues.[41]

Gerald Ford came across to the people as they watched him on television as honest and decent, a straight shooter. But a month after assuming the presidency, he all but destroyed his moral character by issuing a complete pardon to Richard Nixon, cutting off the legal process then in train to bring him to trial. Many interpreted this to mean that Ford had made a deal with Nixon. At his August press conference, and at one held in September, reporters badgered him with almost nothing but questions about Nixon and the pardon.[42]

Ford, like previous television-age incumbents, conducted a no-campaign campaign, the "I am your president" approach now dubbed the Rose Garden strategy since all political campaign activity emanated from the Rose Garden of the White House. Ford adopted this strategy only after a near-disastrous primary campaign to secure the Republican nomination where he almost lost to Ronald Reagan. During the primaries, he appeared on many television shows as a candidate. In January, for example, Ford filmed an interview with NBC's John Chancellor, answered questions for forty minutes on CBS's "Sixty Minutes," and appeared on CBS's "Face the Nation" and ABC's "Issues and Answers." Yet, these appearances as a candidate had made him seem opportunistic, anxious, even desperate. After securing the nomination, he became more "presidential," supplementing the Rose Garden strategy with television ads that displayed his leadership qualities. But these slick commercials that showed Ford demonstrating competent leadership were contradicted by the candid shots television viewers had of a president who walked into helicopter doors; who slipped, stumbled, and knocked things over; who confused the names and locations of cities, states, and universities; and who became halting and inarticulate in interviews. Ford's campaign slogan was The Man Who Made Us Proud Again. But TV watchers found him to be "the man who made us laugh again," as confirmed on "Saturday Night Live," where Chevy Chase, in a weekly imitation of Gerald Ford, would stumble down stairs, knock over his podium, or strangle himself with his phone cord.

In his nomination acceptance speech, which was a highly polished performance (the result of a dozen rehearsals), Ford called for a series of televised debates with the Democratic candidate, Jimmy Carter. In the second debate, Ford once again disclosed his bungling incompetence to a nationwide TV audience when he declared there was "no Soviet domination of Eastern Europe and there never will be under a Ford administration." This, of course, was merely a verbal error; what he had meant was that the United States did not accept Soviet domination of the region. But an event on television is never simply an event; the viewer makes sense of whatever is presented by weaving it into a story, a theme. The theme concocted by many, with the help of TV commentators, was that Ford was an inept bungler. The verbal slip in the debate now became part of the story.

Jimmy Carter: Prime-Time Morality

The Democratic candidate, Jimmy Carter, ran not just against Gerald Ford but against Washington. After Vietnam, after Watergate, the public, he said, wanted a less imperial president. He made much of the fact that he was not a lawyer but only a decent, honest, hard-working peanut farmer form Plains, Georgia. Early ads showed him in blue jeans and work boots walking through a field, running his hands through fresh-picked peanuts, and joking with his mother. His mother, Lillian, his wife, Roslyn, and his ten-year old daughter, Amy, frequently showed up in television ads to attest to his high moral character. Carter's whole television campaign focused on his moral character. Over and over, Carter would stare into the camera, smile, and softly say he wanted to give the nation "a government as good and as honest and as decent and as competent and as compassionate and as filled with love as are the American people." He declared: "I'll never tell a lie," adding, "If I ever lie to you, if I ever mislead you, if I ever avoid a controversial issue, then don't vote for me, because I won't be worthy of your vote if I'm not worthy of your trust" (his pollster, Pat Cadell, later said, "without that trust thing, he couldn't have made it").[43] As a born again Christian, Carter presented his deep religious commitment as evidence for his moral character. He told one television interviewer that he prayed about twenty-five times a day and always asked "Got to help me do the right thing."[44]

Carter not only disclosed and enacted his moral character before television viewers, he used television to entreat voters to vote for him for moral reasons. To southerners—white and black—he pointed out that he was not like George Wallace, nor like Lester Maddox. He recognized that the time for racial discrimination was over. As governor, he had told the citizens of Georgia that no "black person should ever have to bear the additional burden of being deprived of the opportunity of education, a job, or simple justice."[45] By voting for him, he explained, southerners would demonstrate their own moral character: They would show the rest of the nation that southerners were not all rednecks and bigots. On election day, Carter did win nine of the ten southern states, losing only Virginia.

In the North, he also provided voters with moral reasons for supporting him. In Massachusetts and Rhode Island, states with large Catholic populations, Carter's television commercials asked for the same display of tolerance Georgians had shown to John Kennedy: "Some people say the nation will never vote for a southerner for president," Carter announced in this commercial, "but they said in 1960 that the South would never vote for a liberal Irish Catholic senator from Boston." Yet, in that election, Kennedy had gotten a bigger margin of victory in Georgia than in Massachusetts. "I believe," Carter concluded, "that the people in New England will be just as open minded in 1976." The New Englanders could display their own moral character by voting for Jimmy Carter.

Like John Kennedy in 1960, Jimmy Carter had two obstacles to contend with in his quest for the office of president. First, he was a southerner, so people suspected that he was a racist. Secondly, he was a born again Christian, so people suspected that he was a weirdo unable to cope with the real world of politics. Television helped Carter overcome both of these problems.

The suspicion of racism came up when Carter used the term "ethnic purity" in an interview published 2 April 1976 in the *New York Daily News:* "I see nothing wrong with ethnic purity being maintained. I would not force racial integration of a neighborhood by government action." Television reporters dug out the quote and asked Carter what he meant by "ethnic purity." He provided new phrases: "A diametrically opposite kind of family," "the intrusion of alien groups," "a different kind of person." Sam Donaldson of ABC asked him, "Are such terms as 'ethnic purity' and 'alien group' almost Hitlerian?" For a week, the badgering went on while Jimmy Carter continued to defend and explain his words. Finally, he apologized and took back the term. The crisis subsided: Carter was not racist. But the media event did reveal an aspect of Carter's character that loomed large in his conduct as president: He was stubborn.

The question about whether a born again Christian understood what the real world is like was laid to rest by Carter's famous November 1976 *Playboy* interview, which was extensively reported on television network news. "I've committed adultery in my heart many times," Jimmy Carter confessed to the magazine. "This is something that God recognizes I will do—and I have done it—and God forgives me for it. But that doesn't mean that I condemn someone who not only looks on a woman with lust but leaves his wife and shacks up with somebody out of wedlock."

The *Playboy* interview revealed that this born again Christian knew what the world is like, but it also revealed a worrisome aspect of Jimmy Carter's character that, in time, proved disabling: his judgment. "Christ says 'Don't consider yourself better than someone else because one guy screws a whole bunch of women while the other guy is loyal to his wife'," Carter had told his interviewers. One clergyman, a supporter of Carter, noted that "screw" is not a good Baptist word. Carter's conduct, or at least his speech, did appear unseemly for a born again Christian. Later, many would question his judgment about what was seemly conduct for the president of the United States, to which office he was elected by a bare majority of 1,682,970 votes.

Four years later, on 3 July 1980, Gerald Rafshoon, President Carter's media consultant, wrote a memo outlining a general media plan for the upcoming election: "The public is now convinced that Jimmy Carter is an inept man. He has tried hard but he has failed. He is weak and indecisive—in over his head. *We have to change people's minds*" [*my emphasis*].[46]

During Carter's administration, both inflation and interest rates rose, approaching 20 percent by 1980. And, on the international front, his failure to secure the release of the American hostages held by Iran since November 1979, overshadowed everything else. Carter, perhaps, was unlucky—crises not of his making dogged his administration. But, more revealing to the electorate were his reactions to these crises. His responses were not presidential; he seemed to lack the characteristics of a leader. When the United States experienced a severe oil shortage because of OPEC's (Organization of Petroleum Exporting Countries) policies, Carter made a televised address to the American people, telling them to lower their thermostats, and he wore a sweater for the occasion. When the terrorists first seized the U.S. hostages at the Embassy in Iran, President Carter appeared on television and asked the American public to join him in prayer. Later, he announced that he would not light the Christmas tree on the White House lawn until the captives were returned. When the Soviet Union invaded Afghanistan, the leader of the free world responded by withdrawing the United States from the Olympic games scheduled in Moscow.

There were other minor incidents captured by television that displayed the president as acting in unseemly ways: the inauguration-day walk down Pennsylvania Avenue to the White House holding hands with Amy and Roslyn; running in a ten-kilometer race until he literally collapsed; delivering a televised "national malaise" speech in which he criticized Americans for being self-indulgent and causing "a crisis of confidence" that strikes at the very heart and soul and spirit of the nation; refusing to control his brother, Billy—a beer drinking, profane gas station owner from the president's hometown—who became a registered foreign agent for the Libyan government in return for $220,000 ("Billy is just Billy," the president explained to reporters). Television news and television commentators exposed two other more serious instances of inept judgment. The first one was a U.S. vote in the United Nations Security Council condemning Israel for its settlements on the West Bank and in Gaza, and calling for their dismantlement—a vote the White House explained was due to an error in communication. The second was the failed rescue mission to recover the hostages in Iran—five months after they had been captured. (The American public had no trouble knowing how long the hostages had been in captivity since Walter Cronkite habitually ended his nightly CBS newscast with a hostage day-count: "This is the one hundred and fifty-third day of captivity for the fifty Americans in Iran.") In this abortive rescue attempt, the helicopters malfunctioned and a helicopter and a transport plane collided, killing eight soldiers.

Prior to the disastrous rescue attempt, many citizens had rallied behind the president. But many had second thoughts when shortly after the failed mission he abandoned his Rose Garden strategy and entered the political campaign because, he explained, the Iran problem had become "more manageable" after the "limited success" of the rescue operation. At this point, the man who promised he would never lie to the American people looked to many as if he had used the hostage crisis to manipulate the electorate.

In the primaries, Carter's principal opponent for the Democratic nomination was Edward Kennedy. Kennedy's character had been tainted by his behavior at Chappaquidick in 1969. In the fall of 1979, a CBS special called "Teddy" traveled the route Kennedy's car took on the night of the accident and cast serious doubts on Kennedy's account of the incident. Later, when he delivered a thirty-minute paid for-television speech where he addressed the matter, Kennedy revealed that he would say no more about it: "While I know that many will never believe the facts of the tragic events at Chappaquidick, those facts are the only truth I can tell because that is the way it happened, and I ask only that I be judged on the basis of U.S. standards of fairness." In his primary campaign against Kennedy, Carter's television ads played up the matter of truth:

You may not always agree with President Carter, but you'll never find yourself wondering if he's telling you the truth. It's hard to think of a more useful quality in any person who becomes president than telling the simple truth. President Carter: He tells you the truth.[47]

Carter defeated Kennedy for the Democratic party nomination and then had to face the Republican challenger, Ronald Reagan. Once again, the issue was the character of the president.

In his acceptance speech as the Republican challenger, Ronald Reagan repeated the central theme of the attack Teddy Kennedy had already made against Carter: "I will not stand by and watch this great country destroy itself under mediocre leadership that drifts from one crisis to the next, eroding our national will and purpose." Later, the Reagan media advisors composed a commercial using a clip from a Kennedy primary speech where he shouted: "I say it's time to say no more hostages (cheers), no more high interest rates, no more inflation, and no more Jimmy Carter."[48]

Ronald Reagan: Made for Television

The Federal Election Campaign Act of 1972 had restricted the amount of money candidates could spend on elections, but a Supreme Court ruling of 1976 allowed independent Political Action Committees (PACs) to spend unlimited amounts. These PACs spent more than $6 million on television ads to support candidates in the presidential campaign of 1980, with "virtually every penny of it on behalf of Ronald Reagan or against Jimmy Carter," according to Jeff Greenfield, author of *The Real Campaign: How the Media Misread the Story of the 1980 Campaign*.[49] Most of these television ads were attacks on Carter's character. One, for example, attacked him for accepting the Democratic platform endorsement of gay rights; another showed Uncle Sam being used as a punching bag by leering Communists, Arab Sheiks, and swarthy Iranians. These negative ads paid for by PACs permitted Ronald Reagan to spend his own advertising money on commercials depicting his leadership abilities. The central message of these television commercials was the American can-do theme: "Don't let anyone tell you that inflation can't be controlled. It can be, by making some tough decisions to control federal spending," Reagan announced in a thirty-second TV ad. "As president, I'm ready to make these decisions."[50] The same "can-do" theme came through in commercials on foreign policy: "We've learned by now that it isn't weakness that keeps the peace, it's strength. Our foreign policy has been based on the fear of not being liked. Well, it's nice to be liked. But it's more important to be respected."[51]

Reagan's greatest liability was his age, and the merciless TV cameras did reveal the lines around his eyes, the jowls, and the "turkey-neck" of the almost seventy-year-old candidate. Moreover, television cameras revealed that he was often confused, unsure, or even wrong about his facts, as well as unaware of recent and past events. Carter's television ads, therefore, pictured Ronald Reagan as uninformed and dangerous—following the successful strategy used earlier against Goldwater in 1964 and McGovern in 1972. In one person-in-the-street commercial, a stream of people reveal their fears about electing Ronald Reagan:

It certainly is risky.

I think it's very risky.

I just don't think he's well enough informed.

I think Governor Reagan in a crisis situation would be very fast to use military force.

Reagan doesn't stop to think of things before he does them. That scares me about Ronald Reagan. It really does.

But Carter's television ads didn't work. They did not convince the electorate that Reagan's character—and lack of intelligence—rendered him unfit to be president. Perhaps Reagan or his media advisors were smarter than Goldwater and McGovern, who did fall into the trap of displaying on camera the very flaws their opponents accused them of having. At any rate, Reagan's television appearance did not corroborate the image portrayed of him by Carter's ads. Indeed, Ronald Reagan usually came off appearing *more* presidential than the incumbent, Jimmy Carter.

In desperation, Carter began to attack Ronald Reagan in his

political speeches. In a speech delivered in the Ebenezer Baptist Church in Atlanta—a church where Martin Luther King, Sr. and Martin Luther King, Jr. had both preached—the president accused Reagan of being a racist. A few days later, on two separate occasions, he implied that Reagan was a war monger. Reagan, however, turned the accusations around. When interviewed on TV, he pointed to a long-suspected character defect of Jimmy Carter: "I think that to assume that anyone would deliberately want a war is beneath decency." Many reporters and commentators had thought that Jimmy Carter was mean and vicious—just as many had thought that Gerald Ford was dumb and that Edmund Muskie had an unstable temper. So, when each of these acted in accordance with expectations, the conduct became part of a television story or theme about the candidate's character. And other instances of this character flaw—previously unworthy of mention—became news.

A few days later, Carter's language became even more strident when, in Chicago, he warned a group that their votes would

> literally decide the lives of millions of people in our country and, indeed, throughout the world.... You'll determine whether or not this America will be unified, or, if I lose the election, whether Americans might be separated, blacks from white, Jews from Christians, North from South, rural from urban.

This attack once again permitted Ronald Reagan to appear presidential before the television cameras as he told his interviewers, more in sorrow than in anger: "I'm not asking for an apology from him. I know whom I have to account to for my actions. But I think he owes the country an apology."[52]

Jimmy Carter tried to recover his moral probity and upright character by backing off and, at the same time, making a virtue of baring his soul. On 8 October, he appeared on ABC for an interview by Barbara Walters. Her first comment was: "Mr. President, in recent days you have been characterized as mean, vindictive, hysterical, and at the point of desperation." Carter admitted that "the tone of the campaign had departed from the way it ought to be between two candidates for the highest office in the land."

"No more name calling?" Barbara asked.

"I'll do my best," Carter replied, smiling.

Carter's final attempt to expose Reagan came in the television debate of late October. But here, once again, Ronald Reagan disclosed that he had more presidential character. According to Roger Ailes, the astute media advisor to Richard Nixon in 1968, the viewers of the 1980 Carter-Reagan debate remembered four things: Carter's reference to his daughter, Amy; Reagan's "there you go again" line; Reagan walking over to shake hands with Carter at the end; and Reagan looking generally comfortable, while Carter "looked constipated." In commenting on these four things in their book on political advertising in television called *The Spot*, Edwin Diamond and Stephen Bates lament that "none of these have anything to do with issues."[53] Of course. They all have to do with the moral character of the candidates. It is true that television has driven "substance" out of political campaigns, but, as voters realize and political commentators sometimes forget, it is the moral character of a political leader that is all important. This is what television campaigns are all about: the disclosure of moral character.

Carter referred to his daughter during the debate when the issue of nuclear proliferation came up. "I had a discussion with Amy the other day before I came here to ask her what the most important issue was," the president said. "She thought nuclear weaponry and the control of nuclear arms." Inside the auditorium, Jeff Greenfield reports, "a faint snicker rippled through the crowd."[54] Once again, Jimmy Carter had trivialized the office of the president.

Later in the debate, Carter presented what he said was Reagan's position on Medicare. "There you go again!" Reagan boomed in a good-natured, humorous way, twitting Carter for misinterpreting him. He was cool, relaxed, gracious, and totally in control. Moreover, the debate showed that he was well-informed, stable, and vigorous. The debates put to rest fears about Reagan's age and intelligence. Most of all, the debate presented to the television audience a can-do presidential candidate who seemed to have the requisite moral character for national leadership. The debate insured a landslide vote of no confidence in the character of Jimmy Carter. In the final tally on election day, Reagan won 489 electoral votes to Carter's forty-nine.

Reagan vs. Mondale: TV Pro vs. TV Amateur

By the next presidential election in 1984, the number of television news programs had proliferated. In addition to the local and network nightly and morning news shows, PBS now offered the "MacNeil-Lehrer News Hour." On ABC, "Nightline" provided a late-hour in-depth news program, while NBC had the late-hour "Overnight" and CBS aired "Nightwatch." A new network, CNN (Cable News Network), provided twenty-four hours of news programming, while INN (Independent News Network) provided syndicated national and international news to independent local stations. Finally, C-SPAN (Cable Satellite Public Affairs Network) had been created to broadcast twenty-four hours of public affairs programming, such as the debates in the House of Representatives. The old standby Sunday network interview shows—"Meet the Press" (NBC) and "Face the Nation" (CBS)—were now joined by "This Week with David Brinkley" (ABC).

In the election year of 1984, this surfeit of news shows (some disappeared after the election) made clear to all what the logical consequences of televised coverage of election campaigns are. First, the selection of a president had become a great game—a great video game. The print media, of course, had always treated presidential elections as a game, a race. But television had changed the nature of the game. The cover of *Time* (22 October 1984) captured this transformation with a picture of the candidates cast as jockeys riding horses with television cameras for heads. In the presidential race, those who competed did it by enacting and disclosing themselves before the television cameras. Second, with television, any number of self-appointed candidates could enter the race—there were twelve candidates for the Democratic nomination in 1984. And, finally, the race was about character, the moral character of each candidate.

The entry of so many candidates in the Democratic primaries heightened the scrutiny each received as they competed against one another. Walter Mondale, who had been Jimmy Carter's vice-president, was the front runner, having created an extensive nationwide organization by traveling extensively throughout the country, setting up personal alliances in all the key states. He had raised lots of money and had reached out to all the major interest group constituencies in the Democratic party. The other candidates attacked Mondale for promising too much to too many special interest groups. "Is this going to be a Democratic party that promises everything to everyone?" John Glenn asked in a television "debate" during the New Hampshire primary.[55]

Television helped to destroy the candidacies of the other Democrats by reporting their inadequacies of character: e.g., the homophobic comments of John Glenn and the anti-Semitic slurs of Jesse Jackson. Gary Hart's campaign was plagued by television reports that raised questions about his authenticity: He had changed his name (from Hartpence) and his age. This conduct, combined with his vague references to his own "new" and "fresh" ideas prompted Walter Mondale to ask "Where's the Beef?" copping a slogan from a TV commercial for Wendy's hamburgers that questioned the lack of substance in the products of a rival company.

Mondale won the Democratic nomination and then selected Geraldine Ferraro as his vice-presidential running mate—the first female ever chosen for that position. Television had made the selection of a woman an easy choice. But now, television scrutiny of Walter Mondale became more intense, and ultimately undid him. "I think you know I've never really warmed up to television," he said at his final press conference, "and in fairness to television, it's never really warmed up to me." What television did, of course, was to relentlessly probe Mondale's character and help people to become doubtful about his leadership abilities.

Traditionally, the Democratic party launches its presidential campaign by having its candidates march in the New York City Labor Day parade. This time, television cameras exposed Mondale and Ferraro traveling through sparse, empty streets, waving at people who weren't there. Mondale's consultants explained that this happened because they had to schedule the parade early in the morning so that Mondale could fulfill his promise to New York City labor leaders and then fly to Wisconsin for another scheduled rally. But this only raised again the questions about Mondale's trying to promise everything to everyone.

Not long after the Labor Day fiasco, television reporters had a field day exposing Geraldine Ferraro's tangled financial arrangements with her husband which, of course, raised questions about *her* character. Her offhand remark that her husband's refusal to reveal his tax returns would be understood by other women married to Italian men did little to improve the estimates of her judgment. A subsequent release of the information called for, and her ninety-minute televised press conference on the matter, did help remove doubts about her honesty and integrity but left doubts about Mondale's judgment in failing to investigate this thoroughly beforehand. It looked to some as if he had opportunistically selected a woman to attract female voters.

The fact that she was a Catholic also came to be classified as political opportunism when Ferraro became embroiled in a controversy over abortion with Cardinal O'Connor of the Archdiocese of New York. Ferraro had claimed that although she personally opposed abortion, she also opposed efforts by the government to limit a woman's right to choose to have an abortion. "The Catholic position on abortion is not monolithic," she said. "There can be a range of personal and political responses to the issue." The cardinal pointed out that this is "not true because abortion is the killing of an innocent creature," adding: "I don't see how a Catholic in good conscience can vote for a candidate who explicitly supports abortion."[56] The television reports of Ferraro's dispute with the cardinal raised more questions about moral character.

Walter Mondale regarded all these matters as distractions from what he wanted the medium to focus on: the issues. "It's the issues that count," he said.[57] But as Brit Hume, an ABC reporter, reflected, "Watching Mondale talk about issues continuously is like watching grass grow" (note that Hume talks about "watching" Mondale discuss the issues).

Yet, it is not just that issues on television are boring; it is that television is not a suitable medium for the discussion of issues: They become muddled. Take the seemingly simple matter of where a candidate stands on taxes. Martin Schram reports that the group of voters he observed during the election were unsure about whether Mondale said he would raise taxes or cut taxes (he said he would raise them).[58] Perhaps even more important, Mondale was wrong: The issues do not count—voters judge candidates not on the issues, but in terms of their character. Here's how one of Schram's interviewees put it: "I look at it as a businessman," said Bud Cherry, proprietor of Cherry's Brake and Parts shop.

> When there's a customer standing over the counter, I'm not going to let them see the problems. I'm not going to let them see me sweat. I portray nice soft music, nice mood, nice everything. All organized, all facade. Mondale lets you see him sweat, lets you see his disorganization.[59]

Mondale's insistence on running a campaign on the issues was, as

Howell Raines observed, a reenactment of "the rituals of elections past."[60] Mondale simply did not understand the medium of television, whereas President Reagan—and his advisors—did understand it. It is true that Reagan had the advantage of incumbency—but so had Carter in 1980 and Ford in 1976, and they both lost their elections. It is also true that economic conditions had greatly improved during Reagan's incumbency. But more than anything else, Reagan was able to present himself as having presidential character—the man, as the slogan said, "who made America proud again." As Michael Deaver, the president's deputy chief of staff, said, "We've got a guy who has been in front of a camera for fifty years or so. He is at ease with himself physically, mentally, spiritually."[61]

A story about a CBS news story illustrates how well the Reagan team understood the medium of television. In her broadcast of 4 October 1984, CBS correspondent Leslie Stahl did a reflexive piece about the television coverage of Ronald Reagan's four years in office. Her intent was to show that the television pictures of Ronald Reagan had conveyed impressions that were quite the opposite of his policies. Here's what she said:

> How does Ronald Reagan use television? Brilliantly. He's been criticized as the rich man's president, but the TV pictures say it isn't so. At seventy-three, Mr. Reagan could have an age problem. But the TV pictures say it isn't so. Americans want to feel proud of their country again, and of their president. And the TV pictures say you can. The orchestration of television coverage absorbs the White House. Their goal? To emphasize the president's greatest asset, which, his aides say, is his personality. They provide pictures of him looking like a leader. Confident, with his Marlboro Man walk. A good family man. They also aim to erase the negatives. Mr. Reagan tries to counter the memory of an unpopular issue with a carefully chosen backdrop that actually contradicts the president's policy. Look at the handicapped Olympics, or the opening ceremony of an old age home. No hint that he tried to cut the budgets for the disabled and for federally subsidized housing for the elderly.

> Another technique for distancing the president from bad news—have him disappear, as he did the day he pulled the marines out of Lebanon. He flew off to his California ranch, leaving others to hand out the announcement. There are few visual reminders linking the president to the tragic bombing of the marine headquarters in Beirut. But two days later, the invasion of Grenada succeeded, and the White House offered television a variety of scenes associating the president with the joy and triumph.... President

Reagan is accused of running a campaign in which he highlights the images and hides from the issues. But there's no evidence that the charge will hurt him because, when people see the president on television, he makes them feel good about America, about themselves, and about him.

As she spoke, four years of Reagan videos flashed on the screen: the president basking in a sea of flag-waving supporters, beaming beneath red and blue balloons floating skyward, sharing concerns with farmers in a field out of Grant Woods, picnicking with Mid-Americans, pumping iron, wearing a bathing suit and tossing a football ... more flags ... wearing faded dungarees at the ranch and a suit with Margaret Thatcher, getting a kiss and a cake from Nancy, getting the Olympic torch from a runner, greeting wheelchair athletes at the handicapped Olympics, greeting senior citizens at their housing project, honoring veterans who landed on Normandy, honoring youths just back from Grenada, countering a heckler, joshing with the press corps, impressing suburban school children, wooing black inner-city kids, hugging Mary Lou Retton ... more flags ... red, white, and blue smoke emissions from parachutes descending, red and blue balloons ascending.

When the program ended, Stahl got an anticipated phone call from the White House:

"Great piece," the Reagan man said. "We loved it."

"You *what?*" Stahl said.

"We loved it!" he said.

"What do you mean you loved it?" Stahl asked. How can you say you loved it? It was tough! Don't you think it was tough?

"We're in the middle of a campaign and you gave us four and a half minutes of great pictures of Ronald Reagan," said the Reagan assistant. "And that's all the American people see.... They don't listen to you if you're contradicting great pictures.... They don't hear what you are saying if the pictures are saying something different."[62]

Ronald Reagan's media advisors kept him away from interviews, away from reporters who might ask him embarrassing questions, away from microphones where he might make a mistake, commit a gaffe. His election campaign became a folksy road show: parades with lots of flags and balloons, appearances at automobile races, picnics and barbecues, where he smiled and bragged "You ain't seen nothing yet." The TV-spectacle kind of campaign brought criticisms from reporters that the president was not discussing issues. But as John Lake, the publicity director for Reagan explained:

The press forgets what its job is sometimes. Its job is to report what's going on. What was going on in the election was what we did. It's our responsibility to set the agenda and meet it; it's the press's responsibility to report what we're doing.[63]

Left unsaid, but implicit in these remarks, is that it is the public who will decide who had the character and ability to be president. And it will decide on the basis of what the television screen discloses—not what the TV reporters say.[64]

The only worry voters had about Ronald Reagan was his age: He was now seventy-three years old. Was he too old to continue as president for four more years? The only way to demonstrate his competency was through a debate with Walter Mondale, which the Reagan team finally agreed to. The first debate was a disaster for the president. The content of Reagan's remarks, as Germond and Witcover point out, was, when examined in print, coherent.[65] It was *how* he spoke, *how* he handled himself; *his manner and style* that seemed confused, uncertain, and incoherent.

The television news programs made much of the debate, replaying those portions of it where Reagan appeared to flub, and then supplementing these with films of the president nodding off during an audience with the pope, as well as the famous scene from an impromptu television press conference where Nancy prompted him:

Reporter: "Is there anything you can do to get them to Vienna?"

President Reagan: "Uh ..."

Nancy Reagan (whispering behind her husband): "We're doing everything we can."

President Reagan (aloud): "We're doing everything we can."

One network, ABC, interviewed its own staff physician about changes in mental acuity that accompany aging. But Ronald Reagan was ready for the second debate. He looked sharper, younger, and more fit than he had looked before. Mondale, in contrast, looked tired and frazzled, with very visible bags under his eyes. Halfway through the debate, the president got the opportunity he was waiting for: One of the reporters raised the "age issue," asking the president whether he could handle a lengthy crisis. Henry Trewhitt, the reporter, apologized for raising the question.[66]

"Not at all, Mr. Trewhitt," Reagan replied in the mock seriousness of the expert funny storyteller. "And I want you to know that I also will not make age an issue in this campaign. I am not going to exploit, for political purposes, my opponent's youth and inexperience."

At this point, Germond and Witcover announced, the presidential campaign was over. The audience in the theater laughed and applauded, and the cameras showed Mondale himself smiling in a helpless way. It was "one hell of a one-liner"[67]—a one-liner that ended then and there all fears about mental debility. In the November election, Reagan won by another landslide, capturing the electoral vote of every state but Mondale's home state of Minnesota.

Bush vs. Dukakis: The Nice Man vs. the Ice Man

In the election of 1988, two of the self-appointed fifteen candidates for the presidency—Gary Hart and Joseph Biden—were eliminated from the race as the result of moral character flaws exposed by television. In Senator's Biden's case, the use of videotapes of the speech of a British politician, juxtaposed with a film clip of one of Biden's speeches, clearly disclosed that the senator from Delaware was guilty of plagiarism. Later, a television film clip of Biden's comments to a reporter exposed him lying about his college and law school career, leading, in turn, to revelations of an earlier charge of plagiarism while he was in law school. Once again, television had helped people select and reject political candidates on the basis of appraisals of moral character. This improved the existing political procedures. Here's how the *New York Times* put it:

> What Senator Biden's withdrawal reflects, as did that of Gary Hart before him, is a dramatic change in the way America chooses party candidates for president.
>
> Once a handful of political professionals did it. Now, it's the candidates who propose themselves. The news media play a role, often uneasy, but it's the public that chooses. This evolving selection process is volatile, messy, sometimes cruel—and yet, welcome. It's the latest extension of the franchise.[68]

Although the primary campaign clearly revealed that the crucial question about a candidate was his character, Michael Dukakis, the

Democratic nominee, decided that the real issue was competence. Now, it is very difficult to demonstrate competence on television, as Dukakis discovered, too late. His attempts to display his competence in his television appearances made him look smug, arrogant, and cold—not usually considered desirable traits in a Democratic leader. Moreover, stress on competence left the Dukakis campaign without a message suitable for television: "I like Mike" simply did not do it. And, since he eschewed negative attacks on George Bush (a competent person doesn't have to stoop to such maneuvers) his staff had difficulty in devising commercials that Dukakis would approve. During the critical weeks in September, the Dukakis campaign was almost completely without advertising.[69]

While Dukakis seemed unable to conduct an effective television campaign, George Bush—relying heavily on his media professionals, led by master wizard Roger Ailes—used television more effectively than any previous presidential candidate. At the time of the Republican National Convention in August, polls placed George Bush seventeen points behind Dukakis. But the "hired guns" of the Bush campaign took this uninspiring, uncharismatic, political figure—a "wimp"—held in low regard by the voters, and turned him into a near-landslide winner, at least in the electoral college.

The people in the Bush campaign knew that the crucial question for voters was the character of their candidate. The task before them was to demonstrate that Bush, who had been a loyal, supportive vice-president to Ronald Reagan, was strong enough to lead the nation. Second, they had to disclose what they called the natural kindness and humaneness of their candidate. And finally, they had to show that George Bush shared the beliefs and dominant values of most Americans. The other side of the agenda, of course, was to reveal that Michael Dukakis had none of these essential traits of character. If this meant a negative television campaign, then so be it.

The opportunity for George Bush to demonstrate that he was strong, and even tough, came as a veritable gift from CBS when Dan Rather interviewed him on his "Evening News" show. Primed by his television guru, Roger Ailes, "to stay on the offense the whole time and wear him out,"[70] Bush turned the interview into a prize fight, taking the initiative so forcefully that Rather wound up losing hold of his emotions. Amazed viewers watched as the TV anchorman ended the interview with the vice-president of the United States by cutting him off in midsentence—sounding rude and sealing Bush's victory.

Bush's TV commercials displayed his humaneness in scenes of him exuberantly hoisting one of his grandchildren into the air in the presence of a loving and affectionate family. And then, there was his goofiness, a tendency to make gaffes, as when he said in a speech on 7 September that it was the anniversary of Pearl Harbor. Following this, gags circulated that Bush did not want to debate Dukakis on 25 September because it was Christmas. During that televised debate, Bush made another one of his goofy gaffes in answering a question on defense: "We are going to make some changes and some tough choices before we go to the deployment of the Midgetman missile, or on the Minuteman, or whatever it is. We're going to have to—the MX. We're going to have to do that." And then, good-humoredly added: "It's Christmas!" He had goofed, but he was not a fool. Taking the point a step further, he came out with: "Wouldn't it be nice to be the ice man, so you never made a mistake?" He, George Bush, was a fallible human being, whereas the cool, unflappable Dukakis seemed to have ice water coursing through his veins. Who would the voters choose, the Ice Man or the Nice Man?[71]

In the second televised debate, Dukakis's on-camera conduct all but guaranteed that George Bush was the hands-down winner of the humanity prize. Dukakis had a flu bug, a sore throat, a 101-degree fever, and a pain in his back, but the television audience didn't know any of this. The first question asked of the Democratic candidate came from CNN anchorman Bernard Shaw: "Governor, if Kitty Dukakis was raped and murdered, would you favor an irrevocable death penalty for the killer?" Ignoring the opportunity to disclose heretofore hidden passionate and compassionate feelings, the governor, without hesitation, blandly replied: "I've opposed the death penalty during all my life." Then, he went on to cite how crime had been reduced in his state without it, and ended with a few paragraphs on the need to fight drug traffic. He made no reference to the hypothetical rape and murder of his wife, Kitty; he did not even mention her name.

Later in the debate, a questioner suggested to him that "the American public admired your performance (in the first debate) but didn't seem to like you much." Dukakis replied that he was a "reasonably likable guy," but that he was "also a serious guy" who addressed issues "in a very serious way."[72]

To demonstrate that George Bush was in the mainstream of U.S.

beliefs and values, his people adopted the strategy of showing that Michael Dukakis was far out of that mainstream, making Bush look better by making Dukakis look worse. In his television speeches, interviews, and televised commercials, Bush relentlessly accused his opponent of "liberal" values, making the term an epithet.

- Dukakis lacked patriotism: As governor, he had vetoed a Massachusetts law requesting teachers to lead students in the pledge of allegiance to the flag.
- Dukakis was soft on criminals: He not only opposed the death penalty, he endorsed a prison furlough program through which a convicted murderer named Willie Horton was released for a weekend during Dukakis's tenure, fled, and later committed rape.
- Dukakis was for gun control, he supported a nuclear freeze, and he was a card-carrying member of the American Civil Liberties Union.

In speech after speech, Bush lamented that Dukakis's values "are too often, in my judgment, out of the mainstream." He was soft on crime, in favor of high taxes, and more skeptical of the United States than were some of its enemies.[73]

Many newsmen labelled the 1988 Bush presidential campaign as one of the most negative campaigns in memory.[74] This is probably true. Yet, it turned out that way because only one side realized that, in the television age, presidential races are all about the character of the candidates. So, the attempts of the Bush campaign to prove that their candidate was the better man—more humane, more strong, and more in sync with the values and beliefs of the citizens of the United States—all came out as unfair personal attacks on Michael Dukakis, who steadfastly, or stubbornly, adhered to a "principled" campaign. Like Jimmy Carter, Michael Dukakis is certainly a man of high moral character, but his character traits are simply not those required for presidential leadership. This became evident to many during the primary campaigns when Dukakis seriously crippled his own staff by suspending his campaign manager, John Sasso, when he found out that it was he who brought Joseph Biden's plagiarism to the attention of the press. To most observers, Sasso had simply been doing his job: trying to demonstrate that his guy was the better candidate, or at least not as bad as the other guy.

The inexperience and disorganization of the Dukakis campaign

team continually handed the Bush people opportunities—
"comparative advertising," Roger Ailes called it. One of the most
memorable came on 13 September when, after delivering a speech on
the relationship between the United States and the Soviet Union, the
governor took a ride in an M-1 tank, wearing a helmet. The stunt
buried the speech on television. The tape showed Dukakis smiling
giddily, looking ridiculous, ineffectual, and inept, while the sound
track recorded reporters in the press stand hooting with laughter. Lee
Atwater, Bush's national campaign manager and a master of negative
attack politics, said later: "I thought it was the biggest bonanza I had
seen in the whole campaign. I could immediately think of three
analogues that everybody could relate to and laugh their ass off at:
Rocky the Squirrel, Beattle Bailey, and Alfred E. Neumann.... It was
a gold mine."[75]

Seizing the opportunity to compare the candidates' leadership traits,
Roger Ailes made a commercial out of the tape with a voice-over
narrator who intoned that "Michael Dukakis has opposed virtually
every defense system we developed ... and now he wants to be our
commander in chief. America can't afford that risk."

In an effort to control the damage, the Dukakis camp made a
television ad about another candidate's television ad. It had Dukakis
watching the Bush campaign commercial and then snapping off the set
and barking: "I'm fed up with it. Haven't seen anything like it in
twenty-five years of public life. George Bush's negative TV ads:
distorting my record, full of lies, and he knows it."[76]

The Democrats' ad, of course, just gave viewers another chance to
watch the silly tank episode. Nothing Dukakis said could offset how
unpresidential he looked. On election night, 8 November 1988, the
return made George Bush the nation's forty-first president. He won
forty states, giving him 246 electoral votes; Dukakis won ten states,
plus the District of Columbia, giving him 112 electoral votes.

TV and the Peaceful Transfer of Power

In addition to enabling citizens to make a moral assessment of
political candidates, television has helped improve the selection of
political leaders in another way: It has guaranteed peaceful succession
in political office. In modern democratic states, the transferring of
power from one leader to another normally takes place through the

procedure of regular elections. But extraordinary circumstances—say, the assassination or the resignation of the head of state—can create a crisis. What television does is to reduce that danger by presenting the new leaders to the public to reassure them that a bona fide leader is in charge and that the government will continue to function according to the same rules and values. Many readers will recall the televised picture of Gerald Ford taking the oath of office on the day Richard Nixon resigned, then turning to the cameras and saying the comforting words, "Our long national nightmare is over."

An even more dramatic memory for some of us perhaps is the television picture of Lyndon Johnson standing in the rain at Andrews Air Force Base where Air Force One had returned the body of John Kennedy the night of the assassination, saying: "I will do my best. That is all I can do. I ask for your help, and God's."

The coverage of the assassination of John Kennedy stands out as the finest hours of television, as it carried the grief-stricken, anxious, and frightened nation through the funeral and burial of its dashing young president. For four days, there was no entertainment programming on national television. The news division filled all the time, twenty-four hours a day, without commercial interruption. According to Nielson, 96 percent of the nation's household television sets were turned to stations covering the assassination and its postludes. People watched an average of thirty-two of the eighty-two hours between the assassination on Friday and midnight on Monday night. Much of the time, everyone was watching the same thing, since the networks pooled most of the coverage scenes in the Rotunda, where the president's casket was on view for the millions of Americans who journeyed to view it. They also pooled coverage of Johnson's swearing in, the cortege, and the funeral procession. As Martin Mayer later wrote: "There can be no question that the instrument of television tied the country together in ways unlike anything that had ever been known before."[77]

How Television Improved Governmental Accountability

Many who have examined the relationship between television and politics have argued that television has a hegemonic function.[78]

Following the work of the Italian Marxist, Antonio Gramsci, they claim that the ruling class uses television to dominate the ruled and to educe consent from them. Such analyses credit agency only to news reporters and to network news teams, not to the viewers—who are simply, according to the argument, manipulated by those representatives of the ruling class. This hegemonic interpretation of television must be wrong if my earlier analysis of the black civil rights movement and the woman's rights movement are correct. I argued that television helped launch both of these movements by making people critical of the existing arrangements. Television did not educe consent to these movements but rather, in time, helped to make people critical of both the civil rights movement and the women's movement. In short, I do not think that any group or class controls television; rather, I think that television encodes what is going on—whether it is the violation of people's rights or protests against such violations—television presents what's happening, thereby facilitating criticism of the existing culture.

Television, like every other medium of communication, helps people become aware of the inadequacies in their culture. Because of its bias toward encoding relationships, television usually educes moral criticism of what's going on. And in the political realm, such criticism comes in two varieties. One form of moral political criticism exposes the evils, the injustices, the bad consequences of the policies, practices, and procedures, carried out by the government. The second kind of moral political criticism chastises the government for not doing what is proper, good, or just. When it engenders the first kind of criticism—uncovering and exposing evils—television helps to improve accountability in the political realm. When it fosters the second kind of criticism—urging political leaders to take good or right actions—television helps to improve the level of public spirit in the political realm. In this section, I will discuss how television improved accountability in government. In the next section, I will discuss how television increases the level of public spirit in the operation of government.

The accountability of government leaders to the citizens is one of the hallmarks of the modern state, and the medium of print made accountability possible. First, the printing of laws and rules and constitutions provided citizens with agreed-upon standards of conduct for government officials. Second, the printing of books, pamphlets, and newspapers kept citizens informed about what the government was doing so that they could hold their government officials accountable to those standards of conduct. Television has enhanced the ability of citizens to hold their officials accountable—accountable to moral criteria.

Because television is an electronic medium, it can convey messages more quickly than print. Television has created a global village where messages about the doings of political leaders can be spread everywhere instantly. Most homes have television, but not all get daily newspapers. Moreover, since newspapers have to be bought and then read, while television is simply turned on and watched, television messages are more accessible to more people. Finally, television news is more incursive than printed news: Whoever watches television news usually watches all of it, not just the sports or the human interest stories, as many people do with newspapers.

This immediacy and pervasiveness of television messages has helped to change the relationship between citizens and their political leaders. The familiarity of people with what they are doing has diminished public deference toward those who hold political office. The manner or mode in which the public often gets those messages further reduces its deference toward government officials. That is, these government officials realize that they are more continually under the relentless surveillance of the omnipresent television cameras—continually in danger of exposing some flaw, some defect, some inadequacy. Because of this, many of these officials deliberately make themselves less accessible to the press and television reporters. This leads to "door stopping"—questions hurled at officials on the run—and impromptu, often unseemly episodes captured by the cameras that sometimes belie the dignity of the office and always diminish the awe of people toward these officials. This decline in deference is connected with the fact, previously discussed, that television has increased the number of independent voters. No longer partisan supporters and no longer deferential toward those who hold office, many citizens are now more ready to be critical of what their government officials do. Television has helped to produce a more vigilant citizenry, a public better able to hold its government accountable.

Yet, the immediacy and pervasiveness of its message are only part of the reason why television has enhanced the accountability of the government. Equally, if not more important, is the bias of the medium. Because it is both nondiscursive and analogic, television puts a face on messages that is different from the face created by print. As a nondiscursive medium (visual rather than auditory, using pictures more than speech), television forces those who watch it to narratize, to create themes, to make sense of the ambiguous, incomplete, indeterminate, contextless scenes that appear on the screen: Everyone who watches television has to make up his or her own story. And the kind of stories people create is primarily a product of television's being an analogic medium: It encodes relationships. So the stories people make up about those they see on the screen are about relationships: "He's strong," "He's weak," "He's humane," and so on. The usual human response to a perceived relationship is affective: "I like it" or "I dislike it." Since every existing relationship has been created by fallible human beings, every relationship is going to be inadequate in some way. So, when television encodes those relationships on the screen for all to see, some people now, perhaps for the first time, recognize the defects and faults inherent in those relationships, and they react emotionally, expressing moral criticisms. In the political realm, such moral criticism helps to keep those who hold office morally accountable.

TV Exposes McCarthy's Obsession, the U-2 Lie, and the Bay of Pigs Cover-Up

One of the earliest examples of the use of television to hold government officials morally accountable was the Edward R. Murrow "See It Now" show of March 1954 on Senator Joseph McCarthy. Composed primarily of film clips of McCarthy with very little additional commentary by Murrow, the TV documentary displayed the senator's tyrannical harassment of anyone he suspected of being a Communist. A month later, ABC broadcast live the so-called Army-McCarthy Hearings, where McCarthy revealed himself a demagogue who consistently disregarded the constitutional rights of witnesses. As Eric Barnouw described it: "A whole nation watched him in murderous close up—and recoiled." By the end of the year, the Senate passed a vote condemning McCarthy sixty-seven to twenty-two.[79]

Perhaps the most significant early instance of the moral accountability television made possible came in 1960 when the medium clearly and dramatically exposed the U.S. government in an act of deception, unprecedented in the minds of most Americans. On 4 May, Soviet leader Kruschev announced that a U.S. spy plane had been shot down over the Soviet Union. (Most Americans knew nothing about the regular reconnaissance flights the U.S. government conducted. Capable of flying at 80,000 feet, these secret U-2 planes could not be shot down by the Russians, U.S. officials believed.) Immediately following the Soviet announcement, millions of American television viewers saw Lincoln White, state department press chief, appear before a battery of cameras and declare there had been "absolutely no—NO—deliberate attempt to violate Soviet air space.... Never has been." The next day, Soviet television released a film of Kruschev giving viewers a guided tour of the U-2 wreckage. The film included a shot of the pilot, Gary Powers, who had confessed the nature of the mission. Television kept the issue of governmental accountability alive when shortly thereafter NBC made the U-2 spy plane affair the focus of one of its hour-long "White Paper" reports.[80]

The next instance of government deception uncovered by television happened early in John Kennedy's administration: the Bay of Pigs invasion of Cuba. President Eisenhower had initiated the plan to have the CIA train and equip Cuban exiles to overthrow the Castro regime. When he became president, Kennedy accepted and endorsed the secret invasion plan, stipulating that no U.S. armed forces should take part in the landings at the Bay of Pigs. In conjunction with the plan, the CIA planted false cover-up stories about an insurrection in Cuba. At this time, the television networks were still dependent upon the wire services and government handouts for most foreign news—and here the CIA manipulated both sources. When news did leak out before the invasion about possible U.S. involvement, President Kennedy, on television, said there would not be "under any conditions, an intervention in Cuba by the United States." After the invasion, the Cuban ambassador to the UN announced during televised proceedings of the General Assembly that the United States had launched a surprise attack on Cuba with mercenaries trained by experts of the Pentagon and the CIA. U.S. ambassador Adlai Stevenson rose, and before the cameras indignantly replied: "No U.S. government airplanes of any kind participated." He then repeated the CIA-fabricated cover story of an insurrection within Cuba itself. Adlai Stevenson was unaware of the whole plot, a victim himself of government deception. But when Secretary of State Rusk said at a television press conference, "The American people are entitled to know whether we are intervening in Cuba or intend to do so in the future. The answer is no," he deliberately deceived the entire nation.[81]

When the full story of governmental deception finally came out, there was some moral outrage, but it was not widespread since the action was a limited one and Castro's Cuba was believed by many to be a threat to the American hemisphere.

TV Gets Serious: Vietnam

It was not until the mid-1960s that the full import of television on the relationship between people and the government became apparent. By the 1960s, television coverage of government activity had greatly increased. Partly as a result of the quiz scandals and partly as a result of the charge made by FCC Chairman Newton Minnow that television was a vast wasteland, the networks expanded their news offerings. CBS began producing "CBS Reports," NBC started its "White Paper" series, and in 1963 both networks increased their nightly news programs to half an hour. On its first half-hour broadcast, CBS featured an exclusive Walter Cronkite interview of President Kennedy. In connection with this expansion, the networks hired a number of top-class, young reporters from newspapers. More aggressive than their predecessors, these reporters now set about doing more than simply accepting government press handouts.[82]

During Kennedy's administration, press conferences were transmitted live for the first time. Eisenhower had "permitted" conferences to be filmed, but these were then edited by the president's press secretary. In an earlier era, presidents had demanded that the press submit all questions in advance, answered only those they wanted to, forbade the press to mention those questions that were unanswered, and banned all unauthorized direct quotations.[83] The expanded news services and the new arrangements with the television press made it more difficult for the government to avoid critical scrutiny. This set the stage for a series of "crises" and "affairs" that brought forth widespread moral criticism of America's leaders—criticisms that resulted in the unmaking of President Johnson over Vietnam, the resignation of President Nixon over Watergate, the failure of President Carter to win reelection because of U.S. hostages in Iran, and the disabled last two years of the Reagan administration over the Iran-Contra Affair. But it was the Vietnam War—"the living room war," as Michael Arlen so aptly dubbed it—that most dramatically altered the relationship between Americans and their political leaders.

From 1954 to 1973, the United States fought an undeclared war against North Vietnam. Because it was undeclared, much of the fighting was clandestine and therefore limited in scope and effectiveness. But, because it was an undeclared war, it was an uncensored war, which meant that television cameras, in time, could and did expose how ineffective U.S. military forces were. Television's exposure of the Vietnam war led to strong moral criticism of the U.S. government, resulting in the unmaking of a president.

Early U.S. involvement in Vietnam under the Eisenhower and Kennedy administrations went largely unreported by television, but what was reported was supported by the public as part of a plan to contain communism in Asia. "You have a row of dominos set up," President Eisenhower explained. "You knock over the first one and what will happen to the last one is a certainty that it will go over very quickly."[84] So when the Communist North Vietnamese defeated France in 1954, the United States stepped in to prevent a Communist victory (through all-Vietnamese elections) by maintaining a friendly noncommunist government in South Vietnam. President Eisenhower sent funds to support and advisors to train the South Vietnamese army, transforming it into a conventional fighting force but one ill-prepared for the guerilla warfare that then erupted. The next step came when President Kennedy sent in five hundred Green Berets—an elite antiguerilla force—to conduct clandestine operations against the North Vietnamese. Their numbers proved to be insufficient, and a steady build-up of U.S. forces ("advisors") continued until, by November 1963, when John Kennedy was assassinated, there were sixteen thousand U.S. troops in Vietnam. Like his predecessors, Lyndon Johnson continued to escalate U.S. involvement. "We love peace," Johnson said. "We hate war. But our course is charted always by the compass of honor.... We are [in Vietnam] because ... we remain fixed in the pursuit of freedom, a deep and moral obligation that will not let us go."[85] The United States had a promise to keep.

War was never declared, and U.S. forces were not supposed to engage in fighting, but they could retaliate and seek revenge if they were attacked. Yet, by February, a few months after taking office,

Johnson authorized a series of secret operations against North Vietnam, including sending clandestine guerrilla teams into the north, engaging in commando raids from sea against North Vietnamese targets, and bombing coastal bases with Vietnamese PT boats operating under the protective umbrella of U.S. destroyers. Then, on 2 March, Johnson sent more than a hundred U.S. aircraft to raid a North Vietnamese ammunition dump. This began "Rolling Thunder," a bombing operation that lasted for three years. Later that month, the president sent the first U.S. ground troops to Vietnam—thirty-five hundred Marines to protect U.S. air bases.

The following August, two U.S. destroyers in the Gulf of Tonkin reported being attacked by North Vietnamese torpedo boats. Johnson ordered retaliatory air strikes and obtained a resolution from both houses of Congress authorizing the president "to take all necessary measures to repel any armed attack against the forces of the United States."[86] The way was now clear for a wholescale escalation of U.S. involvement. By June of the following year, nearly ninety thousand U.S. troops were stationed in Vietnam, and U.S. aircraft were flying more than thirty-six hundred sorties a month.

As troop ships and commercial airlines began pouring U.S. soldiers into Vietnam, the networks dispatched television crews where they were pretty much "free to go where they pleased and report what they wished."[87] In 1966, NBC inaugurated "Vietnam Weekly Review," hosted by Garrick Utley. Beginning in February 1966 ABC's "Scope" devoted its weekly program to the Vietnam War. U.S. press and TV contingents rose to 131 in 1965 and to 207 by the end of 1967. In January 1968, NBC and CBS each had six reporters in Vietnam, while ABC had four. The increased television and press coverage soon uncovered a war different from that described in the information supplied by government sources in Washington, leading to what came to be called Lyndon Johnson's "credibility gap." Most of the television reports sent back to the United States were strange, disconnected—contextless. They lacked breadth or depth. The viewers—aided perhaps by the TV reporters—created stories to make sense of the two- or three-minute vignettes that appeared on the screen nightly. Here's an account of one such vignette by Michael Arlen:

> CBS showed a five-minute film of a company of South Vietnamese troops on patrol coming under Vietcong sniper fire. The technical quality of the

film, as of NBC's, seemed remarkably good. You could see a handful of soldiers, under cover of some trees, firing into a line of trees that appeared to be several miles away. The rifle fire sounded clear and sharp. The camera work was expert and agile. There was a sequence, very close up, of a U.S. adviser asking someone over a field telephone to send in a couple of armed helicopters. You could hear everything the adviser said (he seemed calm and matter of fact, and he was terribly young). Then there were more scenes of soldiers, crouching and standing, firing toward the distant line of trees, and later, up in the sky, far in the distance, the two helicopters. At the end, CBS correspondent Morley Safer came on the air to say that there had probably been only three or four Vietcong snipers, that nobody knew whether or not the southern troops had killed them, and that that was they way it often was in Vietnam.[88]

The Vietnam war was a war without military fronts; a war mostly of hit and run skirmishes and sniper attacks instead of classic conventional battles; a war against enemies not in uniform. Most of the television reports came from crews traveling with U.S. troops in the brush. The film went back to Saigon, where it was airlifted to Hong Kong, Bangkok, or Tokyo, then beamed by satellite to 47 million American television viewers each evening. Most of the TV coverage before the Tet offensive did not include combat scenes or pictures of dead or wounded Americans, in part because this is what the war was: Most operations in Vietnam involved little contact with the enemy. For the average combat unit a bloody fight was not an everyday occurrence. For most, the Vietnamese war was endless plodding across flooded rice fields and tangled jungle trails in search of an elusive enemy.

The most important sources for television news were the U.S. soldiers in the field; television reported the war from their point of view. And from 1965 to 1967, they supported it. Televised interviews with individual soldiers described their high morale: "Better to be fighting the Communists here than back in San Diego," one corporal told John Lawrence of CBS news. "I'd be lying if I said I was glad to be here," one soldier admitted to Morley Safer of CBS, "But since I am here I'm glad to be doing what I'm doing."[89]

Yet, such scenes raised a critical question in the minds of some viewers: "What is that American soldier doing in Vietnam?" And the answer that came back from the soldiers themselves did not ease the doubts about whether Americans ought to be there. In an interview by Morley Safer conducted over beers with the crew of an attack helicopter recently returned from a mission, he asked them: "How do you feel when you make a kill like that?"

Pilot: I feel sort of detached from the whole thing. It's not personal.

Captain: I feel real good when we do it. It's kind of a feeling of accomplishment. It's the only way we're going to win, I guess, is to kill 'em.

Third Pilot: I just feel like it's just another target. You know, like in the States you shot at dummies, over here you shoot at Vietnamese. Vietnamese Cong.

Another pilot's voice (interrupting): Cong. You shoot at Cong. You don't shoot at Vietnamese.

Third pilot (laughing): All right, you shoot at Cong. Anyway, when you come out on the run and then you see them, and they come into your sights, it's just like a wooden dummy or something there, you just thumb off a couple pair of rockets. Like they weren't people at all.

Yet, in spite of some moral misgivings, most viewers supported the war. After all, we were winning, weren't we? Night after night, television reports about U.S. "search and destroy" operations developed this theme. A typical report was the 27 October 1967 NBC news segment showing a U.S. platoon landing by helicopter in the bush, moving into the village of Cong Phu, searching out the Viet Cong, and then destroying the village. Reporter Greg Harris summarized: "The war in First Corps is changing for the enemy. Today, the Viet Cong lost the use of Cong Phu. Tomorrow, they will lose the use of another village, then another."

Throughout the period 1965-67, TV anchormen in New York repeated and elaborated the theme that the United States was winning the war:

Walter Cronkite (CBS, 23 August 1965), before a map of Southeast Asia with the words RED CHINA arching over the top: U.S. Air Force jets gave Communist Vietnamese their heaviest clobbering of the war today, hurling almost half a million pounds of explosives at targets in the north. In one thrust, our bombers hit the Long Bon railroad bridge only thirty miles from Red China's border. Other bombs smashed a hydroelectric power station and dam at Bahn Thuc, southwest of Hanoi. In that raid, the first at purely economic targets, they dropped one-and-a-half-ton bombs, believed to be the biggest used yet in this war. In the south, Vietcong mortars fired into the big U.S. air base at Bien Hoa, fifteen miles from Saigon, and light U.S. casualties were reported. And the International Red Cross in Geneva today got an urgent plea from the Vietcong for medical and surgical supplies, an indication that our bombing raids and infantry sweeps are taking a heavy toll of all kinds of Red equipment.

Chet Huntley (NBC, 10 January 1966): American and allied forces were on the offensive on three fronts today in Vietnam. An assault by units of the First Air Cavalry Division, kept secret for six days, wound up on the east bank of a river separating South Vietnam and Cambodia. The enemy was clearly visible on the other bank, but refused to fire. The sweep has netted virtually no enemy personnel, but three large camps and tons of equipment and supplies have been destroyed. In the Iron Triangle twenty-five miles north of Saigon the story is about the same.... The South Koreans ten miles north of Qui Nonh have turned in one of the big victories of the war, catching an enemy regiment and killing 185 and capturing 609 suspects. In air operations over South Vietnam, four U.S. airplanes were lost yesterday and today.

Walter Cronkite (CBS, 31 October 1967): In the war, U.S. and South Vietnamese troops smashed the second Communist attempt in three days to capture the district capital of Loc Ninh, some seventy-two miles north of Saigon. The allies killed more than 110 VC [Viet Cong], boosting the enemy death toll since Sunday to 365. American losses were reported at four dead and eleven wounded.[90]

During the period 1965-67, according to Daniel Hallin, who conducted extensive analyses of network coverage of Vietnam, 79 percent of the television accounts of the overall military situation from 1965 to 1967 described it as favorable to the United States.[91]

Yet, many viewers found these reports of progress morally repulsive. The body count, or kill-ratio figures, could satisfy only those willing to equate the lives of Americans with those of the enemy. Many reacted against the increasing U.S. losses, no matter how many of the enemy were wiped out. And, as the number of Americans in Vietnam increased (four hundred fifty thousand by 1967), and the number of casualties mounted (fourteen thousand GIs killed by 1967, six hundred planes shot down, and hundreds of air force crews captured and imprisoned in the north), opposition to the war increased at home. Television reported this, too. For, television coverage of the Vietnam war consisted of more than reports from Vietnam and spot reports from anchormen culled from the AP and UPI wire services. There was also film of antiwar statements by

Senator William Fulbright, Senator Eugene McCarthy, and others, as well as dramatic films of antiwar protestors. To counter this, President Johnson and members of his administration made repeated appearances on TV issuing pronouncements about the progress the United States was making in defeating the Vietnam Communists.

Public Opinion Turns Against the War

As the war escalated, protest against it increased. Sparked, in great part, by college students, protest demonstrations took place at many universities—against ROTC programs, against recruitment visits by representatives of companies that manufactured napalm or chemical defoliants being used in the war, against university research supported by the Defense Department. Most of these demonstrations were widely reported on the nightly news, as were the larger protest marches in Washington in April 1965 (twenty thousand marchers) and in New York in the Fall (thirty thousand marchers). Widespread television coverage of massive, peaceful protests against the war raised the expectations of the protesters that they would have an impact on America's Vietnam policy. When this didn't happen, many set out to escalate the protests: A draft resistance program was organized that supplied television viewers with dramatic, even shocking, pictures of students burning their draft cards and engaging in sit-ins and other acts of disobedience at draft boards around the country.

Throughout 1966 and 1967, the anger, bitterness, and stridency of the protesters mounted. Television cameras filmed students surrounding the secretary of defense and beating on the roof of his car when he came to Harvard University. By the end of 1967, no government official could make a public appearance without having to confront masses of protesters. The president himself became a virtual prisoner of the White House, able to travel forth to speak only at "safe" locations, like military bases. By this time, a growing number of established, respectable political figures had joined the protest against the war. Some senators now began voting against war appropriations.

To counteract growing opposition to the war, the Johnson administration in November 1967 launched a full-scale "progress campaign" on national television. At his press conference on 17 November, the president said:

We are making progress. We are pleased with the results we are getting. We are inflicting greater losses than we are taking.... The fact that the population under free control has constantly risen ... is a very encouraging sign.... Overall, we are making progress.[92]

Following this, Ellsworth Bunker, ambassador to South Vietnam, appeared on "Meet the Press" on 10 November to talk about pacification progress:

Q: Mr. Ambassador, you speak of progress in extending the proportion of population under government control. What is the proportion under government control? What is the proportion now and how does that compare with six months ago?

Bunker: I don't know about six months or a year ago. A year ago it was about 55 percent under government control. Now the Vietnamese figure is 70 percent. Ours is a little more conservative. We say 67 percent. About 17 percent according to our figures is under VC control and the rest is in contested areas.

Q: Are you talking about population?

Bunker: Yes.[93]

The following week, Vice-President Humphrey repeated the progress line on the same CBS program: "I do think it is fair to say that there has been progress on every front in Vietnam: militarily, substantial progress; politically, very significant progress, with the Constitution and the freely elected government. Diplomatically, in terms of peace negotiations, that is the place where there has been a stalemate. There is no military stalemate. There is no pacification stalemate."

The most convincing progress report came from General William Westmoreland, U.S. commander in Vietnam, in a speech to the National Press Club on 21 November that was widely reported on television:

I am absolutely certain that whereas in 1965 the enemy was winning, today he is certainly losing. We are making progress. We know you want an honorable and early transition to the fourth and last phase. So do your sons and so do I. It lies within our grasp—the enemy's hopes are bankrupt.

With your support we will give you a success that will impact not only on South Vietnam but on every emerging nation in the world.

Westmoreland concluded by assuring the audience that "we have reached an important point where the end begins to come into view."[94]

The North Vietnam Tet offensive launched on 30 January 1968 totally undermined all reports of U.S. progress. Within twenty-four hours, the Vietcong attacked virtually every significant target in South Vietnam: five major cities, sixty-four district capitals, thirty-six provincial capitals, and fifty hamlets. In Saigon, Vietcong suicide squads broke into the presidential palace, the national radio station, and even the American Embassy compound. The first reports from Vietnam reached the networks in time for the evening news on 30 January. By the following night, the networks all had film of the fierce fighting in South Vietnam: the destruction, the vast numbers of refugees, the wounded GIs. The viewers saw the grounds of the American Embassy in rubble. The next night, they watched the chief of South Vietnam's national police execute a Vietcong suspect in the middle of a Saigon street. On 1 February, NBC presented a special, portraying the havoc and casting doubts on Washington's claim that the offensive was a military failure for North Vietnam (today, most analysts agree that it was a failure). After showing the impact the attacks had made, Robert Goralski concluded: "The Communists may not be winning the war, as the Pentagon claims, but they don't seem to be losing it either."[95] That same evening, ABC commentator Joseph C. Harsch, reporting from Saigon, reminded viewers of the Johnson administration progress reports:

What this city yearns for is someone like a Winston Churchill, who would admit frankly the fact that after two years of massive U.S. military intervention in Vietnam, the enemy has been able to mount and to launch by far the biggest and boldest and most sophisticated offensive of the whole war.

Maybe it is the last wild throw of the dice; let us profoundly hope so. But it is also the exact opposite of what U.S. leaders have, for months, been leading us to expect.[96]

The most significant television explanation of the meaning of Tet came from Walter Cronkite who had gone to Vietnam himself to assess the situation. On 13 February, he reported his findings to the nation in a Special CBS broadcast. He cast doubt on official estimates of enemy losses and civilian damage, describing the ruins of the ancient city of Hue and the kinds of refugees in the countryside. He summed up by saying:

> It seems now more certain than ever that the bloody experience of Vietnam is to end in a stalemate.... On the off chance that military and political analysts are right, in the next few months we must test the enemy's intentions, in case this is indeed his last big gasp before negotiations. But it is increasingly clear to this reporter that the only rational way out then will be to negotiate, not as victors, but as honorable people who lived up to their pledge to defend democracy, and did as best they could.[97]

At that point, Lyndon Johnson, who had three televisions sets in the oval office so he could simultaneously watch the news on all networks, turned to those with him and said: "That's it. It's all over." It was true. The shock and anger of the public to the first reports of the Tet offensive gave way to futility and despair. A majority of the U.S. public had supported the war prior to Tet; now a majority opposed it.

The following month, Johnson announced that he would halt the bombing if the North Vietnamese would agree to peace negotiations. At the end of his speech, the president revealed to an amazed television audience that: "I shall not seek, and I will not accept, the nomination of my party for another term as your president." Television had helped Americans hold their president morally accountable for his disastrous Vietnam policies. Those policies had dragged the United States deeper into a war some said we shouldn't be fighting, a war others said we should fight to win. Johnson's policy of a limited U.S. involvement had been judged to be immoral by both sets of critics.

Just as it helped to unmake the presidency of Lyndon Johnson, so did television help to undermine his successor, Richard Nixon. Once again, it was televised coverage of the Vietnam war that led to the downfall of a president.

Nixon's Private War

Richard Nixon entered the White House in 1969, pledged to end the war in Vietnam. His "secret plan" for peace was the deamericanization of the war, or, as it was better known, "Vietnamization": the withdrawal of U.S. troops while, at the same time, the build-up of South Vietnamese military forces. In June, he announced the withdrawal of twenty-five thousand troops; by December, U.S. troop strength had been reduced by sixty thousand. By the end of 1970, he had reduced U.S. troops in Vietnam to two hundred eighty thousand, half the number that had been there before he took office. By December 1971, U.S. troop strength was down to one hundred forty thousand men.

Yet, President Nixon did not simply want to withdraw from Vietnam. He wanted peace, but peace "with honor." And his truly "secret" plan for this war was to escalate the bombing. Prior to March 1965, the United States had conducted only retaliatory raids on North Vietnam—responding directly to deliberate attacks on U.S. forces in the south. At that point, President Johnson began Operation Rolling Thunder—the continuous, but restrained, bombing of North Vietnam, graduated in order to increase pressure on the enemy to negotiate a peace. There were eight complete halts and five partial cessations of the bombings lasting from twenty-four hours to thirty-six days at a time—all related to peace feelers. By mid-1965, the total number of sorties (one aircraft flight) had risen to almost nine hundred a week, and the escalation continued. By the end of 1966, the number of sorties and the number of bombs dropped had tripled. Rolling Thunder continued for three years, until President Johnson stopped it in November 1968—just before the election. It had not worked: The limited bombing had not significantly impeded the flow of supplies to the south, nor had it eliminated any important sector of North Vietnam's military establishment. Johnson had not dared to change his policy of limited bombing for two reasons: first, because of fear of protest at home over this illegal bombing of another nation against whom Congress had not declared war; and second, out of fear of the possible entry of China or the Soviet Union into the war.

When he took office, Richard Nixon believed that unlimited bombing of the enemy could make them beg for peace. He called it the "madman theory," designed, as he told H. R. Haldeman, his chief of staff, to make the North Vietnamese believe that he was obsessed about Communists and would do anything to stop the war. Because this was still an undeclared war, the bombing had to be either completely secret or concealed by false or deceptive reports. During 1969, Nixon's first year in office, U.S. fighter bombers flew a total of 285 "retaliatory" sorties against North Vietnam. In March of that year, U.S. planes began the secret bombing of North Vietnamese supply and staging areas in the neutral country of Cambodia. This bombing of Cambodia continued for fourteen months along with the thousands of sorties against the Ho Chi Minh trail in the neutral country of Laos.

As early as August 1969, Henry Kissinger, head of Nixon's Security Council, began a series of secret meetings in Paris with the North Vietnamese to negotiate a peace. In 1970, Nixon escalated the bombing. Now, U.S. planes engaged in "protective reaction strikes," i.e., attacks on enemy sites before they actually opened fire.[98] In all, Americans flew 1,113 "limited-duration, protective-reaction air strikes" against Vietnam in 1970. In 1971, the attacks against antiaircraft installations were secretly expanded to include attacks on personnel and supplies in North Vietnam.

Television provided little coverage of the bombing war other than oral summaries of the wire service reports by TV anchormen. Without television pictures, the bombing reports caused little public outcry—not even the televised reports of the *New York Times* revelation of the secret bombing of Cambodia caused much stir. But the Nixon administration did react strongly to such press revelations and responded by installing wiretaps on telephone lines of five journalists and thirteen government officials in an effort to prevent "leaks."

During this period, television continued to produce filmed reports of U.S. ground forces showing soldiers engaged in meaningless operations for no understandable purpose. In May 1969, there was extensive coverage of one of the fiercest battles of the war: Hamburger Hill, so called because the fighting ground up so many GIs. After finally capturing the objective, the North Vietnamese reoccupied it a month later. Television reporting of such futile engagements deepened the despair and revulsion of people at home. Protest against the war increased. In October and November, moratoriums against the war took place in Washington, Boston, New York, Miami, Detroit and other cities. A quarter of a million people marched in Washington alone. The protesters now included not only students but people from all walks of life, including political leaders and former statesmen, like Ambassador Averill Harriman and former Supreme Court Justice Arthur Goldberg. Television supplied extensive coverage of the October demonstrations—before, during and after they took place. The news reports of these protests further lowered the morale of U.S. GIs who, ever since Nixon had begun to wind down the war, had each begun to worry about being the last casualty in this lame duck war. This lowered morale was evident in the increase in drug use, racial conflict, refusals to obey orders, and "fragging"—assaults with fragmentation grenades on U.S. officers considered too willing to risk their men's lives. Television reported this decline in the morale of U.S. troops, which, in turn, increased domestic opposition to an enterprise that caused such brutality and breakdown of military discipline.

As President Nixon saw it, the press was sabotaging his efforts to secure peace with honor. The leaks about bombing, the disclosures about "futile" ground operations, simply fomented more antiwar protest and lowered the morale of the troops. Moreover, the reflexivity of television—television stories about the protesters and the demoralized U.S. troops—served to strengthen the will of the enemy to continue fighting the war instead of coming to the bargaining table. So, as he would later do in his campaign for reelection, Richard Nixon used television to reach out directly to the U.S. public. Two weeks after the October moratorium, he went on television to give a quintessential Nixon speech appealing to the "silent majority"—those who supported his efforts to secure peace with honor, but who, so far, had been silent, while the media publicized the antics of the minority who opposed his policies. "And so tonight," he intoned, "to you, the great silent majority of my fellow Americans—I ask for your support. Let us be united for peace. Let us be united against defeat. Because let us understand: North Vietnam cannot defeat or humiliate the United States. Only Americans can do that."[99]

Although the television analysts derided the speech, the public response was enthusiastic—telephone calls of support jammed the White House switchboard, and thousands of positive telegrams and letters arrived. Next, Nixon dispatched Vice-President Agnew to deliver a televised address on 13 November, two days before the November moratorium, intended to harass and intimidate the news media—a small and unelected elite "that do not—I repeat not—represent the views of America." Prudently—since the federal government issues and renews the licenses to broadcast—television network executives began to censor and modify their reporting of the war.[100]

The November moratorium demonstrations were the largest in U.S. history—more than half a million people marched in Washington alone. There was no television coverage at all by any of the three networks.

The Public Turns Against TV and Nixon Forges Ahead

The Nixon people were convinced that they had contained the protest movement when they saw the public reaction to the My Lai Massacre. On 16 November, the day after the November moratorium, all the media disclosed that a U.S. platoon, on a search and destroy mission, had murdered three hundred fifty civilians in the village of My Lai. This massacre had taken place twenty months earlier, but had only now been discovered by a *New York Times* reporter. Television reports showed still pictures a photographer had taken of screaming women, dead babies, and a mass of bodies piled up in a ditch. But this time, the moral shock and dismay of people after seeing how atrociously brutalized some U.S. soldiers had become, was more than matched by the moral outrage others expressed toward the press for disclosing information that gave aid and comfort to the enemy. Once again, we can see that television does not determine how people will act or think. Television viewers are agents who themselves decide what is wrong, what is bad.

President Nixon next moved to escalate the conduct of the war by sending U.S. troops into Cambodia to attack Communist sanctuaries there. He unveiled the Cambodian invasion in a televised addressed on the evening of 30 April 1970, announcing that he had spurned "all political considerations," preferring to follow his conscience rather than to "be a two-term president at the cost of seeing America become a second-rate power," and adding: "If, when the chips are down, the world's most powerful nation, the United States of America, acts like a pitiful, helpless giant, the forces of totalitarianism and anarchy will threaten free nations throughout the world."[101]

A large proportion of the U.S. people supported the Cambodian invasion, but student protest exploded at colleges and universities across the nation—including many colleges where there had been previously very little sign of dissent. Disaster struck at Kent State University where, as at other campuses, antiwar students attacked the reserve officers training building. The governor of Ohio sent the National Guard to restore order to the campus. On 4 May, nettled by the demonstrators, some National Guardsmen opened fire on the students, killing four and wounding eleven. The televised reports of the Kent State killings sparked protest across the country. More than four hundred universities and colleges shut down as students and professors staged strikes. In Washington, nearly a hundred thousand demonstrators marched, circling the White House.

In response, President Nixon appointed a commission to assess the unrest at colleges and universities. At the same time, he ordered the formation of a covert intelligence team that included the CIA, the FBI, and the Defense Intelligence Agency for the surveillance of domestic critics. During the summer, the president pulled U.S. combat troops out of Cambodia and followed this up with a televised speech on the war, stressing that Vietnamization was working: Already one hundred sixty-five thousand GIs had come home, and ninety thousand more would return by the following Spring, he promised. But when the first test of Vietnamization took place in February 1971, it became clear that the South Vietnamese troops could not be relied upon. Given the task of destroying the Ho Chi Minh Trail in Laos, the South Vietnamese infantry found itself routed as a smaller contingent of North Vietnamese troops forced it to retreat. Television coverage of the debacle showed a route littered with corpses and abandoned vehicles, with U.S. helicopters trying to evacuate the wounded, some of whom dangled from the skids as the choppers skimmed through the tree tops.

The bombing of North Vietnam would have to increase. But first, China and the USSR had to be headed off. Plans for President Nixon to visit China were laid in 1971. In February 1972, he made his much-publicized trip there with worldwide television coverage. After securing concordance with the Chinese leaders, Nixon, in April, met with Soviet leader Breshnov in Moscow, where they entered into a détente. The way was now clear for "decisive action" in Vietnam.

The North Vietnamese gave Nixon the opportunity to act when it launched a full-scale invasion of South Vietnam at Easter, capturing the provincial capital of Quantri on 1 May. On 8 May, Nixon announced the mining of Haiphong harbor and the intensification of the bombing of North Vietnam. Known as operation "Linebacker," this full-scale bombing campaign destroyed the war-related resources of North Vietnam and interdicted the movement of men and supplies to the south. In August, the North Vietnamese resumed peace talks with Henry Kissinger, who was now secretary of state. On 23 October, President Nixon suspended all bombing and three days later, Kissinger announced at a televised press conference that "peace is at hand." But within a month, negotiations broke down. Nixon resumed the bombing on 23 December. The Christmas bombing, called Linebacker II, lasted twelve days, comprising the largest bombing raid of the war. U.S. planes made about two thousand sorties, dropping 23,370 tons of bombs that crippled North Vietnam's electrical power supply, shattered its air defenses, and laid waste to factories, hospitals, residential districts, airports, and bus and train stations. When North Vietnam returned to the negotiating table in Paris in early January, it took only one week to complete the peace settlement.[102]

Over the course of the war, the United States had dropped on North Vietnam, an area the size of Texas, triple the bomb tonnage dropped on Europe, Asia, and Africa during World War II.[103] It had taken Richard Nixon four years to carry out his pledge to end the war through his "secret plan." He blamed the media for the delay. As he saw it, by broadcasting leaks about military operations in Vietnam and by exploiting antiwar protests at home, the media had thwarted the national interest and undermined national security.

TV Undoes Nixon: Watergate

It was this second war, his war with the media that brought about Richard Nixon's downfall. Not content with using wiretaps and the CIA, the FBI, and the Defense Intelligence Agency to spy on his enemies, Nixon ordered the creation of a special clandestine group to plug "leaks," jokingly known as the "plumbers." The plumbers were created originally to investigate Daniel Ellsberg, a Pentagon official who had released a mammoth collection of confidential governmental memoranda on the war that the Defense Department had compiled during the Johnson administration. In spite of Nixon's attempts to stop it—including an unsuccessful appeal to the Supreme Court—the *New*

York Times published extensive excerpts from these "Pentagon Papers." The plumbers, in an attempt to secure damaging information about Ellsberg's sexual activities, broke into his psychiatrist's office and later tried to bribe the judge who tried Ellsberg for the theft of the classified documents. Then came Watergate.

On 17 June 1972, five men were caught in the sixth-floor office of the Democratic National Committee in the Watergate Office building. Over the summer, newspaper reporters revealed them to be "plumbers" working for the Committee to Re-elect the President (CREP). In October, CBS news devoted considerable time to the story, but nothing came of it before the election. After the election, the Senate created a select committee, headed by Sam Ervin, to investigate the affair. After months of preliminary investigation, the Ervin committee began televised public hearings in May 1973 that were rebroadcast on PBS every evening. As the public watched in fascination, the top aides to the president—who had by now all resigned—appeared before the cameras to testify: Jeb Magruder, deputy director of CREP; John Mitchel, director of CREP and former attorney general of the United States; John Dean, counsel to the president; John Ehrlichman, assistant to the president; H. R. Haldeman, the president's chief of staff. As the story unfolded on the television screen, it became clear that those in the White House had abused their power, committed crimes, lied about them, and then attempted to cover up both the crimes and the lies. The central questions, of course, concerned the president of the United States: Was he involved? Or, as Senator Howard Baker constantly inquired of every witness: "What did the president know, and when did he know it?"

In his televised testimony, John Dean reported that on 15 September 1972 the president had congratulated him for the good work he was doing "containing" Watergate. Since at that time only a small-fry burglar had been indicated with grand jury action not as yet touching the White House, the reported conversation was significant. Dean also told about a conversation in March during which the president had agreed to pay "hush money" to the plumbers. In response to these charges, the president delivered a nationally televised speech denying vigorously any knowledge of the crime or involvement in the cover-up.

The next crucial development in the continuing television drama was the revelation from Alexander Butterfield, a staff assistant at the White House, that tape recordings existed of all conversations that took place in the oval office. Once it became known that evidence existed that could resolve the Dean-Nixon conflict, both the Ervin committee and William Cox, the special prosecutor the president had appointed to examine the Watergate affair, requested the pertinent tapes. Nixon refused. They obtained subpoenas, and he again refused to release them on grounds of executive privilege. This set the stage for a televised dramatic sequence. On Friday, 19 October, the president gave a speech to the nation explaining why he would not release the tapes. The next day, Cox, the special prosecutor, held a televised press conference to explain why he continued to request the tapes. Then came the "Saturday Night Massacre," when viewers were treated to the extraordinary spectacle of continuous program interruptions as White House reporters conveyed a series of astonishing bulletins. Nixon had fired Cox. Elliot Richardson, the attorney general, and his deputy had both resigned rather than carry out the president's order to fire him. The actual firing of Cox had been done by Robert Bork, who had been appointed acting attorney general.

Within an hour of the televised reports of the firing, cars with horns honking circled the White House, holding up signs calling for impeachment. NBC and CBS followed up the next day with ninety-minute special shows. On Monday, the House of Representatives requested the House Judiciary Committee to conduct an impeachment inquiry. On Tuesday, Nixon agreed to release the tapes in question to the court that had subpoenaed them. Two of the requested tapes were said not to exist, and one of those turned over had an eighteen-and-half-minute gap where it had been manually erased. The court turned them over to the House Judiciary Committee. The Judiciary Committee requested additional tapes. Nixon again refused, but finally on 30 April 1974 appeared on television with bound copies of 1,308 pages of transcribed tapes that were then turned over to the Judiciary Committee.

The penultimate television installment of the continuing Watergate saga came in July of the following year as the country watched for four days as the House Judiciary Committee debated and then decided to impeach the president of the United States. In the week following the decision to impeach, the release of additional tapes—by order of the Supreme Court—revealed that the president on 23 June 1972, six days after the Watergate burglary, had ordered the CIA to prevent the FBI from determining that it was Nixon campaign money that had paid for the burglary. The last televised installment came on the evening of 8 August, when President Richard Nixon resigned from office. Once again, television had helped the citizenry hold its political leaders morally accountable.

TV Exposes Other Public Officials

In this discussion of how television has heightened the accountability of elected officials, I have focused on the office of the president, but the same condition holds for congressman and senators. The most dramatic recent example of this is the savings and loan scandals of the late 1980s. Here, television exposed that savings and loan executives had contributed millions to lawmakers for use in their election campaigns. The congressmen and senators all denied any wrongdoing, but in this television age of heightened moral sensitivity, the public saw it differently. In 1988, the chairman of the House Banking Committee, Fernand St. Germain, of Rhode Island, was defeated for reelection because of revelations about his connections with savings and loan lobbyists. The following year, two top Democrats in the House of Representatives—Jim Wright of Texas, the Speaker of the House, and Tony Coelho of California, the majority leader—were forced from office as a result of questionable dealings with savings officials. All these elected officials protested that they were only doing what elected officials had always done. Probably so, but television has raised the standards of moral accountability for elected officials. Similar protests came from the five senators—John Glenn of Ohio, Allan Cranston of California, Dennis DeConcini of Arizona, Donald Riegle of Michigan, and John McCain of Arizona— who came under investigation in 1989 for their relationship with Charles Keating, head of Lincoln Savings and Loan Association in California. None of these five were up for reelection until 1992, but public opinion polls in 1990 showed that the standings of all five had slipped among voters.

How Television Improved Public Spirit

So far, I have argued that television has made political arrangements more moral in two ways: It has enabled voters to select political leaders on the basis of their character, and it has enabled citizens to hold those in office morally accountable. A third way television has improved our political arrangements is to make our leaders more public spirited. By this I mean that since the coming of television there has been more inclination among those in government to make an honest effort to achieve good public policy.[104] In other words, television has reduced (not eliminated) self-interested behavior. In the television era, we find fewer participants in policy making who only ask what policy would be best for themselves, and more participants who ask what policy would be right overall. I think it important to point out that here, as in the matter of selecting political leaders, I am talking about procedures, not results. I argued earlier that the coming of television has enabled each voter to assess the moral character of political candidates. I did not argue that television has enabled us to make correct assessments. So, here, in the matter of policy decisions, I am not arguing that television has brought us wiser or better public policy, but only that it has increased the effort, the inclination, to do what is right.

One way television has infused more public spirit into policy making is through the increased surveillance of public officials it allows. The ever-present threat of media exposure of self-serving actions has reduced such conduct. There are numerous instances in recent legislation that reveal how congressmen have eschewed self-serving decisions. Take, for example, the large increases in government welfare spending during the 1960s and 1970s. This aid has not been in the form of federal grants to localities, which provide visible constituency benefits, but in general transfer programs that do not allow congressmen to demonstrate that they have gotten something special for their district. Moreover, since the beginning of the 1970s, Congress has tended to avoid categorical grants (localities must apply for categorical grants, so congressmen can take credit for helping districts get them). Instead, Congress has substituted formula grants, which are allocated automatically. And these formula grants, as Kelman points out, are not even tied to specific projects where congressmen can be present at opening ceremonies and cut a ribbon."[105]

Congress has further demonstrated an increase in public spirit in recent years in depriving itself of opportunities to provide visible constituency benefits by granting more formal authority to the executive branch, or by legislating automatic formulas. Thus, Congress has foresworn tariff power to the executive branch—thereby giving up the opportunity to save constituents in trouble from foreign imports. It has indexed social security benefits—thereby denying itself the chance to vote politically visible benefit increases. When it approved the Gramm-Rudman budget-balancing legislation, requiring certain budget cuts, it gave up the opportunity to save politically popular programs. In each of these cases, members of Congress have deprived themselves of power and of the chance to provide visible constituency benefits, and they have done this so as to bring about good public policy: free trade, modest benefit increases, a balanced budget. The argument, once again, is not that today's congressmen are better political leaders than their predecessors, but rather that television has created an environment such that self-interested policy making is more readily exposed and instantly and widely broadcast; hence, this kind of conduct has diminished.

Yet, although increased media surveillance of policy makers has resulted in more public-spirited legislation, the most important way television has increased public spirit in government is by facilitating criticism of existing political and government arrangements: criticism of laws, policies, practices, and procedures. Such criticism then leads to the search for new policies, practices, and procedures that will be more in the public interest.

Electronic Credal Passion

Clearly, of course, the television age is not the first time people have become critical of existing political arrangements. In the United States, as Samuel Huntington has analyzed it, there have been three previous periods of criticism (what he calls credal passion periods or eras of disharmony, when there was widespread criticism and sweeping political changes): the Revolutionary Era, the Jacksonian Era, and the Progressive Era.[106] Significantly, Huntington recognizes that in each of these credal passion periods new forms of media emerged. During the Revolutionary period, we find widespread circulation throughout the colonies of (printed) petitions, remonstrances, sermons, and orations, as well as almanacs, broadsides, newspapers, and, most important of all, pamphlets—"the most effective weapon of political argument."[107] During the Jacksonian period, we have the rise of the "penny press," which greatly increased the number and circulation of newspapers—from two hundred forty two newspapers with a circulation of two hundred thousand in 1800, to one thousand newspapers with a circulation of over a million by 1829. During the Progressive years, cheap, national magazines—*McClures, The American*—set afoot the era of muckraking journalism. Finally, in the fourth period, which Huntington calls the "Sixties and Seventies," we have the electronic medium of television.

Since my interpretation of the effects of media on culture is different from his, I see the period of the 1960s and 1970s as radically different from the three earlier periods, whereas Huntington sees this period as a replay of those earlier periods. Here's how I see the "1960s and 1970s" as different from those earlier eras of criticism: The political reforms and changes of those earlier periods were all concerned with "rights." Thus, the printed pamphlets of the Revolutionary Era helped the colonists become critical of those policies of the mother country that deprived them of their natural rights. This led to the creation of a new constitutional government that identified and secured rights to all citizens. Then, during the second period—the Jacksonian Era—the penny press helped Americans become critical of the practice of restricting the rights of citizenship to white male property holders. This led to the expansion of suffrage to all white males, demands for female suffrage, and agitation to abolish Negro slavery. Such media-generated criticism also led to the creation of social institutions to protect the rights of children (schools and orphanages), criminals (penitentiaries and reform schools), the sick (hospitals), and the insane (asylums). During the third period—the Progressive Era—the muckraking magazines facilitated criticism of those policies and procedures that deprived the immigrants of their rights. There was also criticism of the social upheaval this deprived group created. The efforts to "Americanize" the immigrant were in effect efforts to prepare them to secure their own rights and at the same time to prepare them to recognize the rights of others. So, in each of these three periods of credal passion, new print media appeared that enabled people to "see" deprivations of rights that they had not seen before.

But, in the 1960s and 1970s (the Television Era), the criticisms that erupted focused on relationships, not rights. (The so-called "children's rights" movement of the 1960s and 1970 and the concern with women's rights were not struggles to secure rights guaranteed by the (printed) Constitution. They were struggles against existing relationships, which lawyers had cast into the language of "rights" when they took the battles to the courts. This, incidentally, explains the frantic opposition of "rights" groups to the nomination of Robert Bork to the Supreme Court: Bork insisted on limiting rights to those specified in print in the original Constitution.) Earlier, we saw how television exposed the inadequate, immoral, unfair relationships that existed between men and women, blacks and whites. There were other immoral and unfair relationships between students and teachers, criminals and police, the handicapped and the healthy, the aged and the young. During the 1960s and 1970s, public policy affecting all these groups underwent dramatic change as each group became conscious of victimization and began to agitate for new public policies that would change the existing relationships. This is a deeper and broader transformation of culture than the mere extension or protection of agreed-upon rights. So the changes that took place in the 1960s and 1970s were much more dramatic, more sweeping, and more upsetting, than those that took place in the earlier periods of credal passion. For this reason, the first widespread stirrings of moral criticism came from the young. The young, by simply being young, were less socialized to the existing arrangements, had less of a stake in preserving the arrangements, so they were more ready to criticize. Moreover, the young, those who came to maturity in the 1960s, unlike their parents, were a television generation: They were being raised on television. Television made young people critical, critical in ways not possible before. "We grew up old," wrote Joyce Maynard. "We are the cynics who see the trap door in the magic show, the pillow stuffing in Salvation Army Santa Clauses, the common tricks in the TV commercials ("That isn't really a genie's hand coming out of the washing machine.... It's just an actor with gloves on").[108] The 1960s generation "saw through" the relationships encoded on television: Television provided the distance that enabled them to become critical of how men treated women, how whites related to blacks, how cops handled criminals, how teachers regarded students; critical of the position in the society of the poor, the handicapped, the mentally ill, the offbeat, and the eccentric.

Activist Students

Television not only helped the 1960s and 1970s generation to become critical of existing relationships in society, it also invited them to try to change those relationships, to try to improve them. It was President John Kennedy who first issued the invitation in his televised acceptance speech at the Democratic National Convention in 1960:

> The New Frontier of which I speak is not a set of promises: It is a set of challenges. It sums up not what I intend to offer the American people, but what I intend to ask of them. It appeals to their pride, not to their pocketbooks. It holds out the promise of more sacrifice instead of more security. Beyond that frontier are uncharted areas of science and space, unsolved problems of peace and war, unconquered pockets of ignorance and prejudice, unanswered questions of poverty and surplus.

> It would be easy to shrink from that frontier, to look to the safe mediocrity of the past ... but I believe the time demands invention, innovation, imagination, decision. I am asking each of you to be pioneers of that New Frontier.

Later, in his stirring inaugural address, he repeated the invitation: "And so, my fellow Americans, ask not what your country can do for you; ask what you can do for your country," adding: "The energy, the faith, the devotion which we bring to this endeavor will light our country and all who serve it, and the glow from that fire can truly light the world." He concluded with an invitation: "Let us begin."

Less than one year later, a group of students assembled at Port Huron, Michigan, to compose and issue the Port Huron Statement on behalf of the newly formed Students for a Democratic Society (SDS). They called for "participatory democracy," a form of government wherein the individual could share in those social decisions determining the quality and direction of his life. Twenty thousand copies of the Port Huron Statement were printed; in time, it became the most widely read pamphlet of the 1960s generation. Significantly, after the meeting in Port Huron, Tom Hayden and Al Huber drove to Washington to take a copy to President Kennedy in the White House.[109] SDS was for a time the vanguard of what came to be called the student movement, or simply, "the movement." Made up of young people who shared a new consciousness, the movement insisted that there was something radically wrong with U.S. society.

Racism was a principal target of criticism. All the time they were growing up, this first television generation had watched white people beat up black people on the nightly news; they had seen blacks tormented and spat upon. Some college students became "freedom riders" in the South, and many participated in the public-spirited Mississippi Summer of 1964. Gradually, they began to see that racism extended beyond the South, infesting many institutions in the North, including their own universities. From 1965 on, college students, usually led by local SDS chapters, protested institutional racism. At the University of Chicago, students protested to demand the integration of university-owned apartment buildings. At City University of New York, students demanded "open admission for minority students." At Columbia University, they demonstrated to oppose the construction of a new university gymnasium on public park land that belonged to the people of Harlem. At Cornell University, students protested in support of the black students' demands for separate living quarters, separate classes, and a black studies program. At San Francisco State University, students demonstrated and went on a strike to support the Black Student Union's demand for the immediate creation of a fully autonomous black studies department. Each of these student demonstrations received nationwide television coverage. And each televised report fanned the public spirit and inflamed and made more fierce the rhetoric of the students who launched the next protest.

A second focus of student criticism was the Vietnam War. Students protested the war in part because they did not want to be drafted and perhaps killed, but, more importantly, they protested it out of public spirit: U.S. involvement was immoral. In 1965, students at the University of Michigan held the first teach-in. Later that year, a fifteen-hour teach-in took place in Washington, with scholars from all over the nation discussing the war in Vietnam. The three major networks televised part of this event, and one educational channel carried the complete discussion. Teach-ins spread across the campuses of the United States. Next came sit-ins to protest draft deferment policies, to eliminate ROTC programs, or to prevent campus recruitment by the CIA and Dow Chemical Company. Another form of protest was the walk-out—staged first by three hundred Berkeley students at a convocation at which Arthur Goldberg, then U.S. ambassador to the United Nations, received an honorary degree. At Amherst, students walked out on Secretary of Defense Robert MacNamara. To secure more television coverage, student demonstrations against the war became more physical and violent, although sometimes this happened out of fury—especially when students uncovered the extent of university involvement in war-related research. MIT ran defense laboratories, Cornell's aeronautical laboratory tested ammunition and radar, the University of California ran counterinsurgency programs and built prototypes of H-bombs in its radiation laboratories, Princeton had a secret code-breaking center patrolled by guards, and the University of Pennsylvania conducted chemical, germ, and biological warfare research.[110]

The students saw themselves in the vanguard of a revolution—a revolution of public spirit. They used the media to raise the moral conscience of the rest of the nation to apprise them of the evils in the United States. They started newspapers: *The Rat* and the *East Village Other* in New York, *Seed* in Chicago, the *San Francisco Express Times*, the *Berkeley Barb*, and the *Los Angeles Free Press* in California. They set up magazines: *Ramparts, Root and Branch, Studies on the Left, New Left Notes,* and *The Realist.* They wrote books: *The Other Side, When Push Comes To Shove, The Strawberry Statement, Up Against the Ivy Wall.* They wrote plays: *Macbird.* And they wrote hundreds of songs: "Eve of Disaster," "Ballad of the Green Berets," "It's all right Ma (I'm Only Kidding)," "For What its Worth," and "Let's Get Together." But most of all, the students used the medium of television. Television exposed how racist and militaristic the society was; it made issues personal and vivid. Television enacts rather than describes, presenting complex issues in a simple, direct way. A strike, a sit-in, a march, got attention from television. This exposed the system, provoked questions, and raised the consciousness of all who watched.

Yet, the logic of television finally undermined the student movement. To attract cameras and secure air time, the protesters had to escalate their antics. On campus after campus, semester after semester, student demonstrations—against racism, against the war, against the draft, against the universities—became more strident and raucous. By 1968, civility gave way to rudeness, civil disobedience had become violent, and strikes had become insurrections as classrooms were disrupted, buildings trashed, barricades erected, and bottles, bricks, and rocks hurled through the air. In the first five months of 1968, nearly forty thousand students participated in 221 major demonstrations on 101 campuses. But the most memorable riot took place not on any college campus but in the streets of Chicago.

Chicago Spawns Violence

The riot in Chicago during the Democratic National Convention was the turning point in the movement. Here is how Todd Gitlin, a member of SDS, later described the melee:

> Some essentials, then. Who beat whom? In brief, again and again, the police came down like avenging thugs. They charged, clubbed, gassed, and mauled—demonstrators, bystanders, and reporters. They did it when there were minor violations of the law, like the curfew; they did it when there were symbolic provocations, like the lowering of an American flag; they did it when provoked (with taunts, with rocks, and, at times, they claimed, with bags of shit); in crucial instances, like the assault outside the Hilton Hotel Wednesday evening, they did it when unprovoked. Sometimes, in the heat of their fury, the police took little or no trouble to distinguish between provocateurs and bystanders. Sometimes they singled out longhairs. Monday night in Lincoln Park, they slashed the tires of some thirty cars bearing McCarthy stickers. They bashed reporters so devotedly that they guaranteed themselves a bad press. More than five demonstrators were injured for every policeman, and a large proportion of the police injuries were to hands—suggesting that they were hurt while colliding with the flesh and bone of demonstrators.[111]

The most violent clash took place on Wednesday night in Grant Park and on Michigan Avenue in front of the Hilton Hotel where the convention delegates stayed and where network cameras were conveniently positioned. During an evening rally in the park, someone pulled down the American flag and raised a red cloth in its place. At this point, the police attacked, clubbing people senseless. Some participants ripped up the slats of park benches to defend themselves. Tom Hayden, an SDS leader and one of the organizers of the rally, grabbed the microphone and shouted:

> The city and the military machinery it has aimed at us won't permit us to protest in an organized fashion. Therefore, we must move out of this park

in groups throughout the city and turn this overheated military machine against itself. Let us make sure that if blood flows, it flows all over the city. If they use gas against us, let us make sure they use gas against their own citizens.[112]

As the crowd tried to get out of the park, they ran into the National Guard armed with rifles, machine guns, and flame throwers filled with tear gas. The soldiers rammed people with rifle butts and sprayed vast clouds of tear gas all over the park. As people ran down Michigan Avenue, they met more cops in front of the Hilton Hotel. There, for seventeen minutes, the network cameras filmed the riot live. Viewers watched in horror as police brutally beat the demonstrators, pushing the trapped crowd so hard that the windows of the Hilton cocktail lounge shattered, shoving people inside, where, slashed by glass, they were pursued by screaming police who clubbed and knocked them down.[113]

Television coverage of the brutal behavior of the Chicago police inflamed the moral outrage of students across the land. Many now believed that the United States was ready for radical change: Instead of "the movement," some now talked about "the revolution." Jerry Rubin, one of the protest organizers at Chicago, later told Milton Viorst:

We wanted to show that America wasn't a democracy, that the convention wasn't politics. The message of the week was of an America ruled by force. That was a big victory.... It was all perfect. After the convention was over, the question was not what had gone on inside, but why did the Chicago police go crazy, and what's wrong with America?"[114]

But Rubin was wrong. The televised riots in Chicago evoked vigorous criticism, but the majority of Americans criticized the protesters. Hubert Humphrey best expressed the public's revulsion with the protesters:

The obscenity, the profanity, the filth that was uttered night after night in front of the hotels was an insult to every woman, every mother, every daughter, indeed, every human being—the kind of language that no one would tolerate at all. You'd put anyone in jail for that kind of talk. And it went on for day after day. Is it any wonder that the police had to take action?"[115]

The protesters, most TV viewers believed, had brought it on themselves.

Once again it was the issue of substance versus procedure. The students believed that their conduct was morally correct because they were protesting concrete, substantive, moral evils in society. The rest of society condemned the students because they had used morally unacceptable procedures. Moreover, they condemned the students for being unpatriotic, even anti-American, since many openly proclaimed their support for the Viet Cong and North Vietnamese.

One of the outcomes of the Chicago riot was the federal trial of the Chicago Eight—the protest leaders—for conspiracy. This bizarre episode in the history of U.S. jurisprudence—during most of which one of the defendants, Bobby Seale, the leader of the Black Panthers, sat in the courtroom bound and gagged—had it been televised, would have raised moral outrage—on both sides—to the boiling point. One gains some notion of what transpired during this shocking trial from a list of some of the twenty-four citations for contempt the federal judge, Julius Hoffman, laid on one of the defendants, Abbie Hoffman (no relation):

26 September: Blowing kiss to jury: one day.

23 October: Showing newspaper in courtroom: seven days.

26 November: Renouncing his last name: one month.

15 December: Laughing at the court: fourteen days.

30 December: Commenting out of turn while on witness stand: fourteen days.

9 January: Laughing at the court: seven days.

4 February: Baring body to jury: four days; insulting Judge: five days.

5 February: Insulting Judge in Yiddish: six days.

6 February: Entering courtroom in judicial robe: seven days.

Total: twenty-four counts, eight months.[116]

At the end of the four-month trial, Jerry Rubin made the following statement:

> We are going to go to jail with smiles on our faces because we are the happiest people in the courtroom because we know what is happening because you are jailing your youth, America. That's what you are doing. You are jailing your youth. And you are jailing it for the crime of dreaming, dreaming of an alternative. You are jailing it for the crime of idealism. Our crime is idealism. That's the only thing. And there is this slogan, "You can jail the revolutionary but you can't jail a revolution."

> What you are doing out there is creating millions of revolutionaries, millions of revolutionaries. Julius Hoffman, you have done more to destroy the court system in this country than any of us could have done. All we did was go to Chicago and the police system exposed itself as totalitarian. All we did is walk into the courtroom and the court system exposed itself as totalitarian.... Maybe now people will be interested in what happened in the courthouse down the street because of what happens here. Maybe now people will be interested.

> This is the happiest moment of my life.

> [The Defendants: "Right on."][117]

But Jerry Rubin was wrong again. Although widely reported in newspapers, the trial of the Chicago Eight was not televised so the moral criticism it engendered was muted—even among students.

Another outcome of the televised Chicago riots was the growth of student radicalism. By the fall of 1969, SDS had opened a hundred new chapters, raising the total to over three hundred fifty. The circulation of underground newspapers increased: By July 1968, *The Los Angeles Free Press* sold ninety-five thousand copies a week, the *Berkeley Barb* eighty-five thousand, the *East Village Other* sixty-five thousand—all up from five thousand or fewer in 1965. During the year following the Chicago riots, nearly three hundred campuses in every part of the country had student demonstrations—strikes, sit-ins, and sometimes fires, bombings and the destruction of property. Major campus confrontations convulsed San Francisco State, Berkeley, Harvard, Stanford, Wisconsin.

As the students became more radical, more militant leaders came forward, advocating more and more violent tactics in order to create

The Revolution. At the SDS 1969 convention, a group calling itself "The Weathermen" created a split in organization. Then, declaring that "we are SDS," it launched "four days of rage" in Chicago in October, intending to "bring the war home."[118] Some three hundred strong, armed with chains, pipes, and clubs, and chanting "HO HO HO Chi Minh, Dare to Struggle, Dare to Win," they charged through the streets of Chicago, trashing cars, smashing windows, and fighting with the cops. The following month, on Moratorium Day, the militants captured all Washington, D.C. television coverage away from the peaceful demonstrators. Throwing bottles, rocks, and smoke bombs, they marched on the Justice Department building, where they took down the "Amerikan" flag and raised the Vietcong flag in its stead.

As the average American TV viewer could see, the Weathermen had become terrorists. This was confirmed when, at their December meeting, they decided to go underground for the purpose of "Making War" on the state. Other radical groups followed suit. By May 1970, there had been more that two hundred fifty major bombings and attempted bombings—at ROTC buildings, draft boards, induction centers, and other federal offices. Terrorists trashed supermarkets (in support of striking farm workers), banks (against imperialism), the corporate headquarters of Socony, Mobil, IBM, and General Telephone and Electric (against capitalism), and several police headquarters (against the pigs).

The last hurrah of the student protest movement came in the spring of 1970. Richard Nixon's 30 April televised speech announcing the "incursion "of U.S. Troops into Cambodia set off protests on hundreds of college campuses, including Kent State University, where, on 4 May, as we saw, National Guardsmen killed four students. Televised reports of the shootings brought about the largest student demonstrations ever—probably 50 or 60 percent of the students in the United States took part. Striking students closed down seventy-five campuses for the rest of the year. By the fall, student protests had subsided—partly out of fear and revulsion about the escalating violence, partly because President Nixon had withdrawn U.S. troops from Cambodia, and partly because a new draft law had gone into effect—a lottery system that limited all men to one year of draft vulnerability after their nineteenth birthday.

Public-Spirited Policy

The students' televised protests had widened the base of antiwar opinion: Now groups of lawyers, doctors, architects, nurses, corporate executives, union leaders,Vietnam veterans, and State Department employees all publicly expressed their opposition to the war. Some actively lobbied in Congress to cut off funds for the war in Southeast Asia. As opposition to the war mushroomed, college campuses ceased being centers of resistance. This widespread opposition ultimately brought about America's withdrawal from Southeast Asia.

Once again, television had helped make U.S. policy more public spirited. Student activism had originally stemmed from the students' moral opposition to the nondemocratic relations they saw encoded on television. The efforts of the young critics to create a more worthy society—efforts encouraged by President Kennedy's televised appeals to do so—came to focus on ending the "immoral" war in Vietnam, a war they saw depicted on television. While the procedures the young used to oppose the war incurred the moral opposition of many adults when they witnessed them on television, the same televised reports helped others to become critical of the government's policies and then to join the moral protest against the war.

The opposition of the young to existing laws and policies went beyond this. As we have seen, and will see later, many of the members of this first television generation opposed laws and policies that oppressed blacks, women, ethnic minorities, and the handicapped; they also opposed laws and regulations that allowed industries to pollute the environment and deplete natural resources. The young, then, were in the vanguard of all the sweeping, public-spirited legislation and policy changes of the 1960s and 1970s. My argument, of course, is not that the young were more moral than their elders, but simply that the young could more readily "see" the evils in existing policies because their knowledge of those policies came mostly from television, a medium that provides distance that enables people to become critical of relationships. Adults, most of whom had direct experience with these policies, took longer to become critical of them. Moreover, the young, having no stake in the existing arrangements, had more freedom to display and "act out" their criticisms.

These changes in society did not all come about easily. In some areas, the young reformers ran into difficulties with long-established rules and laws. They had to break new ground, destroying existing public policies and constructing new ones that reflected more public-spirit policies that enhanced people's life chances.

The young reformers triumphed because so many went to graduate and professional schools and were able to use their specialized knowledge to do good—to change and alter unfair relationships in the existing culture. Take the field of law, for example, a profession that attracted many young activists. Between 1961 and 1971, law school enrollment more than doubled and continued to rise throughout the 1970s. Concurrent with this was an increase in the number and size of organizations dedicated to using law to protect the powerless. Between the early and late 1960s, the ACLU had changed from an organization with ten thousand members and half a dozen affiliates to an organization with over a hundred thousand members with affiliates in practically every state. Prodded and goaded by the young radical lawyers who now joined its ranks, the scope of the organization broadened to become active in cases involving women's rights, rights of the gay community, abortion, academic freedom, and the rights of children. Moreover, many young lawyers helped create a number of state-situated programs to help the poor with their legal problems. By 1977, there were 265 legal services programs in the country operating nine hundred offices and employing two thousand lawyers. At the same time, a number of university law schools had established centers and institutes to provide research, consultation, and coordination of the people's law movement.[119]

In 1969, a young Harvard Law School graduate, Ralph Nader, established the Center for the Study of Responsive Law. By 1970, the center had four thousand applicants for summer internships, including one-third of Harvard Law School. Since then, it has publicly criticized a great variety of institutions and industries, usually securing changes in policies and practices that are against the public interest, including the automobile industry, the dental industry, meat inspection, mouthwashes, the FTC, the ICC, the Food and Drug Administration (FDA), air polluters, medicines, nursing homes, coal mines, banks, supermarkets, the antitrust division of the Justice Department, the Department of Agriculture, citizen access to regulating agencies, the pulp and paper industry, tractor manufacturers, air lines, and so on.

In Chicago and Newark, young lawyers established legal communes or collectives to protect the powerless and to bring about changes in the laws. Minority lawyers set up national organizations for the same purpose, such as the National Conference of Black Lawyers and the Native American Rights Fund.

In addition to carrying this fight against existing relationships to the courtrooms of the United States, the one-time student protesters also entered government service: as law clerks, as aides to congressmen (the Legislative Reorganization Act of 1970 increased the number of aides each congressman could have), and as members of the bureaucracy in various federal agencies. They even won elective office: as congressmen and, at the local level, as mayors and councilmen.[120] Another kind of occupation that attracted the brightest of the one-time student protesters was the think tanks devoted to research and government consultation on such matters as welfare, housing, education, economic planning, and the like.

Once they had become part of the "system," the political system, this first television generation helped to infuse public policy with a new public spirit. Much of this consisted of legislation directed at imposing requirements and restrictions on educational institutions. To help the non-English speaking, Congress passed the Bilingual Education Acts of 1968 and 1974 that reversed the long-standing tradition in U.S. education of English being the language of instruction. To offset discrimination against the handicapped, Congress passed the Education for all Handicapped Children Act of 1973 that forced schools to accept and provide places for handicapped children in the "mainstream" of education. To protect women from discrimination, Congress passed the Women's Educational Equity Act of 1974. Basic Opportunity Grants were provided to low-income college students. The upshot of all this legislation was to provide improved life chances in this society for the non-English speaking, the handicapped, women, and children of the poor.

A second area where Congress passed laws that dramatically affected another U.S. institution was in the area of safety and environmental protection. Here, conservationists, environmentalists, and health and safety groups lobbied Congress to secure new regulatory legislation. Throughout the decade, year after year, new regulatory legislation appeared. This legislation expanded the work of the staff of existing federal commissions and created new commissions.

The many bureaus, boards, commissions, and agencies had to interpret and implement the sometimes vague legislation providing aid, support, and protection to various groups. It was in the Department of Labor in 1970, for example, that the present doctrine of affirmative action was first announced. The doctrine migrated to the Office of Civil Rights and the new "results-oriented doctrine was applied to all college and universities receiving federal support."[121] Thereafter, federal courts began to apply this doctrine in discrimination cases. Thus, in January of 1980, the Federal District Court for the Southern District of New York forbade New York City from using its existing test to screen applicants for the police force unless 50 percent of the recruits selected were black or Hispanic.

The federal courts were the third branch of government where one could see public-spirited policy making. Here, the battles were waged as issues of "rights." These cases were not about rights, however—at least, not as traditionally understood. In the past, rights had been construed negatively, as restrictions on the government; rights referred to what a government could not do to its citizens. Now, most of these issues of rights were positive. They were claims about what an individual, or more likely, a group, was entitled to. What they were really about, of course, were relationships, each case representing a rejection by a group of the existing and traditional relationships between it and others in the society. These cases concerned the relationships between children and adults, whites and blacks, cops and criminals. They concerned the relationships between the rest of society and those identified as panhandlers, drunks, addicts, rowdy teenagers, prostitutes, loiterers, and the mentally disturbed. These court cases have invalidated such "traditional" crimes as "disturbing the peace," "disorderly conduct," "the use of obscene and abusive language," and "vagrancy." They rendered meaningless in courts of law such words as "vagrant," "offensive," "obscene," "disrespectful," and "inflammatory." Such words and such traditional crimes stood revealed as masks for authoritarian relationships.

Under the banner of "judicial federalism," the courts allowed people to bring class action suits against federal, state, and local administration officials for violation of constitutional and legal rights. These cases brought about vast administrative and fiscal reforms of state and local school systems, educational arrangements, personnel practices, and prisons and mental health facilities. Some of the most important decisions were in the area of racial discrimination. The Supreme Court decision in *Swann vs. Charlotte Mecklenberg Board of*

Education in 1971 instructed the federal courts to eliminate all vestiges of state-imposed segregation from public schools. This created a new role for the courts since the decision required some degree of racial balance in all public schools. And the court sanctioned busing as a "normal and accepted tool of educational policy." This provided the authority necessary for the extensive busing of pupils ordered by district courts in the 1970s and 1980s. In 1978, in *University of California Regents vs. Bakke*, the court upheld the affirmative action program for admission to the medical school of the University of California at Davis. The following year, in the case of *United Steel Workers v. Weber*, the court maintained that affirmative action covers employers who engage in interstate commerce.

In a series of cases in the 1970s, the court upheld the rights of children. In 1969, in *Tinker v. Des Moines*, the court declared that high school students could wear black armbands in protest against the government's policies in Vietnam on the grounds that the speech guarantees of the First Amendment protected their right to "symbolic speech." In 1975, in *Goss v. Lopez*, the Supreme Court ruled in favor of nine students temporarily suspended by their high school principal for spiking the punch at a school dance because the students had been deprived of due process. The same year, in *Wood v. Strickland*, the court established the right of school children to bring actions for damages against individual school teachers and administrators. These cases, and others, permanently altered the relationships between students and educational authorities: The schools could no longer be autocratic; they had to respect the rights of students in their admission policies, in their disciplinary practices, and in their operating procedures.

Yet, even though criticism of existing arrangements led to changes that improved the life chances of many, did such protest really make things better? Has not television simply exacerbated discontent and fragmented the society? By creating yet another credal passion period, a period of criticism, has not television, in the words of Edmund Burke, "undermined the pleasing illusions that make power gentle and obedience liberal?" In the place of the normal rhythms of political change, we have had a succession of crises and problems and a reduction of all goals to impulsive appetite. There is a loss of historical and social connectedness, a lack of contact with other people—past, present, and future. Everyone now looks only for his or her entitlements.

The episodic activism that television generated among various oppressed groups brought a backlash from other groups who felt that they now suffer as a result of the government's efforts to improve the condition of oppressed groups. The working class, for example, complained of paying taxes to support those who would not work. Business groups attacked government for its regulation of hiring practices, promotions, product contents, and safety conditions. Educators complained of losing control over schools and students. Moreover, since the new policies never worked as intended—they didn't go far enough, or they went too far, or they had unwanted or unanticipated consequences—people became more and more convinced that those in government are incompetent as well as imprudent. Distrust and skepticism about government increased.

All these criticisms are true. The polity is less stable, more fragmented. There is more disharmony, less trust, and more skepticism about government. Yet, I believe all of this signals an improvement in the polity. The government has become more responsive to the public. It is true that the original framers of the U.S. Constitution had considered responsiveness to public opinion a vice to be avoided. They had sought to protect government officials from public opinion by various institutionalized devices, such as the electoral college, fixed terms of office, the election of senators by state legislatures rather than through direct popular election, and so on. Today, however, we regard responsiveness to the public as a virtue—we think it is a characteristic of good government, a necessary condition for an open society. An open society is one in which all arrangements, all policies, all practices, all procedures, are open to criticism. The idea of an open society rests on the conception that fallible human beings have created the political arrangements, so they cannot be perfect. But they can be improved—through criticism. Criticism can, and will, uncover the inadequacies, the bads, the insufficiencies in what exists. Those arrangements, policies, procedures, and practices are bad insofar as they adversely affect people, or a group of people. So, in an open society, those people or groups who suffer from the existing arrangements can criticize and seek change in order to reduce their suffering. Television has helped to make the polity more open.

Television has helped people to recognize that ours is not, nor can it ever be, a perfect society. Yet, it has revealed how our society can

get better—continually. In place of utopianism, many Americans have
come to see that improvement consists of the diminution of concrete
evils. This way is in keeping with our condition of human fallibility.
We learn from our mistakes. Throughout the 1960s and 1970s, the
first television generation made things better. And the improvements
have been ratcheted into public policy—despite the efforts of some to
eliminate them. Thus, when President Nixon provided no funds for the
1974 Office of Economic Opportunity, which meant closing down its
nine hundred community action agencies, a federal judge ruled the
action illegal. The courts have also ruled that a governing authority
failing to provide social or welfare services in such a way as to
infringe upon the civil rights of citizens was liable for damages; that
an authority that reduced prison staff as an economy measure
damaged the civil rights of prisoners; and that all government
departments and all private companies receiving government funds or
contracts must employ races by quota.[122] And when Ronald Reagan
was elected to the presidency by a landslide vote in 1980 with a
mandate to change the direction of U.S. government, instead of
dismantling these public-spirited policies of the previous twenty years,
instead of making "a 180-degree turn in the course of government,"
the Reagan administration merely tried to modify and refine them in
an attempt to eliminate or reduce some of their unwanted, and
unanticipated consequences. In short, the Reagan administration
responded to the moral criticism about fraud, waste, and
mismanagement, but the policies themselves remain ratcheted into the
political arrangements of the culture. As Lawrence Brown has pointed
out, there were no major policy "breakthroughs" under Reagan, but
simply "rationalizating" policies—policies intended to eliminate or
reduce the evils inherent in or caused by already existing policies.[123]
Reagan made cuts in Medicaid, Medicare, and education, but the
programs were not eliminated, and federal expenditures actually
increased in order to support the "truly needy." Nor was any of the
legislation or judicial decisions that benefited blacks, women, Indians,
Chicanos, children, criminals, the mentally ill, or the handicapped
repealed or overturned, although some of it has been modified or
changed with the intention of making it better public policy.[124]

The Impact of TV on Eastern Europe

Since I am looking at the effect of television on U.S. politics, consideration of the remarkable political changes that took place in Eastern Europe in 1988-89 are beyond the scope of this chapter. Yet, I cannot resist a few brief remarks to point out how television facilitated these dramatic changes.

First, during the 1980s, the relaxation of censorship brought about by the doctrine of "glasnost" enabled more Eastern Europeans to watch television shows broadcast from Western nations. Significantly, the democratic uprisings began in those Communist countries closest to the West: Poles, Hungarians, East Germans, and residents of the Baltic countries could watch programs broadcast by Scandinavian, West German, and Austrian television.[125] These programs provided a glimpse of life in the West that made viewers in Communist countries more critical of their own life chances under existing (Communist) arrangements. According to *Time* magazine, a poll conducted for the Ministry of Intra-German Relations revealed that all those who fled to West Germany across the Hungarian border in the fall of 1989 had been watching West German broadcasts regularly.[126] In the Baltic countries, many of the viewers could not, of course, understand the Scandinavian language of the television programs they received, but they could understand the visual images that encoded relationships among people, workers and employers, police and citizens, leaders and followers—all of which helped them become critical of the relationships existing in their own nations.

Television further facilitated these political changes in Eastern Europe by providing continuous coverage within each Communist country of the actions taken by protesters and the counteractions of the government. This television coverage mobilized the popular support within each country that kept the resistance alive and growing. But more than this: Television helped make political arrangements in Eastern European nations more moral. For, as it had already done in the United States and other Western nations, unfettered television coverage of the goings-on in the political world helped make viewers more critical of the moral character of their government leaders, helped hold them accountable for their unacceptable conduct, and helped infuse a new public spirit into political decision making.

Here a comparison of political events in China and Eastern Europe during 1989 is enlightening. Some commentators have correctly pointed out that the crucial difference between China and Russia in dealing with protesters in their countries was that China decided to send in tanks to quell the democratic uprising while Russia decided not to do so. But this raises the question: Why did each nation make the decision it did? The answer is that Russia could not decide to send in tanks because of its prior decision—in accord with its commitment to "glasnost"—to allow televised reports of what was going on in each eastern country. It could not send in tanks because televised reports of such violence against unarmed citizens would inflame the rest of the country and the world, thereby strengthening opposition to the Russians.

China snuffed out its democratic revolution because it first banned and banished all television coverage of the events in Tianamen Square. Consequently, it could, with impunity, send in tanks ... and then deny it did so! For, even if many people ended up believing that the Chinese government violently suppressed and murdered the protesters, the written and oral accounts of this would never have the affective power to whip up moral outrage in the way television pictures would. Moreover, without television pictures, there could be no "proof" to support the accusations of the student protesters and newspaper reporters who claimed that the government had murdered thousands. Television pictures have become the criterion for truth, as became clear in December 1989 when newspapers in the United States dutifully, and ironically, reported that the new Romanian government had corroborated the execution of former Prime Minister Nicolai Ceaceascu and his wife, Elena, by releasing television pictures to the nation.

Notes

1   Reedy, *Twilight of the Presidency*, passim; Mayer, *Making News*, passim.
2   MacNeil, *The People Machine: The Influence of Television on American Politics*, 157.
3   Graber, *Mass Media and American Politics*, 217.
4   Patterson, *The Mass Media Election*, 63.
5   Some analysts have argued that television creates a "bandwagon" effect in the selection of political leaders. That is, voters support candidates simply because

they are popular. This "propaganda" analysis of the effect of television, once again, rests on an associationist epistemology that denies agency to the individual voter. Voters, this theory seems to be saying, are mindless creatures who "become what they perceive." While popularity does figure preeminently in the reasons people give for their choice of candidates, it is reasonable to assume that for most people popularity is not the reason they chose the candidate they did. Rather, popularity simply corroborates their own personal assessment of the character of the candidate. Thomas Patterson, who is a leading advocate of the "bandwagon" thesis, reported some of the responses he got from voters during the presidential primary races in April 1976, when people were asked why they favored Carter. Patterson does not entertain the possibility that people had first decided, on the basis of television viewing, that Carter's moral character qualified him to be president and then took the opinions of others as corroboration of their own assessment. Yet, the quotations Patterson supplies (Patterson, *The Mass Media Election*, 128) lend themselves to such an interpretation:

He is the person the majority of the public is backing. He seems to be a nice man.

He seems to be forthright, a good man. The voters like him and he is way ahead.

I respect him. He doesn't have a machine behind him and yet is going to be nominated.

I guess we haven't heard as many bad things about him as the others. He's popular, too.

I know that he's doing good. He seems down to earth. He seems honest and sincere. He has a nice smile.

He appeals to many people.

I guess I like him best because I hear more about him.

He seems to be honest. I don't necessarily really favor him, but I think he's going to be the one.

I don't see anyone else with a chance. He's a fresh and engaging personality. Not committed to Washington, either.

He must be doing the right thing. He's in popular demand.

6   Ibid., 5; Ranney, *Channels of Power: The Impact of Television on American Politics*, 107.

7   Ranney, *Channels of Power: The Impact of Television on American Politics*, 109; Patterson, *The Mass Media Election*, 4.

8   Barnow, *Tube of Plenty*, 277.

9   White, *The Making of the President, 1960*, 352.

10   Diamond and Bates, *The Spot: The Rise of Political Advertizing in Television*, 112.

11   Porter, *Assault on the Media: The Nixon Years*, 13; MacNeil, *The People Machine: The Influence of Television on American Politics*, 309.

12   Shadegg, *What Happened to Goldwater: The Inside Story of the 1964 Campaign*, 167.

13   Barber, *The Pulse of Politics*, 167.

14   Barber, *The Pulse of Politics: Electing Presidents in the Media Age,* 167.
15   Jamieson, *Packaging the President,* 198.
16   Barber, *The Pulse of Politics: Electing Presidents in the Media Age,* 165.
17   Jamieson, *Packaging the President,* 206-7.
18   Lang and Lang, *Politics and Television,* 200.
19   Witcover, *The Resurrection of Richard Nixon,* 17-21.
20   Jamieson, *Packaging the President,* 217.
21   Herblock was a well known political cartoonist of the 1960s.
22   McGinniss, *The Selling of the President, 1968,* 198.
23   Ibid., 10.
24   Chester et al., *An American Melodrama: The Presidential Campaign of 1968,* 687-8.
25   Jamieson, *Packaging the President,* 261.
26   Halberstam, *The Powers that Be,* 514.
27   Chester, et al., *An American Melodrama: The Presidential Campaign of 1968,* 584-5.
28   Barber, *The Pulse of Politics: Electing Presidents in the Media Age,* 295.
29   Chester, et al., *An American Melodrama: The Presidential Campaign of 1968,* 513.
30   Barber, *The Pulse of Politics: Electing Presidents in the Media Age,* 296.
31   White, *The Making of the President, 1968,* 318.
32   Porter, *Assault on the Media: The Nixon Years,* 255-62.
33   Ibid., 50-51.
34   Spear, *Presidents and the Press,* 185.
35   Jamieson, *Packaging the President,* 303.
36   Ibid., 305.
37   Barber, *The Pulse of Politics: Electing Presidents in the Media Age,* 99.
38   Roseboom and Eckes, *A History of Presidential Elections,* 307.
39   Diamond, *The Tin Kazoo,* 196.
40   Barber, *The Pulse of Politics: Electing Presidents in the Media Age,* 188.
41   Ibid., 189.
42   Spear, *Presidents and the Press,* 258.
43   Barber, *The Pulse of Politics: Electing Presidents in the Media Age,* 209.
44   Ibid., 202.
45   Ibid., 190.
46   Jamieson, *Packaging the President,* 401.
47   Diamond, *The Tin Kazoo,* 276.
48   Jamieson, *Packaging the President,* 389.
49   Greenfield, *The Real Campaign: How the Media Misread the Story of the 1980 Campaign,* 257.
50   Jamieson, *Packaging the President,* 429.
51   Diamond and Bates, *The Spot: The Rise of Political Advertizing on TV,* 271.
52   Germond and Witcover, *Blue Smoke and Mirrors: How Reagan Won and Why Carter Lost the Election of 1980,* 25;6-7.
53   Diamond and Bates, *The Spot: The Rise of Political Advertizing on TV,* 392.
54   Greenfield, *The Real Campaign: How the Media Missed the Story of the 1980 Campaign,* 240.
55   Henry, *Visions of America: How We Saw the 1984 Election,* 102.
56   Albert R. Hunt, "The Campaign and the Issues," in Ranney, *The American Election of 1984,* 143.

57   Schram, *The Great American Video Game: Presidential Politics in the Television Age, 194.*

58   Ibid., 261.

59   Ibid., 53.

60   Blume, *The Presidential Election Show: Campaign 84 and Beyond on the Nightly News,* 13.

61   Schram, *The Great American Video Game: Presidential Politics in the Television Age,* 32.

62   Ibid., 24-25.

63   Ibid., 201.

64   On this point, see Michael Robinson, "Media and the Media Elite," in Ranney, *The American Election of 1984,* 166-202.

65   Germond and Witcover, *Blue Smoke and Mirrors: How Reagan Won and Why Carter Lost the Election of 1980,* 2.

66   Ranney, *The American Election of 1984,* 158.

67   Germond and Witcover, *Blue Smoke and Mirrors: How Reagan Won and Why Carter Lost the Election of 1980,* 9

68   Editorial, *New York Times* 27 September 1987.

69   Black and Oliphant, *All by Myself,* 234.

70   Germond and Witcover, *Whose Broad Stripes and Bright Stars? The Trivial Pursuit of the Presidency, 1988,* 121.

71   Ibid., 433.

72   Ibid., 447.

73   Black and Oliphant, *All by Myself,* 233-4.

74   Germond and Witcover, *Whose Broad Stripes and Bright Stars? The Trivial Pursuit of the Presidency, 1988,* 465.

75   Ibid., 407.

76   Black and Oliphant, *All by Myself,* 233.

77   Mayer, *Making News,* 137.

78   One example of this appears in Gitlin, *The Whole World is Watching.* The Introduction mentions others who have made this argument.

79   Barnow, *Tube of Plenty,* 181.

80   Ibid., 256.

81   Ibid., 294, 296.

82   Hodgson, *America In Our Time,* 142-44.

83   Meyerwitz, *No Sense of Place,* 28.

84   Chafe, *The Unfinished Journey: America Since World War II,* 258.

85   Ibid., 274.

86   Ibid., 278.

87   Hallin, *The Uncensored War: The Media and Vietnam,* 129.

88   Arlen, *The Living Room War,* 7.

89   Ibid., 65, 88.

90   Hallin, *The Uncensored War: The Media and Vietnam,* 140-41.

91   Ibid., 146.

92   Braestrup, *Big Story: How the American Press and Television Reported and Interpreted the Crisis of Tet 1968 in Vietnam and Washington,* 49.

93   Ibid., 50.

94   Karnow, *Vietnam: A History,* 514.

95   Braestrup, *Big Story: How the American Press and Television Reported and Interpreted the Crisis of Tet 1968 in Vietnam and Washington,* 133.

96   Ibid.

97   Ibid., 134.

98   Lewy, *America in Vietnam*, 407.

99   Karnow, *Vietnam: A History*, 600.

100   Hodgson, *America in Our Time*, 370.

101   Karnow, *Vietnam: A History*, 609.

102   A critical assumption of the negotiated peace was that the United States would monitor and punish the North for any violations. But Congress thwarted this by passing a bill to block funds for any U.S. military activities in Indochina. In 1975, the North violated the agreement, marching into Saigon as U.S. officials scrambled for helicopters on the roof of the American Embassy compound. The domino theory became a fact: Once South Vietnam fell to the Communists, Laos and Cambodia followed, leading to genocidal horrors in Indochina—none of which appeared on U.S. television, so they evoked no widespread moral outrage.

103   Ibid., 415.

104   In this section, I have leaned heavily on Kelman, *Making Public Policy*.

105   Ibid., 65.

106   Huntington, *American Politics: The Promise of Disharmony*, ch. 5.

107   Ibid., 99-100.

108   Maynard, *Looking Back: A Chronicle of Growing Up Old in the Sixties*, 3.

109   Hayden, *Reunion: A Memoir*, 103, 33.

110   Ridgeway, *The Closed Corporation: American Universities in Crisis*, 327.

111   Gitlin, *Sixties: Days of Hope, Days of Rage*, 327.

112   Ibid., 332.

113   Ibid., 331-5.

114   Viorst, *Fire in the Streets*, 459.

115   Gitlin, *Sixties: Days of Hope, Days of Rage*, 338.

116   Levine et al., eds., *The Tales of Hoffman*, 288.

117   Ibid., 285-6.

118   Gitlin, *The Sixties: Days of Hope, Day s of Rage*, 393.

119   James, *The People's Lawyers*, 30, 46, 61.

120   Norman J. Ornstein, "The New House and the New Senate," in Mann and Ornstein, eds., *The New Congress*, 374.

121   Morgan, *Disabling America*, 146.

122   Johnson, *Modern Times*, 663.

123   Brown, *New Policies, New Politics*, 7.

124   Ibid., 22-26.

125   Messerer, "Is Television a National or an International Medium?" (Unpublished manuscript) 3.

126   *Time*, 25 September 1989, page 32.

4

Television and the Economy

The central feature of capitalism is the market. The wealth of nations, as Adam Smith pointed out, depends upon the market. The buying and selling of goods on the open market creates wealth since it leads to a larger and cheaper aggregate output. The market creates wealth for the entrepreneur; it distributes wealth to others. Competition in the marketplace causes the entrepreneur to improve his means of production. This usually takes the form of some kind of division of labor, which increases the number of aggregate jobs available and thus distributes the wealth created by the entrepreneur.

Since competitive markets force entrepreneurs to be efficient in self-defense, capitalists have eschewed any interference with the market that would reduce efficiency and thereby constrict economic growth. Capitalists, therefore, favor a general policy of laissez-faire. With the development of industrial capitalism in the nineteenth century, however, the doctrine of laissez-faire became a dogma used to defend the exploitative practices of capitalists who, in their unrestrained pursuit of profits, paid their workers—many of whom were children—starvation wages to work in unsafe and unhealthy working conditions. As the capitalists accumulated wealth, the workers accumulated misery, low wages, long hours, brutalization, moral degradation, sickness, disease, and early death.

But in the latter part of the nineteenth century and continuing into the twentieth, governments intervened to tame this unrestrained capitalism and reduce the exploitation of workers. Laws regulating child employment as well as health and safety and hours and wages became commonplace in all capitalist countries. Yet, the basic principles of capitalism have remained intact. The purpose of economic activity was still the creation of wealth. Economic growth was limitless. The pursuit of profits was good. The marketplace was the authority for all economic decisions. And laissez-faire was acceptable as a general policy.

Television changed all this. With the coming of television, the economic arrangements changed. Instead of the creation of wealth, the *transfer* of wealth became the aim of economic activity. In place of continuous and limitless growth, people, for the first time, discovered limits to growth. And now, the entrepreneur's pursuit of profits became subordinated to moral considerations.

Television and the Transfer of Wealth

During the early period of industrial capitalism in the first half of the nineteenth century, Karl Marx produced a scathing moral criticism of capitalism. Agreeing with Adam Smith that under capitalism there is a tendency toward increased productivity, Marx protested that, because they own the means of production, the bourgeoisie alone profit from this increase. And, as the bourgeoisie, or ruling class, becomes more wealthy, the ruled class, the workers—what he called the proletariat—become increasingly miserable. They become not only poorer, their very development as human beings is thwarted since they are naught but "labor" in the capitalist system. As Marx saw it, these two classes would, in time, become more rigid and more polarized from ever-increasing tension and conflict until finally a revolution would break out, which the workers would win, enabling them to create a society consisting of one class only—in effect, a classless society.

Marx was a determinist and so saw these happenings as inevitable. Living in the age of print, and therefore having access to works of history that the printing press made possible, Marx concluded from his studies that there were historical laws that determined the course of events. Marx's historicism was wrong-headed, of course, and his prophecies proved to be false. Since the time of Marx, the working class has become more and more wealthy, not more immiserated. Moreover, since his time, there has been considerable social mobility—not the rigidification of classes he had prophesied. It is, of course, true that the early period of industrial capitalism in England, and probably in other Western countries, exacted considerable human costs, if not in actual decline in material living standards, then in social and cultural dislocation. But advanced industrial capitalism has generated and continues to generate the highest standard of living for large numbers of people in human history.[1] Yet, some one hundred years later, in the 1960s, some Americans began to look at their capitalist economy in decidedly Marxist, or neo-Marxist, ways. At this time, in the age of television, a new variant of determinism took hold in the minds of many: structural determinism.

America Discovers its Poor

In the 1960s, Americans discovered (or rediscovered) poverty in their supposedly affluent society. The explanation usually given has it that this came about through the medium of print. Books like *The Other Americans: Poverty in the United States* (1962) by Michael Harrington, and articles like Dwight MacDonald's "Our Invisible Poor" (*New Yorker* 19 January 1963), are said to have influenced President John Kennedy, who then proceeded to work out a new federal program that ultimately became, under President Johnson, the "War on Poverty."

Now, it may be that the writings of intellectuals did help to launch the war on poverty, yet one cannot ignore that in the 1960s television helped the poor to become conscious of themselves. Once the poor saw the reality of their situation, once they saw their position in society, they became outspokenly critical of the economic arrangements of society. Thus, it is not so much that other people discovered in the 1960s that poor people lived in the United States as it is that poor people in the 1960s made public their presence—and their discontent.

Television shattered the isolation of the poor. Living in Appalachia or in the ghettoes of large cities, the poor had interacted only with others like themselves, having little or no contact with the rest of the United States. Here is a man from Wolfe County, Kentucky, talking about one of the "Appalachian Volunteers" in 1966:

The one with us, his name is Richard and he comes from someplace near New York. I think outside the city there. His mother writes him these letters and tells him to be real careful and not to get sick. You'd think he was someplace over in China. But he's O.K. We've never before met anyone from where he comes, or like him, but he's pretty good, and he likes the singing we do. He's a little jittery we notice. He can't sit for too long. He has to be doing something or moving about. I guess that's his way. A while back I never thought we'd see people like him hereabouts— ever. But I've lived to see them. First it was in the army, where you meet all types, and we got sent over there to England and France. Yes, and it's television, too. I've never seen so much in all my life as TV brings into your home. It's the thing that my kids pay most attention to—more than to me or their mother, even. Nowadays, they've seen everything before a father has a chance to talk.[2]

With the coming of television, the poor could observe how people with money lived. They saw the quality of their lives, their standards of living, their attitudes, and their opinions. Inevitably, the poor became aware of how deprived they were. In absolute terms, of course, the poor in the United States were better off than the poor of earlier times or the poor in other nations. Moreover, the number of the poor had markedly decreased during the twentieth century.[3] But by comparing themselves to the rest of the nation—a comparison television made possible—these people saw themselves as relatively deprived. Moreover, the poor could see that they not only had less money than other people in society, they were living in a different culture—a culture of poverty. They lived lives different from the lives of the rest of America. Most devastating of all, it now seemed that to be poor was not to live in a category out of which one could climb; rather, being poor was to belong an entity, a group, with more or less stable membership—not a social class but a racial or ethnic group. In the United States, it seemed to many, to be black was to be poor, to be Hispanic was to be poor, to be an Appalachian was to be poor. Television brought about this realization. There were no blacks on television in mainstream American culture, no Hispanics, no people from Appalachia. There were, of course, "The Real McCoys" and later "The Beverly Hillbillies," but these shows simply strengthened the notion that the rural poor were living in a different culture, a culture of poverty out of which they could never really escape, even if they miraculously became rich.

The racial and ethnic rigidity now discovered in U.S. society was not unlike the social class rigidity Marx saw emerging in nineteenth-century England. And the relative immiseration of blacks, Hispanics, and the people of Appalachia corresponded to the immiseration of the working class Marx had observed in the nineteenth century. The Marxist theme of alienation also reappeared, although now it took the guise of powerlessness. Television not only exposed their poverty, it also disclosed how powerless blacks, Hispanics, and Appalachian types were relative to other groups in society. Both the entertainment shows and the nightly news stories on the civil rights struggles revealed the power structure of American society. Whereas Marx in the age of print had concluded from his reading of history that historical laws determined the course of events, television viewers in the 1960s now believed that it was the structure, the power structure, that determined the course of events. Just as the medium of print had earlier lured people into believing in historical determinism, so the bias of the medium of television lured many now into becoming structural determinists. As an analogic medium, television focuses on relationships, revealing the structure of relationships in existing economic arrangements. As people now saw things, the structure of these relationships determined the course of events.

So, through television, the poor became conscious of their (relative) immiseration, they confronted the racial and ethnic rigidity of society, and they recognized how powerless they were. All that remained to complete this replay of Marxist analysis was to trace these conditions to capitalism. In time, some did.

Television not only made the poor aware of the reality of their situation, it also heightened the awareness of the rest of the nation. John Kennedy's national television appearances from West Virginia during the primary campaign of 1960 brought home the misery of the poor in America to most U.S. homes. One of the most dramatic revelations of poverty in the United States came in November 1960, three weeks after the presidential election and the day after Thanksgiving: "A Harvest of Shame," an Edward R. Murrow/CBS Report that showed tens of thousands of migrant workers who were miserably paid, ill-housed, uneducated, and undernourished. In addition, local television reports on juvenile delinquency and the slums that were said to cause it also prepared people to try to do something to combat the problem of poverty in the United States.

Much was already being done for the poor. In 1960, almost 15 million people received old age, survivors, and disability insurance. Another 3 million received Aid to Families with Dependent Children (AFDC) assistance, which was the largest federal welfare program. But many complained that these expenditures were not comprehensive enough, nor as generous as they could be (AFDC, for example, was slightly over $100 a month). Another problem was the professional bureaucracy that administered welfare benefits. Television reporters did much to expose the mean-spirited, niggardly, paternalistic system the bureaucracy had created. Many state agencies denied aid to families with "employable mothers," dawdled in processing applications, established lengthy residence requirements, and intimidated prospective applicants. In New York City in 1960, welfare workers certified families of four to receive $2,660 per year only if they met the following conditions:

> Such families were permitted to rent a five-room flat. The living room could have two chairs, a mattress and spring on legs to serve as a couch, a drop-leaf table for eating, and two straight chairs. The floor could be covered with linoleum, not rugs. There could be one or two lamps, but electricity was to be carefully used. The family could have a refrigerator and an electric iron and could play the radio an hour a day—there was no provision for using TV. The weekly budget allowed for meat, but not for frozen foods, tobacco, beer, or telephone calls. The clothing allowance provided for protection against the weather but left no room for impulse buying or fashion and barely coped with the problem of wear. A woman's coat was to last for five years. Breakage (say of light bulbs) or spillage (of flour) meant that the family did without. This budget provided no "frills"—haircuts more than once a month, home permanents more than once a year, drugs other than aspirin, candy or ice cream for the children, movies, coffee for visitors.[4]

Mobilization for Youth

Recognizing that any new programs had to bypass the dead hand of the welfare bureaucracy, social scientists now advised government officials to include the poor people themselves in the administration of such programs. When adopted, this participatory strategy gave the poor a chance to make themselves visible in dramatic ways. One of the earliest of these participatory programs, Mobilization for Youth (MFY), was set up in New York City in 1961, after four years of planning. Created as a program to combat juvenile delinquency, MFY used a broad-based effort to effect social changes in the community that would provide opportunities for youth to conform to accepted ways of "making it" in the United States. The theory underlying MFY was that young people became juvenile delinquents because they lacked such opportunities.

Participation of the poor in both planning and implementing the program became the cornerstone of MFY. Launched with elaborate television coverage and lavish fanfare, MFY created unrealistic expectations in the minds of the poor about what would change and how fast it would change. Funded with federal money that the poor themselves administered, MFY came into conflict with established city and state officials and existing laws and regulations at every turn as it sought to reform community schools, create jobs, provide adequate housing, secure building repairs, and prevent police harassment. But the frustrated leaders of MFY soon discovered the power of television. The MFY could and did organize the unaffiliated poor to overturn the status quo by means of rent strikes, school boycotts, mass demonstrations against police brutality, and voter registration drives. To protest living conditions in the community, they dumped dead rats on Mayor Wagner's doorstep. All these antics took place under the glare of television cameras. Through television, the powerless could become politically powerful; they could and did fight city hall, the state, the system. When their demands were met, new and larger demands were put forth in order to maintain the dynamics of conflict and confrontation.

In the eyes of the poor who ran MFY, the enemy was no longer the petty bureaucrats, nor even the obtuse, unfeeling politicians; the enemy was the system itself. So, instead of becoming an agency for integrating the poor into the system, MFY had become an agency to mobilize the poor to bring down the entire system. At least, this is how it seemed to many TV observers, and, indeed, this is how the inflamed rhetoric of MFY people often described what was going on. Yet, I do not think they wanted to destroy the system but only to modify it, to change it. They were not Marxists (although some were, according to Moynihan),[5] but they did use Marxist analysis to uncover the inadequacies of the existing capitalist system. The system, as it stood, both created and perpetuated an unacceptable inequality. Institutionalized racism and ethnic discrimination kept blacks and Hispanics alienated from the mainstream culture of affluence.

Moreover, blacks and Hispanics suffered increasing immiseration as a group. The system simply would not, could not, accept them as they were. What the poor who ran the MFY were saying was: "We are not going to change ... the system has to change." Earlier, in the analysis of the black revolt and the women's movement, we saw this same dynamic in action. Here it was the poor. MFY was the vanguard of a new poor people's movement, as became clear when the federal government launched its war on poverty and provided the poor across the nation the chance to replay the story of MFY.

Johnson's War on Poverty

On 16 March 1964, President Lyndon Johnson presented his Economic Opportunity Act (EOA) to Congress, announcing that with it he thereby declared a national war on poverty. Like the MFY, on which it was modeled, the war on poverty was intended to give poor people an opportunity—an opportunity to escape from poverty forever. As President Johnson put it: "The war on poverty is not a struggle simply to support people, to make them dependent on the generosity of others. It is a struggle to give people a chance."[6] To this end, the EOA provided youth programs: work training programs, work study programs for needy college students, and a Job Corps. It also provided for small business loans and incentives for employment of the unemployed. The central feature of the act was the setting up of community action programs in which there was to be maximum feasible participation of the poor. Like the MFY, the EOA focused on changing the environment of the poor. As Sargent Shriver, the first director of the Office of Economic Opportunity (OEO), the office set up to carry out the Economic Opportunities Act, put it: The war on poverty is

> an attempt to change institutions as well as people ... [it] starts with individuals—with a man, a woman, a child—taking them one by one. But it does not stop there, because poverty is not just an individual affair. It is also a condition, a relationship to society, and to all the institutions which comprise society. Poverty is need. It is lack of opportunity. But it is also helplessness to cope with hostile or uncaring or exploitive institutions. It is lack of dignity. And it is vulnerability to injustice. The treatment the poor get, at the hands of bureaucrats and politicians, at the hands of private industry, at the hands of landlords and merchants and agriculturalists, is

more than the sum of the individuals involved. A pattern of response, a way of reacting to and treating the poor has become entrenched, and institutionalized.[7]

Through the OEO, cities and rural areas across the nation set up community action centers with maximum feasible participation of the poor. Within a short time, local television news shows, and sometimes the network news, carried stories about Puerto Ricans, Mexicans, Native Americans, Asian Americans Appalachian types, and blacks who disclosed themselves and their miseries to the rest of the nation. And as they engaged in tactics to overcome their powerlessness, these groups exposed the inadequacies and moral evils of existing economic arrangements. In community after community, the poor were overturning the status quo.

Robert Coles reported that in Kentucky and West Virginia he saw mob scenes unheard of in "mountain history." He quotes a shopkeeper in a West Virginia town who complained to him about the local community action program:

> The people in this action program ... do so much talking when they meet that I think they're all primed up and looking for trouble, for something to go fight and win, if you ask me. I admit we have plenty of things to fight about down here, but it's not so easy to find who the enemy is. From what I see, if they can't fine a mine-stripper, they turn on the school people or the mayor, or the federal government who's paying to "organize" them in the first place. It all goes round and round from what we can figure out. Now they're talking about marching on the state capital, and Washington, and letting the country know about conditions down here. So, you see, they don't just sit together and talk; they look for trouble and go out and make it when they can't find it.[8]

In Syracuse, the community action center called the Crusade for Opportunity started out with a white executive director and a white majority on its board. Through systematic agitation, blacks took over the directorship and the board. As the Crusade for Opportunity went black, it also became more abrasive: "How else do you gain power for the poor?" asked the new executive director. The center issued remedial reading manuals that informed struggling functional illiterates: "No ends are accomplished without the use of force.... Squeamishness about force is the mark not of idealism but of moonstruck morals."[9] The pattern repeated itself in community after community: An action program was set up, largely controlled by the nonpoor; the poor agitated for greater participation; a more effective community action program was formed with a new leadership from among the poor; the new leadership was then denounced by even more militant poverty warriors for having sold out to the existing power structure; even more effective community programs were formed, and so it went.

Television, of course, escalated the disruptions. Community action programs were inaugurated with extensive television coverage, broadcasting promises that raised immediate expectations. When promises were broken and tangible benefits not forthcoming, the poor became disappointed, frustrated, and outraged. Perhaps the most bizarre demonstration of outrage took place 22 December 1966 when a busload of poor made their way to Timberlawn, Sargent Shriver's home in suburban Washington. There, the poor sang specially composed songs to Shriver and his family:

O come all ye poor folk,
Soulful and together,
Come ye, O come ye to Shriver's house.
Come and behold him, politicians' puppet.
O come and let us move him,
O come and sock it to him,
And send him on his way to L.B.J.

Keep the money in the kitty,
Fa la la la la la la la la.
Let's get down to nitty gritty,
Fa la la la la la la la la.
Put us poor folks in the cold,
Fa la la la la la la la la.
Shriver you ain't got no soul,
Fa la la la la la la la la.[10]

Television coverage of the protests, the demonstrations, and the riots stirred moral backlash against the OEO. When rioting hit Detroit, Mayor Jerome Cavanaugh blamed that federal agency: "What we've been doing at the level we've been doing it, is almost worse than nothing at all.... We've raised expectations, but we haven't been able to deliver all we should have."[11] At the annual meeting of the U.S. Conference of Mayors in 1965, the mayors of San Francisco and Los

Angeles presented a resolution that decried the tensions created by insisting on maximum feasible participation of the poor in planning community action programs. This policy, they insisted "failed to recognize the legal and moral responsibilities of local officials who are accountable to the taxpayers for expenditures of local funds."[12] The resolution was shelved in favor of a meeting between a group of aggrieved mayors and Vice-President Humphrey. The community action programs, manned by poor people with little or no experience in handling finances, patronage, and power, also came under fire for waste and mismanagement. Senator Dirksen of Illinois called the program "the greatest boondoggle since bread and circuses in the days of the ancient Roman empire, when the republic fell." He insisted that the program was "the very acme of waste and extravagance and unorganization and disorganization ... a colossal disgrace, and in some cases, an absolute fraud upon the taxpayer of this country. We are on a binge," he said, "it can't last."[13]

The community action programs did on a national scale what MFY had done in New York City. First of all, they made the poor conscious of their relationship to the rest of society and galvanized them into militant action to overcome their powerlessness. Secondly, like the MFY, which had also started out as an attempt to provide opportunity to the poor to become a part of the system, the community action program became a vehicle through which the poor could attack the system. Finally, although the antics of the poor did trigger much moral backlash, those antics did make many public officials, and much of the public in general, more responsive to criticism against the system. None of this could have happened on a national scale without the medium of television which continually and instantly broadcast the ongoing conflicts and counterconflicts to just about every home in the United States.

The community action program did change the power structure in the United States—first at the local, then at the state, and finally at the national level, as people who were once poor moved into public office, into industrial and commercial firms, into the professions, and into social and cultural organizations. As James Sundquist observed in 1969: "Throughout the United States, the most common phrase on the lips of those who talk of community action is: 'This town will never be the same again'."[14]

Community action also gave birth to the National Welfare Rights

Organization (NWRO), founded in 1966 to publicize the cause of the welfare poor and to help them receive what they were entitled to. The NWRO supported many of the court cases that dramatically changed the practices, policies, and procedures of the welfare system in the United States—such as the various state residency requirements for welfare payments and the absent father rule, which prohibited payments to families unless the father was absent. In 1970, the NWRO helped defeat the Family Assistance Plan (FAP) of President Nixon, which threatened to reduce federal funds below that already provided by welfare as well as to introduce mandatory workfare: All able-bodied people receiving aid would have had to work or accept work training. With characteristic hyperbole, the NWRO asserted that the FAP was "an act of political repression: welfare for state and local governments and ill fare for poor people." The organization brought busloads of welfare mothers to Washington to testify during the congressional hearings. "You can't force me to work," one of them responded to shouts in the hearing room. "You better give me something better than I'm getting on welfare. I ain't takin' it."[15]

What had become increasingly clear is that the poor expected government help. And there was nothing shameful about receiving such help. The poor were entitled to it. Even those who had jobs deserved to receive a supplement to their income.

The government now provides Supplementary Security Income, Food Stamps, public housing, Social Security, and other forms of welfare for working people. "Ten years ago," Charles Murray wrote in 1984, "hardly anyone would have argued that it was right for the government to take tax dollars from one worker and give them to another worker whose paycheck the government had decided was too small."[16] Critics like Murray argue that the change in welfare policies comprises a shift from the notion of equality of opportunity to equality of results. The purpose of these new welfare programs, he argues, is to redistribute the wealth in the United States.[17]

This, I think, considerably overstates what has happened. The original premise shared by Americans was that the United States is, and should be, a land of equality of opportunity. But people have come to see that for those who lack equal opportunities, a "handout" is not enough. Nor is a "hand" enough, as the earliest poverty warriors of the Johnson administration had believed. To have equal opportunities, the poor need help getting training for jobs, and they need income to sustain them when they do not have a job, or when their job provides insufficient income. In spite of what critics like Murray say, the welfare services do not, could not, lead to equality of results. The poor will not become rich through them. Nor will the rich become poor by supporting such programs.

What troubles Murray and other critics is that the changes in the policies and procedures have made it easier for the poor to obtain welfare benefits. During the 1960s and 1970s, the federal agencies, Congress, and the courts liberalized the eligibility requirements and increased the benefits. The most popular welfare benefits were in-kind transfers: Medicaid (for low-income persons), Medicare (for Social Security beneficiaries), Food Stamps, and housing programs. And here again, television—through news stories, talk shows, and documentaries on nutrition, medical care, and housing, helped many people to become critical of a society that did not provide these necessities to the needy. As a result of in-kind benefits, nutritional inequality decreased noticeably: Both caloric intake and protein consumption of the poor increased relative to the middle class, and life expectancy in the United States rose more during the 1970s than during either the 1950s or 1960s.[18]

In the 1960s, television made the poor visible and increasingly critical of existing economic arrangements. The war on poverty was the initial response to such awareness. This led to a complete restructuring of the relations of the government to the poor, and brought about a new conception of the purpose of economic activity: Now the purpose was not simply to create wealth but to transfer some of that wealth to the poor—not in order to make everyone equal but in order to provide real opportunities to the poor to enhance their life chances.

The Subordination of the Profit Motive to Moral Concerns

Television not only helped change the purpose of economic activity, it also helped subordinate the profit motive to moral considerations. That is, just as TV exposure of the economic power structure in America generated criticism that led to attempts to change it through poverty programs, so TV exposure of the consequences of the single-minded pursuit of profits generated criticism that led to other changes in economic arrangements. The first change to note is government regulation of business and industry.

Government regulation of economic activity is not a recent phenomenon. One hundred years ago, Congress established the Interstate Commerce Commission (ICC) to oversee the nation's railroads. Later, it established the Federal Trade Commission and the Food and Drug Administration, as well as other regulatory agencies. However, in the 1960s and 1970s, a new kind of federal regulation emerged. Called "social regulation," it was directed at protecting the health and safety of workers and consumers as well as at protecting the quality of life against pollution. In the area of health and safety, Congress passed the following acts between 1960 and 1975:

1960	Federal Hazardous Substances Labeling Act
1965	Service Control Act
1966	National Traffic and Motor Vehicle Safety Act
1966	Federal Metal and Nonmetallic Mine Safety Act
1968	Natural Gas Pipeline Safety Act
1968	Flammable Fabric Act
1969	Federal Coal Mine Health and Safety Act
1969	Child Protection and Toy Safety Act
1970	Federal Railroad Safety Act; Hazardous Materials Transportation Control Act
1970	Occupational Safety and Health Act
1971	Federal Boat Safety Act
1972	Ports and Waterways Safety Act
1972	Consumer Products Safety Act
1974	National Mobile Home Construction and Safety Act
1974	Motor Vehicle and School Bus Safety Act
1975	Hazardous Materials Transportation Act

Two points are worthy of note here. One is that during this period government regulation of the economy broadened dramatically. Earlier, old-line government regulation had applied to the operation of specific economic sectors and had been concerned with matters such as licensing, market entry, rate making, and so forth. But the new regulations applied to a broad spectrum of industries and activities.

The two most sweeping acts were the Consumer Products Safety Act (CPSA) of 1972 and the Occupational Safety and Health Act

(OSHA) of 1970. The CPSA created a new federal regulatory agency, the Consumer Product Safety Commission (CPSC), and empowered it to deal with the safety of practically every consumer product in use.[19] Equally sweeping in the broad regulatory power it gave the federal government was the Occupational Safety and Health Act Congress passed in 1970 "to assure, as far as possible, every working man and woman in the nation safe and healthful working conditions." Prior to passage of the OSHA, federal health and safety rules had covered a limited number of workers, including federal employees, miners, longshoremen and workers employed under certain federal contracts. Each of the states had regulated occupational safety and health, although their laws varied widely in stringency and coverage and many were only weakly enforced. All states had also had workmen's compensation laws to provide for medical expenses and partial replacement of lost wages due to occupational injuries and illnesses. But most of these laws had only limited coverage, low benefits, and brief time constraints. The new Occupational Safety and Health Act created a new federal agency—OSHA—that was responsible, either directly or through supervision of state programs, for the health and safety of about 60 million workers employed in roughly 5 million workplaces.[20]

The second point to be made about this new federal social regulation is that—in addition to broadening the scope of federal regulation over the economic realm—it launched the federal government into the practice of issuing and enforcing federal standards for health and safety. Thus, OSHA has promulgated several thousand standards covering the physical conditions of workplaces. Most of these specify in great detail the required physical characteristics of plants and equipment. OSHA has tried to enforce these standards through on-site inspections. By 1977, it had a budget of $130 million and authorization to staff over twenty-seven hundred positions.

The CPSC has a mandate "to reduce unreasonable risk of injury from the use of household products," and it alone has the power to decide what "unreasonable risk" is and how to reduce it. To do this, CPSC relies on a sophisticated information system called the National Electronic Inquiry Surveillance System, which draws upon daily computer reports from 119 hospital emergency rooms giving information on admissions involving product-related injuries. This information is categorized according to product and injury, rated according to severity and frequency, and then analyzed to set priorities for in-depth investigations at the local level. Investigators check for possible violations of existing safety standards as well as for new or unusual products that might be unsafe. Out of all this, the commission then creates a priority list of products ranked by degree of danger, thus constructing, in effect, a risk index.

The same two themes of broader federal control over matters traditionally regulated at the local and state level, and the promulgation of federal standards, runs through federal environmental legislation enacted since 1960. In the case of water pollution control, the early Water Pollution Control Act of 1948, with its amendments of 1956 and 1961, left primary responsibility for pollution control with the states. In 1965, the Water Quality Act created the Federal Water Pollution Control Administration, which established for the first time a national policy for controlling pollution. This so-called "clean water" approach departed dramatically from the older regulatory notion of simply requiring industries to "use the rivers so as to maximize the waste dilution and assimilation capacity of the nation's waters." Now, under the "clean water" approach, industries were not allowed to discharge treatable waste without providing "the best practicable treatment or control"—insuring, thereby, "clean water." Moreover, the legislation authorized the secretary of Health, Education and Welfare (HEW—where the Federal Water Pollution Control Administration was housed) to issue federal standards for water quality.

In 1970, Congress passed the Water Quality Improvement Act, which established liability standards for owners of vessels that spill oil. The Federal Water Pollution Control Act amendments of 1972 finally provided for the establishment of federal effluent limits for individual sources of pollution. Two years later, the Safe Drinking Water Act provided federal standards for all public water systems "to protect human health from organic, inorganic, and microbiological contaminants."

In the matter of air pollution, the earliest legislation came with the 1955 Air Pollution Control Act, which authorized a modest $5 million annually for federal research and training. Then in 1963 Congress passed the Clean Air Act, which changed the role of the federal government from that of a mere professional research agency in the matter of air pollution to that of an enforcing agent: The act authorized the secretary of HEW to establish nonmandatory air quality criteria and gave it the right to intervene in the pollution problems of a state if the state itself could not deal appropriately with those problems. This legislation, however, applied only to stationary sources of pollution, thus excluding pollution caused by automobiles. Congress remedied this with the Motor Vehicle Pollution Control Act of 1965, which authorized HEW to prescribe emission standards for automobiles— standards that went into effect in 1968.

The Air Quality Act of 1967 enlarged the federal government's enforcement role by requiring the secretary of HEW to establish both air quality control regions and clean air criteria. The states were to implement these standards; if a state failed to do so, the secretary of HEW was authorized to bring suit.

The Clean Air Act amendments of 1970 solidified the federal government's role as environmental protector by establishing more stringent emission standards for automobiles and by expanding the federal role in setting and enforcing standards.

During this period, Congress also passed other major environmental legislation in the following areas: solid waste and resource recovery,[21] noise pollution control,[22] chemicals,[23] and water resources and land use.[24]

On New Year's Day 1969, President Nixon signed the National Environmental Policy Act (NEPA), declaring to the television cameras: "The 1970s absolutely must be the years when America pays its debt to the past by reclaiming the purity of its air, its water, and our living environment. It is literally now or never." The act provided a coherent national policy for the environment,

> which will encourage productive and enjoyable harmony between man and his environment; to promote efforts which will prevent or eliminate damage to the environment and biosphere and stimulate the health and welfare of man, to enrich the understanding of the ecological systems and natural resources important to the nation; and to establish a Council on Environmental Quality.

These stated purposes sound more symbolic than real, but NEPA also created a Council on Environmental Quality that became an advisory and policy-making body for the executive branch. One of its most far-reaching actions was to require environmental impact statements from federal government officials for every major federal action—like building a dam, developing an off-shore oil field, or constructing a housing project. NAPA, like the Clean Air Act amendments of 1970, also provided for judicial review and citizen suits. This allowed environmentalist groups to turn to the courts to make government agencies more responsive to environmental concerns. By June 1975, there had been 332 suits against federal agencies and another 322 suits still pending. Of the completed cases, the courts had sustained sixty-four, and the defendant agencies were obliged either to prepare a new Environmental Impact Statement or to remedy the existing one. These victories "substantially enhanced the power of environmental groups."[25]

Finally, just as it did with both occupational safety and consumer protection, Congress created a special, comprehensive, federal regulatory agency for the environment: the Environmental Protection Agency (EPA). The EPA consolidated the various programs formerly scattered among various federal agencies and took over the job of enforcing pollution standards for air, water, solid wastes, pesticides, and radiation.

TV Exposure of Pollution and Polluters

How can we account for this burgeoning social regulation of the economic realm? Why did the federal government assume such broad and sweeping controls over business and industries, forcing them to subordinate their quest for profits to a concern for air quality, clean water, and the health and safety of workers and consumers? Obviously, the federal government took on this responsibility because local and state governmental bodies were not exercising such controls. States and localities did not do it because of opposition from business and industry. The simple threat of their relocating plants and factories to another area—thereby causing unemployment and lost tax revenue—deterred local and state governments from interfering with those businesses and industries that polluted the air and waters or disregarded the health and safety of the public. Industry and business had no such leverage at the national level.

Yet, the question remains: Why did this type of federal regulation come at this particular time? After all, business and industry had been polluting the air and water for many decades, and they had long conducted themselves with little regard for the health and safety of the public. Moreover, pollution problems had been far more deadly in a literal and immediate sense in the 1940s and 1950s.[26] Why did federal government social regulations not begin until the 1960s?

The conventional explanation credits the medium of print. In 1961, the story goes, Rachel Carson published *The Sea Around Us* and, the next year, *The Silent Spring*, books that drew attention to the alarming pollution of natural resources and the destruction of organic life caused by business and industry. In 1965, Ralph Nader published *Unsafe At Any Speed*, accusing the U.S. automobile of being a death trap. According to one typical account, these books "introduced an era in which the protection of the environment and the consumer became a quasi-religious crusade, fought with increasingly fanatical zeal."[27]

Most people in the United States never read those books; not even many congressmen read them. However, almost everyone got the message, and not from print but from television. Television did this in two ways: First, through local and national news programs and special documentaries, people began to see that the present economic arrangements posed a threat to health and safety. Secondly, television, through its entertainment shows—its comedies and dramas, its regular series, and its feature films—presented businessmen as evil and uncaring, solely concerned with their profits.

People have always known that they are vulnerable to dangers from the environment: Floods, fires, earthquakes, storms, cold and heat, and a host of other natural disasters can strike at most any time. But people have not always recognized how vulnerable they are to dangers from the cultural environment they have created. Suddenly, with the coming of television, people became increasingly aware that they had created an environment that in many unforeseen ways was dangerous to their health and safety, dangerous to the quality of their lives, dangerous to their very survival. The relationships between human beings and some aspects of the existing economic arrangements were potentially lethal.

When television presented these relationships to the viewing public, people became angry, afraid, and critical. During the 1960s, all the network news shows at one time or another presented segments and series on various toxins and poisons in our air, in our water, and in our food: Mercury, kepone, and other carcinogens and pollutants each had their time on camera. At the same time, local reporters—often called "consumer reporters"—presented news segments exposing dangerous products such as unsafe drugs, dangerous automobiles, inflammable fabrics, and stepladders that collapsed when you stepped on them. In January 1969, a Union Oil Company well in the Santa Barbara channel blew out, releasing two hundred thirty-five thousand gallons of oil in the Pacific Ocean. TV viewers saw thirty miles of fouled beaches and millions of dead and dying fish and birds. In September 1969, NBC had a two and a half hour special entitled "Who killed Lake Erie?" In April of the following year, ABC produced a special on the U.S. environment called "This Land is Mine."

In addition to raising the environmental conscience of the nation, television also helped people zero in on the villain in this matter. A fundamental theme of most television shows is that the world is run by hardened businessmen without consciences who satisfy their greed for profits at the expense of the public well-being. In *The View from Sunset Boulevard*, Ben Stein credits this animosity to the small group of writers and producers of television shows who live in the Los Angeles area—a group, he claims, whose views are atypical[28] However, it seems unlikely that the views of these writers and producers were atypical since, during the 1960s and 1970s, most people did become critical of businessmen—highly critical. During this period, they watched news reports of how businessmen in the largest and wealthiest companies in the nation—including General Electric and Westinghouse—had illegally conspired to fix prices. In February 1961, seven executives in the heavy electrical equipment industry were fined and sentenced to jail. Between 1962 and 1964, seven more criminal indictments were leveled against various companies, the most shocking being that against sheet steel companies in April 1964, when eight major companies and ten officials were indicted for illegally conspiring over a six-year period to fix prices. Earlier, on 11 April 1962, the president of the United States had attacked executives of the steel industry on national television for their "irresponsible defiance" of the public interest. This came about when Roger Blough, chairman of U.S. Steel, raised steel prices after leading President Kennedy to believe he would not do so because Kennedy had persuaded the steel workers to limit their wage demands. In a bitter, televised address to the nation, Kennedy blasted these business executives:

In this serious hour in our nation's history, with grave crises in Berlin and Southeast Asia, when ... restraint and sacrifice are being asked of every citizen, the American people will find it hard, as I do, to accept a situation in which a tiny handful of steel executives, whose pursuit of private power and profit exceeds their sense of public responsibility, can show such utter contempt for the interest of 185 million Americans.[29]

Given such television exposure of the goings-on in the real world of big business, it would seem that the depiction of businessmen in television entertainment shows was not simply the creation of a small group of Los Angeles writers and producers but a view shared by many. At any rate, television comedies during the 1960s depicted businessmen in a variety of stereotypical roles—conmen, bullies, pompous fools, cheats, and knaves—on popular shows such as the "I Love Lucy Show," "The Beverly Hillbillies," "The Dick Van Dyke Show," "Petticoat Junction," "Green Acres," and "Get Smart" as well as on less popular shows like "Pistols and Petticoats," "The Pruitts of Southampton," and "Hey, Landlord." In adventure shows, businessmen were almost always criminals in disguise—often murderers or drug dealers. These stereotypes appeared regularly on "The Defenders," "Perry Mason," "Peyton Place," "The F.B.I.," "Mission Impossible," "Hawaii Five-O," "Mannix," "Naked City," and "The Fugitive." On all of these shows, businessmen were often the behind-the-scenes manipulators of small-time hoods and criminals. Businessmen frequently used their connections and power for various nefarious purposes. They continually tried to bribe or bully their way out of getting caught. This characterization of businessmen continued in the 1970s. On "Columbo," for example, the murderer was always a businessman, while on "Dallas," the infamous J. R. Ewing was the prototypical businessman: surly, scheming, and evil. The short-lived "Stockard Channing Show" provided pointed commentary on the ethics of American businessmen by focusing on the activities of an enthusiastic consumer advocate who hosted a television show called "The Big Ripoff." As Stein summarizes: "The murderous, duplicitous, cynical businessman is almost the only kind of businessman there is on TV adventure shows, just as the cunning, trickster businessman shares the stage with the pompous buffoon businessman in situation comedies."[30]

TV and the Improvement of the Environment

During the 1960s, people became increasingly critical of the man-made pollution they saw exposed on television. At the same time, they became increasingly critical of and cynical about the businessmen they saw depicted as criminals on the evening news and in the entertainment shows they watched nightly. What was lacking was a forum through which this criticism could be expressed and galvanized.

At this time, as we have already seen, protection of the environment still lay with the states, each of whom usually had some state commissioner in charge. In accordance with normal procedure, these commissioners held hearings on proposed policies and programs. In the late 1960s, these hearings frequently became the forum wherein environmental-minded critics presented their views. The outpouring of criticism was such that these events got extensive local and even national television coverage, thereby mobilizing support for the environmentalists. In September 1969, for example, the Pennsylvania State Air Pollution Commission was astonished to confront fifty witnesses and an audience of four hundred fifty. To accommodate the audience, the hearings had to be moved from the state office building to the auditorium of a nearby Catholic church. According to Charles Jones, all the witnesses at this hearing were hostile to the proposed statewide air quality standards. The witnesses included representatives of citizens' groups, women's clubs, garden clubs, labor unions, tuberculosis and health associations conservation groups, experts from the Universities of Pittsburgh and California, public officials and citizens representing themselves. All protested that the proposed air quality standards were too weak and a threat to the health and well-being of people in the community.[31]

Televised reports of this and similar meetings helped to gather more and more public support for stronger governmental regulation. Moreover, such hearings usually led to the creation of local environmental action groups who engaged in demonstrations, rallies, and happenings that secured further TV coverage for the cause of environmentalism.

During the 1960s, the federal government gradually assumed broader and deeper regulatory control over various arrangements in the economic sector, culminating in the creation of the Consumer Safety Protection Agency (CSPA), the Occupational Safety and

Health Agency (OSHA)and the Environmental Protection Agency (EPA). By 1970, environmental pollution had become the big issue, its status helped by television coverage of nationwide demonstrations on Earth Day in April of that year. On Earth Day, schools, colleges, and civic groups staged demonstrations, parades, sit-ins, automobile burials, debates, and harassment of various industries—most of which the television cameras recorded. A highly-publicized air pollution alert in Washington and other east coast cities later in the year further heightened environmental consciousness. By 1970, Gallop Poll reported that 53 percent of the population named reducing air and water pollution as the most serious national problem, second only to crime. Just two years earlier, in a similar poll, Americans had not even mentioned pollution among their top twenty-three concerns. By 1980, a number of polls revealed that a substantial majority of Americans opposed any relaxation of environmental standards. Pollster Louis Harris, appearing before the House Commerce Subcommittee on Health and Environment in October 1981, reported:

> I am saying to you just as clear as can be that clean air happens to be one of the sacred cows of the American people, and the suspicion is afoot that there are interests in the business community and among Republicans and some Democrats who want to keelhaul that legislation. And people are saying, "Watch out. We will have your hide if you do it." That is the only message that comes out of this as clear cut as anything I have ever seen in my professional career.[32]

Perhaps Irving Shapiro, former chairman of the board of the Dupont Company, summed it up most succinctly when he said, "I don't know anyone who believes in dirty air or dirty water."[33] People supported the social regulation Congress passed in the 1960s and 1970s because it helped to make things better. During the 1960s and 1970s, the nation experienced an absolute reversal in air pollution trends and avoided further deterioration of its waters. In many instances, water pollution declined significantly. Lake Erie and Lake Ontario, once the chief exhibit of the nation's dying waters, had, by 1981, improved so much that they now teemed with fish.[34] The improved quality of air and water meant that fewer people got sick from the environment. And improved job and product safety meant that there were fewer accidents and injuries. Moreover, following passage of the National Traffic and Motor Vehicle Safety Act of 1966, some 40 million automobiles had been recalled for safety reasons, and the death rate per passenger-mile had declined to such an extent that more than fifty-six thousand drivers, passengers, and pedestrians were saved from death on the road.[35] Between 1973 and 1980, the Consumer Product Safety Commission (CPSC) recalled more than 120 million products in more than twenty-six hundred actions. The Center for Policy Alternatives at the Massachusetts Institute of Technology completed a study in 1980 that concluded that the American people had saved billions of dollars each year as a direct result of federal social regulation. The study's major findings included the following:

- Air pollution control benefits ranged from $5 billion to $58 billion annually.
- Up to sixty thousand lost workday accidents and three hundred fifty deaths were avoided in 1974 and 1975 because of OSHA rules on workplace safety, thereby reducing the $15 billion society paid yearly for industrial accidents.
- Cleaning up water pollution resulted in a $9 billion gain due to increased recreational use, such as camping, fishing, and vacationing.
- Crib safety standards reduced crib-related injuries to infants by 44 percent since 1974.[36]

Not just the public at large but the business community itself found federal regulations advantageous—at least in some ways. Automobile manufacturers, for example, realized that it was easier to build automobiles to meet federal safety and pollution standards than to try to comply with such regulations for fifty different states. In the realm of consumer products and occupational safety, companies also recognized that compliance with federal regulations for health and safety did help to forestall liability suits. And safety regulations meant fewer accidents, therefore higher worker productivity, just as pollution controls also increased productivity by reducing energy consumption through heat reuse, by encouraging recycling, or by creating marketable byproducts out of materials previously regarded as process wastes.

The Cost of Regulation

But businessmen did bellyache about social regulation; many felt that they were victims of overregulation. It is true that social regulation interfered with management decision making. Often, these regulations were nothing more than nit-picking, silly rules. OSHA, for example, required that fire extinguishers in workplaces be hung precisely thirty-nine inches above the floor; it also promulgated over one hundred forty standards covering portable wooden ladders. Yet, it wasn't so much the interference with management that business complained about as it was the costs that social regulation imposed on them. By the end of the 1970s, private industry was paying more than $6 billion each year to comply with environmental regulations. When the indirect costs were added—such as the redirection of funds away from research and advertising to regulatory compliance, or the costs of well-paid executives devoting their time to redesigning operations, setting up government relations departments, and becoming versed in the subject matter of regulation—the price industry had to pay increased tremendously. Murray Weidenbaum estimated the costs of regulation to business to be $102.7 billion in 1979. Here are some examples he included in his book, *The Future of Business Regulation:*

- The Small Business Administration reported in December 1979 that paperwork requirements by regulatory agencies cost small businesses an average of $1,270 a year apiece.
- Data Resources, Inc. estimated that the cost of meeting environmental regulations during 1979 was $12.3 billion, up from $9.6 billion in 1978.
- Louis Lasagna, a professor at the University of Rochester Medical Center, reported in the November/December 1979 issue of *Regulation* that premarket testing of new drugs required by the Food and Drug Administration cost up to $50 million.
- In January 1978, Dow Chemical Co. released a study showing that compliance with federal regulations cost the company $186 million, a 27 percent increase over 1975.[37]

Not only private businesses but the government, too, had to pay dearly to administer regulatory programs. The budgets of regulatory agencies went up from $0.9 billion in 1970 to $6.6 billion in 1981.

In addition to being costly, many businessmen argued that federal regulations curtailed economic growth. Rather than comply with regulations by making costly changes in their operations, some companies closed down plants and factories. Others decided not to expand old plants or build new ones. According to one analyst, the National Environmental Protection Act of 1969 alone was

> responsible for stopping the building of nuclear power plants; for preventing oil exploration on the outercontinental shelf; for sharply curtailing oil production in off-shore fields already explored and tapped; for prohibiting the building of the Alaska pipeline; for preventing the leasing of oil shale lands; and for reducing the production of coal.[38]

In addition to being costly and slowing down growth, many complained that federal social regulations had an adverse effect on innovation. Manufacturers were loathe to put out new products that could in any way be found unsafe; they could not employ workers for hazardous work—even at higher pay; they were careful and cautious about introducing new equipment and new routines. Government approval for new products—e.g., drugs—was both time consuming and costly. According to one estimate, it takes seven years to bring a drug to market.[39]

All these adverse economic consequences of federal social regulation, critics said, debilitated the economy by causing both inflation and unemployment. Indeed, in the 1970s, most realized that the country was experiencing both inflation and unemployment. And, when television news reporters reported the latest figures, they usually went on to explain these problems, as they always do, by asking experts—in this case, businessmen, economists, and politicians. In most instances, these experts explained that government interference was responsible for plant closings that brought unemployment, and that government interference was also responsible for inflation, since the government-imposed regulations increased both production costs and government spending. The engaging antiregulation economist, Milton Friedman, made this point over and over on his ten-week television series broadcast on PBS early in 1980.

By the 1980s, the United States was ready to relax some of the social regulations it had imposed on the economic sector. A *New York Times*-CBS news poll in 1981 found that nearly two-thirds of adult Americans wanted to keep clean air laws "as tough as they are now" even if "some factories might have to close." But another poll by the

Council on Environmental Quality the same year found that only 27 percent agreed that economic growth should be sacrificed to protect the environment—compared with 58 percent in 1978.[40] Americans wanted it both ways: environmental protection and economic growth, and at the same time. The time had come to modify and refine existing federal regulations.

One of the first steps at modification came from the Supreme Court in July 1980 when, in a case against the Occupational Safety and Health Administration (OSHA), it declared that "a safe workplace need not be completely risk-free."[41] The court found that OSHA had not provided substantial evidence to show either that workers exposed to benzene levels higher than OSHA proposed would contract cancer, or that workers exposed only to the proposed level would not contract cancer. The following November, voters elected Ronald Reagan as president on his promise "to get the government off the backs of the people." In a television address to a joint session of Congress soon after taking office, the new president announced:

> American society [has] experienced a virtual explosion in government regulation during the past decade. The result has been higher prices, higher unemployment, and lower productivity growth.... We have no intention of dismantling the regulatory agencies—especially those necessary to protect the environment and to ensure the public health and safety. However, we must come to grips with inefficient and burdensome regulations—eliminate those we can and reform the others.[42]

Later that same month, Reagan issued an executive order that required all agencies to make a cost-benefit analysis for every rule or regulation they proposed, listing potential benefits, potential costs, and potential net benefits. In the early months of 1981, scores of federal regulatory rules were revised, rescinded, or postponed. Reagan also cut the budgets of all the regulatory agencies, and he appointed key personnel to those agencies who were "business types," not the "environmental activist types" favored by his predecessor, Jimmy Carter.

Some critics have accused Ronald Reagan of dismantling the environmental protection programs of the government.[43] This is hyperbole. None of the social regulatory agencies were abolished; none of the major congressional legislation was scrapped. The moral consensus remains that the profit motive had to be subordinated to the moral considerations of public health and safety, but that the profit motive was not to be expunged.

TV and Working Conditions

In addition to subordinating the profit motive to moral considerations of health and safety, television also helped to subordinate the profit motive to another moral consideration: the human development of workers and employees. Television helped to change the patterns of management in many of America's business corporations. Television, as we have seen, helps people become critical of relationships they had hitherto accepted. In this case, we find television helping workers to become critical of their working arrangements and then helping others to become critical of those arrangements that alienated workers.

Worker alienation was rooted in those arrangements that had come about as the result of the development of corporate capitalism during the nineteenth and twentieth centuries when U.S. industries had adopted new inventions and techniques that dramatically changed the production process. Continuous-process machinery markedly increased the output of industries that processed tobacco, grain products, soap, and canned foodstuffs; new heat and chemical technologies vastly increased the refining and distilling processes of petroleum, sugar, animal and vegetable fats, alcohol, and chemicals; more efficient machine tools benefitted the metal working industries. The rapid expansion of high-volume production of standard goods was followed by new patterns of organization that standardized and coordinated the entire production process through managerial hierarchies that used sophisticated techniques to monitor and supervise all workers. In keeping with the lietmotif of modern civilization, this pattern of organization was rational. The basic principle of rational organization was the separation of planning from execution, of thinking from doing. Professional managers did the planning. First, they created numerous specialized jobs by simplifying individual tasks in the production process; second, they constructed rules to coordinate all these jobs; and third, they exercised detailed monitoring of all performances by means of task reports, budget controls, inventory controls, cost accounting, and other information-gathering tools. It is important to note that labor unions embraced this pattern of organization since it offered security against arbitrary acts by the company.[44]

The division between management and workers occurred in offices as well as in factories, in the public sphere as well as the private. Bureaucratic rules and regulations controlled and guided the work of clerks, typists, secretaries, teachers, social workers, and other service and information personnel.

This division of labor between brain work and manual labor, between the design and the execution of production,became the seed bed of worker alienation. Unable to plan or control their jobs, workers did nothing but carry out orders. However, as long as the industrial work force consisted of displaced farm laborers and immigrant peasants with little or no acquaintance with worker autonomy or knowledge of the larger world of work, most workers remained disciplined and willing to function as cogs in the system. Furthermore, as long as the clerical staffs of most businesses were females who would work only until they could get married and raise a family, they too endured the existing arrangements without much protest.

Television helped workers become aware of the larger world of work; it helped them become conscious of the work lives of others, which enabled them to take a critical look at the quality of their own work lives. Most blue collar and white collar workers, of course, had always disliked their jobs, but they had believed that nobody else liked his job either—that, they thought, was the nature of work. But, through television, workers saw that most middle-class jobs allowed people to function as autonomous workers, as intelligent agents, not like robots who simply took orders. This threw new light on their own condition.

Here are some samples of that heightened consciousness Studs Turkel found among Ford workers he interviewed in the early 1970s:

Pete Stallings, a spot welder: I don't understand how come more guys don't flip. Because you're nothing more than a machine when you hit this type of thing. They give better care to that machine than they will to you. They'll have more respect, give more attention to that machine. And you know this. Somehow you get the feeling that the machine is better than you are [laughs].[45]

Fred Williams, a stock chaser: Sometimes I felt like I was just a robot. You push a button and you go this way. You become a mechanical nut.

You get a couple of beers and go to sleep at night. Maybe one, two o'clock in the morning, my wife is saying, "Come on, come on, leave it." I'm still working that line. Three o'clock in the morning, five o'clock. Tired. I have worked that job all night. Saturday, Sunday, still working. It's just ground into you. My wife taps me on the shoulder. Tappin' me didn't mean nothing [laughs].[46]

Jim Grayson, a spot welder part-time student at Roosevelt University: There's no time for the human side in this work. I have other aims. It would be different in an office, in a bank. Any type of job where people would proceed at their own pace.[47]

Television rarely presented workers "on the job"; indeed, few shows on television were about workers, and those that were—"The Honeymooners," "The Life of Riley," "All in the Family"—confined themselves to the workers' domestic and neighborhood interrelationships. But in these shows, workers saw how others in society viewed them: primarily as figures of ridicule—boorish, narrow, intolerant, and dumb. Television did not create this stereotype of the blue collar worker, it simply encoded the view that the rest of society had of them. But once these views were exposed on the screen, blue collar workers became critical—and angry. In one of Studs Turkel's interviews, a steel worker talks about a "college boy" who worked part-time in his plant:

He saw a book in my back pocket one time and he was amazed. He walked up to me and he said, "You read?" I said, "What do you mean, I read?" He said, "All these dummies read the sports pages around here. What are you doing with a book?" I got pissed off at the kid right away. I said, "What do you mean, all these dummies? Don't knock a man who's paying somebody else's way through college." He was a nineteen-year-old effete snob.[48]

White collar workers also appeared on television shows: "Private Secretary," "Meet Millie," "The Doris Day Show." Teachers and other public employees showed up in programs like "Our Miss Brooks," "Mr. Peepers," and later "Room 222." In these shows, too, the status and prestige—or lack of it—of such occupations stood exposed and even held up to ridicule.

Once television had helped workers become aware of the reality of their situation in the job hierarchy, they became increasingly alienated; they came to care less about what they produced, or about the services they performed. Realizing that they had no control over what they did or what they produced, workers gave up responsibility for it. Society gave them no respect, so how could they respect themselves? Indeed, the only way they could sustain their own self-respect as a person was to alienate themselves from their jobs, from their work. Many began to see how limiting their jobs were. Working all day at a narrow, confining job with no autonomy whatsoever curtailed their own growth and development as human beings.

Concern about the rising tide of dissatisfied workers brought the secretary of HEW to create a special task force in the early 1970s that prepared a report under the title, "Work in America." The major finding of the task force was that significant numbers of U.S. workers were dissatisfied with the quality of their working lives. Workers in all occupations found the opportunity to grow lacking in their jobs, challenge missing from their tasks.[49]

Worker alienation became clearly manifest in increased absenteeism, higher job turnover rates, a lowering of worker morale, and increased antagonism toward management and customers. Workers became nonchalant, lackadaisical, irresponsible, surly and rude. Most important of all for the economy, the quality of American-made products deteriorated. In the late 1960s and 1970s, customers and consumers began to complain that nothing seemed to work anymore. Marvin Harris, an anthropologist, listed some of these complaints in his book, *America Now:*

> The United States has become a land plagued by loose wires, missing screws, things that don't fit, things that don't last, things that don't work. Push the handle on the pop-up toaster and it won't stay down. Or it stays down and burns the toast.... Faulty thermostats also plague hair dryers and coffee makers. Electric fans used to work forever; now the plastic blades develop cracks and have to be replaced. Vacuum cleaners have plastic handles that wobble and break; their cords come loose from the switch; their motors burn out. Tug hard on your shoelaces when they're a month old and they'll come apart. Or the little plastic tips come off and you can't pass the frayed ends through the holds. Go to the medicine chest for a band-aid. "Tear off end, pull string down," it says. But the string slips to the side and comes out. On the same principle, there is the packing bag for books. "Pull tab down." But the tab breaks off, sending a shower of dirty fluff over the floor.[50]

Automobiles perhaps caused the most headaches for Americans. In the 1970s, Ford and General Motors recalled hundreds of thousands of their cars for safety problems: defective steering, unsafe engine fans, defective brake hoses, collapsing seat backs and gear shift levers that fell apart. Not only did safety defects plague owners, but there were complaints about leaking doors and windows, rattling bodies, peeling paint, and loose-fitting interior panels and upholstery. Television, of course, kept the public informed about automobile recalls, about shoddy and unsafe products. Most local news shows had consumer advocates who fanned the consumer revolt against the quality of U.S. products and services. A 1979 poll found two-thirds of the public "deeply worried" about the poor quality of American products; 70 percent reported that they had returned one or more unsatisfactory products to the place of purchase during the preceding twelve months. As Marvin Harris put it, the social relationship between producer and consumer has been shattered.[51] Alienated workers had destroyed the bonds of responsibility that had heretofore prevailed.

What about the managers? How could they have permitted this to happen? The answer is that the existing economic arrangements had alienated the managers, too; alienated them from the criticisms of the market.

They were alienated in a number of ways. First of all, the success of a large, corporate enterprise depends on a great number of factors present over a number of years. These factors are not subject to managerial control, so corporate managers could not be readily or solely judged by demonstrable results. Other criteria applied:

> The forcefulness of the manager's personality, as evident by his ability to shape the organization, to put his "stamp" upon it; his cleverness at analysis, in manipulating numbers, juggling organizational units, and diagnosing problems; his professional detachment, which enabled him to make difficult decisions like laying off employees or firing subordinates— quickly and dispassionately.[52]

These "internal" criteria of "good management" isolated executives from contact with the real world of the market. According to John DeLorean, one-time head of the Chevrolet Division of General Motors, "top managers probably haven't purchased a car for themselves or sat in a line outside a dealer's service garage in twenty years."[53]

Their concern with mass consumption also alienated managers from the pressures of the marketplace. For, to secure the mass consumption of their products, many manufacturers emphasized the constant upgrading of those products, coming out with frequent model changes. Many of these "improvements" in products were merely cosmetic, or simply the addition of accessory features of dubious value that increased the likelihood of product failure. Managers wanted their products to last the lifetime of the warranty—but no longer. This created what amounted to planned obsolescence. The ideology of "new is better" immunized managers from the marketplace complaints about product failures.

Finally, many managers had moved into the business of buying and selling companies rather than producing goods. In these conglomerates, managers frequently jumped from one company to another, becoming what Robert Reich has called, "paper entrepreneurs."[54] Such managers brought no loyalty to a company, little interest or pride in its products, and no passion for quality or craftsmanship.

At the very moment Americans began to register their rejection of shoddy U.S.-made goods, more and more foreign-made goods appeared on the market. In 1970, Americans imported 9 percent of the goods they used; by 1980, this had risen to 20 percent. By 1981, the United States imported 26 percent of its cars, 25 percent of its steel, and 60 percent of its televisions, radios, tape recorders, and phonographs. It was not just that these foreign-made products were cheaper, but that they were of a higher quality than U.S.-made products.

U.S. corporate management tried to fight back through the medium of television advertising. But television advertising has a way of boomeranging. Television viewers cannot ignore or avoid commercials in the same way readers can ignore and avoid printed advertisements. Moreover, the costs of television commercials encourages advertisers to repeat the same ones over and over. As a result, people become more critical of television advertising. Earlier, many people had become angered and annoyed by the commercials of the early 1960s that had portrayed customers as simple minded, gullible victims who became ecstatic when their clothes came out the laundry "whiter than white," or their toilets and sinks scrubbed sparkling clean. Martin Mayer, in *Madison Avenue, USA*, provides the quintessential appraisal of television commercials of that era in a reported conversation between an advertising man and his young son:

> The other day the kids were watching television and one of those cartoon commercials came on. It showed two big wrestlers in a ring, one with the label "pain" on his robe and the other with the label "ordinary pain killer." The "pain" then threw "ordinary pain killer" out of the ring. Then another wrestler climbed into the ring with this brand stenciled onto his robe, and he threw "pain" out of the ring, knocking him out completely. My own boy called me aside and said, "Dad, am I to understand that a bunch of grown men sat down and said that was a good idea, and another bunch of grown men went to all the trouble to make a movie out of it?"[55]

The television commercials of the 1970s also boomeranged. Designed to convince consumers of the high quality of U.S.-made products, these commercials made claims that often turned out to be false or deceptive. Consumer complaints led the Federal Trade Commission (FTC) to challenge the companies involved. Thus, the General Electric Company found itself being asked to prove that its air conditioners reproduced the "clear freshness of clear, cool, mountain air." North American Philips was asked to prove that its electric razor shaved "up to 50 percent faster." And there were others the FTC got after when they uncovered exaggerations, half truths, vague claims, weasel words, and outright lies in many commercials: coffee laced with molasses to make it look rich and dark, whipped egg whites used to look like foaming shampoo, marbles in the soup so that meat and vegetables would not sink, towels that looked soft and springy because of the sponges hidden beneath them, electric razors that shaved sandpaper that was actually sand glued on glass. One study of young children, reported in the Harvard Business Review, found that by the time they reached ten, many children had concluded that commercials always lie. By eleven and twelve, the report added, children begin to "become tolerant of social hypocrisy"—i.e., they become cynical.[56]

Ultimately, many advertisers abandoned making claims about the quality of their products and simply presented images of people happily using the product: driving cars, listening to music, taking photographs, shopping. But by this time, many of the advertised products were foreign made.

As managers came to realize that touting the merits of their products on TV commercials would not recapture U.S. consumers, many corporate managers turned to more drastic tactics: massive worker layoffs, factory closings, and plant moves to less costly locations. These actions did not improve the quality of U.S. goods and they did not eliminate worker alienation. If anything, they threatened to create worker obsolescence.[57] In some industries, managers tried automation, hoping thereby to better control and standardize product quality. But this only increased worker alienation—and public awareness of worker alienation.

At their Lordstown, Ohio, plant, General Motors managers in the early 1970s built the most advanced and automated plant in the country. At its designated speed, the assembly lines turned out one hundred Vegas an hour (in 1966, the line had produced sixty an hour). This gave each worker thirty-six seconds to complete work on each car and get ready for the next. Furthermore, management ordered compulsory overtime, laid off "unproductive" workers, employed time-and-motion studies to set up new production standards, "buried" hundreds of grievances filed by union reps, and attacked informal agreements work groups had made with foremen.[58] The workers went on a wildcat strike, provoking nationwide attention to the issue of worker alienation. The strike leader, Gary Bryner, explained to the television camera that they were not concerned with the "almighty dollar" but with the social aspects of their jobs, the assertion of their "human rights."

The Lordstown strike became the subject of a great deal of television commentary—as were the other managerial decisions to lay off great masses of workers, close down factories, and relocate plants. All of these management decisions heightened public conviction that U.S. business was concerned solely with profits. In 1971, the *Wall Street Journal* reported that the percentage of people who thought that business achieved a good balance between securing profit and serving the public had suddenly slumped—to 26 percent from the 55 percent it had been for years.[59]

During the late 1970s, some U.S. firms began to change their patterns of organization in order to address this problem of worker alienation. Going under various names—"collective entrepreneurship," "participative management," "development management," "De-management," "group consensus"—this new concept of organization overcame the traditional division between planning and execution so as to upgrade and use all the human capital in the business enterprise. Workers now began to perform complex (not simple) tasks without fixed sets of rules covering all contingencies and without the same kind of officious monitoring of performance that takes place in high-volume, standardized production.[60]

By the late 1970s and 1980s, this form of collective entrepreneurship characterized many small firms producing service-intensive goods. In these firms, coalitions of designers, engineers, fabricators, marketers, salespeople, and financial specialists all worked together to get new products to market. The same patterns of organization appeared in technology-based production in the Massachusetts area around Route 128 and in California's Silicone Valley.[61] Under these new patterns of management, the pursuit of profit was connected to the mutual obligations and mutual responsibilities of all engaged in the economic enterprise. Profits would be had, but not at the expense of worker alienation. Here's how Robert D. Haas, president of Levi Strauss, put it in an interview in the mid-1980s:

> I think what an effective executive needs to do (and I say this because it's a goal for me, not something that I practice) is to try and stand back from all the day-to-day demands and understand really the two things that I think are the senior executive's responsibility: How do I provide a vision for this organization that will carry the organization into the future? And how do I liberate the talents of all the people in my organization to make the most effective contributions that they can to be satisfied, to be fulfilled, to be motivated, and to devote themselves to the welfare of this enterprise and its stakeholders? ... I try as hard as I can to involve as many people in our company as possible in sharing the responsibility for shaping the destiny of this company, for analyzing the issues in our environment, and possibly to shape the course of our business rather than to react to events as they come to us. My effort is really to reaffirm the values that are important around Levi Strauss & Co., and at the heart of it is a respect for people—a respect for our associates who work with us, a respect for our partners who are our suppliers or our customers, a respect for the people in the communities in which we operate. That's the vision I have— to make everyone who is associated with Levi Strauss and Company a spiritual stakeholder in the company.[62]

These changes in the pattern of organization presage what Clark Kerr has called "industrialism with a human face."[63] At the root of this change, as Courtney Brown has pointed out, is the fresh comingling of the modern values of individualism, competition, and objective rationalism, with the long-ignored, premodern, tribal values of collectivism, cooperation, and subjective well-being. In these emerging patterns of economic organization in the postmodern world, business judgments are increasingly based on purposes that include, but extend beyond, the bottom line.[64]

Television and Limits to Growth

Capitalism helped the West to grow rich. As the standard of living kept rising in capitalist countries over the centuries, the doctrine of economic growth became tantamount to a secular religion. Economic growth provided full employment and a steady increase in consumption. It also served as a "political solvent"—the means for financing social welfare expenditure and military defense.

In the second half of the twentieth century, following World War II, the United States assumed the mantle of leadership in the West. The tasks the nation now assumed—both foreign and domestic—could not be undertaken without expanding economic growth. These tasks included defending the free world against Communist aggression, providing economic aid to speed up the development of both war-ravaged and underdeveloped countries, improving the health, education, and welfare of its citizens.

By 1960, economic growth had become the central issue in the presidential campaigns. Nelson Rockefeller, who sought the Republican nomination, had, two years earlier, convened a panel of eminent citizens to prepare a report called "The Challenge of the Future," which turned out to be all about the key importance of growth to the nation's economic goals. Rockefeller lost the bid for the nomination to Richard Nixon, who, as Eisenhower's vice-president, had chaired a cabinet committee that had identified economic growth as the nation's first economic objective. John Kennedy, the Democratic candidate, won the election in part because of his promise to get the country moving again by pledging a 5 percent growth rate.[65]

Actually, although the United States did not enjoy the fastest rate of growth during this period, the West as a whole did. The quarter of a century following World War II witnessed the highest rate of sustained growth in the recorded history of Western civilization.

Between 1948 and 1973, the world's total industrial production expanded three and a half times. This period of unprecedented economic growth eliminated mass unemployment and doubled the average income. But, by the end of the 1960s, doubts were being cast on all sides as to whether economic growth was a boon after all. Many now argued that the moral price paid for economic progress had been too high: increasing pollution, general deterioration of the environment, the danger of running out of supplies of raw materials, and the destruction of essential spiritual and aesthetic values. By 1974, the British sociologist Julius Gould could report "a general feeling (now converted to a near certainty), that endless economic growth is neither feasible, nor desirable."[66]

What had happened?

Television Commercializes Life

The conventional historic explanation blames it on the medium of print.[67] In the late 1950s, books like David Reisman's *The Lonely Crowd* and John Galbraith's *The Affluent Society* raised questions about a consumer-oriented society that regarded production as "the goal of preeminent importance in life." These works did not directly oppose economic growth, but, the argument went, they set the stage for later authors who did—like E.F. Schumaker, who in 1962 published *Roots of Economic Growth*, criticizing present-day economics for propagating "a philosophy of unlimited expansionism" without any regard to the true and genuine needs of man, which are limited."[68] A few years later, another economist, E.J. Mishan, published *The Costs of Economic Growth*, a protest against the blind pursuit of material progress, urging readers to ponder "the effects on the welfare of ordinary people of a gathering eruption of science and technology in pressure sufficient to splinter the framework of our institutions and to erode the moral foundations on which they have been raised."[69] The most dramatic printed criticism came in 1972 with the publication of *The Limits to Growth*, a report for the Club of Rome's project on the predicament of mankind. Using a model developed by Jay Forrester, a group from the Massachusetts Institute of Technology (MIT) investigated major trends of global concern. From their study, they concluded that "if the present growth trends in world population, industrialization, pollution, food production, and resource depletion continue unchanged, the limits to growth on this planet will be reached sometime within the next one hundred years."[70] According to one typical account of the emergence of ecological concern during this period, the report of the Club of Rome "caught the imagination of a large part of the idea-moving community."[71]

I want to argue that it was not the medium of print, but rather the medium of television that brought about the widespread questioning of the doctrine of limitless economic growth. Television did this by bringing about the commercialization of life—the conversion of almost all human activities into market transactions. First, by exposing us and our possessions to one another, television helped to make each of us critical—dissatisfied—with our share of goods. Not just possessions, like cars and clothes and home furnishings, but life styles too: We saw that other people had more freedom than we or more friends, or were more aggressive, or luckier, or more confident. We saw this, and we wanted what they had. We saw exotic vacation spots on our TV screens, where people like us were having more fun than we ever had. I am not talking here only about television commercials but also about entertainment shows, documentaries, talk shows—all of television—that continually exposed the lives of others, revealing that they have more life chances than we. This discontent became a demand for these goods, and, in a capitalist society, energetic entrepreneurs were soon creating and packaging products to fill the demand.

In no time at all, most of life's activities became commercialized: The clothes we wear, our leisure time (sports and entertainment have become completely commercialized), our relationships with one another, our education, our diet, our weight, our health and medical care, our child-rearing practices—all have become market transactions. Some commentators on this commercialization of life, like Ivan Illich and Christopher Lasch, have deplored it because it has debilitated people, making great numbers of us dependent upon professionals who, for a fee, will tell us how to conduct our lives, how to raise our children, how to care for our bodies, how to settle disputes, how to dress, where to go, and what to see.[72] There is undoubtedly some truth to this charge, yet I do think that the commercialization of life has enabled more people to purchase life chances denied to them heretofore.

Yet, at the same time that the commercialization of life has helped to improve the life chances of some people, it has also exposed the limits to growth—the social limits, the psychological limits, and the health and safety limits. Now, of course, there were people who pointed out the limits to growth long before the coming of television. But these were usually Marxists who were anxious only to point out the limits to growth inherent in capitalism.

Like Adam Smith and the classical economists, Marx had favored economic growth, since only increased productivity could provide the wealth necessary for the equitable distribution of goods that would guarantee the well-being of all. He argued that capitalism set limits to growth because of increasing antagonisms between the forces of production it set in motion and its arrangements for distribution. Under capitalism, ownership of the means of production became concentrated in fewer and fewer capitalist hands, who limited the production of goods in order to increase their profits. Thus, when the supply of goods exceeded demand, capitalists would limit production, which put workers out of a job. As Marx saw it, this exploitation of workers was coupled with exploitation of the environment. Under capitalist agriculture, for example, he pointed out that "all progress in increasing the fertility of the soil for a given time is a progress toward ruining the lasting sources of that fertility."[73] In the 1960s and 1970s, the followers of Marx elaborated upon his original arguments against capitalism.[74] But, by this time, the argument had moved beyond Marx to become arguments against growth itself. Television had made the Marxist arguments against the capitalist limits to growth irrelevant.

Social Limits to Growth

Television played a key role in making people conscious of social limits to growth, which came from the fact that some goods are possible only for a minority. They cannot be enjoyed by everyone because it is their scarcity that makes them good.[75] Vacation travel is a good example. If everyone, or hordes of people, travel to a particular vacation resort, then that resort is no longer good—congestion, crowding, higher prices, increased ugliness, and noise all destroy what had made it an appealing resort in the first place. Through travel commercials, news reports, talk shows, and entertainments filmed in exotic locations, television has made more people aware of the existence of such places, provoked discontent, and stimulated mass tourism to vacation resorts heretofore frequented by a few. U.S.

national parks, the Costa del Sol in Spain, not to mention the Olympic Games, the seashore, and ski resorts, have all become less attractive as a result of more crowding and congestion.

The automobile is another example of social limits to growth. Through commercials and entertainment shows, television has created "America's love affair with the automobile," linking it to adventure, romance, independence, and prestige. But, as more and more people purchase automobiles, the roads become more congested, and travel by car becomes slower and less enjoyable.

Education, or schooling, is another "good" subject to social limits. One of the most persistent and continued messages of television is that schooling is a good everyone should seek. Yet, the greater the number of people attending schools and getting diplomas and degrees, the lower the worth of those diplomas and degrees. Moreover, with increased numbers, the quality of education provided usually declines.

Status symbols are perhaps the quintessential example of social limits to growth. With status symbols, the satisfaction consumers desire is not from the goods as such but from the exclusivity that possession of the good provides. Yet, when many people share possession of such goods—whether they be cars, clothes, or life styles—then they can no longer function as status symbols. By exposing the status symbols of the rich and famous, television cultivates imitators and imitations. This commercialization of status symbols deprives their owners of the satisfaction of being in front, of being superior to other people.

Television not only creates social limits to growth (by stirring up demands for goods), it also exposes the social limits. That is, television dutifully reports traffic conditions, accidents, and road construction delays—all brought about by the ever-increasing number of automobiles on the roads. On weekends, viewers see resorts and beaches teeming with people ... and later with litter. Regularly, news reporters feature interviews with highly schooled people unable to get jobs, including Ph.D.s who wind up driving taxicabs. And on television commercials, owners of costly automobiles can see cheaper models advertised that look identical to the ones they own.

One of the consequences of increased awareness of social limits to growth has been the growth of laws and regulations that curtail individual freedom and choice: licenses to operate motorcycles, motorbikes, speed boats, snowmobiles, and the like; rationing of visits to national parks, wilderness areas, and town beaches; the creation of community colleges and junior colleges to draw off some of those seeking "higher education"; antinoise and antilitter ordinances; and strict zoning regulations to discourage tourism in many localities, as well as beefed up police forces to maintain peace. All of these changes reveal a recognition of the social limits to growth, a tacit admission that capitalism must pay some heed to the public interest.

Psychological Limits to Growth

A second kind of limit to economic growth that television helped to uncover can be called the spiritual or psychological limit to growth. The strongest criticism of the commercialization of life brought about by television came from those who can be called "the simple-lifers." Most of the simple-lifers were raised on television from their earliest years and had come to resent the constant, relentless bombardment on the screen that tried to manipulate their lives. Advertising, as they saw it, was a device to create artificial wants, an obsession with which destroyed all hopes of living a simple life: A simple life was nothing more than the satisfaction of truly limited human needs.

Then, there were game shows, like "The Price is Right," and "Let's Make a Deal." On "The Price is Right," contestants bid on merchandise, with the merchandise going to the contestant who had bid the highest without going over the manufacturer's suggested list price. The studio audience constantly exhorted the contestants to stop bidding, or "freeze." To play, or watch, one had to be an avid consumer. In "Let's Make a Deal," contestants were presented with a choice: whether to take one prize or another, some of which were described fully while others remained hidden in a box or behind doors; some of the prizes were cash, others worthless merchandise. A player could take one prize, say $1,000, trade it for what proved to be a mink coat, and decide to trade the coat only to wind up with a wheelbarrow. The game was based on consumer greed. And consumer greed paid off: The two players who won the most could trade their winnings for the "big deal"—a $10,000 prize hidden behind one of three doors.

The simple-lifers resented the way of life presented on television— life, they insisted, was not simply a race to accumulate commodities— and they were particularly hard on Americans, who, with only 6 percent of the world's population, actually consumed more than a third of the world's natural resources. During the 1960s, they excoriated American materialism, preaching in its stead a somewhat shallow simple-life message: material simplicity and all-embracing love, which included long hair, bell bottoms, rock music, nature walks, and drugs. People, they counseled, should exchange wealth, status, and power for love, creativity, and liberation. The simple-lifers tried to construct a counterculture outside of mainstream culture, a counterculture that, in the words of Jerry Rubin, "signifies the total end of the Protestant Ethic: Screw work, we want to know ourselves."[76] Some set up collective enclaves in San Francisco's Haight-Ashbury district, New York's East Village, or Atlanta's Fourteenth Street; and in rural areas, too: in Vermont, California, Colorado, Oregon, Arizona, and New Mexico. Founded usually on nothing more substantial than an exchange of the materialist hedonism of the consumer culture for the sexual and sensory hedonism of the counterculture, most of these experiments lasted but a few months or years.

Yet, the counterculture had tapped a spring of discontent with the commercialization of life television had brought about in sports, entertainment, transportation, diet, education, careers, and vacations. Television had not only brought about the commercialization of life, it had glorified it on its programs, daily and nightly. Now, less preposterous advocates of the simple life began to reject the spiritually bankrupt way of life displayed on television. Rather than be spectators of the professional, competitive games shown on television, they preferred participating in amateur cooperative games. They sought out personal, intimate entertainment rather than the professional, packaged entertainment on commercial television. If a simple-lifer had an automobile—often he had a bike instead—it was not a late model but simply a functional vehicle. The simple-lifers avoided the fast foods, the processed foods, the chemically-laced foods found on TV in favor of natural foods, organically grown. They avoided the glitzy vacation resorts featured on television in order to go backpacking in the wilderness. Instead of pursuing the kind of education provided on television that would put them on the fast lane to a career in the corporate world, they took up carpentry, leather work, weaving, or some other necessary elemental craft or trade. They sought jobs not in the large corporations glamorized on television but in small companies and firms where they could remain a person pursuing their own goals rather than mindlessly subscribing to the goals of the corporation.

Since the simple-lifers were anticonsumers and preached anticonsumerism, commercial television networks certainly did nothing to propagate their message or point of view—except to disparage and make fun of it in situation comedies. Yet, the reaction against the commercialization of life continued to grow in the 1970s as more and more people became conscious of the spiritual limits to economic growth. In the mid-1970s, the Stanford Research Institute found that "evidence is mounting that an increasing segment of the U.S. population is voluntarily taking up a simpler way of life."[77] They found support for human-scale technology and decision making, and they discovered an ecological consciousness as well as conscientious consumption among young, white, well-educated, middle- and upper-middle-class Americans. According to Duane Elgin, these people were not ideological extremists of any sort; they simply preferred products that were functional, healthy, nonpolluting, durable, repairable, recyclable or made from renewable raw materials, energy cheap, authentic, aesthetically pleasing, and made through simple technology.[78]

Some of these simple-lifers did create cooperatives, alternative enterprises, and worker-owned and -managed firms in various parts of the nation. One estimate in the late 1970s claimed that more than ten thousand such enterprises were in operation.[79] A Lou Harris Poll in 1977 concluded that a "quiet revolution" was occurring in national values in the United States: "People have begun to show a deep skepticism about the nation's capacity for unlimited economic growth and they are wary of the benefits that growth is supposed to bring."[80]

Health and Safety Limits to Growth

In addition to the social limits to growth and the spiritual limits to growth, television also brought about increased consciousness of the health and safety limits to growth. In the early 1980s, the Public Broadcasting System produced a program entitled "The Doomsayers." In the opening sequence, the narrator announced:

Now there are those who say that Western civilization has run its course. That our efforts to create a society of peace and prosperity have nearly failed. That ahead of us waits the prospect of a new dark age. Around us rise the voices of the doomsayers.

We have always had doomsayers among us, but the environmental doomsayers who appeared in the 1970s were the first to have television on their side. They presented a two-fold moral argument against limitless economic growth. Continued economic growth endangered the health and safety of everyone because it destroyed the environment through production processes, waste disposal practices, or consumer use: first, by depleting and eventually using up our finite natural resources, and secondly, by polluting the environment.

Night after night during the 1960s and 1970s, television carried bad news about our unhealthy society: DDT in the food chain, radiation, mercury, toxic waste, oil spills, Kepone, and a list of carcinogens long enough to lead the evening news on any day nothing else was happening. Not only the news, but public affairs programs, documentaries, talk shows, and interview programs carried pictures of seagulls covered with oil on a Santa Barbara beach; of babies burned from inflammable nightshirts or contaminated by chemically treated nonflammable nightshirts; of faces in Harrisburg, Pennsylvania, worried about exposure to radiation; of terrified mothers at Love Canal, fearful about birth defects, miscarriages, and cancer; of supersonic airplanes that threatened to deplete the ozone supply; of the snail darter threatened with extinction.

As instances of environmental pollution mounted, moral criticism became more widespread and the message of the doomsayers more accepted: Limitless economic growth was leading to ecocide; we were hurtling toward an ecotastrophe that threatened not only our own culture but the environment, the biosphere, as a whole.

Television also helped raise people's consciousness about the depletion of our natural resources. Over the decade, television reported that the world was running out of tin, copper, phosphate, zinc, and iron. Yet, although many environmentalists had long warned that continuous economic growth would soon use up the finite supply of metals, minerals, and fuels available to us, it was not until the oil crisis of 1973 that the message really struck home.

In 1973, the Arab States of OPEC embargoed oil exports to the United States, causing higher prices and shortages. The oil crisis of 1973 was followed a few years later with a similar crisis in 1979, when the overthrow of the Shah again interrupted the flow of Iranian oil to the West. During both of these crises, television showed the long lines of motorists waiting for gas; it carried extensive coverage of truckers protesting huge fuel prices by blockading major interstate highways. Television showed airports where passengers were stranded because airlines had canceled flights due to fuel shortages. During both crises, television showed the impact of oil shortages on the tourism and recreation industry. One report by NBC's Dan Oliver concluded with these words:

> We wanted to show that Disneyland and seaside and mountain resorts have also had a loss of business. But you'll have to take our word for it. We didn't have enough gas to get to those places.[81]

There were also reports on a wide assortment of adversely affected industries: textile, recorded music, toys, plastic, and slaughter house industries, to name but a few. According to Leonard Theberge, the effects of the crises on service stations commanded fully 25 percent of all television coverage.[82] Aerial footage of interminable gas lines wrapping around city blocks was a favorite story. Most of the stories and pictures were complemented by interviews of environmental pundits who warned that we were running out of oil. We live, they told us, in an era of limits: Oil was limited, as were other nonrenewable resources, like natural gas, coal, and metals.

Television converted the energy crisis into a moral crisis. While everyone agreed that OPEC had caused the shortage, television continually pointed out that American overconsumption and waste of oil and gas was exacerbating the crisis. In one report, ABC's Robert Peterson noted that

> economists who study the oil situation are divided on whether they think governmental action will become necessary. But there is general agreement on one thing: If Americans would start using their common sense and stop wasting energy, we wouldn't be faced with mandatory conservation, much less rationing.[83]

If the energy crisis was at bottom a moral crisis, then the solution lay in self-sacrifice and self-discipline. In 1973, President Nixon asked gas stations to remain closed on Sundays. Shortly thereafter, Anne Kaistner of ABC news asked a skier in California, "Do you feel guilty buying gas on Sundays?" During the second energy crisis, President Jimmy Carter brought out the William James phrase, "the moral equivalent of war," as the slogan for his energy program, which was intended to lead the country away from its wasteful habits.

Carter was not successful in extorting self-sacrifice from Americans primarily because people now thought the oil companies were to blame for the shortage. During the first shortage in 1973, television had depicted a public that was fearful, concerned, or alarmed. On CBS, Congressman Silvio Conte stated that his constituents "come in here with trembling hands and show me their gas bills and their oil bills and say, 'Mr. Conte, I—I just can't exist'." But, during the second crisis, the networks portrayed a more indignant and outraged public. According to Theberge, over one-third of the television discussion of the cause of the crisis blamed the oil companies.[84] John Chancellor reported in March 1979 that "a lot of people wonder if the shortages are for real or part of a scheme to make more money for the oil companies." There were frequent reports that oil companies were withholding supplies in order to make excessive profits through price gouging. In February 1969, ABC showed Senator John Durkin exclaiming, "How in God's name can you ask the American public to make a sacrifice when you have the horrendous, unconscionable oil company profits for the last quarter?" Television had shifted its moral gaze to identify the oil companies as the bad guys.

Blaming the energy crisis on greedy oil companies diverted attention from the environmental doomsayers' message that we were depleting our finite natural resources. Few people seemed to want to hear this message. Moreover, as the energy crisis subsided, laissez-faire economists like Wilfred Beckerman, Charles Maurice, and Charles Smithson remounted their counterattacks on the doomsayers' warnings about the limits to growth. While admitting that the natural resources of the world are finite, they rejected the environmentalists' assumption of exponential growth, which assumes that prevailing trends will continue in the future. Instead, these economists argued, either shortages or surpluses will change the price of a commodity, which, in turn, will alter the growth of both consumption and production: Price changes alter growth trends.[85] But, for this to happen, of course, there had to be a free market where prices would reflect actual supply and demand. Ronald Reagan, when he succeeded Jimmy Carter as president, announced that he did not accept the limits to growth beliefs of his predecessor but subscribed instead to those of the laissez-faire economists. Therefore, he set afoot the process of deregulation of energy, airlines, interstate trucking, and a host of other industries to allow the free market to moderate economic growth and preserve our natural resources.

In the matter of pollution, the laissez-faire economists did not deny it existed, nor that it was bad, but they did argue that air pollution, for example, had been worse in the nineteenth century. More to the point, they insisted that pollution resulted not from economic growth but from the misallocation of resources. That is, those who polluted did not pay the costs of pollution, the public did. Therefore, to diminish pollution, those who polluted should pay the cost—in the form of taxes, for example. Here, too, Ronald Reagan followed the laissez-faire economists, forswearing increased regulation of industries for economic incentives to encourage them to reduce pollution. But, according to one sober assessment of the Reagan record, this administration, which supposedly espoused the free market approach, actually made "little progress in furthering the use of economic incentives as tools of environmental policy."[86]

Television has helped us see that the economic problem is not simply a scarcity of goods, as the traditional theorists of capitalism had thought. Today, the problem is also a plethora of bads. Television has brought about an increased consciousness of some of these bads and, by casting these bads as moral bads, has helped to make us care. The recognition and acceptance of social, spiritual, and health and safety limits to economic growth have profoundly changed the face of capitalism.

In this chapter, I have tried to show how television facilitated moral criticism of capitalism. This criticism led to a subordination of the pursuit of profits to moral concerns; it led to a recognition of the social, the spiritual, and the health and safety limits to economic growth; and it led to increased efforts to transfer wealth from the rich to the poor. In these ways, the coming of television brought about moral progress in the economic realm.

Notes

1   Berger, *The Capitalist Revolution*, 41-43.
2   Robert Coles, "Rural Upheaval: Confrontation and Upheaval," in Sundquist, ed., *On Fighting Poverty*, 121.
3   Patterson, *America's Struggle against Poverty 1900-1980*, 79.
4   Ibid., 86.
5   Moynihan, *Maximum Feasible Misunderstanding*, 104.
6   Ferman et al., eds., *Poverty in America*, 508.
7   Ibid., 508.
8   Robert Coles, "Rural Upheaval: Confrontation and Upheaval," in Sundquist, ed., *On Fighting Poverty*, 123.
9   Moynihan, *Maximum Feasible Misunderstanding*, 132-3.
10   Ibid., 140-1.
11   Patterson, *America's Struggle against Poverty 1900-1980*, 152.
12   Ibid., 146.
13   William C. Selover, "The View from Capitol Hill: Harassment and Survival," in Sundquist, ed., *On Fighting Poverty*, 167.
14   Sundquist, *On Fighting Poverty*, 240.
15   Patterson, *America's Struggle against Poverty 1900-1980*, 195.
16   Murray, *Losing Ground*, 46.
17   Ibid., 43-44.
18   Ellwood and Summers, "Is Welfare Really the Problem?" 57-78.
19   Kelman, "Regulation by the Numbers," 83-102.
20   Nichols and Zeckhauser, "Government Comes to the Workplace: An Assessment of OSHA," 39-69.
21   Solid Waste Disposal Act, 1965
      Resource Conservation and Recovery Act, 1976
22   Air Act to Require Aircraft Noise Abatement Regulation, 1968
      Noise Control Act, 1972
23   Federal Environmental Pesticide Control Act, 1972
      Toxic Substance Control Act, 1977
24   Water Resources Act, 1964
      Water Resources Planning Act, 1965
      Coastal Zone Management Act, 1972
      Marine Mammal Protection Act, 1972
      Endangered Species Act, 1973
      Federal Land Policy and Management Act, 1976
      National Forest Management Act, 1976
25   Bardach and Pugliaresi, "The Environmental Impact Statement vs. the Real World," 23.
26   Jones, *Clean Air*, 27.
27   Johnson, *Modern Times*, 661.
28   Stein, *The View from Sunset Boulevard*, iii.

29   Rowen, *The Free Enterprisers: Kennedy, Johnson and the Business Establishment,* 90.

30   Stein, *The View from Sunset Boulevard,* 18-19.

31   Jones, *Clean Air,* 162.

32   Gottron, ed., *Regulation: Process and Politics,* 113.

33   Tolchin and Tolchin, *Dismantling America: The Rush to Deregulate,* 12.

34   Schwarz, *America's Hidden Success,* 58-68.

35   Lodge, *The New American Ideology,* 237.

36   Gottron, ed., *Regulation: Process and Politics,* 30.

37   Weidenbaum, *The Future of Business Regulation: Private Action and Public Demand,* passim.

38   Bach, ed., *The Environmental Crisis—Opposing Viewpoints,* 34.

39   Tolchin and Tolchin, *Dismantling America: The Rush to Deregulate,* 11.

40   Gottron, ed., *Regulation: Process and Politics,* 113.

41   Ibid., 28.

42   Ibid., 4.

43   Tolchin and Tolchin, *Dismantling America: The Rush to Deregulate,* 1.

44   Reich, *The Next American Frontier,* 67.

45   Terkel, *Working,* 160.

46   Ibid., 175.

47   Ibid., 168.

48   Ibid., xxxvii.

49   U.S. Department of Health, Education and Welfare, *Work in America.*

50   Harris, *America Now,* 18.

51   Ibid., 22.

52   Reich, *The Next American Frontier,* 33.

53   Harris, *America Now,* 31.

54   Reich, *The Next American Frontier,* ch. 6.

55   Mayer, *Madison Avenue, USA,* 165.

56   Price, *The Best Thing on TV: Commercials,* 144-45.

57   Barnet and Miller, *Global Reach: The Power of Multinational Corporations,* 305.

58   Green, *The World of the Worker,* 219.

59   Wright, *The Day the Pigs Refused to be Driven to Market,* 12.

60   Reich, *Tales from a New America;* Sevareid, *Enterprise: The Making of Business in America;* Dunlop, *The Quiet Revolution;* Cornuelle, *De-Managing America;* Brown, *Beyond the Bottom Line.*

61   Reich, *Tales from a New America,* 126.

62   Freudberg, *The Corporate Conscience,* 209.

63   Kerr and Rosow, eds., *Work in America,* xxvii.

64   Brown, *Beyond the Bottom Line,* xxxiii.

65   Arndt, *The Rise and Fall of Economic Growth,* 55-56.

66   Anthony Wiener, "Some Functions of Attitudes Toward Economic Growth," in Wilson, ed., *Prospects for Growth,* 66.

67   Arndt, *The Rise and Fall of Economic Growth,* ch. 7.

68   Schumacher, *Roots of Economic Growth,* 13.

69   Mishan, *The Costs of Economic Growth,* xvii.

70   Meadows et al., *The Limits to Growth,* 23.

71   Robert Theobald, "Managing the Quality of Life," in Wilson, ed., *Prospects for Growth,* 74.

72   Illich, *DeSchooling Society*; Illich, *Medical Nemesis*; Lasch, *The Culture of Narcissism*; Lasch, *The Minimal Self.*
73   Marx, *Capital*, I:506.
74   Harris, *The Death of Capital.*
75   Hirsch, *Social Limits to Growth*, passim.
76   Shi, *The Simple Life*, 251.
77   Ibid., 268.
78   Elgin, *Voluntary Simplicity*, 36-38.
79   McRobic, *Small is Possible*, 153.
80   Shi, *The Simple Life*, 268.
81   Theberge, *TV Coverage of the Oil Crises*, 33.
82   Ibid., 44.
83   Ibid., 14.
84   Ibid., 31.
85   Beckerman, *Two Cheers for the Affluent Society*; Maurice and Smithson, *The Doomsday Myth.*
86   Paul Portney, "Natural Resources and the Environment," in Palmer and Sawhill, eds., *The Reagan Record*, 175.

5

Television and Science

The continual advancement of scientific knowledge over the past four centuries has marked not only a path of continuous improvement in human knowledge but an improvement in the human condition as well. For, as Francis Bacon pointed out early in the seventeenth century, knowledge is power, and power can be used for the betterment of the human estate, "for the merit and emolument of man." The systematic application of science to the affairs of man brought prosperity, health, and happiness to ever-increasing numbers. Applying science to the affairs of man was the faith of the men of genius of the seventeenth century; it was the faith of those responsible for the eighteenth-century enlightenment, and it was a faith shared by men of good hope in the nineteenth and twentieth centuries. In the 1930s, the historian George Sarton wrote: "The history of science is the only history which can illuminate the progress of mankind. In fact, progress has no definite and unquestionable meaning in other fields than the history of science."[1]

As recently as 1950, the American Nobel laureate I.I. Rabbi writing in *The Atlantic* monthly, restated that Baconian faith, assuring us that science

inspires us with a feeling of hopefulness and infinite possibility. The road ahead may be invisible, but the tradition of science has shown that the human spirit applied in the tradition of science will find a way toward the objective. Science shows that it is possible to foresee and to plan, and that we can take the future into our hands if we rid ourselves of prejudices and superstitions.

Then, suddenly, during the third quarter of the twentieth century, this faith in the beneficence of science came into question. The public grew increasingly more critical of science and scientists. In the early 1970s, the Ciba Foundation reflected this new animus toward science when it held a symposium in London on "Civilization and Science: In Conflict or Collaboration." The chairman of the symposium defined the problem by pointing out that "in the minds of many, science all the way from nuclear physics and engineering to biology and medicine has become a most dangerous evil."[2] At about the same time, *Daedelus*, the journal of the American Arts and Science, sponsored a conference on "Science and its Public: The Changing Relationship." The bulk of criticism, the editor of the collected papers of the conference pointed out, "is not simply the ephemeral reaction of isolated individuals or small groups to specific political and moral dilemmas, but ... may be the sign of a more basic discontent— possibly even a harbinger that our world view, which until recently has been generally supportive of science, may be about to turn."[3]

There had always been critics of science. These critics were often literary people, like Ben Johnson, Mary Shelly, William Blake, and Goethe, who worried about the hubris of the scientists and the consequences that might ensue from their intellectual probings. Even earlier, the comic poet of ancient Greece, Aristophanes, railed against one Socrates who insulted the gods by prying into the secrets of nature. But now, in the 1960s, criticism of science and scientists came not from a few literateurs but from large segments of the public. National surveys revealed that, between 1957 and 1964, the proportion of people who saw science as a disintegrating force nearly doubled, increasing from 23 percent to 42 percent. And from 1966 to 1971, confidence in science dropped from 56 percent to 32 percent.[4] Jerome Wiesner, one-time science advisor to President Kennedy, lamented in 1973 the "deep distrust of science and technology ... expressed by many in our society today."[5] That same year, *Time* magazine summarized the public's reaction to science as one of "deepening disillusionment."

What had happened, of course, was the appearance of television. Science was now encoded on the video screen. George Gerbner and his colleagues, on the basis of a study conducted in the 1970s, reported that six out of ten prime-time programs on commercial television involved a "theme or aspect of life explicitly and unambiguously related to science, technology, or engineering." He calculated that, because the average viewer spends thirty hours per week in front of the television set, and because one-third of that viewing is of prime-time dramatic shows, at least one hour of viewing in each weekday evening can include a program that "involves" science. "No other cultural or educational source," he noted, "comes near to the magnitude of that exposure period."[6]

What television did was to create a new critical community, a community quite different from the critical community that the printing press had created centuries earlier. The printing press had created (and still creates) a community that focused its criticism on the rationality of science, uncovering the contradiction inherent in proposed scientific theories. But because of the bias of the electronic medium of television, it created a community critical of the moral relationships inherent in the scientific enterprise. Once science was encoded on television, viewers could see it in a way not possible before. Now, for the first time, large segments of the public became critical of science, critical of it on moral grounds. Gerbner and his associates found a remarkable negative correlation between the amount of television viewed and public confidence in the scientific community. The confidence level in the scientific community declined, he found, among those who watch more television.[7]

Some have accounted for this by reminding us that television presents dubious, sensationalized, or fictional images of science—so, the argument goes, people who watch a lot of this lose confidence in science. I think, rather, that confidence declines because television does encode the actual relationships between science and people, thereby facilitating (moral) criticism of those relationships. There are at least three kinds of relationships that are of moral concern to people: the relationship between science and the survival of the human species; the relationship between science and human nature; and the relationship between science and human dignity.

Science and Human Survival

Many commentators on TV coverage of science have complained that the medium has failed to provide viewers with accurate and comprehensive information.[8] Although we get more information about science than before, public understanding of science and technology is often distorted. "In terms of continuing discourse between science and citizen," David Perlman claims, "commercial television is the most bankrupt of the mass media."[9]

Exactly. And that goes for public television, too. Television generates no discourse because it is a nondiscursive medium. It deals in images and pictures. For example, the PBS series "The Ascent of Man" generated no discourse—it simply entertained. The "show" presented lots of unusual pictures of Jacob Bronowski appearing in exotic locations, showing fascinating artifacts and items while he recounted interesting anecdotes about science and scientists.

Yet science, when it appears on television, does more than entertain. As an analogic medium, television presents science in a way that reveals what it means to us. Sometimes, there are scientific achievements that make us proud: the moon landings, the winning of a Nobel prize; or hopeful: a new cure for cancer, a new treatment for mental illness, a new miracle drug, a new procedure in surgery. But more often, television shows what science has wrought to make us fearful: the bomb, radioactive fallout, fluorocarbons in the ozone layer, carcinogenic food additives—all produced through the ingenuity of modern physics and chemistry. It is through the medium of television that most of us learned about Bhopal, Three Mile Island, Chernobyl, Love Canal, and the explosion of the space shuttle *Challenger*. We saw these events as they happened, or, more importantly, we saw the effects these scientific catastrophes had on our fellow human beings. We watched, and we became afraid and critical—critical of the scientists responsible for these tragedies, critical of science itself. When he was interviewed on television many years after it had happened, Clement Atlee, the British prime minister who had concurred with President Truman's decision to drop the atomic bomb on Japan, uttered a *cri de coeur:*

> All I knew was that it was a bigger bomb. I knew nothing at all about fallout, nor the genetic effects. And as far as I know, President Truman

and Winston Churchill knew nothing of those things either. Whether the scientists directly concerned knew, or guessed, I do not know. But, as far as I am aware, they said nothing of it to those who had to make the decision. I am no scientist, you know.[10]

Television does not present scientific news objectively. Because of its inherent bias, it personalizes the events it depicts. When it reports about Nobel prize winners, television frequently shows pictures of them with their families, and reporters frequently ask spouses and children: "How does it feel to have a Nobel prize winner in the family?" When it reports scientifically related crises and tragedies, television shows people who are adversely affected: people in pain, anxious people, fearful people, people who are grief-stricken and in a state of shock. Through this personalization of the news, television moralizes about science. ("Dr. Blank, would you live in Love Canal?") As a result of what they have seen on television, many people doubt that science always improves the quality of life for all. As they see it, science lacks a public morality; science is unconcerned with the public good.

TV Shows that Science Threatens Humanity

As one of the central features of modern civilization, science has always been rooted in individualism, always concerned with the pursuit of private goods. Modern science and technology have improved life chances by enabling people to do and get what they want. But in many instances, the efforts of some to secure their wants have caused pain and suffering to others. Thus, science has helped the people of one nation to win a war, but only by creating ever-increasingly horrible weapons that kill and maim the people of the defeated nation. Science has enabled entrepreneurs to increase their profits by developing more efficient methods of production, but these methods exploit workers and pollute the environment. Science has created food additives that improve the taste of food products and lengthen their shelf life, but which, at the same time, impair the health of consumers. Science has reduced mortality and increased life, thereby increasing world population, but to such an extent that the planet can no longer support everyone with adequate food, clothing, and shelter. Science has enabled physicians to transplant vital organs and to keep the "brain dead" alive, but only by husbanding money, time, manpower, and equipment that might have been utilized for other people or for other purposes more attuned to the public good. Science has advanced through continual experimentation, but often these are dangerous experiments conducted on unsuspecting subjects sometimes coerced or duped into participation.

All of these tales of lack of concern for the public good displayed by scientists have come to us through the medium of television. Moreover, in recounting these stories on news programs, in documentaries, docudramas, and special programs, television has not only called forth increased public criticism of the immoral consequences wrought by modern science, it has also raised fears that science and technology have escaped from public control and threaten to destroy us all.

Here are a few of the reports about life-threatening happenings that television viewers received during the 1960s and early 1970s:

1962	Thalidomide: a drug developed for use in sleeping tablets and tranquilizers, is found to cause birth defects. Television viewers see pictures of limbless and deformed babies
1963	CBS Reports airs "The Silent Spring of Rachel Carlson," revealing the harmful effects of DDT in pesticides.
1964	Asbestos is found to be a cause of lung cancer: Television reporters interview frightened and tearful people who have had long exposure to asbestos.
1965	Nonbiodegradable detergents are found to cause large amounts of foam in rivers and tap water.
1966	Concern that oral contraceptives ("the pill") cause blood clotting and other illnesses leads the FDA to study the problem. Later, the agency releases a report that it found no evidence it is "unsafe."
1967	General Electric recalls one hundred thousand color television sets because they emit low levels of x-rays.
1968	Over six thousand sheep in Utah sicken or die from nerve gas accidentally released during tests made at the U.S. Proving Grounds. First reports of this appear on NBC's "First Tuesday" on 4 February 1969.
1969	Phosphates in detergents are found to contribute to the eutrophication of the nation's waterways.
1969	Cyclomates—widely used in diet sweeteners—are found to cause cancer. The FDA removes them from the market.
1970	Public protest prevents the Atomic Energy Commission from using

1970 an abandoned salt mine near Lyons, Kansas, as a repository for
radioactive waste.

1970 Mercury is found to be polluting rivers and lakes, and is also found
to contaminate canned tuna fish.

1971 Diethylstilbesterol (DES), used since the 1930s to prevent
miscarriage, is found to be carcinogenic for children of those
pregnancies

1971 Hexachlorophene (HCP), used in some three hundred to four
hundred products ranging from baby cleansers to tooth pastes to
feminine deodorant sprays, is found to cause brain damage.

Coupled with these spectacular news stories about how science and technology endanger our lives and even threaten our survival is the picture of scientists television presents on its entertainment shows. A 1980 University of Michigan study of how U.S. television characterizes fictional scientists concluded that they were usually shown as somewhat unstable, often threatening, usually unpleasant, and (the kiss of death) short in stature.[11] Scientists are rarely heroes on television shows. More likely they appear as villains who use their knowledge for evil purposes. If he is not malevolent, the television scientist is cold and unfeeling—like Dr. Spock, the science officer of the space ship *Enterprise* in "Star Treck," who expresses virtually no emotion and firmly rejects female advances (he has a mating urge once every seven years, preferring to amuse himself by playing three-dimensional chess). Usually isolated from the rest of society, the TV scientist spends most of his time seeking the knowledge that will consolidate his dominion over nature and therefore over mankind.

The villainous scientist is a staple of many Saturday morning cartoon shows. A number of these cartoon characters first appeared in comic books, but television in the 1960s and 1970s gave them and their characterizations of science and scientists much wider exposure than ever possible before. On "Birdman and the Galaxy Trio," Birdman fights against a bevy of evil scientists, including Dr. Millenium, Dr. Freezoids, Professor Nightshade, and Vulturo, the Mind-Taker. The nefarious Dr. Gizmo appears in "George of the Jungle," while Dr. Sivana (Thaddeus Bodog Sivana) "the world's maddest scientist," is a longtime adversary of Captain Marvel. Dr. Doom, the sworn enemy of Spiderman, possesses the greatest arsenal of technological weapons, including a miniature index-finger gun, an ether gun, a machine that can pluck objects out of the past, and a boxing device that clobbers rooms full of people at a time. On "Flash Gordon," one finds Ming the Merciless, emperor of the planet Mango, where science is far in advance of that on earth. ("The reason for our success is that we possess none of the human traits of kindness, mercy, or pity! We are coldly scientific and ruthless.")

In addition to displaying the destructive forces of scientific technology, television entertainment shows frequently provide warnings about accidents in scientific experiments that could have dire consequences. Such accidents could bring about dramatic and dangerous changes in the makeup of people—as happened, for example, in the case of the Incredible Hulk, where a research scientist, after being accidentally exposed to an overdose of gamma rays, found himself transformed into a green-skinned, white-eyed behemoth whenever he became enraged.

The Public Loses Faith in Science

Television exposure of how modern science threatens human survival brought out in the public a new critical perspective on science that resulted in significant cultural changes in the 1970s. One of the most dramatic was the decline in numbers of students who chose to become scientists. In 1977, about 40 percent fewer Ph.D. degrees were conferred in physics than in 1969.[12] During this period, scientists suffered severe cutbacks in funding for research, and, when they received funds, had less freedom to use them as they wished. An era had ended. Ever since the end of World War II, the federal government had supported basic research with no immediate connection to any applied purpose, allocating funds on the basis of the scientific merit of specific projects as judged by eminent scientists in private life. But, beginning with President Nixon's 1973-74 budget, a reaction set in. Now, instead of providing money for general categories that allowed grant recipients to determine the purpose and direction of research, federal funds were earmarked for categories of applied research directed toward politically popular ends.[13] It is true that this may have been, in part, retribution to the scientific community for not supporting the administration's SST and ABM programs, but this cutback and reduction of funds seems to have been more an expression of a widespread critical reaction to science and an attempt to make it more accountable to the public. Another indication of the critical reaction to scientists was the abolition in 1973 of the president's Science Advisory Committee and the transfer of the Office of Science and Technology out of the Executive Office. The congressional hearings on this dismantling "evoked little debate either within or outside the government."[14]

The growth of government control and regulation of the conduct of science provides additional evidence of the decline of public faith in science. After banning cyclomates in 1969, the FDA banned saccharine in 1977. In 1978, the Environmental Protection Agency imposed a ban on the use of chloroflurocarbons as aerosol propellants. In the nuclear energy field, the Nuclear Regulatory Commission has continually tightened and ratcheted safety requirements, not in response to the assessments of scientists but in response to political activists. Thus, between the early and late 1970s, the government, for safety reasons, increased the building requirements for nuclear power plants, raising the poundage of steel used by 40 percent, the amount of concrete by 27 percent, and the linear footage of piping by 50 percent and of electric cable by 36 percent.[15]

One of the most controversial areas of regulation has been in the field of genetic engineering. Early in the 1970s, scientists devised a technique for cutting and splicing the basic substance of life forms (DNA), thereby creating hybrid (recombinant) DNA molecules. Reports of this scientific breakthrough raised widespread fear of human genetic manipulation. This resulted in the creation of scientific committees and study panels, as well as the passage of state and local ordinances and laws and the introduction of a dozen bills in Congress to regulate all cases of gene splicing. In addition, the National Institute of Health issued guidelines that set forth a moratorium on some cases of experiments. The swiftness—and the depth and breadth—of the critical response of the public could only have happened in an age of electronic communication.

Since the coming of television, another significant change has occurred within the scientific community itself: the appearance of "public interest" science. Sometimes called "critical science," it emphasizes the role of the scientist as critic. Public interest scientists use their knowledge to try to protect the public as a whole from what they regard as possible harm from emerging technologies. But rather than recapture public faith in science and scientists, public interest science has further eroded that faith by politicizing the field and laying bare the controversies and disagreements among scientists about safety and danger, about causes and consequences.

This same picture of furor among scientists also surfaces whenever the government seeks to ban or regulate certain kinds of scientific products. Then, we are faced with entrepreneurial scientists, who are employed by the chemical and technological companies who fight the government's scientists. Academic scientists also enter the battle, each group putting forth intransigent positions on the issues under consideration. Television news reports have heightened the controversies by adopting a policy of "equal time," which allows each of the contending parties, or their representatives, to give a thirty-second explanation of his position to the TV audience. The spectacle of such disarray in the field and such contumacious conduct among scientists only deepens public distrust.

Nothing more strongly reveals the impact of a decade and more of moral criticism than the loss of credibility in the matter of nuclear energy.

In the 1950s, there was little or no antipathy toward nuclear energy. Neither was there any in the early 1970s, when reactors began sprouting all over the country. A 1956 Gallup Poll found that only 20 percent of the public opposed having nuclear plants in their communities. By 1977, that number rose to 33 percent. However, the proportion of "anti-nukes" by 1979 was 56 percent. Meanwhile, as Bernard Cohen points out, the 1956 Windscale accident in England was much more severe than the Three Mile Island accident. Yet, its effect on public opinion was not nearly as great—in either England or the United States—as that of Three Mile Island. The reason why Three Mile Island had such an impact, of course, is that it happened in the age of television and received massive TV coverage.

In a 1980 Gallup survey of the top three preferred energy sources, only 27 percent of those responding included nuclear energy. In a survey taken in Oregon the year before, groups of college students and members of the League of Women Voters were asked to rank 30 technologies and activities according to the "present risk of death" they pose to the average American. Both groups ranked nuclear power number one. Yet, at the same time, 89 percent of all scientists, and 95 percent of all scientists engaged in energy-related fields, favor proceeding with the development of nuclear power. Moreover, a poll of radiation health scientists shows that 82 percent of them feel that the public's fear of radiation is "substantially" or "greatly" exaggerated.[16]

Bernard Coehn, a nuclear scientist, blames television and other news media for public withdrawal from a path advocated by almost all U.S. scientists. The media do not transmit scientists' views to the public, he argues; instead, they present stories that create "wildly exaggerated fears of radiation, a highly distorted picture of a reactor meltdown accident, greatly unjustified fears about the disposal of radioactive waste, and romantic ideas about the feasibility of solar energy."[17]

The trouble with his explanation is that it denies agency to television viewers. Cohen, like most of those who talk about the influence of television, assumes that people are simply receptors who ingest what they observe on the screen. What has to be explained, I think, is why public faith and trust in scientists is so low. Cohen's own experience as a public proponent of nuclear energy clearly shows that the key issue is the credibility of scientists. He reports that when he gives public lectures presenting the scientists' case for nuclear energy, he always gets hostile questions from the audience like these:

- Why should we believe scientists when they have made nuclear bombs and all sorts of devastating weapons?
- Since nuclear scientists rely on the nuclear industry for their livelihood, how can we believe them?
- With nuclear scientists split on the question of dangers of radiation, how do we know which side to believe?
- The nuclear establishment told us that there could never be a reactor accident, but there was Three Mile Island. How can we trust them?[18]

Dr. Cohen can answer all these questions in an objective, rational way. But rational discussion, or rational arguments, cannot restore the public's trust. The widely shared fear and distrust of scientists has come from television, or, more accurately, it has evolved through the moral criticism of science and scientists that television has engendered. Scientists have not become more evil or more untrustworthy than they were before. It is the critical perspective of the public that is new, a critical perspective made possible by television and one likely to last, a critical perspective that helps people better protect themselves.

Science and Human Nature

By the 1950s, science had become the established religion in the United States and scientists its priests and ministers.[19] Science had disclosed wonders and miracles far more astounding than any religious vision. Moreover, the knowledge that science had revealed had made things better. Everyone recognized and applauded the contributions of science to the well-being of society, recognizing that the gross national product of industry reflected the gross national product of science. Expanded federal support for scientific research provides one indication of how much respect Americans had for science: From 1940 to 1965, appropriations rose from $74,000,000 to $15,287,000,000—a two-fold increase.[20]

Most people assumed that the remarkable contribution of science to the improvement of the human estate rested upon scientists' objective, dispassionate pursuit of truth. Their search for truth, it was further assumed, had provided us with a true understanding of the universe we inhabit. However, the coming of television raised questions in the minds of many about both of these assumptions: Were scientists really objective, dispassionate seekers of truth? Did science provide a true understanding of the universe? In short, could human beings know the truth?

Television personalized science. For a long time, the image the public had had of a scientist was that of a pale, balding, bespectacled professor in a white laboratory coat. More than this, the scientist was different from the rest of us. He was thought to be logical, objective, dispassionate, and devoted to the pursuit of scientific truth— seemingly divorced from feelings, from emotions, and from moral and aesthetic values. Television changed this by making real scientists visible—exposing them as human beings like the rest of us: fallible, passionate, subjective, emotional, and morally concerned, but also concerned about fame and fortune. During the 1960s and 1970s, television converted certain scientists into celebrities—not because of their scientific achievements but because of their passionate, articulate advocacy of some cause. Paul Ehrlich, for example, an entomologist and an authority on butterflies, became a famous personality for his hyperbolic pronouncements on television talk shows about the population explosion. Linus Pauling, the recipient of a Nobel prize for his work on chemical bonds, became well-known to television viewers for his political activities promoting a nuclear weapons test ban and for his promotion of megadoses of vitamin C. Barry Commoner, a biologist, became a leading television environmentalist. William Shockley, another Nobel laureate (for inventing the transistor) became famous through the medium of television for his genetic views—specifically, his belief that blacks are genetically inferior to whites.

In news interviews, talk shows, and various TV specials, these visible scientists appeared as celebrity experts. Aggressively taking advantage of the medium, they helped to influence people and policy on such matters as pollution, overpopulation, genetics and IQ, nuclear power, and arms control. They were invited to serve on the boards of directors of various groups, used for all sorts of fund drives, and asked to appear at congressional hearings—giving added publicity to whatever hearings they attended.

TV Values Trivialize Science

Inevitably, these visible scientists became what someone has labeled "Anything Authorities"—experts whose credentials in one field are taken as valid for others: George Wald, the biologist, and Benjamin Spock, the pediatrician, became authorities on war and foreign policy while Linus Pauling, a chemist, became a psychologist: "For years, I have studied insanity. I saw the eyes of President Nixon on television and there is madness, paranoia." The anything authority always gets good reactions from the audience of television panel shows—whether cheers or boos did not matter—and he is never stuck for an answer ... on anything.[21] As scientists, they all had impeccable credentials in their respective fields, but when they turned to areas outside their expertise, they seldom seemed to apply the same standards of research and documentation they applied to their own discipline. Of course, there had always been scientists like this. But television now made them visible to a wider public. Moreover, people generalized and took them to be representative of the scientific community as a whole. In consequence, the credibility of scientists declined as they were revealed to be human, all too human, beings.

Television also trivialized their work. It did this in several ways. First, as a nondiscoursive medium, it subordinated scientific content to the personality of the scientist. After watching a science program, viewers usually remember little of the content but do recall that Dr.

Carl Sagan wore a turtleneck sweater, or that Dr. Jonathon Miller has a cultured British accent. Another thing television does is to present science in bits and pieces: brief snippets that leave out the context, the qualifications. This impoverished scientific information leaves people with a distorted understanding of the meaning, significance, and relevance of what scientists are up to. David Perlman, a science writer, describes how spectacular science news may typically reach the public:

> A major meeting takes place in a large city—a meeting say, on geophysics. A press conference is held at which scientists from Columbia University, the California Institute of Technology, and the U. S. Geological Survey discuss efforts at earthquake prediction. They explain a new theory of crystal dilation and describe how they and Soviet geophysicists have used such parameters as changes in strain gauges, changes in well-water levels, and changes in the radioisotope content of ground water to foretell earthquakes. They contend that a few quakes have been predicted—although not yet with precision as to time, magnitude, or exact epicenter—and that new analyses of old records before the 1971 San Fernando quake show how that devastating tremor might have been forecast.

> This press conference lasts, perhaps, an hour. Science writers for a handful of newspapers and the two wire services take notes, ask questions, and prepare to write articles that may run between a few hundred and a thousand [words]. Their deadlines will come in a very few hours, but some reporters will later write more reflective, interpretive, longer feature articles based on further interviews and fresh background reading.

> At the end of the conference, the television reporters will seek out the scientist whose explanations have seemed the most colorful and articulate, and ask him if he can please explain the whole matter in two or three minutes. The scientist, if he is adroit and cooperative, may take four or five minutes. On the six o'clock news that night, his explanation will be cut down to thirty seconds or a minute, with another minute for the TV reporter's summary, often rewritten from a press release prepared earlier by the public relations office of the scientist's institution.[22]

Television further trivializes science by its adherence to the doctrine of equal time in matters of scientific controversies. By presenting "balancing" opposing views—sometimes giving as much time to pseudo-science as to science—television does not enhance public understanding of the controversy but simply trivializes science by implying that one opinion is as good as another, or that verity can be established by balancing conflicting claims—hardly a scientific approach.

A further consequence of the personalization of science by television is increased commercialization of the field. Televised reports of scientific investigations usually take the form of race track terminology: a race, a competition, a victory. In 1975, for example, televised reports of the American Cancer Society's support of research on interferon focused on the hot competition among scientists for a solution. With the growth of "big science," conducted only by means of costly experiments far beyond the means of individual scientists, or the universities they work for, scientists have become engaged in competition with one another for public support of their research. This has led many scientists to pay a great deal of attention to public relations activities, most of which take place through the media, especially television. The American Institute of Physics (AIP), which was founded in 1935, expanded its publicity programs in the 1960s, running seminars for journalists and news conferences to summarize newsworthy developments in physics. The AIP now routinely issues press releases and provides instructions to physicists on how to deal with reporters. Universities use their own public relations agencies (public information offices) to publicize the work of their science faculty. Even government agencies engaged in costly technological developments play the same game. NASA, for example, has been described as a "public affairs office."[23] Individual scientists have also tried to use television to attract funds, or to establish their competitive position in "hot" fields of research. All this "grandstanding" on the public airways sometimes leads to promises and claims that cannot be fulfilled. Such television exposure of opportunistic, self-seeking scientists demeans not only them, but the entire community of scientists.

The commercialization of science, with its promise of fame, glory, and money, has also brought about an increase in the number of scientific frauds. Prior to 1960, there had been only seven cases of scientific fraud, four of them coming to light only in the 1960s. But from 1960 to 1981, there were nineteen cases of reported fraud in science. Public concern with these startling revelations promoted a congressional investigation by the House Committee on Science and Technology in late 1981. The most dramatic finding the committee came up with was the arrogance of the scientific community. Scientist after scientist gave testimony denying that a problem existed. Albert

Gore, who chaired the hearings, summarized the chagrin of his fellow congressmen—and the public—when he declared: "I cannot avoid the conclusion that one reason for the persistence of this type of problem is the reluctance of people high in the science field to take these matters very seriously."[24]

A few months later, yet another major instance of scientific fraud surfaced, this time at the Harvard Medical School, where a young cardiologist had forged one experiment and probably others as well. In a televised interview, a senior official at the National Institute of Health chided Harvard for the delay in reporting this incident of fraud.

Then there were the scientific failures, the most dramatic and tragic being the explosion of Challenger Ten—an event replayed over and over on television. The most ridiculed was the nonappearance of the highly heralded comet, Kahoutek, which became the butt of many television comedians. Scientists, of course, had failed before, but with the advent of television, their failures became more widely exposed.

How TV Created a Nonscientific Public

Since the 1960s, television has exposed scientists as self-aggrandizing know-it-alls, engaged in what are often trivial pursuits in a quest for fame and fortune—in short, scientists live lives not unlike those of the rest of us. Television has also exposed the prevalence of fraud in the scientific community, and relentlessly revealed scientific mistakes and errors. By showing us scientists' feet of clay, television has helped reduce their credibility and disestablished science as the religion of the United States. By 1980, Daniel Yankelovich found that the 30 percent who in 1970 believed "everything has a scientific explanation" had shrunk to 27 percent, and the 42 percent who said they had given up the belief that science would explain the mysteries of nature had increased to 48 percent.[25] Yet, the declining faith in science was not due solely to the exposure of scientists on television as fallible human beings. It also came about because television helped to demythicize science.

This sounds paradoxical, since, prior to the advent of television, most everyone thought that science had replaced myth; i.e., prescientific explanations were held to be mythological, while scientific explanations were held to be true. Prescientific explanations had imputed purpose and agency to the nonanimate world. Science had displaced this animism by explaining physical events as simply mechanical acts that follow discernable physical laws—laws that could be encoded in mathematical formulae and equations. (However much physics has, in our time, modified this mechanistic imagery of its classical period, the determinism of the Newtonian world view has continued to dominate the scientific view of nature.) Science disenchanted the world, reducing it to a purposeless, meaningless collection of events. Television helped people become critical of this scientific world view.

Here's how it happened.

Recall, first of all, that modern science is a human creation—a human creation that seeks to approximate physical reality. So we have two worlds, as it were: the real world (world one), and the world created by scientists (world three). There is also a world two: the world of human minds or human consciousness. Now, because it is a nondiscursive medium, television is not suitable for presenting science that consists of world three conjectures: conjectures made in language or in mathematical formulae. But television is an excellent medium for presenting world one: the actual, natural, or physical world. This is why most "science shows" on television are natural history shows: "Wild Kingdom," "The Wild, Wild World of Animals," "Natural Geographic Specials," and most "Nova" shows. Or they are shows about the stars ("Cosmos") or the oceans ("The Undersea World of Jacques Cousteau). On these shows, viewers directly perceive world one: The earth, the sky, the sea, flora and fauna, the cosmos, are all directly experienced through television. But whenever it attempts to deal with world three—the world of scientific problems and conjectures about world one—television usually personalizes them and winds up trivializing science, as happened, for example, on Public Television's "Newton's Apple," where some of the questions discussed were: "Are we alone in space?" "Why do people faint?" "Why do we get goose bumps?" "Is there any way to cut onions without crying?"

Television is a medium of color and sound, form and images, that enables viewers to view the universe (world one) in ways never possible before. Through the technology of television, people saw beneath the seas and beyond the clouds, they saw the interiors of volcanoes and observed minute bacteria, cells, and microorganisms. Through the technology of time-stop photography, they saw the growth of a flower and the breaking of waves on the shore. For the first time, millions saw birds, mammals, and insects close up and in living color, observing their daily conduct in their natural habitats. They saw the interior of the human body with all the organs fully displayed and actually functioning. They saw exotic locations of the globe they had never even known existed. In a sense, through television, people recaptured the experience of their prescientific ancestors by once again directly experiencing the wonder, the splendor, the grandeur, and the mystery of the universe—without the mediation of science or scientific explanations.

These televised presentations of world one enabled people to become critical—not of the world of nature, but of world three. More precisely, they became critical of science—that part of world three that claimed to describe and explain world one. The reductionist, mechanistic, picture of the universe that scientists had produced did not adequately describe the universe people witnessed on television. That experienced universe could not be reduced to mathematical formulae, could not be described in theories inscribed in books. Scientific explanations were too limited, too insufficient to capture the beauty and the grandeur of the universe television now revealed. Scientific explanations seemed paltry and trivial in contrast to the wonder and mystery, the awesomeness of the world, people experienced through television. Television then, helped people see that science had ignored the aesthetic and spiritual qualities of nature. More than this, television gave birth to, or rebirth to, those questions people had raised in the prescientific era. Television, once again, is an analogic medium that focuses on relationships. So, the so-called "science" programs on television evoked questions about the relationships between man and nature: What is the purpose of these goings-on in the universe? What do they mean for me and for the conduct of my life?

Modern science had swept these kinds of questions under the rug, dismissing them as irrelevant simply because science claims there is no purpose in the universe, that it has no meaning for us, and that it contains no messages telling us how to conduct our lives—except in the sense of power. A scientific understanding of the universe does give us power to carry out our projects, whatever they may be. But the universe does not tell us what we ought to do. Therefore, according to modern science, the correct relationship to nature is for human beings to be detached, dispassionate, objective. We should treat nature as alien to us. Only then will we be able to truly understand it.

In the age of television, when people could and did directly experience world one, the scientific outlook seemed barren—aesthetically diluted, spiritually impoverished, psychologically unsatisfying. The scientific outlook provides no insight into the meaning of things, no revelations about the place and purpose of human existence in the universe. It gives us no knowledge that can enhance our lives, no wisdom to broaden and deepen our human potential. Some people, therefore, concluded that science does not really provide knowledge of the nature of things. It is only a partial knowledge, only an inadequate approximation of true reality.

This criticism of the incompleteness of science gave birth to a heightened and widespread interest in the occult and the mystical, ushering in what has come to be called "The New Age."

According to Dr. José Arguelles, author of *The Mayan Factor*, the New Age began on 16-17 August 1987. At that time, the "human convergence" predicted by the Mayan calendar took place, marking the final twenty-five-year cycle of this planet. The return of harmonic convergence, Arguelles said, "is like an awakening from a cultural trance. It is the opportunity for all to engage in the Mayan Factor, and, in a word, to receive the galactic imprint."[26] According to other sources, however, the New Age had begun earlier, coincident with increased watching of television. *Time* magazine (19 June 1972) reported that "books on witchcraft, satanism, spirit phenomena, etc. had had steady but not spectacular sales until about 1965, when they began to skyrocket." The same article reports that Sybil Leek, ("America's most famous witch") made close to a million dollars from her writings after 1965. Since that time, psychics, mediums, and spiritualists, have appeared on TV shows like "Good Morning, America," "Donahue," and "Today." Television movies and specials have flooded the screen with information about spiritual awareness, heightened consciousness, spirit entities, and prophecies.

It is not just weirdos and wackos who make up this New Age movement. People from all walks of life participate in it: College educated people, people in responsible jobs, practicing professionals—all consult astrologers, use the *I Ching* and tarot cards, and carry crystals. They accept numerology, palmistry, graphology, and oracles. New Age businessmen credit their success to intuition (not science). New Age physicians tell us that the true healer lies within each of us.

In 1982, the magazine *Body, Mind, Spirit* first appeared; by 1988, it had over one half million readers. Presently, there are over twenty-five New Age magazines and newsletters published in the United States. In 1988, the 244-page *New Age Catalogue* appeared, listing the books, tapes, magazines, services, organizations, and companies available "to help you travel down your unique pathway to awareness."[27]

The New Age has reintroduced practices and beliefs not too long ago looked upon as ridiculous and laughable, beliefs and practices once thought to have been permanently dumped into the dustbin of superstition and ignorance. These include the following (all descriptions taken from the *New Age Catalogue*).

- Channeling: the communication of information to organisms thorough a physically embodied human being from a source that is said to exist on some other level or dimension of reality than the physical as we know it.
- Clear Quartz Crystals: reflect the pure white light that can be channeled into daily thoughts, feelings, words, and actions. They stimulate the finer, more subtle realms of our being, which can then be integrated and manipulated into our lives.
- Out-of-Body Experience: an event in which the experiencer seems to perceive some portion of some environment that could not possibly be perceived from where his physical body is known to be at the time, and knows at the time that he is not dreaming or fantasizing.
- Rebirthing: to remember and reexperience one's birth. Negative energy patterns held in the mind and body start to dissolve. "Youthing replaces aging and life becomes more fun. It is learning how to fill the physical body with divine energy on a practical, daily basis."
- Near Death Experiences: people who complete NDEs often completely transform, their spiritual values change, and they sometimes glimpse, during their other worldly experience, the fate of planet Earth.
- Reincarnation: the reason for reincarnation is to further the human evolution, specifically the evolution of the mind ... Through reincarnation, we develop our understanding of the universe and of our place in it. Our destiny is to become fully what we are now only potentially—centers of the authentic life, wisdom, and activity of the ground of all-being.
- Walk-Ins: high-minded entities from the spiritual plane who are permitted under certain conditions to take over the unwanted bodies of other human beings ... to help others along their spiritual path and to benefit all mankind.

- Holistic Healing: includes acupuncture, acupressure, biofeedback, body cleansing, flower essence therapy, herbology, macrobiotics, polarity therapy, reflexology, reike (the laying on of hands), rolfing (stringent muscular realignment therapy), yoga.
- Responsible Investing: investing only in those companies, countries, and industries that care for the earth and everything that lives on it.
- New Age Music: the power of sound to actually vibrate the body's psychic energy centers and transform our awareness. To awaken within us that spark of universal love and oneness with all that is.
- Visionary Art: works that include at least two distinctly unique paradigms of reality represented naturalistically and expressing an uplifting message—containing a spiritual content.
- New Age Gardening: communicating with the nature spirits (called Devas), working with them in creating and maintaining your garden, selecting what to grow, improving the soil, fertilizing, humanizing with seasonal and astrological cycles.

The focus of the New Age is on relationships: new, purposeful, meaningful relationships with nature, or more specifically, with the stars, with minerals, and with other beings living and dead—relationships all once proscribed, prohibited, or ridiculed by science. These new relationships are participatory rather than detached, holistic rather than analytical, and sacramental rather than secular. As the New Agers see it—with visionary insight, be it noted (not the reductionist view of the scientist)—the universe is something to be loved as a living presence, endowed with soul or mind. Here is David Spangler, one of the leading philosophers of the New Age:

> What is the New Age? The simplest answer for me is that it is the condition that emerges when I live life in a creative, empowering, compassionate manner. It manifests when I recognize and honor both the intrinsic wholeness of my world and the value and importance of everything within it. It arises when I honor each person, animal, plant, or object as unique, yet also as a part of myself, imbued with a spirit of personhood, sharing whatever worthiness and sacredness I claim for myself.[28]

Does the New Age mark an advancement in Western culture? Has knowledge improved? Have things become better? Or is it a retrogression to irrationality? In answering this, the first thing to note is the subjectivism that characterizes all New Age pronouncements.

Here's Paul Zieremoski, editor of *Body, Mind, Spirit* magazine: "What we perceive in this reality is just illusion created by each one of us for the grand and important purpose of learning."[29] Shirley MacLaine puts it more colloquially in her enormously popular book, *It's All in the Playing:* "The way I look at it, this is all my dream. I'm making all of it happen, good and bad—and I have the choice of how I'll relate to it and what I'll do about it. What is the lesson in this? Perhaps we are all telling the truth—our truth as we see it. Perhaps everyone has his own truth and truth as an objective reality doesn't exist.[30]

It is important to note that this New Age subjectivism is actually very much in keeping with the Copenhagen interpretation of quantum physics developed in the first half of the twentieth century by Niels Bohr and Werner Heisenberg. Quantum physics falsified determinism: The universe is not a machine such that if we know the laws of nature and the present or past state of the world we could predict every future event. Quantum physicists, in trying to understand particles, discovered that the light necessary to measure one interfered with the particle they were trying to measure. Therefore, it is not possible to make predictions about them: One could measure the position of a particle only by interfering with its motion, or one could measure its motion only by disturbing its position. According to the Copenhagen interpretation, we cannot observe a particle without disturbing it. From this, they concluded that we should then drop the idea that anything exists without our observing it. Here is how Werner Heisenberg put it: "The concept of objective reality ... has thus evaporated ... into the transparent clarity of mathematics that represents no longer the behavior of particles but rather our knowledge of their behavior." According to this interpretation, nothing is real and we cannot say anything about what things are doing when we are not looking at them: Nothing is real unless it is observed. The U.S. physicist, John Wheeler, has suggested that the whole universe may only owe its "real" existence to the fact that it is observed by an intelligent being.[31]

It can be argued, then, that the theories put forward by the New Agers are simply popularizations of the metaphysical theories subscribed to by a very influential group of quantum physicists. Michael Talbot has made this point in *Beyond the Quantum.*[32] So the New Age may indeed represent a popularization of the advancement of knowledge made in quantum physics: declaring that the determinist, mechanistic, reductionist world view of classical physics is inadequate to explain all there is in the universe.

The majority of scientists simply ignore these metaphysical or philosophical questions about truth and reality; they perceive theories as nothing but instruments or calculating devices. But instrumentalism provides no way to demarcate science from nonscience, so such scientists are deprived of any critical arguments against the claims that New Agers make about mystical relationships with the universe. For, if all theories are simply instruments, then if a New Ager's theory "works" for that New Ager, it is as acceptable as any so-called "scientific" theory.

Yet, there is a serious problem with the subjectivism of the New Age (and with the subjectivism of the Copenhagen interpretation of quantum physics). Subjectivism signals the end of any further advancement in knowledge. This is because, as Karl Popper has frequently pointed out, subjectivism makes criticism impossible: If all knowledge is subjective, then my "truth" is just as good as your "truth," and vice versa. But as I hope I have made clear in this book, knowledge advances through criticism. The logic of subjectivism, then, cuts off further progress in knowledge; knowledge cannot improve.

It may turn out, however, that the very excesses of the New Agers will expose the poverty of subjectivism, its untenability as a metaphysical foundation for knowledge. At the very least, then, the New Age may introduce a new period of critical discussion of the metaphysical theories of objectivity and subjectivity, realism and idealism, determinism and indeterminism—theories crucial to the continuation of our endless quest for ever-improved knowledge.[33]

Science and Human Dignity

The attack on science that burst forth in the 1960s was, at bottom, an attack on rationality—the hallmark of modern culture.[34] As I understand it, a rational culture is objective, egalitarian, competitive, and individualistic.

In the premodern era, culture was not rational. First of all, it was not objective. Premodern man had felt himself a part of nature simply because he was not able to objectify it. The coming of the printing press enabled people to look at nature objectively. Printed descriptions and explanations of natural phenomena allowed readers to distance themselves from such phenomena and to study them as disenchanted things and events, as the actions of objects that lacked agency. Nature became a world where goings-on were explained by rational laws. This rational understanding of the material world greatly enhanced man's power, as Bacon had said it would. Now man could predict and control much that happened in the world.

Understandably then, many moderns wanted to construct a rational human world, a world with the same predictable characteristics of the physical world, a world where human conduct and human relations would be rational. From Thomas Hobbes to B.F. Skinner, we find persistent efforts to construct a rational understanding of human beings by explaining conduct as a result of mechanical interactions with the environment. Human conduct, these moderns insisted, functioned in accordance with natural laws. Knowledge of these laws would enable us to predict and control human actions. Lacking such knowledge, it still remained possible to create rational machines that could do the physical and mental work of human beings, and that could do it more efficiently and more effectively. Yet, some who thought and wrote about such matters lamented that all these attempts to make the world more rational wound up affronting human dignity. For, when everything, including man, is viewed objectively, then the human being becomes a thing; he is no longer a free agent.

A rational world is not only objective, it is also equal. All entities, including human beings, are treated the same—they become abstract. Whether the scientist studies stars, atoms, societies, or human beings, he seeks not what is unique about each star or each atom, each society or each person; rather, he looks for what is common to all. Only by viewing all atoms equally—i.e., abstractly—can the scientist establish laws or theories that explain and predict their behavior. Likewise with the institutions and arrangements of the modern world. In the modern world, a rational organization is one that ignores the unique, personal qualities of all the individuals who make up the organization; it ignores the personal qualities of each person who interacts with it. The people who work in a rational organization become abstractions: clerks, machinists, stockmen, guards, secretaries, etc.—they become personnel. And the people who interact with the organization also become abstractions: suppliers, customers, clients, etc. Once viewed as abstractions, then all their actions can be ordered by means of specially constructed functional rules and regulations that insure the most efficient and efficacious attainment of the goals of the organization. So, when we say that this industry, or that institution, has been made rational, we mean, in the words of Mannheim, that it has been organized in such a way that "all actions become part of a series that leads to a previously defined goal, with every element in the series receiving a functional position and role."[35]

We usually call such a rational organization a bureaucracy. In a bureaucracy, everyone is treated fairly, which means that they are treated equally, in accordance with established rules. This means that everyone is treated as an abstraction. So, with rational organization everyone assumes a role. Those who play the same role—clerk, secretary, guard, whatever—have the same goals and are expected to behave more or less the same way, i.e., in accordance with the rational rules designed to attain the goals of the organization. In schools, people assume the role of teacher, student, or administrator; in a hospital, people become physicians, nurses, or patients. People also play roles as lawyers and clients, judges and jurors. When people assume these roles, others treat them the same as other people who are playing the same roles. Personhood disappears.

So, a rational world, one that treats people objectively and equally, ends up denying them agency and personhood. Nor is this all. In a rational world, people become uncertain and anxious about how they will be treated, how other people will relate to them. In the premodern world, when people were firmly ensconced in a caste, a class, or an estate, they were always treated the same in all situations. If one were royalty, for example, then one was always treated as royalty; if one were born a serf, then one was always treated as a serf. But, in the modern world, this hierarchical structure no longer exists. Now everyone is treated equally, which means that each is treated in accordance with the role he has assumed in any given situation: a customer, a student, a client, a patient, a salesperson, a teacher, a lawyer, a physician. But everyone plays many different roles, daily, which means that not only must each person continually shift roles but each must continually see to it that he or she is treated fairly or equally in the competition with others playing the same role in this endless quest for goods and services dispensed by modern organizations. Thus, the secretary who is waiting in line as a customer at the delicatessen, must see to it that she is treated the same as the physician who is also standing in line as a customer. In this rational world, people continually engage in competition with others. This is in sharp contrast to the premodern hierarchical world where rank always had its privileges and thereby established a more secure, stable, set of relationships among people.

Finally, in the modern world, each individual's fate and fortune depends primarily upon himself. In the more collective organization of the premodern world, the group, the tribe, or all those living together on the manor, cooperated in solving the elemental problems of survival. Securing an adequate supply of food and adequate shelter was a communal project. The entertainment and recreational activities were communal, too. But in the modern world, each person is pretty much on his own. Each individual must plan and organize his own activities in order to survive and flourish. Everyone is isolated.

TV Restores Value ... and Moral Criticism

Clearly then, the rational modern world was not perfect. The relationships that existed among people were inadequate—some said immoral: The relationships demeaned human dignity. In the rational world human beings had created, people were treated as things, as mechanical robots, as depersonalized entities who lacked agency. And in the rational world, each person was isolated and alone, locked in competition with others for the goods and services they needed and sought.

Some keen observers of the human condition during the first half of the twentieth century had pointed out these discontents and evils of the modern world. But, once again, few, save intellectuals, read these depressing books, and most people seemed oblivious to the moral inadequacies of the abstract society in which they lived and died. With the coming of television, however, that abstract society could be encoded on the screen, giving everyone, for the first time, the distance that allowed them to become critical of it. And critical they became. As Peter Berger reminds us, the 1960s produced widespread complaints about depersonalization, authoritarianism, the competitive "rat race," powerlessness, alienation, and isolation. People, especially young people, were suddenly antihypocrisy, antisuperficiality, antiplanning, antiorganization, antiorder. In sum, they were against the system—the abstract system that denied them their humanity.[36]

In tracing this increased awareness in the popular consciousness of the moral evils of abstract society to television, we can begin with the sitcoms, the westerns, and the quiz shows that dominated television during the late 1950s and early 1960s.

The vapid and innocuous sitcoms of the late 1950s ("I Love Lucy," "My Little Margie") presented weekly episodes built upon lies and hypocrisy. If Ricky Ricardo or Vern Albright brought an Important Person home to dinner, everyone in the family would lie about life styles, wealth, or tastes. Lucy would lie about buying a new dress or burning the roast. To critical young viewers, domestic life, as presented, was full of pretense and sham. While adults seemed to accept the TV portrayal of relations between husband and wife, worker and employee, parents and children, many young viewers became critical of those relationships.

But even adults were morally shocked when the quiz show scandals exploded. Indeed, nothing on television has ever shocked the moral sensibilities of viewers as much as the quiz show scandals of the 1959-60 season.

It began back in 1955, when CBS upped the ante of the old radio show called "The $64 Question," producing the first prime-time television big money game show, "The $64,000 Question." The show became an instant hit, spinning off "The $64,000 Challenge" (for alumni who had won on "Question") while the other networks launched imitations, like "Twenty-One," "Dotto," and "Break the $250,000 Bank." On NBC's "Twenty-One" during the 1956-57 season, a thirty-year-old Columbia University English instructor, Charles Van Doren, became a national celebrity—a "shining" example of American intellect and youth who gained the affection and esteem of millions throughout the nation as week after week he stood in the "isolation booth" frowning, mopping his brow, and chewing his lip as he answered questions for money that finally reached the unbelievable sum of $143,000. Millions tuned in, making "Twenty-One" the first regular series to beat "I Love Lucy" in its time slot. In February, Van Doren was on the cover of *Time*.[37]

By 1958, quiz shows had become a staple of TV, with networks producing additional shows, like "Top Dollar," "Name that Tune," "Tic Tac Dough," "Dough Re Me," and "Concentration." Suddenly, in August, Colgate cancelled "Dotto"; a few days later, the New York

City district attorney's office announced that it was beginning an investigation of possible rigging of the show. Two weeks later, one of the former contestants on "Twenty-One" charged that the producers had supplied him with answers during his reign as champion and that after he had been on top for four weeks (winning $49,000) they told him to "take a dive" in the match with Charles Van Doren in December 1956. Van Doren, who was guest hosting the "Today" show at the time, issued an on-the-air denial: "I am sad and shocked.... It's enough to shake your faith in human nature.... I myself was never given any answers or told any questions beforehand, and, as far as I know, none of the other contestants received any coaching of this sort." The producers of "Twenty-One" called the charges of rigging "utterly baseless and untrue."[38]

By the following month, however, contrite contestants and producers of all the big money shows confessed that contestants had been supplied the correct answers. By mid-October, the networks had cancelled "Dotto," "Twenty-One," and "The $64,000 Question." The case then went to a grand jury, who, after deliberating for a year, issued a "presentment"—a report calling attention to illegal acts without holding specific people responsible. The inconclusive investigation prompted congressional public hearings conducted by the House Committee on Interstate and Foreign Commerce. In November 1959, Charles Van Doren, who was now a regular "Today Show" staff member, appeared before the committee to confess that he had been living a lie since 1956. He admitted that the producer of "Twenty-One" had coached him in both answers and demeanor, instructing him "how to answer the questions, to pause before certain of the answers, to skip certain parts and return to them, to hesitate to build up suspense, and so forth.... He gave me a script to memorize and, before the program, he took back the script and rehearsed me in my part."[39]

The public was shocked. Van Doren had not only cheated, he had been playing a role. Viewers felt betrayed. President Eisenhower, during a televised news conference, called it a latter-day equivalent to the 1919 Black Sox World Series scandal. Perhaps the most dismaying comment came from the creator of "Twenty-One" when he appeared before the congressional committee: "Deception is not necessarily bad," he explained. "It's practiced in everyday life."[40] The TV quiz show scandals made many people wonder if modern society was inherently corrupt.

Then there were the westerns.

In television westerns like "Maverick," "Have Gun Will Travel," and "The Rebel," viewers saw a version of the nineteenth-century cowboy they could resonate to: the outsider. Weekly, each of these shows demonstrated that when the west was young, the existing legal system could not insure that justice would be done. In fact, justice could be had only when a committed, dedicated, strong believer in justice—a Maverick, a rebel, a Paladin—went around the system, or through it, or over it.

The TV western was not a new genre of entertainment. Printed fiction and Hollywood films contained a long tradition of the hero as outsider. The outsider actually embodied all the values of the modern world, which is why people admired him. The outsider was a true individual, an egalitarian who treated all men fairly. He was a competitor who saw the world as it is: objectively. The question these TV westerns raised, therefore, was: Could justice be secured in the modern world? Children, who were, of course, confronting the outsider for the first time—and in a profusion of shows—became skeptical about the contemporary "system." But most adults—who had encountered the outsider before—simply found the shows entertaining. They believed that the existing system was an acceptable moral order.

Most dramatic shows of the early 1960s supported the notion that we lived in a moral society. The common theme permeating many of the dramatic shows of the early 1960s was socialization of the idealistic young rebel. It was usually an older, wiser colleague who worked to help the young neophyte to understand and accept the traditional arrangements. On "The Defenders," a young defense attorney was initiated into the legal system by a wise and understanding father. On "Dr. Kildare," an impetuous, idealistic intern, who put principle before tradition, was counseled by an older mentor, Dr. Gillespie, who weekly preached patience and understanding. On "Ben Casey," viewers saw a more rugged, unbuttoned character than Kildare, a young physician more angry with the system, but one who was also guided by a mentor into an understanding and appreciation of existing medical arrangements. "The Nurses" had the same format: continual socialization of an idealistic student nurse by a crusty, but understanding, older guide. In the field of education, there was Mr. Novak, a young teacher who was the Dr. Kildare of the classroom, while Dean Jagger played his Dr. Gillespie. All these shows dealt with real problems—on the medical shows, for example, there were cases of syphilis, thalidomide babies, drug abuse, abortion, and teenage pregnancy. But these problems were always dealt with, in the end, according to the rules. And the story line always, in the end, endorsed the wisdom and rightness of the traditional, established arrangements.

Yet, by raising these issues and presenting them in dramatic form on the screen, television allowed many people to begin to question the moral rightness of the established order. The system of relationships embedded in existing institutions was not perfect, most everyone would admit, even though everyone was expected to adjust to and accept those relationships. The first television generation became increasingly critical and restless.

Youth Revolts

The initial outburst of criticism from the young began in the universities. Earlier, we saw that the university and college students of the 1960s led the wave of public-spirited protest against racism and the Vietnam War. But there was another target of student protest: the university itself. More than any institution in the culture, the university had come to stand for abstract society—society that denied one's human dignity. Since World War II, universities had grown enormous. Whereas only one-third of U.S. high school graduates went to college in 1940, almost half were entering college by the mid-1960s. Moreover, as a result of the "baby boom" after the war, there were, in absolute numbers, more youth of college age in the 1960s than there ever had been in U.S. history. At the beginning of World War II, in 1940, the nation's colleges and universities enrolled 1,494,000 students and employed 110,885 faculty. By 1960, this had risen to 3,583,000 students and 281,506 faculty.

To cope with this unprecedented growth, colleges and universities became rationalized: they hired more administrators and administrative staff to handle admissions, registration, record keeping, financial aid, housing, classroom space, and student advisement. In this complex bureaucracy, students attended large classes (some as large as a thousand students) and had little or no personal contact with their professors. As their numbers increased, the faculty became more and more specialized, which resulted in the creation of new departments of instruction. Yet, as specialists, more and more faculty members, by choice or through pressure, found themselves doing research rather than teaching. Moreover, since new and valid knowledge was necessary in devising foreign and domestic policy, in securing technical and industrial advancement, and in analyzing basic economic and social trends, faculty members in certain fields and in the prestigious universities found themselves in demand as consultants to government, to foundations, and to private industry.

In keeping pace with social and economic changes in society, the university served many different functions. It was, in Clark Kerr's memorable label, "a multiversity." Yet, the multiversity had one critical purpose: the production and transmission of knowledge. "Knowledge," Kerr wrote,

> has certainly never in history been so central to the conduct of an entire society.... What the railroads did for the second half of the twentieth century and the automobile for the first half of this century may be done for the second half of this century by the knowledge industry: that is, to serve as the focal point for national growth. And the university is at the center of the knowledge process.[41]

When the students looked at the multiversities, they saw them as "knowledge factories" that, like most factories, affronted the human dignity of those who labored there. Jerry Farber, a professor at California State University, explained the reality of the students' relations to the faculty in his widely reprinted pamphlet, "Student as Nigger."

> Students are niggers. When you get that straight, our schools begin to make sense. It's more important, though, to understand why they're niggers. If we follow that question seriously enough, it will lead us past the zone of academic red tape, where dedicated teachers pass their knowledge on to a new generation, and into the nitty-gritty of human needs and hang-ups. And from there we can go on to consider whether it might ever be possible for students to come up from slavery.

> First let's see what's happening now. Let's look at the role students play in what we like to call education.

> At Cal State, L.A., where I teach, the students have separate and unequal dining facilities. If I take them into the faculty dining room, my colleagues

get uncomfortable, as though there were a bad smell. If I eat in the student cafeteria, I become known as the educational equivalent of a nigger lover. In at least one building, there are even restrooms which students may not use.

Students at Cal State are politically disenfranchised. They are in an academic Lowndes County. Most of them can vote in national elections—their average age is about twenty-six—but they have no voice in decisions which affect their academic lives. The students are, it is true, allowed to have a toy government of their own. It is a government run for the most part by Uncle Toms and concerned principally with trivia. The faculty and administrators decide what courses will be offered; the students get to choose their homecoming queen. Occasionally, when student leaders get uppity and rebellious, they're either ignored, put off with trivial concessions, or maneuvered expertly out of position.

A student at Cal State is expected to know his place. He calls a faculty member "Sir" or "Doctor" or "Professor," and he smiles and shuffles some as he stands outside the professor's office waiting for permission to enter. The faculty tell him what courses to take (in my department, English, even electives have to be approved by a faculty member); they tell him what to read, what to write, and, frequently, where to set the margins of his typewriter. They tell him what's true and what isn't. Some teachers insist that they encourage dissent, but they're almost always jiving, and every student knows it. Tell the man what he wants to hear or he'll fail you out of the course.

When a teacher says "jump," students jump. I know of one professor who refused to take up class time for exams and required students to show up for tests at 6:30 A.M. And they did! Another, at exam time, provides answer cards to be filled out—each one enclosed in a paper bag with a hole cut in the top to see through. Students stick their writing hands in the bags while taking the test. The teacher isn't a provo; I wish he were. He does it to prevent cheating. Another colleague once caught a student reading during one of his lectures and threw her book against the wall. Still another lectures his students into a stupor and then screams at them in a rage when they fall asleep.

Just last week, during the first meeting of a class, one girl got up to leave after about ten minutes had gone by. The teacher rushed over, grabbed her by the arm, saying, "This class is NOT dismissed," and led her back to her seat. On the same day, another teacher began informing his class that he does not like beards, mustaches, long hair on boys, or Capri pants on girls, and will not tolerate any of that in his class. That class, incidentally, consisted mostly of high school teachers.

As students saw it, the policies and practices of the universities helped reproduce the "system." Like the rest of the educational establishment, the university socialized the young to the system, socialized them to accept the existing network of relationships. In the system, everyone played a role—lawyers, doctors, teachers, policemen, nurses, salesmen, secretaries, and factory workers. All were imprisoned by the roles the system imposed on them, enclosed by the relationships prescribed and proscribed by their occupations. Had not the young witnessed the imposed relationships in television shows like "Dr. Kildare," "The Doctors," "Medic," "The Defenders," "Perry Mason," "Our Miss Brooks," "Mr. Peepers," "Dragnet," "Naked City," "The Nurses," and "The Ann Southern Show"? The role constraints of every occupation, it seemed to the young, made people's lives sterile, empty of experience. Everyone had to be mechanical, never expressing their own feelings, doing only what was dictated by the functional requirements of the job. Not only work time but all of life seemed to be prescribed by the system.

Yet, as the students realized, the universities demeaned the human dignity of students not by design, not through malevolence, mean spiritedness, or even mindlessness. No, universities demeaned students by their rationality. Universities treated all equally, which meant that everyone was treated the same, i.e., as an abstraction: a student. Universities treated everyone objectively, i.e., as an object— an IBM card, a number. They treated everyone fairly, i.e., in accord with his or her merits—which meant that all students engaged in endless competition with one another: They competed for admission to the university, they competed for scholarships, they competed to register for courses, they competed to get the attention of the professor, they competed for grades, they competed to graduate. (For males, competition became even more anxiety-producing during the Vietnam War, when failure or low class standing could result in being drafted into the army.) Finally, and perhaps most important, the rational university treated each student as an individual (although not as a person). This meant that each student was isolated, alone, unaware of the depth of discontent the university caused in all students through the competition each had to engage in, and the objective and equal treatment each experienced.

This isolation of students becomes clear from a sociological survey taken of Berkeley students in November 1964, two months after the birth of the Free Speech Movement (FSM) there. Launched to secure students the right to engage in political activity, the FSM in early October had dramatically confronted the police by holding a police car in captivity. For thirty-two hours, radical students had stood atop the car and lectured hundreds of students on the rights of free speech. That sociological survey taken of students in November reported that 82 percent of Berkeley students were "satisfied" or "very satisfied" with "courses, examinations, professors, etc." while 92 percent agreed that "although some people do not think so, the president of the university (Clark Kerr) and the chancellor are really trying very hard to provide top quality educational experiences for students here."[42] Within a few weeks, however, great numbers of students became "radicalized"—they became severely critical of the university and its president. In the very act of becoming radicalized, students discovered a commonly shared deep dissatisfaction among their fellow students— a dissatisfaction few had previously recognized. They suddenly realized they no longer believed in the official beliefs they had thought they believed in; and most surprisingly, they found that thousand of others shared their disbeliefs.[43]

What had radicalized the students? It is true that Berkeley had the largest undergraduate student body of any institution in the country, and was one of the most bureaucratized universities in the world, so one might expect student dissatisfaction to begin on this campus. Yet, until the end of November, the Free Speech Movement (FSM) was largely ignored by most students, who saw it as a political battle between radical students and a harried administration. Most students had shrugged off the many printed broadsides put out by FSM that urged them to "begin an open, fierce, and thorough-going rebellion on this campus," and they had disregarded printed demands "to bring the university to a grinding halt."[44] But on 2 December, Mario Savio, the student leader of FSM, recruited a thousand students to sit in Sproul Hall, the Administration Building on the Berkeley campus. The students joined the sit-in largely as a result of Savio's dramatic plea, broadcast by television cameras called to the scene:

> There is a time when the operation of the machine becomes so odious, makes you so sick at heart that you can't take part; you can't even tacitly take part, and you've got to put your bodies upon the gears and upon the wheels, upon the levers, upon all the apparatus and you've got to make it stop. And you've got to indicate to the people who run it, to the people

who own it, that unless you're free, the machines will be prevented from working at all.[45]

The following morning, at 3:45 A.M., 635 police, sent by Governor Brown with the concurrence of the university administration, physically, and often violently, removed the students. Televised reports of the police bust on their campus and arrest of 814 people radicalized Berkeley students. It made them see that, yes, the university was a machine that denied the human dignity of the students. Television exposed the university as an instrument of oppression. Clark Kerr's elegant, but bureaucratic, televised explanation of the police bust merely confirmed student criticism of the administration.

> The university is an institution whose primary obligation is to educate its students. It has shown patience. This patience has been met with impatience and with violation of the law. The university has shown tolerance. This tolerance has been met with intolerance and distortion of the truth. The university has shown reasonableness. This reasonableness has been met with irrationality and intransigence. The university has shown decency. This decency has been met with indecency and ill-will. When patience and tolerance and reasonableness and decency have been tried, yet democratic processes continue to be forsaken by the FSM in favor of anarchy, then the process of law enforcement takes over.[46]

Television helped radicalize students by presenting the university as a system that cared little about the human dignity of students. On 3 December, the students of Berkeley went on strike.

The strike lasted less than a month and brought about the creation of the Select Committee on Education at Berkeley to make recommendations for restructuring the university. Meanwhile, the nationally televised happenings at Berkeley raised questions in the minds of many students on other campuses about their own universities and colleges. Soon, they too, began to criticize existing arrangements. They criticized them orally—preferably for television reporters—and they criticized them through action: protest demonstrations, marches, sit-ins, and strikes. They criticized the parietal rules the universities imposed on them, and they rejected the very notion of it acting *in loco parentis.* They criticized the departmentalization of subject matter because it fractured knowledge and isolated teachers and students. They denounced the combative competition that informed all aspects of their entire university career. They even criticized the architectural design and decoration of university classrooms. ("All surfaces are hard, paint is tough and nonchip. Academic spaces are designed to turn over their occupants six times daily or once a semester and leave no trace.")[47]

Students also criticized those teaching methods that treated them like products on an assembly line. They objected to the lecture method of instruction, not only because of the size of classes it allowed, but because it cast the professor into the role of an authority figure. They demanded the right to evaluate their courses and their professors. They criticized the universities for not being a community, for not including students in educational planning, in curriculum development, and in the hiring of faculty.

While on some campuses these demands for increased student power emerged spontaneously, in most cases they were sparked by some external struggle, such as civil rights or the Vietnam War. The logic of the situation usually went like this. These external protests, usually sponsored by a small group of radicals like an SDS chapter, inevitably brought about a negative reaction from university authorities: restrictions and restraints that often took the form of a "police bust." The ever-present television cameras recorded the confrontations and in all cases the university stood exposed as a repressive institution. Once they saw their university in this light—the light of television—students became critically conscious that the university system was morally wrong in failing to respect them as human beings. On many campuses, student pickets carried signs declaring: "I am a human being. Do not fold, spindle or mutilate." During the student strike at Harvard in 1968, a student poster was plastered all over the campus that said:

STRIKE FOR THE EIGHT DEMANDS STRIKE BECAUSE YOU HATE COPS STRIKE BECAUSE YOUR ROOMMATE WAS CLUBBED STRIKE TO STOP EXPANSION STRIKE TO SEIZE CONTROL OF YOUR LIFE STRIKE TO BECOME MORE HUMAN STRIKE BECAUSE THERE'S NO POETRY IN YOUR LECTURES STRIKE BECAUSE CLASSES ARE A BORE STRIKE FOR POWER STRIKE TO MAKE YOURSELF FREE STRIKE TO ABOLISH ROTC STRIKE BECAUSE THEY ARE TRYING TO SQUEEZE THE LIFE OUT OF YOU STRIKE.[48]

The spontaneity, force, and anger of the student protesters revealed a substantial substratum of discontent with the university that the external issues simply unleashed. Moreover, once they became conscious of the reality of their situation, aware of the unfair relationships the university subjected them to, many students decided that they did not want to be students any more—they dropped out. By 1967, tens of thousand of young people flowed off the campuses and out of the suburbs to converge on cities like San Francisco and New York to form city-sized communities of their own. Tearing themselves out of the system, they became, as Bob Dylan put it, like a rolling stone: "How does it feel to be on your own, with no direction home, a complete unknown, like a rolling stone?"

These "drop outs" grew shoulder-length hair, put on beads and granny glasses, grooved on rock music and drugs, and created a youth culture—the very antithesis of university culture, a counterculture. Only a small percentage of college students actually dropped out of college, but almost all college students joined the cultural revolution and adopted, in whole or in part, the new attitudes, beliefs, values, and styles that the revolution had created. The counterculture had its own music, art, language, clothing, and life styles. More importantly, it rejected existing societal ideas about family, work, careers, religion, and authority. In place of hard work, deferred gratification, achievement, and material possessions that the mainstream culture valued, the counterculture prized sensual experiences, immediate gratification, and unrestrained naturalism.

In his book, *Revolution for the Hell of It*, Abbie Hoffman, one of the founding fathers of the counterculture, reprinted a pamphlet called "Fuck the System." This guide for ripping off the system had been the manual used by dropouts in New York's East Village, telling them how to get free food, clothing, transportation, medical care, and entertainment. "What would happen," Hoffman asked,

> if large numbers of people in the country started getting together, forming communities, hustling free fish on Fulton Street, and passing out brass washers to use in the laundromats and phones? What if people living in slums started moving into abandoned buildings and refusing to move [out] even to the point of defending them[selves] with guns? What if this movement grew and busy salesmen sweating under the collar on a hot summer day decided to say "fuck the system" and headed for welfare?

What if secretaries got tired of typing memos to the boss's girlfriend in triplicate and took to panhandling in the streets? What if when they called a war, no one went? What if people who wanted to get educated just went to a college classroom and sat-in without paying and without caring about a degree? Well, you know what? We'd have ourselves one hell of a revolution, that's what. Who would do the work? Fuck it. There's always some schmuck like Spiro Agnew lying around. Let him pick up the garbage if he's worried about the smell. We'll build a special zoo for people like that and every weekend we'll take the kiddies over to Queens to watch them work.[49]

What the counterculture did, of course, was to reintroduce the tribalism that modern rational society had abandoned. In place of the isolation and combative competition endemic in the university and the society it served, the counterculture stood for communal or collective living and cooperation. Here's how Charles Reich put it: The counterculture (he called it Consciousness III)

does not believe in the antagonistic or competitive doctrine of life.... They do not measure others, they do not see others as something to struggle against. People are brothers, the world is ample for all.... In place of the world seen as a jungle with every man for himself or the world seen as a meritocracy leading to a great corporate hierarchy of rigidly drawn relations and maneuvers for position, the world is a community. People all belong to the same family, whether they have met one another or not. It is as simple as that.[50]

The counterculture also rejected objectivity, which, as we saw, results in human beings being treated as objects. Insisting that human beings are agents, autonomous selves, the counterculture demanded respect for everyone's subjective feelings, beliefs, values, attitudes, and understandings. Here are two bits of advice from Abbie Hoffman:

Trust your impulses. Trust your impulses. TRUST- TRUST—TRUST— TRUST—TRUST—TRUST—TRUST -TRUST—TRUST—TRUST
   Test
      Test
         Test
            Relax

Revolution is in your head. You are the Revolution.
Do your thing.
Do your thing.

Do your thing.
Do your thing.
Do your thing.
Do your thing.[51]

Finally, in addition to reintroducing the tribal values of cooperation, collectivism, and subjectivity, the counterculture also restored hierarchy, which took the form of a new moral elitism. Those in the counterculture believed that they were unequivocally morally correct—just as did the new left, the civil rights activists, the Vietnam protesters, and the feminists. And, like all these other groups, the counterculturists viewed those who disagreed with them as being morally depraved.

Concerned that the relationships common in the society were false and hypocritical, members of the counterculture prided themselves on their honesty. Honesty, the expression of one's true feelings, they claimed, should be the basis for all relationships. The television shows they had watched while growing up had exposed the falsity and inadequacy of all the contractual relationships of modern society. They decried the "artificial bonds" of duty, obligation, law, oaths, and promises. The relationships they sought with others were based on love and friendship, not contractual arrangements. The Beatles put this moral elitism to music: "All you need is love."

Not rationality, but emotions, they insisted, were the basic characteristics of human beings. Feelings, not intellect, should be the basis for all human relations, they claimed. Thus was set afoot the widespread efforts among the young, and among their epigones, to "get in touch with their feelings," and the quest for relationships that would be intimate, trusting, and candid. These searches often took place in therapy or encounter sessions in "Growth Centers" that sprang up in the 1960s from Bethel, Maine to La Jolla, California. These included the Esalen Institute (Big Sur, California), The Center for the Whole Person (Philadelphia), GROW (New York), The Explorations Institute (Berkeley), and The Athena Center for Creative Living (with intimacy labs in Mexico and Aliquippa, Pennsylvania). Jane Howard, who wrote a popular account of this "human potential" movement in 1970, listed eighty-four such growth centers and kindred establishments—forty-four of them in California. It wasn't just kooks and weirdos who wanted to get in touch with their feelings—Howard lists forty different U.S. corporations that conducted various forms of group therapy sessions for their personnel.

The central assumption of the human potential movement was that thinking is bad—it creates stress, anxiety, hypertension, coronary disease, alienation, etc. If we stop thinking and start feeling, things will get better. Howard reports that in one of the groups she attended, a school teacher who declared "I think this is a lot of crap!" was reprimanded with the words: "Don't say think; say feel." She also tells about a girl named Elaine who was criticized in one of the therapy sessions: "There's Elaine over in her corner, thinking again. That thinking! It'll get you in trouble every time."[52]

Different therapists adopted various techniques to discourage "intellectualizing." In "Mind Control," one is taught to minimize the beta brain waves normally associated with active thought. In "Rolfing," one is massaged; in "Scream Therapy," one screams disorders away; at Esalen, one engaged in free-for-all physical combat in a variety of exercises.

Like most everything connected with the counterculture, the human potential movement encouraged irrationalism. Yet, it did make things better insofar as it increased awareness of the emotional relationships among people that the abstract society had ignored or had tried to suppress.

The students' countercultural criticism of the arrangements in higher education had a dramatic impact on university operations, radically transforming them in less than five years. The student uprisings toppled university presidents from Berkeley and Stanford to Columbia and Harvard. Throughout academia, universities and colleges eliminated the unfair and demeaning relationships between faculty and students and between administrators and students. Almost all institutions of higher learning abandoned the doctrine of *in loco parentis*, and everywhere students experienced greater freedom in their personal behavior—particularly with respect to sexual activity. Coeducational dormitories became common. Health services distributed contraceptives. (It is hard to believe that in 1968, a few weeks before the Columbia uprising, a girl was suspended from Barnard, the women's college associated with Columbia, for surreptitiously living off-campus with her boyfriend.)

Schools suspended college rituals. Class jewelry, proms, fraternities, and sororities all lost their appeal. For the first time in their history, fraternities declined in both membership and prestige. Student government seemed unnecessary, especially since students now were members of university and college senates, committees, councils, and commissions that exercised governance. Students now became part of all disciplinary committees, and all student discipline took place with careful attention to due process. Students now served on the selection committees that hired faculty and university presidents. Many schools dropped course requirements in fields like mathematics and foreign languages. New, more relevant courses and programs emerged, including black and other ethnic studies programs and women's studies and family or sex-role studies.

The students' freedom to create their own curriculum, to move through it at their own pace, and to do so with greater autonomy, all profoundly changed. A 1972 survey of academic deans in 115 select colleges and universities showed that

> three-fourths of these institutions permitted students to plan their courses of study and define their major. Eighty-three percent of the colleges granted credit for individual work or study away from the campus.... Three-fifths of these selective colleges allow students to initiate new courses. More significantly, 28 percent permitted undergraduates to conduct these courses for credit.[53]

Professors continued to grade students but they now inflated the grades: Until 1965, only 10 percent of students graduated with honors; by 1970, 16 percent of the class graduated with honors; 19 percent of the 1971 graduates, 23.5 percent of the 1972 class, and, in 1973, 27 percent.[54] At the same time, it became commonplace for students to evaluate the courses they took and the professors who taught them.

Because of the military deferment such a choice allowed, many male college graduates chose to become teachers during the Vietnam War. Here, they led a similar educational revolution against the authoritarian relationships that prevailed in most elementary and secondary schools. They criticized the irrelevant curriculum, the authoritarian teaching methods, and the lethal atmosphere in most classrooms and schools. In many instances, they succeeded in introducing new, relevant courses and expanded the freedom of the students to decide what was worth knowing. Their "thrust" was to make the educational engagement more student-centered, and to this end, they introduced new methods of instruction: the inquiry method, the discovery method, and the "open" classroom, where students "messed about" with objects and stuff that provoked their natural curiosity. In some school systems, they succeeded in establishing "alternative" schools where they could experiment with these innovative educational schemes. In some cases, they set up "free" schools—private schools unconnected to the established schools of the system.

The youthful critics of the abstract society succeeded in changing more than the educational institutions. By the early 1970s, pollsters like Daniel Yankelovich found that the unorthodox values "formerly confined to a minority of college youth" had achieved "an astonishingly swift transmission" to noncollege youth and had "now spread throughout the generation.... The enduring heritage of the 1960s," Yankelovich wrote, "is the new social values that grew on the nation's campuses during the same fateful period and now have grown stronger and more powerful."[55]

By the mid-1970s, sexual customs, practices and even laws had changed with regard to premarital sex, abortion, divorce, homosexuality, and extramarital relations. Changed, too, was adherence to the work ethic: People now talked about self-fulfillment rather than economic security. With old roles shattered and abandoned, gender differences faded as men and women wore similar clothes (unisex) and used the same language. Interpersonal relations became more casual and informal. Husbands now performed tasks— cooking, cleaning, tending to children—previously fit only for wives; many wives worked from nine to five. Children became more like adults in dress and style; they were seen everywhere and heard by everyone; the notion of "a child's place" had disappeared. The relations between worker and employer, doctor and patient, lawyer and client, teacher and student, all underwent dramatic change.

Television and Moral Backlash

Television encoded these cultural changes in relationships in the new shows that began to appear in the late 1960s and early 1970s— encoded them for all to see and become critical of. The initial indications of cultural change came in the comedy shows, which became increasingly satirical, ridiculing traditionally accepted relationships. Political relationships became the first target when, during the election year of 1964, "That Was the Week That Was" poked fun at candidates Goldwater and Johnson in irreverent, topical skits. President Johnson's infamous beagle episode (when LBJ lifted one of his pet dogs by its ears) inspired a send up featuring hand puppet HBJ (Him Beagle Johnson) being snatched by giant presidential hands before it could reveal LBJ's choice for his vice-presidential running mate.

The following year, the relationship between the good guys and the bad guys became the object of a new kind of satire in the camp adventures of "Batman." Staged as a television comic book with all the comic book elements grossly exaggerated, the program became a huge tongue-in-cheek joke. The words "POW!" "SMASH!" and "CRUNCH!" appeared on the screen during every fight scene. Batman, "The World's Greatest Detective," and Robin, "The Boy Wonder," were caricatures of gung-ho, positive-thinking, very serious crime fighters. But the characters were so naive they became preposterous. As a parody of kiddie shows, these vapid and hokey crime fighters were good fun. But the show did make a mockery of good citizenship. The battle between good and evil was depicted as silly, and the criminals were made appealing while the good guys appeared to be nerds and the police dummies.

Another tongue-in-cheek comedy show that lampooned the system was "Get Smart," a parody of the CIA that starred Maxwell Smart as Secret Agent 86, a bumbling idiot who continually fouled up ("Sorry about that, chief"). The military came in for ridicule in "F Troop," a comedy farce set in the post-Civil War period that ridiculed traditional military values and relationships by showing that both the Indians and the men of F Troop were far more interested in drinking, sleeping, gambling, and turning a profit than in fighting each other. The only major threats to the happy, profitable life of the F Troop and the local Indian tribe, the Hekawis (as in "where the heck-are-we?"), were the visiting brass, who wanted the troop to have reveille, drills, and exercise, and wandering Indian tribes with the foolish notion of teaming up with the Hekawis for a raid on the fort ("Hekawis not fighters; we lovers," the chief explained).

"Hogan's Heroes," which also debuted in 1965, broke new ground in satirizing institutional authority by showing how total-control institutions, like prisoner of war camps, could be undermined. The inmates of Stalag 13 had more power than their captors. They had a complete system of tunnels under the prison camp, housing supplies and services (including custom tailoring), munitions, gourmet food, and direct radio contact with the allies. Here, the inmates thwarted, outwitted, and humbled the Nazi authorities.

Later, "M.A.S.H." presented more serious and powerful criticism of the military through the portrayal of Korean war physicians, Hawkeye Pierce and Trapper John McIntyre, who continually disregard military regulations and military discipline in order to perform their heroic and compassionate deeds as surgeons.

During the 1966-67 season, the "Smothers Brothers Comedy Hour" introduced a controversial, antiestablishment, politically topical tone quite different from anything else on television. The show included a stock character, Officer Judy, who came on stage whenever the barbs against some lawful authority went too far, and warned the Smothers they were under either suspicion or arrest for violating some rule of society, usually for abusing the "privilege" of free speech.

By the late 1960s, the weekly dramatic shows began to present the new relationships that had emerged in the culture. One of the first of these was "The Mod Squad," a show about an undercover unit of the Los Angeles police department. Made up of three former criminals— "one black, one white, and one blonde"—these young crime fighters were hip and cool, totally unlike the square-jawed, straight cops on "Dragnet" and "The FBI." Gone was the Dr. Kildare theme of socializing the young, idealistic neophytes to the established system. Now it was the system that had to change to accommodate the radical styles of the young. Other cop shows, like "Toma," "Baretta," and "Starsky and Hutch," displayed the same pattern of the police department adjusting to the new breed of young radicals.

In 1969, "The Bold Ones" introduced hip, brash, young doctors and lawyers into the establishment professions, where their wisdom, honesty, compassion, and moral outlook helped to improve medicine and law. In "Room 222," an integrated, middle-class urban high school showed how young teachers and students helped a school to effectively overcome racial tension and recognize the rights of students.

By 1970, the new breed of lawyers, physicians, and teachers who were initiating new standards of morality into the professions appeared regularly in shows like "The Young Lawyers," "Storefront Lawyers," "The Interns," and "The Headmaster." In most of these shows, the new breed of hero was a former outsider won over to help the establishment correct its moral shortcomings. Some of these shows did include wise old men who were supposed to be mentors to the young, but frequently an episode revealed that these "mentors" lacked the wisdom, the moral fortitude, or the compassion of their young charges.

All these shows oversimplified complex social problems and put forth superficial solutions. Often, hip jargon would topple the unfeeling bureaucracy. Viewers, of course, realized that matters were more complex and solutions not so easy to come by, so these shows were all short lived. Yet, these shows did reveal that the traditional system was morally inadequate. And all the shows carried the message that it was the young, the morally insightful, honest, and forthright young, who would and could set things right.

By the end of the 1960s, TV movies and special dramatic shows also began to portray the changes that had taken place in the culture. At Christmas time in 1969, NBC presented an adaptation of Robert Anderson's play, *Silent Night, Lonely Night*, a favorable account of an adulterous romance between two married people. The next month, viewers watched "My Sweet Charlie," a positive treatment of a chance-encounter interracial romance. It proved to be the highest-rated movie on TV that year. One by one, the traditional taboos fell, and even the weekly series displayed unpunished extramarital affairs, teenage pregnancy, and abortion. The first sympathetic portrayal of homosexuality came in 1972 in the made-for-TV film, "That Certain Summer." Hal Holbrook played a building contractor and Martin Sheen a sound engineer, two very masculine figures, who became homosexual lovers.

Truly, the moral and social values of society had changed. The "system" itself had changed. And the changes had largely been wrought by the young. Instead of the young adjusting to fit into the system, the system had adjusted to the young—or better: The system had changed in response to the moral criticisms of the young. Yet, not everyone welcomed these changes they saw portrayed nightly on the television screen. Many doubted that these changes had improved society. The traditional relationships had changed, they agreed, but had the society really become more moral? They were critical of the postmodern world that had risen in response to the criticism of the 1960s. The sexual candor repulsed them, the acceptance of abortion angered them, and the endorsement of homosexuality dismayed them.

They were "fed up" with the coddling of criminals and rejected the story that crime was caused by discrimination and a lack of compassion for the poor, the unfortunate, and the minorities. Furthermore, the self-righteous youths who were running the schools and universities disgusted them.

To these new critics, morality rested upon tradition, order, authority, restraint, and duty—all of which society seemed to have abandoned. At least, one would think so from watching the nightly news and the weekly television shows. These critics yearned for the order and stability of the pretelevision world, a time before moral criticism had been unleashed. In the 1970s, they began to fight back; they began to criticize the postmodern culture. On moral grounds, they condemned homosexuality, abortion, pornography, crime in the streets, and lack of discipline in the schools.

In January 1971, these new moral critics found a voice on television in the person of Archie Bunker, who, on the weekly comedy show, "All in the Family," presented the traditional culture point of view on such topics as racism, homosexuality, premarital sex, abortion, drugs, sexual candor, crime, feminism, patriotism, and the counterculture. But there was a hitch: Archie was a crude, dumb, ignorant bigot. So his arguments against the changed relationships in U.S. society became tirades against: "spades," "spics," "spooks," "schwartzes," "coons," "chinks," "commies" and "their commie crapola," "pinkos," "pansies," "hebes," "yids," "bleeding hearts," "tamale eaters," "atheists," "weirdos," "dumb pollacks," "dingbats," "meatheads," "fairies," "fruits," and "fags." Through the lovable bigot, Archie Bunker, the show presented a double message: It gave Archie all the good lines, but it condemned bigotry. So, while seeming to strengthen the attitude held by those viewers who shared Archie's prejudices, "All in the Family" actually helped people become critical of those prejudices. "We have received hundreds of letters from individuals who wrote to say, 'Right on, Archie!' " Norman Lear, the producer of the show reported. "But without exception, every one of them went on to say, one way or another, 'But why do you always make Archie a horse's ass by the end of every episode?' "[56]

The metamessage of "All in the Family" was that the new social relationships were not going to be reversed. The new relationships between men and women, between the old and the young, between blacks and whites, and between an ever-increasing variety of ethnic groups were all morally better relationships than had existed before. Even Archie, in time, seemed to accept this message ... grudgingly.

So far, I have argued that television facilitated widespread moral criticism of abstract society. Specifically, it helped raise criticism of the functional rationality of that society. Abstract society, the criticism went, treated people like objects, not like human beings, thrusting them into a fierce, competitive war against one another in the quest for satisfaction of their wants. In abstract society, people experienced ever-deepening feelings of isolation, alienation, and anxiety. Intellectuals, of course, had long before this raised such criticism of the contemporary world, and had written books and scholarly articles to elaborate upon them in print. But television enabled more and more people, especially the young, to come up with the same kinds of criticism.

The criticism and protest that television facilitated brought about changes in the relationships among groups of people—changes that restored tribal values of cooperation, collectivism, and subjectivity, all of which had been displaced by the rationalization of culture that had taken place in the modern world. The postmodern culture that emerged in the 1960s, combining as it did the values of modern and tribal cultures, was morally superior to both. But the attempt to reconcile antithetical values—individualism and collectivism, competition and cooperation, objectivity and subjectivity—placed a tremendous strain upon people—so much strain that some now sought a return to a closed society, a society immunized from criticism. The society those people sought to create was to be beyond criticism simply because it would be founded on true and permanent moral values. Frightened by the strains of living in an ever more open society, they rejected the message of "All in the Family" that the cultural changes were here to stay, and that all who opposed them were ignorant bigots. They believed that there were permanent values—values that were true for all times and all places; values that ordained the correct relationship that should hold in every society. These were the values decreed by God, values found in the Holy Bible. To recall people to true Christian morality and restore correct Christian relationships, these true believers turned to the medium of TV, creating what has been called the electronic church.

The Electronic Church

And so it came to pass that, after being a medium that facilitated moral progress, television now became a conservative medium. And the evangelical Christians who brought about this transformation of television truly believed that this would make things better.

The word "evangelical" comes from the Greek root, evangelion, which means "the good news." Evangelicals believe that Christ's greatest commandment was "Go ye into all the world and preach the gospel to every creature" (Mark 16:15). Electronic communication, some evangelicals believe, is literally a gift from God that makes possible the fulfillment of the Great Conversion.

The Federal Communications Commission (FCC) paved the way for the development of the electronic church by its 1960 ruling that local stations could sell air time for religious programs and still get "public interest credit"—required of all who used the air waves. Thus encouraged, many stations began to sell air time to religious groups rather than donate it to them. This opened the way for the evangelical preachers to buy TV time. They had never benefited from free donations of air time, but now they could raise the money to buy television air time through fundraising appeals made in the course of their broadcasts.

Under this new arrangement, the audience for religious programs greatly expanded. By his own account, Rex Humbard, who televised a weekly show from the five thousand-seat Cathedral of Tomorrow in Akron, Ohio, was appearing on sixty-eight stations by 1968, on 175 by 1975, and on 207 by 1981. Oral Roberts, who originally broadcast his religious services from a tent in Oklahoma, soon folded up his tent and, beginning in 1969, televised his show from his own multimillion-dollar station on the campus of Oral Roberts University in Tulsa, Oklahoma. By 1980, he was being shown on 165 TV stations and had the largest audience of any syndicated evangelical program.

Syndication, made possible by the development of videotape recording, contributed to the explosive growth of the electronic church, introducing the superstars of evangelical Protestantism: Jerry Falwell, Jim and Tammy Bakker, Jimmy Swaggart, and Pat Robertson. With the additional development of cable technology and the communications satellite, it became possible to create nationwide cable networks that competed with commercial networks that broadcast over the air. Pat Robertson, who had purchased his own television station in 1961, created the Christian Broadcasting Network (CBN) in 1977. By 1988, it had 37 million subscribers and was growing at an average rate of eighteen thousand members daily.[57] There are presently four Christian television networks and ninety-five nationally syndicated religious programs. Pat Robertson's CBN is by far the largest network, owning and operating four TV stations that transmit to twenty-seven hundred cable systems. Its closest competition is the PTL (Praise the Lord) network, until recently headed by Jim and Tammy Bakker.

Because of the absence of Nielsen ratings and the lack of mechanisms to measure cable television viewing, it is difficult to tell how many people actually watch these television evangelist shows. But, according to Jeffrey Hadden and Anson Shupe, who have carefully reviewed all the claims, estimates, and actual research on the matter, the cumulative national audience for the top ten religious programs by 1988 was 67.7 million households: An average of 40 percent of all U.S. households watch at least one segment of religious television each month. Pat Robertson's Show, "The 700 Club," is the top drawing card, reaching approximately 2.5 million viewers; on a monthly basis 16 million tune in.[58]

Those who watch the electronic church are believers, true believers. Curious nonbelievers may occasionally watch, but usually only to marvel and scoff. Thus, the most significant aspect of evangelical television is that it does not facilitate criticism of what it presents to its viewers. It turns television into a conserving medium. Like all of television, evangelical television encodes relationships, but here the encoded relationship is that between man and God—a personal God, a transcendent God who is interested in the affairs of the world, an accessible God, a God who interacts with the world and all that occurs in that world. There, on the screen, viewers can see the preacher relate to God—through prayer, supplication, entreaty. There, too, television reveals God's reality to man: through the inerrant word of the living God—the Bible—that the preacher reads, quotes, interprets, and applies to the goings-on in the world. Since the Bible is inerrant, infallible, and without contradiction, believers cannot criticize the relation between God and man encoded on the television screen; they can only accept and bear witness to the correctness, the appropriateness, and the necessity of that relationship.

Some of the television evangelical preachers, like Robertson and Bakker, are charismatics who claim to receive messages and powers directly from God: the power to prophesy, to heal, and sometimes to speak in tongues. These are presented as further television evidence of the continuing relationship of God and man. Pat Robertson, for example, has identified the European Common Market with the ten-nation confederacy mentioned with prophetic vision in Daniel in the Old Testament (Daniel 7:24). According to Robertson, the entry of Greece into the Common Market brought the membership to ten countries and set the stage for the rise of the Anti-Christ, a charismatic and winning person who is simply Satan in disguise.

In the realm of healing, here's how Jim Bakker did it on the PTL show:

> Bakker, attired in an egg-blue suit, standing against a velvet background, begins quietly: "There's a prostate gland condition that God is healing right now.... There is a spinal condition, perhaps a missing disc that is being restored.... Someone to my left has a kidney ailment.... There are growths and in the name of Jesus those growths are gone.... You will not need surgery.... There is something that goes into the marrow of the bone, maybe it's leukemia.... The Lord is healing it.[59]

The "PTL Club" also provides healing for viewers at home. During the show, viewers are urged to call in and discuss their personal and spiritual problems with one of seven thousand trained volunteers staffing some sixty regional telephone centers strategically placed across the country. The operators have a computer form in front of them listing ailments in alphabetical order, starting with arthritis. Other boxes list major emotional and spiritual problem areas. Under each subject is a list of inspirational Bible verses. Here's a report from one counselor about one caller:

> Phew! She was in bad shape. She's divorced and depressed and misses her husband very much. She had her toes cut off and they were sewn back on and she's in pain.... I said she should focus her eyes on Jesus. She said she was. I said she should focus more. She said every time she picked up the Bible she couldn't concentrate on it. So I gave her some verses (she pointed to a printed blue card all the counselors had before them, on which inspirational Bible verses were grouped by subject). I gave her some from "Depression," "Divorce," and "Fear."[60]

Televangelists further demonstrate the continuing relationship of God to human beings through interviews with "successful people." A singer, a well-known businessman, an actor, an athlete, a beauty queen—each describes how "bad" things were before God came into the picture, and how all is now wonderful. Praise the Lord!

Evangelical Christians believe that all human beings are sinners. As originally created by God, man and woman were good, but their nature was corrupted by the Fall (in the Garden of Eden). Human beings, therefore, cannot save themselves or cleanse themselves of sin. Each person can be cleansed and saved only by God, by God's grace. Once saved, or born again, through God's grace, the evangelical believes that he must lead a life of service to his fellow human beings as a continuing sign of the presence and glory of God's future kingdom.

For the evangelical Christian, the greatest of all sins is the sin of pride, or hubris—the belief that human beings can go it alone, that they can solve their problems independently of God. Those who believe that man can improve the world without God's help the evangelicals call "secular humanists.

Secular humanists, the evangelicals contend, now have control of all our social, political, and economic institutions; and they run the media, including television. Through their control of the government, the media, and the schools, the secular humanists have, the evangelicals insist, undermined Americans' relations with God. Moreover, by encouraging and supporting feminism, homosexuality, pornography, children's rights, and disobedience to authority, secular humanists have all but destroyed the correct Christian relationships that should prevail between men and women, parents and children, teachers and students, and citizens and their government leaders. Everywhere the evangelicals look—and especially when they look at commercial television—they spy sin: stealing, mugging, killing, sexual hedonism, drug abuse, wife and child abuse, unwed mothers, welfare cheats, and corruption and greed in all of society's institutions. By casting these evils as "sins," the evangelicals can whip up moral fervor to stamp them out.

One of the battlefields of the evangelicals' crusade against secular humanism is the public school. They have tried to censor textbooks and curriculum materials; they have succeeded in banning books from school and public library shelves; they have secured "equal time" to teach creationism in science classes; they have defeated sex education programs in schools; and they have fought for the restoration of prayer in public schools:

> The educators have taken religion out of our schools and now they are wondering why people are dishonest, smoke drugs, don't pay attention, and are juvenile delinquents. (Rev. Pat Robertson, "700 Club" broadcast, 2 December 1981)

In addition to the public schools, the TV evangelists have zeroed in on the influence of secular humanism on the courts, the media, and the policies of the U.S. government.

> But each of these judges (of the Supreme Court) has extraordinary powers and they influence our lives more than we realize. None of these judges are elected; they are accountable to no one really; they can be impeached but that's rare and they exercise what amounts to a type of dictatorship. (Rev. Pat Robertson, "700 Club" broadcast, 2 October 1981)

> You and I, whether we like it or not, we are opinion makers; we are leaders; the way we go, millions will go with us. We have an obligation to present life not the way it is but the way it ought to be. (Rev. Jerry Falwell, speaking to an ABC-TV official, *Penthouse*, March 1981)

> The Constitution of the United States, for instance, is a marvelous document for self-government by Christian people. But the minute you turn the document into the hands of non-Christian people and atheistic people, they can use it to destroy the very foundation of our society. And that's what's been happening. (Rev. Pat Robertson, "700 Club" broadcast, 20 December 1981)

In the battle to protect the Christian family, to preserve the correct relationships within the family, the evangelical preachers have condemned feminism, homosexuality and abortion:

> I know this is painful for the ladies to hear, but if you get married you have accepted the headship of man, your husband.... Christ is head of the household, and the husband's the head of the wife and that's just the way it is.... This is the way the Bible sets it up. (Rev. Pat Robertson, "700 Club" broadcast, 8 January 1982)

Remember, homosexuals do not reproduce! They recruit! And many of them are out after my children and your children. (Rev. Jerry Falwell, fundraising letter, 13 August 1981)

The judgment of God will surely fall on a nation which allows the mass murder of millions of preborn human beings. For this horrible sin, America must reckon with the Holy and Just God of this Universe. Every godly citizen should use his influence to help put a stop to this pervasive curse in our society. ("The Religious Roundtable")

Religion Takes a Room at the White House

During the 1980s, the rest of the nation became aware of the power the televangelists had to redirect moral criticism in the United States. On 29 April 1980, a crowd estimated at a quarter to a half million poured into the Mall in Washington, D.C., for a marathon prayer meeting that its organizers called "Washington for Jesus." The network news gave it brief notice, failing to mention that it was the largest crowd ever to assemble on the Mall—larger than any of the civil rights marches of the 1960s, larger than the antiwar protests, larger than the crowd that had attended Mass with Pope John Paul II on the same site a few months earlier. But the CBN, PTL, and Trinity Broadcasting Networks all televised the proceedings live, adding several million more to witness this historic happening. It was Pat Robertson, cochairman of the event, who announced it "a historic moment for our nation." His fellow cochairman, William Bright, founder and president of Campus Crusade for Christ, gave the keynote address. Bright told the assembled throng and the millions who watched on television that something had gone terribly wrong with the United States. It had gone wrong, he explained, because the United States had broken its covenant with God; the relationship between the U.S. people and God was not as it should be:

It's no mystery. We've turned from God and God is chastising us. Laugh if you will. The critics will laugh. And they'll make fun. But I'll tell you, this is God's doing. You go back to 1962 and 1963 and you'll discover a series of plagues that came upon America. First, the assassination of President Kennedy. The war in Vietnam accelerated. The drug culture swept millions of young people into the drug scene. The youth revolution. Crime accelerated over 300 percent in a brief period of time. Racial conflict threatened to tear our nation apart. The Watergate scandal. The divorce rate accelerated. There were almost as many divorces as marriages. And there was an epidemic of drug addition, an epidemic of alcoholism. And now, we are faced with a great economic crisis.... God is saying to us, "Wake Up! Wake up! Wake up!"[61]

Those who participated in "Washington for Jesus" comprised an almost full roster of who's who in the electronic church. Besides Robertson and Bright, Jim and Tammy Bakker were there, as were Ben Armstrong, Rex Humbard, James Robinson, and Robert Schuller. One by one, they went to the microphone to speak, to preach, and to pray for the nation.

The following August, Ronald Reagan, then campaigning for election to the presidency of the United States, addressed an assembly of preachers in the Reunion Arena in Dallas, gathered for what was called the National Affairs Briefing. After being introduced by Jerry Falwell, Reagan made the comment that brought the crowd to its feet, a comment broadcast that evening on all the network news shows:

A few days ago, I addressed a group in Chicago and received their endorsement for my candidacy. Now, I know this is a nonpartisan gathering and so I know you can't endorse me, but I only brought that up because I want you to know that I endorse you and what you are doing.

After Dallas, and after further reports of his influence at the Republican National Convention, Falwell became one of the most sought after figures in the 1980 campaign, making guest appearances on "Meet the Press," "Today," and "Donohue." When the election was over, some evangelical preachers, including Jerry Falwell, claimed credit for Ronald Reagan's victory. More credible perhaps, was the defeat of incumbent liberal senators that Falwell and other ministers had targeted as enemies. The Moral Majority, a political action group headed by Falwell, had issued report cards on the enemies. All were defeated for reelection in 1980: Frank Church, Birch Bayh, John Culver, George McGovern, Warren Magnuson, and Gaylord Nelson.

Reagan's first term in office saw evangelists enjoying unprecedented access to the presidency and the White House, with Jerry Falwell serving as the president's unofficial chaplain. Frequently, the president called Falwell to persuade him to give support to an action, or sometimes to explain an action—as, for example, the nomination of Sandra Day O'Connor to the Supreme Court. Reagan also appointed Robert Billings—executive director of the Moral Majority Political Action Committee—to director of regional offices in the Department of Education. He appointed Morton Blackwell, who had performed liaison duties between evangelicals and the Reagan campaign, as a coordinator of political strategy in the White House staff. The president often spoke before gatherings of evangelicals and expressed solidarity with their religious beliefs. (The Bible, he said, "contains all the answers to all the problems that face us today.") On 23 August 1984, just hours before his acceptance of the Republican party's nomination for a second term, President Reagan spoke at a prayer breakfast in the Reunion Arena in Dallas and delivered another memorable line: "The truth is politics and morality are inseparable. As morality's foundation is religion, religion and politics are necessarily related."

On election day, 81 percent of white evangelicals voted for Reagan—an increase of about one-third over 1980. Even more important, 77 percent of white evangelicals voting in congressional elections supported Republican candidates for the House of Representatives.[62]

What about the 1988 presidential campaign? Whom would the evangelicals support? Early in Ronald Reagan's second term, Pat Robertson indicated that he himself would seek the office of president of the United States. In a 1985 broadcast on his own Christian Broadcasting Network, he declared: "We have enough votes to run the country.... And when the people say 'we've had enough,' we are going to take over the country." Paul Kirk, the Democratic National Committee chairman, warned his fellow Democrats in November that, although he had at first not believed that this relatively unknown man could be a major candidate for the presidency, he now realized that "Pat Robertson has the most powerful political organization in America."

In May 1986, Robertson registered nearly as many delegates in the Michigan delegate selection as did George Bush. Later that month, he raised more than a million dollars at a Washington dinner, and almost 3.5 million three months later in Texas. His most striking victory came in the Republican Straw Poll conducted in Iowa in September 1987, when Robertson beat both the incumbent vice-president, George Bush, and the Senate minority leader, Robert Dole.

But shortly, without warning, the evangelical bid for the presidency derailed. It had begun back in March 1987 when follow televangelist, Oral Roberts, set off his "donate or I die campaign." God, according to Roberts, had threatened Oral that this would be his last month on earth if Oral's followers did not come up with $8 million in ransom money. With that, Oral sequestered himself in the top of a tower in his church until the payoff took place.

The commercial news shows and the talk shows had a field day of fun with the Oral Roberts story, but the next revelation spelled real trouble for Pat Robertson's bid for the presidency. Late in March, the PTL network announced that Tammy Bakker, wife of Jim Bakker and costar of the Jim and Tammy show, had entered the Betty Ford Center for Drug Rehabilitation. Shortly thereafter, the world found out that Jim Bakker had had an adulterous affair with the church secretary in a Florida motel. Bakker was a former colleague of Pat Robertson and had been a host on his Christian Broadcasting Network. The final bombshell was the revelation of the incompetent, sloppy and probably dishonest, handling of funds by Bakker's PTL ministry.

Nightly, the network news shows had stories about the sex, the hypocrisy, the pillaged coffers of PTL, along with the unholy name calling among some of the biggest stars of the electronic church. Soon there were reports of investigations by the Internal Revenue Service, the Federal Bureau of Investigation, the U.S. Postal Service, the South Carolina Tax Commission, and the U.S. Congress. The sordid elements of a seemingly endless, sleazy, real-life soap opera were more fully explored on ABC's "Nightline," which devoted eleven full programs to the scandal. In their television appearances, Jim and Tammy seemed unrepentant ... and arrogant to boot: "We've been accused of so many things that we've just decided to let our accusers do what they would like. We're just going to forgive them. We're going to go on, and we're going to love."

Within a short time, Jerry Falwell took over the Bakker's PTL Network along with Heritage, USA—a Disney World-like community the Bakkers had created. Following this, elders of the Assembly of God defrocked Jim Bakker.

Yet another scandal erupted among the evangelicals when Jimmy Swaggart, who had blown the whistle on Jim Bakker's sexual indiscretions, tearfully confessed on his own television broadcast that he, too, had committed sexual sins. He had, it turned out, consorted with a prostitute in New Orleans. He, too, was banished from his ministry by the elders of the Assembly of God. But he, too, like the Bakkers, defied the elders and continued to preach.

In the face of such carryings-on by his fellow ministers, the candidacy of Pat Robertson for president of the Untied States faltered and sputtered out. After a poor showing in the Super Tuesday primaries, Robertson withdrew his candidacy. Yet, he was not the last hope of the new Christian right. There will most likely be another. Television has created a strong conservative movement among fundamentalist evangelical Christians. There are 1,370 religious radio stations and 221 religious television stations in the country today. Twenty-four hours a day the Christian networks broadcast programs that can be picked up via satellite nationwide. Television has mobilized the Christian evangelicals, and locked them into a struggle against the dark forces of secular humanism—a battle of right against wrong, good against evil.

Through the power of television, some 10 million evangelical Christians have constructed what approaches a total Christian community: In addition to Christian schools, Christian orphanages, and Christian senior citizen homes, there are now Christian shopping centers, Christian nightclubs (no dancing and no drinking), and Christian business directories (a born again Christian can be trusted, and it is God's will that Christians take their business to him); there are Christian business associations, whose members can call upon the services of Christian management consultants and, when needed, Christian industrial chaplains; there are Christian women's clubs, Christian charm schools, and Christian counseling services, as well as the Fellowship of Christian Athletes.

In June 1972, Roger Staubach, Dallas Cowboy Quarterback, addressed a rally of the Campus Crusade for Christ at the Cotton Bowl in Dallas: "The goal line we must get across is our salvation.... God has given us a good field position." At that, the eighty thousand fans broke out in wild applause and began a spontaneous chant:

Two bits, four bits, six bits, a dollar.
All for Jesus, stand up and holler!

The electronic medium has not only mobilized evangelical Christians, it has allowed them to seal themselves off from the rest of the culture, from which vantage point they can view it critically. Here's how Jeremy Rifkin describes a typical day of an evangelical Christian:

> In the morning, husband and wife wake up to an evangelical service on their local Christian-owned and operated radio station. The husband leaves for work where he will start off his day at a businessman's prayer breakfast. The evangelical wife bustles the children off to their Christian day school. At midmorning, she relaxes in front of the TV set and turns on her favorite Christian soap opera. Later in the afternoon, while the Christian husband is attending a Christian business seminar and the children are engaged in an after-school Christian sports program, the Christian wife is doing her daily shopping at a Christian store, recommended in her Christian business directory. In the evening, the Christian family watches the Christian world news on TV and then settles down for dinner. After dinner, the children begin their Christian school assignments. A Christian babysitter arrives—she is part of a baby-sitter pool from the local church. After changing into their evening clothes, the Christian wife applies a touch of Christian makeup and then they're off to a Christian nightclub for some socializing with Christian friends from the local church. They return home later in the evening and catch the last half hour of the "700 Club," the evangelical Johnny Carson Show. The Christian wife ends her day reading a chapter or two from Marabel Morgan's best-selling Christian book, *The Total Woman.* Meanwhile, her husband leafs through a copy of *Inspiration* magazine, the evangelical *Newsweek,* before they both retire for the evening.[63]

The evangelical Christians are leading the retreat from the postmodern morality that (commercial) television has helped create. Postmodern morality is a morality in transition, emerging as people painfully try to construct new and more moral relationships. Yet, it is not just the new morality that offends the evangelical Christians. Even more, it is the emergence of a world, a postmodern culture, bereft of any final authority. With the help of television, the rampant criticisms of the 1960s and 1970s destroyed the authority of science and scientific rationality that had served as the final authority in the modern world. Without a final authority to anchor them, many people fear that all coherence is gone. The televangelists have stepped into this breach to lead us back to the Bible, which is to become the final authority.

But there are no final authorities. Human beings, alone, are responsible for their culture. In recognizing and accepting responsibility for our culture, we confront our own fallibility. We human beings can never create a perfectly moral world. But the real good news is that it can always get better. By uncovering and reducing or eliminating the evils that are part of our culture, we can improve it … continually. We uncover evils by being critical. Television can help us approach our culture critically, can help us to make things better.

Notes

1   Holton, "From the Endless Frontier to the Ideology of Limits," 240.
2   Ciba Foundation Symposium. *Civilization and Science: In Conflict or Collaboration?* 1.
3   Holton and Blanpied, eds., *Science and its Public: The Changing Relationship,* 65.
4   Etzioni and Nunn, "The Public Appreciation of Science in Contemporary America." 231.
5   Ibid., 230.
6   Gerbner et al, "Scientists on the TV Screen," 41.
7   Ibid., 42-44.
8   Goodfield, *Playing God*; David Perlman, "Science and the Mass Media," in Holton and Blanpied, *Science and its Public: The Changing Relationship,* 245-260.
9   Perlman, 254.
10 Dubos, *Reason Awake*, 241.
11 Rybczynski, *Taming the Tiger: The Struggle to Control Technology,* 27.
12 Holton and Blanpied, *Science and its Public: The Changing Relationship,* 78.
13 Don K. Price, "Money and Inluence," in Ibid., 198.
14 David Z. Beckler, "The Precarious Life of Science in the White House," in Ibid., 121.
15 Cohen, *Before It's Too Late: A Scientist's Case for Nuclear Energy,* 23.
16 Ibid., 1-2, 255-6.
17 Ibid., 17-25, 57-58.
18 Ibid., chapter 11.
19 Klaw, *The New Brahmins: Scientific Life in America,* 12.
20 Krieghbaum, *Science and the Mass Media,* 9.
21 Goodell, *The Visible Scientists,* 202.
22 David Perlman, "Science and the Mass Media," in Holton and Blanpied, *Science and its Public: The Changing Relationship,* 255.
23 Nelkin, *Selling Science,* 4, 7, 137.
24 Broad and Wade, *Betrayers of the Truth: Fraud and Deceit in the Halls of Science,* 11, Appendix.
25 Burnham, *How Superstition Won and Science Lost,* 254.
26 *New Age Catalogue,* 216.
27 Ibid., ix.
28 Ibid., xi.
29 Ibid., ii.
30 MacLaine, *It's All in the Playing,* 6-7.
31 Gribbin, *In Search of Schrodinger's Cat: Quantum Physics and Reality,* 172.

32   Talbot, *Beyond the Quantum,* passim.
33   For a lucid discussion of these issues, see Popper, *Postscript to the Logic of Scientific Discovery.*
34   Holton and Blanpied, *Science and its Public: The Changing Relationship,* 72.
35   Mannheim, *Man and Society in an Age of Reconstruction,* 53.
36   Berger, *The Homeless Mind: Modernization and Consciousness,* passim.
37   Castleman and Podrazik, *Watching TV,* 115.
38   Ibid., 114.
39   Ibid., 134.
40   Ibid., 133.
41   Kerr, *The Uses of the University,* 87-88.
42   Robert H. Somers, "The Mainsprings of the Rebellion: A Survey of Berkeley Students in November 1964," in Lipset and Wolin, eds., *The Berkleley Student Revolt,* 536.
43   Searle, *The Campus War,* 69.
44   Bradford Cleaveland, "A Letter to Undergraduates," in Lipset and Wolin, eds., *The Berkeley Student Revolt,* 66-94.
45   "Chronology of Events," in Ibid., 163.
46   "Statement by President Clark Kerr," in Ibid., 246-7.
47   Rossman, *On Learning and Social Change,* 165.
48   Kelman, *Push Comes to Shove,* 169.
49   Hoffman, *Revolution for the Hell of It,* 219.
50   Reich, *The Greening of America,* 236-7.
51   Hoffman, *Revolution for the Hell of It,* 10-12.
52   Howard, *Please Touch,* 234.
53   Grant and Riesman, "An Ecology of Academic Reform," 176-7.
54   Ibid., 182.
55   Yankelovich, *The New Morality,* 23.
56   Adler, ed., *All in the Family: A Critical Appraisal,* 255.
57   Donovan, *Pat Robertson: The Authorized Biography,* 120.
58   Hadden and Shupe, *Televangelism: Power and Politics on God's Frontier,* 156, 158.
59   Jorstad, *The Politics of Moralism,* 42.
60   Rifkin and Howard, *The Emerging Order,* 108.
61   Hadden and Shupe, *Televangelism: Power and Politics on God's Frontier,* 22-23.
62   James Reichly, "The Evangelical and Fundamentalist Revolt," in Neuhaus and Cromartie, eds., *Piety and Politics: Evnagelicals and Fundamentalists Confront the World,* 88.
63   Rifkin and Howard, *The Emerging Order,* 125-6.

6

Conclusion:
Television and Postmodern Morality

Sometime during the sixteenth century, the modern world began to emerge. Its elements included new political, social, and economic arrangements—the nation-state, the open society, and capitalism—and a new intellectual climate—modern science. What gave the modern world its coherence was the embodiment in all the new arrangements of a common set of values: the values of individualism, competition, equality, and objectivity. These values embodied in the arrangements of the modern world contrast sharply with the values of collectivism, cooperation, hierarchy, and subjectivity found in the political, social, economic, and intellectual arrangements of the premodern world.

The modern world lasted over five hundred years, up until the advent of television. Television helped people recognize the moral inadequacies of the modern world—the injustices, the evils, the bad things it caused and condoned. In this book, I have tried to show how television did this.

In brief, the argument is that television helped people become aware of the moral inadequacies of the values of the modern world— the values of individualism, competition, equality, and objectivity. This has resulted in the creation of a postmodern world, a world where people rediscovered those long-discarded, premodern values of collectivism, cooperation, hierarchy, and subjectivity and infused them into our political, social, economic, and intellectual arrangements. It is difficult to create arrangements and institutions that embody both sets of values, which is why our world now appears to lack coherence. Yet, this postmodern world is morally superior to the modern world; it provides more life chances to more people.

It is not fashionable to profess a belief in progress. But this is what I have tried to argue in this book. I do not believe there is a law of progress that causes things to get better. Rather, it is human beings who improve their culture. They do this by modifying, changing, and refining the culture they have inherited. And they make these changes or modifications when they uncover inadequacies and insufficiencies in the existing culture. People uncover these inadequacies in their culture when they become critical of it, and media—the so-called communication media—I have argued, facilitate such criticism. What happens is that the medium encodes the culture, thereby allowing people a new and different perception of the culture, enabling them to ascertain faults and insufficiencies not apparent heretofore. This is the case especially when a new medium first appears.[1] This explains why historians have found such dramatic and far-reaching cultural changes at specific periods in the past: changes that took place after the emergence of speech; again, after the invention of writing; again, after the advent of the printing press; and most recently, with the coming of television.

One reason many today do not subscribe to the notion of progress in history is their lack of belief in human agency. They think that human conduct is determined—determined by factors, conditions, and structures, over which humans have no control; determined by the environment: by what one sees, hears, and perceives. This determinist outlook prevails widely among those who study television so that they continually look for the influence television has over people. In this book, I have tried to show that television does not influence people; it does not cause people to do this or that. Rather, television encodes the existing culture, enables people to criticize it, and thereby facilitates its improvement.

A second reason why many today do not believe in progress in history is their acceptance of cultural relativism. This is the notion that no culture, at any time, or any place, is better, or worse, than any other culture at any other time, or at any other place. I maintain that human culture has improved over time. The culture created by homo sapiens was better than that created by his ancestors; the culture of the Greeks was better than that of their predecessors; modern culture was better than the culture of the ancients; and the postmodern culture emerging today is better yet. By "better" I mean that the culture contains fewer inadequacies, limitations, "bads"; in short, in a better culture, people's life chances improve.

In the last analysis, this book is an argument against these twin intellectual maladies of our time: relativism and determinism—maladies that prevent people from seeing that things do get better, maladies that prevent people from understanding how they get better. Things can continue to get better—if we can shake these maladies. For improvement is up to us. We must continue to be critical of our culture, and, for this to happen, we must continue to speak, continue to write, continue to read, and—*mirabile dictu!*—continue to watch television.

Note

1   With the proliferation of television channels and networks, and the coming of the VCR, the impact of television on culture has declined. Fewer television programs have the mass audiences that existed in the 1960s and 1970s, so there is less concentrated focus on the moral inadequacies of our culture, and less mobilization of moral criticisms. In consequence, the pace of cultural change has slackened—in the United States, if not in the rest of the world.

Epilogue

Since the first edition of this book appeared, the power of the original three networks has diminished: They no longer dominate television. With hundreds of channels now available through cable and satellite dishes people no longer watch the same programs. Moreover, many more people now use their television screens to watch videos, or play video games, while increasing numbers surf the Internet on their home computers. Another media development that has drawn viewers away from network TV is the growth of radio call-in shows.

By 1990, the decline in the number of viewers caused a loss of revenue for the big three networks as advertisers sought other outlets. The Persian Gulf War of 1991 did not help. In its first days the war cost each network $6 million a day in lost advertising. NBC calculated that the Gulf War cost it $50 million all told.[1] The collapse of network revenue brought on drastic economic changes: layoffs, downsizing, outsourcing, reorganization—and a rethinking of program strategy.

The one TV habit that did persist among erstwhile viewers was watching television news, or shows about topics in the news. But by the 1990s CNN, with continual news all the time, had garnered a large chunk of this audience. During the Persian Gulf War, for example, most people tuned to CNN for on-the-scene coverage. Now, too, people could watch C-SPAN for live coverage of public affairs and government proceedings. And PBS offered both nightly hour-long news shows and news discussion shows like "Firing Line," "Washington Week in Review," and "Frontline."

To try to snag more of this audience the networks expanded the number of their own news shows. To weekend perennials like "Meet the

Press," "Face the Nation," and "Sixty Minutes," the networks added weekly, prime time, news magazine shows, like: "Prime Time Live," "Forty-Eight Hours," "20/20" "Day One," "Eye to Eye with Connie Chung," and "Dateline NBC" (which appeared twice a week). The networks also blanketed Sunday morning with additional news shows, and on Sunday night one or another network usually presented a docudrama on some topic currently in the news. During the week the network daily morning talk/news shows—"Today," "Good Morning America," and "This Morning"—were followed by talk shows—"Phil Donahue," "Jenny Jones," and "Regis and Kathie Lee"—that often took up current news stories. To attract more viewers to their nightly news programs the networks bracketed them with tabloid news shows, like: "A Current Affair," "Inside Edition," "Hard Copy," and infotainment shows, like: "Entertainment Tonight," "Extra: Entertainment Magazine," and "American Journal."

So in the early 1990s news shows dominated television programming, and most people got all, or most, of their news from television. Television news programs—on NBC, CBS, ABC, CNN, and PBS—all pretty much carried the same news stories, including the same sound bites. And the news magazine shows all pretty much carried the same kinds of stories: investigative reports exposing some social injustice, or some economic injustice, or some political injustice—about which the reporters could and did moralize, explicitly or implicitly.

So although people no longer watched the same television entertainment programs in the 1990s, they did watch the same news and the same kind of news analysis. In consequence, in spite of the great increase in the number of television channels, the diffused use of television sets, the rise of radio call-in shows, all of which had tempered the influence of television on American culture, television, nevertheless, through its vastly expanded news shows, did continue to have an effect, a moral effect, on the culture.

One rather remarkable consequence of the centrality that television news now had in the lives of Americans was the heightened focus on the news reporters and news analysts: they became, not just celebrities, but the message, the subject, the content. This happened because television is a medium that provokes an affective response to the relationships encoded on the screen, and now the relationships most viewers saw were those between reporters and the people they interviewed. Many people did not like what they saw—especially during the Persian Gulf

War when the radio call-in shows were flooded with denunciations of TV reporters.

In that highly censored war TV reporters found that their coverage was restricted to the "structured" briefings conducted by high-ranking military personnel. And when they tried to transform these briefings into "good television" the reporters' interviewing techniques backfired; they became the message.

In the interviews and press conferences held in Saudia Arabia and in Washington reporters treated U.S. generals as if they were duplicitous politicians, or suspected embezzlers, with some flaw to hide, or as military leaders who had lost face. But what most viewers saw on their television screens were straight arrow, dedicated officers who had a job to do, as they were fond of saying. So when news reporters were adversarial or skeptical or suspicious, they appeared unpatriotic. When they feigned naivete (a frequently used tactic), they wound up sounding ignorant and stupid. When they were persistent and critical in their questioning, they sounded ambitious—with no thought for the lives of the troops the general was trying to protect. Whatever trusty interview tactic they tried, the television news reporters appeared arrogant, insensitive, and despicably preoccupied with their own self-aggrandizement.

When they interviewed experts—retired generals and admirals, think-tankers, university professors—the reporters appeared to be trying to undermine the war effort. If the expert was hawkish, as many were, the TV reporters would present the contrary point of view. If the expert was trying to be objective, the TV reporters would try to push him or her with facial expressions and vocal inflections into revealing the expert's real feelings about the president's policies or the commanding general's plans or what other experts had said. To elicit viewer compassion, reporters would show tearful family good-byes to soldiers being shipped to the gulf. In these scenes reporters often asked the children how they felt about daddy, or mommy, going to war. People reacted to all this as attempts to manipulate the viewing audience and foment opinion against the war.

Bernard Shaw, a CNN reporter who was on the scene in Baghdad at the beginning of the war, intensified public moral indignation when he returned to the United States and refused to be debriefed by government officials. Shaw explained that doing so would compromise his integrity and neutrality as a journalist. "CNN is a global network," he said, "we can't take sides."

In November 1992 television reporting got another moral black eye when "Dateline NBC" aired a news story about an alleged flaw that caused some models of GM trucks to explode in side-impact crashes. The Dateline team set up a test crash of a GM truck for the televised segment. But they rigged the crash by placing an incendiary device near the truck's gas tank and putting the wrong cap on the gas tank so that it would fall off on impact. The public outcry over this incident— channeled, fueled, and fanned by radio call-in talk shows—deepened the suspicion that TV reporters were trying to manipulate viewers.

Television's handling of the Rodney King affair throughout 1991-1992 darkened this suspicion in the minds of many. Initially television provoked a near unanimous public revulsion against the four Los Angeles policemen who savagely beat Rodney King, a black man, as he lay helpless on the ground. But the relentless presentation of this twenty-second clip, over and over, every time the story came up on television news not only dulled the horror of the act, it raised suspicion in the minds of some that television was trying to influence public opinion and the outcome of the trial. The jury acquitted three of the four policemen and deadlocked on the one who had struck Rodney King the most times—a mistrial was declared in his case. When the verdict was announced riots erupted in Los Angeles, causing 58 deaths, and property damage estimated at $750 million. Throughout the nation people reacted with a complex compound of moral outrage: some were outraged that the jury could find the cops innocent in spite of the televised video clip that captured them savagely beating a defenseless black man; others were outraged by the rioters captured on television beating a truck driver who just happened to drive by, and by film that showed gleeful looters wantonly destroying the property of innocent Korean shop owners. When, in the aftermath of the riots, President Bush ordered a new (federal) trial of the involved policemen for violating Rodney King's civil rights, this brought forth moral criticism, too. Throughout the entire period television news shows presented the twenty-second video clip of the beating every time they covered each new development in the "story." So, ultimately, moral criticism converged on television and television reporters: instead of simply presenting the news, they were mediating it, trying to manipulate public opinion.

Another incident took place during the Democratic primary campaign of 1992 when Phil Donahue's own audience turned against him for subjecting his guest, Bill Clinton, to a barrage of questions about his marriage, his draft dodging, his marijuana smoking, and his reputation as "slick Willie." When Clinton told him that if he kept up that line of inquiry, "we're going to sit here a long time in silence, Phil," the audience applauded. Later, when Donahue turned to that studio audience, one woman said, "I think, really, given the pathetic state of most of the United States at this point—Medicare, education, everything else—I can't believe you spent half an hour of air time attacking this man's character. I'm not even a Bill Clinton supporter, but I think this is ridiculous." The studio audience cheered and applauded.[2]

In each of these cases the public backlash against television reporters was directed at their haughty and arrogant attempts to mediate the news. In this electronic age, as William Galston has observed, "People believe increasingly that they can make their own judgments, based on direct access to the primary sources of information. They don't need or want others pre-chewing their political food."[3]

But there was more to the public backlash against television reporters than resentment of reporters' attempts to mediate the news. Coupled with this was a growing reaction against the "liberal outlook" of television news.

That "liberal outlook" came out in the point of view of many news stories where reporters almost always saw matters from the perspective of victims. Stories about sexual harassment, racial discrimination, the homeless, the disabled, were always told from the angle of vision of the victims. Stories about police brutality always included interviews with the victim, or witnesses sympathetic to the victim. Stories about legislation usually focused on those groups whom the legislation would affect adversely. Stories about the economy usually described how economic goings-on hurt the poor and the working class, or how they were bad for consumers and customers.

Television news programs and news magazine shows painted businessmen, corporation executives, and entrepreneurs as villains engaged in bilking, overcharging, defrauding, cheating, and stealing from the rest of us. In *Out of Focus*, Burton Yale Pines charts what economic information viewers got from television news on a typical week in January 1992:[4]

• GMAC Mortgage Company overcharged 365,000 borrowers.
• Dow Corning Wright, according to ABC "World News Tonight" and NBC "Today," was balking at releasing documents on the safety of its silicone breast implants.

• Bethlehem Steel continued to lose money and was laying off 6,500 workers.

• Unscrupulous home repair contractors, according to NBC "Nightly News," were bilking many Americans.

• Telephone scams, according to CBS "This Morning," were selling inferior, fake, or nonexistent merchandise.

• Art galleries, according to CBS "Evening News" and NBC "Nightly News," had sold at least 88,000 counterfeit prints by claiming that they had been done by Picasso.

• Those whom NBC "Nightly News" labeled "Merchants of Greed, the biggest financial crooks of their time" who "traded Wall Street for prison cells," were doing relatively well after leaving prison.

• An unidentified congressional researcher asserted that top American executives were paid fifty-three times more than workers.

During the same week (January 25–31, 1992) television news reported that both Macy's and TWA had filed for bankruptcy. After the inevitable interview with the soon to be laid off workers about how they felt, reporters explained that TWA's financial problems resulted from the complicated junk bond schemes used by Carl Ichan to buy TWA some years earlier. Macy's, they explained, had come on hard times because of a leveraged buyout and poor management. Reports like these raised the moral ire of conservative viewers like Burton Yale Pines, who was dismayed by the television reporters' lack of understanding of how markets work and by their animus against capitalism.

The subjective focus on victims revealed a hierarchical, or elitist outlook: a concern for the weaker or lesser folk who were being oppressed by those who television reporters obviously considered to have incorrect moral values. The elitism of television news stems in great part from the fact that television—like print—is not an interactive medium. Neither television, nor newspapers, nor news magazines allow feedback from viewers. It is true that print media publish letters from readers, and some TV news show, like "Sixty Minutes," read and show viewer mail, but this is limited, at best. It was not until the advent of call-in radio shows that people began to realize how elitist newspapers, news magazines, and television news shows are. Call-in radio is much more egalitarian than print and television media since anyone can call in to complain and criticize and interact with the radio show host. The public's heightened sensitivity to elitism in the media was primarily directed at television news simply because it is a visual medium, which means that viewers observe the facial expressions, the body language, as well as the vocal intonations of reporters—all of which more readily reveal the self-righteousness inherent in news reporting.

One aspect of the elitism inherent in television news shows was that their concern for victims carried with it an implied, or sometimes an actual, condemnation of America's competitive social and economic arrangements. Especially in docudramas and news magazine stories, the implicit message was that in the struggle to get ahead, the poor, women, blacks, the disabled, were all handicapped by the existing arrangements. This, too, elicited a reaction from conservative viewers, who reproved television for its smug moralizing and its negativity.

Television news was on the side of cooperation, not competition, and all its upbeat news stories were ones that described how society had cooperated with victims and incorporated them into the mainstream: by making physical changes to buildings, sidewalks, motel rooms, and buses, in order to accommodate the disabled, for example; or by making changes in rules and procedures to facilitate the hiring and promotion of black and female employees. Other upbeat stories revealed how teachers had adapted to students who had mental and physical disabilities. Often this story was told from the point of view of a dedicated and zealous parent who had fought long and hard to get the school to accommodate her child.

The "liberal outlook" of television news—in addition to taking the point of view of victims and condemning the existing social and economic arrangements—also came through in its celebration of group rights. Beginning in the 1960s, as I have recounted in the book, the traditional conception of individual rights had been trumped by group rights: women's rights, the rights of people of color, gay rights, the rights of the disabled and the homeless, and even the rights of other (endangered) species. This rights revolution, I argued in the book, grew out of the moral compassion that television had helped create for the poor, the disabled, black people, and for women in the 1960s and 1970s.

By the 1990s these group rights—created by federal and state legislation, and confirmed by the courts—had shifted power to the victims, who now became special interest groups waging a moralized political war against everyone else, as they struggled to secure what their rights entitled them to: quotas for blacks and women; welfare benefits for the poor; access and accommodation for the disabled; care and protection for the homeless and criminally accused; and expanded health care and educational provisions for all victimized groups.

What increasingly troubled conservatives about the "liberal outlook" of television reporters was what they excluded from the news. The rights revolution had profound economic, social, and psychological consequences—most of which were unanticipated, and all of which were largely ignored by television. The people who were upset about this voiced their dismay on the growing number of radio call-in shows. Many of these call-in shows had generated a deep loyalty and community among their largely conservative listeners—a loyalty based on gratitude that they were not alone; that in spite of what they watched on television there were others "out there" who shared the same moral values and had the same moral indignation about certain goings-on in the world.

What were the complaints about?

First of all, the enforcement of group rights was costly. Although television paid little heed to the matter, taxpayers and consumers recognized that they had to pay for the physical changes made in public buildings, and in buses to accommodate the disabled; taxpayers also realized that they had to pay for the ever-increasing welfare benefits extended to the poor; as well as pay for the widened social, health, educational, legal, and police services now provided to victims. Callers to the radio talk shows decried the morality of using taxation to redistribute wealth. Even protecting the rights of endangered species cost the taxpayers: $1.3 billion to retrain loggers who no longer had trees to cut down in the Pacific Northwest because it would endanger the spotted owl.

Second, although television frequently carried news stories about social tensions and social disharmony—between male and female workers, between black and white students, between environmentalists and property owners—television reporters, viewers complained, rarely traced these phenomena to the rights revolution. Yet it was clear to people in their daily lives that the rights one group sought often could be secured only at the expense of another group. The moral dilemmas this created emerged poignantly in the televised confirmation hearings for Supreme Court nominee Clarence Thomas when Anita Hill accused him of sexual harassment. The moral perplexity of the Senate Judiciary Committee captured by the television cameras reflected the moral perplexity and moral polarization of the public. Should someone accused of sexual harassment be appointed to the Supreme Court? Should unproven charges of sexual harassment prevent a black man from being appointed to the Supreme Court? Whose rights were to be enforced? This moral dilemma was a product of group rights, in so far as the rights in question were not the individual rights of Clarence Thomas or Anita Hill, but rights of women versus the rights of black people.

More recently, the O.J. Simpson trial riveted the nation to TV screens. (CNN viewing went up 80 percent as a result of its live coverage of the trial.) Here people wanted to see if the American judicial system could provide a fair and just trial in a case where a black super athlete was accused of murdering his ex-wife, a white woman. Everyone watched the proceedings from the perspective of his or her own reference group: white people, black people, athletes, sports fans, police officers, women, feminists—each wanted to see if one of their own could be treated fairly. (In passing, I would note that public dismay with the TV circus that the O.J. Simpson trial became will most likely lead to judicial reforms that will improve court procedures. Already analysts have suggested limiting peremptory challenges in jury selection;[5] a universal, constitutional gag rule to prevent leaks of damaging evidence by insiders—the police, the prosecutors, and the defense;[6] restrictions on questions about the political affiliation and cultural practices of potential jurors.[7])

The group rights movement not only raised moral dilemmas about social justice, it also triggered moral resentment and moral recrimination against the preferential treatment given to some groups at the expense of the rest. Television rarely carried stories about this, but angry protests flooded the call-in radio shows where the callers were praised and the complaints usually expanded upon by the radio host. Callers protested the altered rules, regulations, and requirements that enabled blacks and women to become fire fighters and cops. A study by the National Opinion Research Center in 1990 found that one in ten white men had been injured by affirmative action.[8] People also called radio talk shows to lament the break up of the family—illegitimacy, teenage pregnancy, single-parent families—which they blamed on the welfare benefits given to unmarried mothers, who were often teenagers. In 1993 William Bennett documented this public umbrage with the publication of *The Index of Leading Cultural Indicators*, which reported that between 1970 and 1990 the number of teenagers getting welfare payments nearly doubled; that births to unmarried women increased more than 400 percent between 1960 and 1990; that single-parent families tripled between 1960 and 1990—one-quarter of all families were single parent families in 1990.[9]

When Vice President Dan Quayle attacked Murphy Brown (a television sitcom character) for "bearing a child alone and calling it just another life-style choice," people called the radio talk shows to complain about the smirking ridicule that TV reporters displayed when they recounted this story.

Finally, some viewers complained that television misinterpreted the deteriorating relationships among workers, and between clients and their professional helpers. Employees in every occupation recognized that the new government-imposed personnel policies for hiring, compensating, promoting, and firing members of victimized groups created work environments that undermined interpersonal relationships among workers—black and white, male and female, able and disabled—making them suspicious, bitter, and demoralized. At the same time, fear of litigation made many employers and supervisors punctiliously adhere to procedural rules and regulations in order to avoid charges of discrimination. What had become clear to many in their daily lives was that the group rights revolution had actually made matters worse for the victims it was intended to help. The political and legal power now in the hands of heretofore victimized groups had bureaucratized not only the personnel policies of private firms and businesses, but also the service professions that were supposed to aid those groups. Thus, welfare and social workers, health care practitioners, school administrators, the police and government employees, were now ensconced in following elaborate federally imposed procedures and rules of due process to avoid transgressing the group rights of their clients. This bureaucratization of the social services provided more fodder for television news and news magazine shows, who righteously disclosed the impersonal, calloused, unfeeling, mean-spirited bureaucrats psychologically victimizing those who turned to them for help. But the moral rectitude of the television reporters came across to many viewers as moral obtuseness, because those viewers recognized that the deteriorated relationships between those helping professionals and their clients, as well as the deteriorated relationships among employees in the work force, had come about as a result of the rights revolution.

Although there was a considerable increase in complaints from conservatives in the early 1990s about the "liberal outlook" of television news, most of the populace still endorsed a liberal political agenda:

They supported group rights and agreed that the society would be better if there was more tolerance and accommodation of victims. In short, most subscribed to the politics of compassion, exemplified by The Americans with Disabilities Act, The Civil Rights Act of 1991, and The Clean Air Act—all of which were enacted during the presidency of George Bush.

By the time the 1992 election campaign rolled around a new group had surfaced who claimed the government had overlooked them: the middle class. Suffering from a recession that had begun in 1990, as well as experiencing unprecedented job losses from the closing of plants, businesses, and firms because of LBOs, takeovers, and shady dealings on Wall Street, the middle class now demanded more economic security. But President Bush seemed to lack compassion and appeared indifferent to the victimization of this group.

The second debate of the campaign, televised from Richmond, Virginia, bore this out when the president was unable to answer a question posed by a woman in the audience: "How has the national debt personally affected each of your lives?" Bush haltingly replied, "I'm not sure I get—help me with the question and I'll try to answer it." When his turn came, Bill Clinton walked right up to the questioner, looked her in the eye, and told her that he knew people who had lost their jobs in Arkansas when a factory closed, and what we have to do is invest in American jobs, American education, and bring American people together again. While Clinton was speaking the television camera panned to President Bush, who was looking at his watch. It became clear to many viewers that George Bush had no time, or empathy for average Americans. Later, the widely reported story about his surprise and amazement over the electronic scanner the clerk used when he purchased a pair of socks, corroborated the opinion that George Bush was out of the loop, behind the curve, and off the wall.

Bill Clinton, on the other hand, had adroitly zeroed in on the theme of the middle class as victim right from the beginning. His televised speech announcing his candidacy sounded themes he repeated over and over in his campaign: "Middle-class people are spending more hours on the job, spending less time with their children, bringing home a smaller paycheck to pay more for health care and housing and education. Our streets are meaner, our families are broke, our health care is the costliest in the world and we get less for it. The country is headed in the wrong direction fast, slipping behind, losing our way, and all we have out of Washington is status quo paralysis. No vision, no action. Just neglect, selfishness and division."[10]

Clinton and his campaign staff masterfully used television during the primaries. On "Nightline," Mandy Grunwald, Clinton's television advisor, turned back the Gennifer Flowers charges by accusing Ted Koppel of sleazy journalism for introducing this womanizing allegation in lieu of a responsible discussion of journalists' ethics. Later, Hillary and Bill appeared on "Sixty Minutes" where the nation saw them holding hands and being mutually supportive under trying circumstances. This appearance turned attention away from questions of marital infidelity. When Clinton himself appeared on "Nightline" he effectively finessed his so-called draft dodging by explaining that yes, he had opposed the war in Vietnam—like many others. And looking straight into the camera he denied ever receiving any special treatment—adding that officials at his draft board had corroborated this.

The main media strategy of the Clinton campaign was to attack the now unpopular TV reporters. He used this effectively to steal the press conference from Paul Tsongas after Tsongas had won the New Hampshire primary election. Clinton blamed his second place showing on the television reporters' poor coverage of his campaign, but promptly announced that he had actually triumphed over them: "I'm the comeback Kid," he chortled, providing reporters with the sound bite they used to report the results of the New Hampshire primary. Pursuing this anti-reporter strategy Clinton proposed a number of debates with the other candidates to counteract the "bad stuff dropped about me" by the media. "At least the people who watch the debates will hear them," he pointed out. The other strategy he used to prevent reporters from mediating between him and the people, was to appear on television talk shows: "Phil Donahue," "Larry King," "The Today Show," and "Arsenio Hall"— where he wore shades and played the saxophone. He also had a "town meeting" with kids on MTV, where he answered a question about what kind of underwear he wore.

Clinton won the election on the basis of the public's assessment of his character. Once again, the medium of television enabled people to ascertain the character of the candidates, and a plurality of the voters judged him to be the best of the lot. For most voters in 1992 character had nothing to do with marital fidelity, nor with patriotism, nor smoking marijuana. No, for them, character meant compassion, and Clinton came through on the television screen as the most compassionate, the most empathic. The talk show format, by eliminating reporters, enabled him to come forth unmediated. As Larry King noted after the election: "When someone says [on the air] 'I'm out of work, what are you gonna do for me?' it gives a totally different perspective, than Larry King or Dan Rather saying, 'What about the people out of work?' You are now hearing a human being out of work talking to a man who can affect his getting work. You can't beat that."[11] During his election campaign Bill Clinton had articulated his politics of compassion by promising a middle-class tax cut. (George Bush had raised taxes while in office, despite his dramatic, televised, "read my lips" pledge of "no new taxes.") Clinton also vowed to end welfare "as we know it," cut federal spending, reduce the deficit, and slash the federal bureaucracy. But a month after taking office, President Clinton proposed and got a $241 billion tax hike—the largest in the nation's history. His budget proposal (passed by one vote) increased federal spending and projected a federal deficit of $401 billion in the year 2001—about the same as it was in 1992. Although there was a Democratic majority in both houses of Congress, the Clinton administration during its first two years had difficulty getting the legislation it sought: on the matter of gays in the military, on the jobs stimulus package, and most important of all, it failed to get its program on health care. Part of the problem, especially with health care, was the long time it took the administration to prepare the proposed programs. In the matter of welfare reform no proposals at all came from the administration during the first two years.

President Clinton, it was true, was distracted by foreign affairs during this period: Somalia, Russia, Bosnia, Haiti, North Korea. But the administration's performance here was dogged by indecision, vacillation, and flip flops. This was due to both inexperience and ineptitude, which also marked the selection of Cabinet and administration officials. A number of the president's nominations had to be withdrawn because the nominees would never be confirmed: Zoe Baird, Kimba Wood, Lani Guinier, Michael Carns; some of those appointed left office before mid term. Secretary of the Treasury Lloyd Bentsen left voluntarily. Others were asked to leave: Secretary of Defense Lee Aspin; White House Council Bernard Nussbaum; Director of the White House Office of Administration David Watkins; Deputy Treasury Secretary Roger Altman; Associate White House Council William Kennedy; and Press Secretary Dee Dee Myers. One was fired: Surgeon General Joycelyn Elders. Two left because of criminal indictments: Secretary of

Agriculture Mike Espy, and Deputy Attorney General Webb Hubbell. And two were still in the Cabinet in early 1995, but under criminal investigation by independent council: Secretary of Commerce Ron Brown, and Secretary of Housing and Urban Development Henry Cisneros. One committed suicide: White House Council Vincent Foster.

And all the while the specter of Whitewater lurked in the background: the suspicion that President Clinton and his wife, Hillary Rodham Clinton, might have been involved in the shady and mysterious financial dealings that took place years earlier in their home state of Arkansas.

By 1994, many voters had concluded that compassion was not enough. Competence and moral responsibility seemed to be more necessary qualifications for political leadership. And that went for Congress, too, where the members seemed only concerned with special interest groups. This was typified by the black caucus, the women's caucus, the farm caucus, and the high-tech caucus, among many others. In serving these special interest groups Congress had driven the deficit to unheard of heights, and given themselves a $23,200 a year pay raise along the way. When they did legislate, this was often done in a sloppy and irresponsible way. Take the 1991 Highway Bill which the House passed without ever seeing. Staff aides were still writing the bill as House members started to debate at 2 A.M. on 27 November. One copy of the more than one thousand page bill was plunked on the Speaker's table at 5 A.M., where it sat unread until the vote was taken at 6 A.M. Although not a single member had read it, the bill was approved by 372 to 47. This action had been presaged some months earlier when the Public Works and Transportation Committee of the House had voted on the original measure without reading it. After passing the Highway Bill, it being the day before Thanksgiving, Congress adjourned for the remainder of the year.[12]

The last straws for many citizens were the House banking scandal and the House Post Office scam. In the latter, Henry Rostenkowski, Chairman of the House Ways and Means Committee cashed constituent's checks made out to him to purchase stamps and then pocket the change. In the bank scandal 355 members of Congress in a three-year period wrote 20,000 bad checks. Fifty-five major abusers were consistently overdrawn. Although the radio call-in shows had a field day with these scandals, characterizing them as typical examples of congressional arrogance, television treated both of them slightly and lightly. On the "McNeill/Lehrer Report," Representative Vic Fazio announced that criticism of the House Bank was merely an effort by conservatives "to avoid the subjects that we really need to be talking about: the scandal in health care, the prolonged recession, the high rates of unemployment, the things we were elected to do." And on C-SPAN, Representative Donald Pease complained that his office had been flooded with the calls generated by the Rush Limbaugh call-in radio program.

The response of the legislators seemed to miss the point. It is true that no public funds were lost in the check kiting that representatives engaged in, but what the public resented was the fact that members of Congress could write checks without worrying whether they could cover them—something no other citizen can do. The moral resentment of the public was directed at the fact that legislators had set themselves up as a privileged class. They had free, or publicly paid for, travel, mail, and office supplies, as well as free parking at Washington's National Airport in a lot that is not only reserved, but which is closest to the terminal, a lot where most members parked for four days of every week since their work week runs only from Tuesday through Thursday.

By 1994 public anger with Washington went deeper than disgust with the lack of moral responsibility and the incompetence of their political leaders; it now extended to the liberal agenda that a Congress controlled by Democrats had pursued for many years. Ross Perot had done much to galvanize that anger in his presidential campaign in 1992. The first Perot organization had been named "The Coalition to End the Permanent Congress." His theme throughout the campaign was: "It's your country"...and now was the time to take it back from the politicians in Washington. In his first appearance on the Larry King show, Perot declared: "The first thing I'd like for you to do, all of you, is look in the mirror. We're the owners of this country. We don't act like owners. We act like white rabbits that get programmed by messages coming out of Washington. We own this place. The guys in Washington work for us. They are our servants.... The second wish is that everybody in this country would start acting like an owner.... The third thing I'd ask for is the electronic town hall.... With interactive television every other week, say, we could take one major issue, go to the American people, cover it in great detail, have them respond and show by congressional district what the people want. Now don't you think that would kind of clear Congress's heads about whether or not to listen to folks back home or listen to their foreign lobbyists on an issue? Sure it would."[13]

Later, on that same show, Perot began his "top-down" grass-roots movement by asking that people kick in five dollars a person for his campaign so that they would feel they had a stake in the effort to get his name on fifty states' ballots as an independent. Like Clinton, Perot avoided reporters, appearing instead on TV and radio talk shows where he had direct contact with "the owners of the country." In addition, he spent millions of his own money on prime time network half hour and hour"infomercials," where he used color charts and a metal pointer to explain to viewers the major problems facing the American economy.

But television revealed Perot as a kook: quirky, arrogant, and paranoid. In the middle of the campaign he dropped out for four months, losing thereby many of his supporters. In the end, however, he did collect 19 percent of the votes cast—the highest ever for an independent candidate.

Earlier, I pointed out that many conservative voters had called radio talk shows to decry the morality of using taxes to redistribute wealth. Perot introduced another moral issue: saddling future generations—"our children and our grandchildren"—with a mountainous federal debt. Moreover, he reminded taxpayers that much of what they presently paid to the government went to pay interest charges on the existing debt. And that debt, many now realized, was the result of the spending habits of an out of control Congress. Most of that spending, by some accounts, was for entitlements of one type or another: Social Security, Medicare, Medicaid, as well as farm subsidies, veterans compensation, food stamps, welfare, nutrition aid, and on and on. Moreover, entitlement programs kept increasing: Medicare's costs had tripled since 1980, Medicaid had quintupled.

As the 1994 elections approached, public anger against Washington broadened beyond fiscal concerns to encompass many of the issues that conservatives had been raising on the radio call-in shows for a number of years: racism, sexism, family values. By this time there were more than 800 talk or talk/news radio stations across the country, double the number five years earlier, and they had captured 43 percent of the radio audience. Yet, although it was on talk radio that the public voiced its moral outrage against Washington, it was television that had evoked that moral outrage.

Television news' "liberal outlook"—its endorsement of the politics of compassion, without paying heed to the psychological, economic, and social consequences of increased federal actions to help victims—

had stirred up opposition to the politics of compassion. Everyone recognized that federal legislation, executive orders, regulatory agencies,
and court decisions had all reduced racial and sexual discrimination.
But the means used to achieve this worthy goal—affirmative action
and quotas—had created a society that was more racist and sexist: or, if
not more racist and sexist, at least more disposed to uncover and condemn racist and sexist conduct.

Television news reported frightening racial incidents: the alleged
Tawana Brawley kidnapping; the Crown Heights, New York, riots following an automobile accident where a black child was killed and a
Hasidic Jew was stabbed to death. There were also news reports about
racially motivated "hate crimes": on 6 January 1992 a fourteen-year
old black boy and his twelve-year old sister complained that four whites
had roughed them up, stolen their lunch money, and shouted "You'll be
white today," as they smeared white sneaker polish on the young blacks'
faces. A month later the story was discovered to be a hoax, but in the
meantime there were racially motivated beatings, stabbings, and rob-
beries against whites, and one rape—all in retaliation.

Some black leaders exacerbated racial tensions by using the "race
card" to ward off criticism. When Mayor Marion Barry of Washington,
D.C., was caught on videotape smoking crack, he, and other black leaders, accused the FBI of racism. In May 1992 a rap singer, Sister Souljah,
was quoted as saying, "if black people kill black people every day, why
not have a week and kill white people?" A month later, at a Rainbow
Coalition conference, candidate Bill Clinton questioned the wisdom of
inviting Sister Souljah to speak at the conference, prompting Jesse Jackson to declare that Mr. Clinton had thereby "disclosed a character flaw";
he demanded that Clinton apologize to Sister Souljah.

In 1992 the Anti-Defamation League of B'nai B'rith commissioned
a poll that found that 31 percent of whites between eighteen and thirty
years old held views that were very prejudicial against blacks.[14] Racial animosity went both ways: a CBS/*New York Times* poll taken in
October 1990 found that a quarter of all blacks were convinced that
the government was deliberately supplying drugs to blacks in order
to destroy them, and another 35 percent were not sure, but thought
such a plan was possible. Thirty percent of blacks thought either that
AIDS had been deliberately invented by the government to kill blacks,
or that there was at least a chance that this was true. Nearly 80 percent
were either convinced that there was a racist, government campaign

to discredit black elected leaders, or thought it possible that there was such a campaign.[15]

Television during this period reported more and more instances of sexism. In 1993 a widely reported study conducted by the American Association of University Women announced that 81 percent of students said they had been victims of sexual harassment. Television also reported stories about wife battering: in January 1993 a coalition of women's groups held a news conference to announce that Super Bowl Sunday is "the biggest day of the year for violence against women." Just before the Super Bowl game in February, NBC broadcast a public service spot reminding men that domestic violence is a crime. During this period television reported an increase in the incidence of rape: in the spring of 1992, Peter Jennings hosted an ABC special, "Men, Sex, and Rape," where viewers were told that 25 percent of women are the victims of rape. And there were television news stories about sexual discrimination in schools: NBC's "Dateline," in April 1992, did a story about gender bias in a sixth grade classroom.

By 1994 more and more people blamed the loss of family values on welfare. Everyone recognized that as a result of welfare legislation that there was less abject poverty in the nation. But now there were more poor. The chronic complaints on television from ever-increasing numbers of poor people and their advocates about the stingy and mean-spirited government signaled to some viewers that liberal welfare benefits had reduced the need for more and more people to work, and had sapped their desire to do so; welfare had increased dependency and undermined self-reliance. Moreover, as they saw it, Aid to Families with Dependent Children (AFDC) had reduced the risk and stigma of illegitimacy, which wreaked havoc with families and family values. Nightly, viewers watched news stories about the increase in teenage pregnancy, single-parent families, and at-risk children.

So by 1994 the moral landscape of America had changed. Now equal treatment of all—blacks and whites, males and females—seemed more moral than preferential treatment of some. Now, too, it seemed more moral to select people for jobs, and for admission to college, on the basis of merit, rather than by quotas. And now individual responsibility seemed of more moral worth than group rights.

In this changed moral landscape the Republican party saw that it had a vote-catching issue for the upcoming congressional election: curtail big government by cutting back federal spending and federal regulations. Instead of the nanny government, Republicans would encourage individual responsibility and self-reliance.

The problem was that congressional elections are almost always about local, not national issues. Congressmen are reelected because they service their constituents, both in individual matters—like straightening out social benefits, or tracking down VA checks—and in community matters—like securing military contracts. Thus, in the 1992 election, voters, as they had in previous elections since the 1970s, reelected over 90 percent of the congressional incumbents. So, even though polls taken just prior to the 1992 election had revealed that voters hated Congress, the election itself showed that they loved (or at least reelected) their own congressmen, rewarding them for their record of constituent service.

The strategy the Republicans hit upon was the "Contract with America." All the incumbent Republicans in the House of Representatives and all the Republican challengers in the upcoming election signed the "contract," which was a promise to bring ten pieces of legislation to the House floor in the first hundred days of the 104th Congress. The centerpiece of the contract consisted of two proposed constitutional amendments intended to constrain legislators, themselves: one calling for a balanced budget, the other setting term limits for congressmen.[16] Also included in the contract was the Personal Responsibility Act, a bill "to discourage illegitimacy and teenage pregnancy by prohibiting welfare to minor mothers and denying increased AFDC for additional children while on welfare, cut spending for welfare programs, and enact a tough two-years-and-out provision with work requirements to promote individual responsibility." Included, too, was the Family Reenforcement Act, containing "child support enforcement, tax incentives for adoption, strengthening rights of parents in their children's education, stronger child pornography laws, and an elderly dependent care tax credit to reinforce the central role of families in American society."[17] There was also a proposal to eliminate unfunded mandate legislation, and proposals to reform federal regulation, including a strengthening of the Regulatory Flexibility Act.

The political strategy of the "contract" was to make the 1994 congressional elections national, not local; that is, to focus voters' attention on national issues, not constituent service. The strategy was spectacularly successful. In the November 1994 election all the Democratic incumbents running for reelection were defeated, and the Republicans captured both houses of Congress.

As the age of moralistic politics took off on a new tack, it inevitably encountered moral resistance: liberal critics appeared on television to accuse the Republicans of mean-spiritedly cutting the social safety net that had been in place since the 1930s. Few of the critics would buy the conservative's moral justification for their proposed actions: to combat the economic, political, and social ills everyone complained about, personal responsibility and individual self-reliance had to be·revived in the society. The Republicans argued that the so-called safety net had created an environment that had extinguished these moral values. To restore them it was now necessary to reduce people's dependence on the federal government.

The era of populist-driven moralist politics, launched and sustained by television, continues.

Notes

1   Ken Auletta, *Three Blind Mice: How the TV Networks Lost Their Way* (New York: Random House, 1991), 563.
2   Jack W. Germond and Jules Witcover, *Mad as Hell: Revolt at the Ballot Box, 1992* (New York: Warner Books, 1993), 276.
3   Quoted in Michael J. O'Neill, *The Roar of the Crowd* (New York: Random House, 1993), 145.
4   Burton Yale Pines, *Out of Focus: Network Television and the American Economy* (Washington, D.C.: Regnery Publishing Co., 1994).
5   William T. Pizzi, *Insight,* 19 October 1994.
6   Howard Felsher, Op Ed, *New York Times,* 29 September 1994.
7   Anthony Lewis, *New York Times,* 12 December 1994.
8   Richard Bernstein, Dictatorship of Virtue (New York: Alfred A. Knopf, 1994), 128.
9   William J. Bennett, *The Index of Leading Cultural Indicators* (Washington, D.C.: The Heritage Foundation, 1993), 9, 10, 16.
10   Germond and Witcover, *Mad as Hell,* 99.
11   Ibid., 515-16.
12   Eric Felton, *The Ruling Class Inside the Imperial Congress* (Washington, D.C.: The Heritage Foundation, 1993), 5-7.
13   Germond and Witcover, *Mad as Hell,* 219.
14   Bernstein, 189.
15   *New York Times,* 29 October 1990.
16   In March 1995, both amendments failed to muster enough votes in Congress.
17   Ed Gillespie and Bob Schellhas, editors, *Contract with America* (New York: Random House, 1994), 9-10.

Bibliography

Adler, Richard P., ed. *All in the Family: A Critical Appraisal.* New York: Praeger, 1979.

Advisory Commission on Intergovernment Relations. *The Federal Role in the Federal System: The Dynamics of Growth.* Washington, D.C.: U.S. Government Printing Office, 1981.

Allen, Richard L., and Leah Waks. "Social Reality Construction: The Evaluation of the Status and Role of Women and Blacks." Unpublished manuscript.

Arlen, Michael J. *The Camera Age.* New York: Farrar, Straus, Giroux, 1976.

————. *The Living Room War.* New York: Penguin Books, 1982.

———— *The View from Highway 1.* New York: Farrar, Straus, Giroux, 1976.

Arndt, H.W. *The Rise and Fall of Economic Growth.* Melbourne: Longman Cheshire, 1978.

Bach, Julie S., ed. *The Environmental Crisis—Opposing Viewpoints.* St. Paul: Greenhaven Press, 1986.

Baker, Robert, and Sandra Ball, eds. *Violence and the Media.* Washington, D.C.: U.S. Government Printing Office, 1969.

Barber, James David. *The Pulse of Politics: Electing Presidents in the Media Age.* New York: W.W. Norton Co., 1980.

Bardach, Eugene, and Lucian Pugliaresi. "The Environmental Impact Statement vs. the Real World," *Public Interest* 49 (Fall 1977): 22-38.

Barnet, Richard J., and Ronald E. Miller. *Global Reach: The Power of Multinational Corporations.* New York: Simon and Schuster, 1974.

Barnow, Erik. *The Sponsor.* New York: Oxford University Press, 1978.

————. *Tube of Plenty.* New York: Oxford University Press, 1982.

Bateson, Gregory. *Mind and Nature.* New York: Bantam Books, 1980.

————. *Steps to an Ecology of Mind.* New York: Ballantine Books, 1972.

Beckerman, Wilfred. *Two Cheers for the Affluent Society.* New York: St. Martin's Press, 1973.

Berger, Peter L. *The Capitalist Revolution.* New York: Basic Books, 1986.

————. *The Homeless Mind: Modernization and Consciousness.* New York: Random House, 1973.

Black, Christine M., and Thomas Oliphant. *All by Myself.* Chester, Conn.: The Globe Pequot Press, 1989.

Blair, Thomas L. *Retreat to the Ghetto.* New York: Hill and Wang, 1977.

Blauner, Robert. *Racial Oppression in America.* New York: Harper and Row, 1972.

Blume, Keith. *The Presidential Election Show: Campaign 84 and Beyond on the Nightly News.* South Hadley, Mass.: Bergin and Garvey, 1985.

Bollier, David. *Liberty and Justice for Some.* New York: Frederick Ungar Publishing Co., 1982.

Bower, Robert T. *The Changing Television Audience in America.* New York: Columbia University Press, 1985.

Braestrup, Peter. *Big Story: How the American Press and Television Reported and Interpreted the Crisis of Tet 1968 in Vietnam and Washington.* Garden City: Anchor Books, 1978.

Braverman, Harry. *Labor and Monopoly Capital.* New York: Monthly Review Press, 1974.

Broad, William, and Nicholas Wade. *Betrayers of the Truth: Fraud and Deceit in the Halls of Science.* New York: Simon and Schuster, 1982.

Bromley, David, and Anson Shupe, eds. *New Christian Politics.* Macon, Ga.: Mercer University Press, 1984.

Brown, Courtney C. *Beyond the Bottom Line.* New York: Macmillan Publishing Co., 1979.

Brown, Lawrence D. *New Policies, New Politics.* Washington, D.C.: The Brookings Institute, 1983.

Burnham, John C. *How Superstition Won and Science Lost.* New Brunswick, N.J.: Rutgers University Press, 1987.

Burnham, Walter Dean. *The Current Crisis in American Politics*. New York: Oxford University Press, 1982.

Burns, James MacGregor. *John Kennedy: A Political Profile*. New York: Harcourt, Brace and Co., 1959.

Butler, Matilda, and William Paisley. *Women and the Mass Media*. New York: Human Sciences Press, 1980.

Califano, Joseph A., Jr. *The Student Revolution*. New York: W.W. Norton & Co., 1970.

Callahan, Daniel. *The Tyranny of Survival*. New York: Macmillan Publishing Co., 1973.

Carroll, Peter W. *It Seemed Like Nothing Happened: The Tragedy and Promise of America in the 1970s*. New York: Holt, Rinehart and Winston, 1982.

Carson, Clayborne. *In Struggle: SNCC and the Black Awakening of the 1960s*. Cambridge: Harvard University Press, 1981.

Castleman, Henry, and Walter J. Podrazik. *Watching TV*. New York: McGraw Hill, 1982.

Chafe, William H. *The Unfinished Journey: America Since World War II*. New York: Oxford University Press, 1986.

Chavetz, Janet S., and Anthony G. Dworkin. *Female Revolt: Women's Movements in World and Historical Perspective*. Totowa, N.J.: Rowman and Allanheld, 1986.

Chester, Lewis, Godfrey Hodgson, and Bruce Page. *An American Melodrama: The Presidential Campaign of 1968*. New York: Viking Press, 1969.

Ciba Foundation Symposium. *Civilization and Science: In Conflict or Collaboration?* New York: Associated Scientific Publishers, 1972.

Cohen, Bernard L. *Before It's Too Late: A Scientist's Case for Nuclear Energy*. New York: Plenum Press, 1983.

Commoner, Barry. *Science and Survival*. New York: The Viking Press, 1963.

Cornuelle, Richard. *De-Managing America*. New York: Random House, 1975.

Cox, Archibald. *Crisis at Columbia*. New York: Vintage Books, 1968.

Crouse, Timothy. *The Boys on the Bus*. New York: Ballantine Books, 1974.

Davies, J. Clarence, III. *The Politics of Pollution*. New York: Pegasus, 1970.

Davis, Glen, and Gary Helfand. *The Uncertain Balance: Government Regulation in the Political Process*. Wayne, N.J.: Avery Publishing Group, 1985.

Deckard, Barbara S. *The Women's Movement*. New York: Harper & Row, 1983.

Diamond, Edwin, and Stephen Bates. *The Spot: The Rise of Political Advertising on TV*. Cambridge: MIT Press, 1984.

Diamond, Edwin. *The Tin Kazoo*. Cambridge: MIT Press, 1975.

Diggins, John P. *The American Left in the Twentieth Century*. New York: Harcourt Brace Jovanovich, 1973.

Donovan, John B. *Pat Robertson: The Authorized Biography*. New York: Macmillan Publishing Co., 1988.

Drew, Elizabeth. *Portrait of an Election: The 1980 Presidential Campaign*. New York: Simon and Schuster, 1981.

Dubos, Rene. *Reason Awake*. New York: Columbia University Press, 1970.

Dunbar, Leslie, ed. *Minority Report*. New York: Pantheon Books, 1984.

Dunlop, Robert. *The Quiet Revolution*. Radnor, Pa.: Chilton Book Co., 1975.

Ehrenreich, Barbara and John. *Long March: Short Spring: The Student Uprising at Home and Abroad*. New York: Monthly Review Press, 1969.

Elgin, Duane. *Voluntary Simplicity*. New York: William Morrow, 1981.

Ellwood, David T., and Lawrence H. Sumers. "Is Welfare Really the Problem," *The Public Interest* 83 (Spring 1986): 57-78.

Emerson, Gloria. *Winners and Losers*. New York: Harcourt, Brace, Jovanovich, 1978.

Endo, Russel, and William Strawbridge, eds. *Perspectives on Black America*. Englewood Cliffs: Prentice-Hall, 1970.

Epstein, Edward Jay. *News from Nowhere*. New York: Vintage Books, 1974.

Etzioni, Amitai, and Clyde Nunn. "The Public Appreciation of Science in Contemporary America," in Holton and Blanpied, eds., *Science and its Public: The Changing Relationship*, pp. 229-244.

Ewen, Stuart. *Captains of Consciousness*. New York: McGraw-Hill Book Company, 1976.

Fadiman, Clifton, and Jean White. *Ecocide*. Santa Barbara: Center for the Study of Democratic Institutions, 1971.

Fair, Charles. *The New Nonsense*. New York: Simon and Schuster, 1974.

Fairlie, Henry. *The Kennedy Promise*. Garden City: Doubleday, 1973.

Farley, Reynolds. *Blacks and Whites: Narrowing the Gap*. Cambridge: Harvard University Press, 1984.

Farmer, Richard N. *Why Nothing Seems to Work Anymore*. Chicago: Henry Regnery Co., 1977.

Ferman, Louis A., Joyce L. Kornbluh, and Alan Haber, eds. *Poverty in America*. Ann Arbor: The University of Michigan Press, 1965.

Florman, Samuel C. *The Existential Pleasures of Engineering*. New York: St. Martin's Press, 1976.

Foster, Julian, and Durward Long. *Protest: Student Activism in America*. New York: William Morrow, 1970.

Freeman, Jo. *The Politics of Women's Liberation*. New York: David McKay, 1975.

Freudberg, David. *The Corporate Conscience*. New York: American Management Association, 1986.

Friedan, Betty. *The Feminine Mystique*. New York: Dell Publishing Co., 1984.

———. *The Second Stage*. New York: Summit Books, 1981.

Friendly, Fred W. *Due to Circumstances Beyond Our Control*. New York: Vintage Books, 1968.

Galbraith, John K. *The New Industrial State*. New York: Signet Books, 1968.

Garrow, David J. *Bearing the Cross: Martin Luther King, Jr., and the Southern Christian Leadership Conference, 1955-1968*. New York: W. Morrow, 1986.

Gerbner, George, Larry Gross, Michael Morgan, and Nancy Signorielli. "Scientists on the TV Screen," *Society* 18 (May/June 1981): 41-44.

Germond, Jack W., and Jules Witcover. *Blue Smoke and Mirrors: How Reagan Won and Why Carter Lost the Election of 1980*. New York: The Viking Press, 1981.

———. *Wake Us When It's Over: Presidential Politics of 1984*. New York: Macmillan Publishing Co., 1985.

———. *Whose Broad Stripes and Bright Stars? The Trivial Pursuit of the Presidency, 1988*. New York: Warner Books, 1989.

Geschwender, James, ed. *The Black Revolt: The Civil Rights Movement, Ghetto Uprisings, and Separatism*. Englewood Cliffs, N.J.: Prentice-Hall, 1971.

Gilberti, Robert E. *Television and Presidential Politics*. North Quincy, Mass.: The Christopher Publishing House, 1972.

Gitlin, Todd. *Inside Prime Time*. New York: Pantheon Books, 1983.

———. *Sixties: Days of Hope, Days of Rage*. New York: Bantam Books, 1987.

———. *The Whole World is Watching*. Berkeley: University of California Press, 1980.

Goethals, Gregor. *The TV Ritual.* Boston: Beacon Press, 1981.

Gold, Philip. *Advertising Politics and American Culture.* New York: Paragon House, 1987.

Goldman, Peter, and Tom Matthews. *The Quest for the Presidency, 1988.* New York: Simon and Schuster, 1989.

Goldsmith, Maurice. *The Science Critic.* London: Routledge, Kegan Paul. 1986.

Goodell, Rae. *The Visible Scientists.* Boston: Little, Brown & Co., 1977.

Goodfield, June. *Playing God.* New York: Random House, 1977.

Gottron, Martha V., ed. *Regulation: Process and Politics.* Washington, D.C.: Congressional Quarterly Press, 1982.

Graber, Doris A. *Mass Media and American Politics.* Washington, D.C.: Congressional Quarterly Press, 1984.

——. *Media Power in Politics.* Washington, D.C.: Congressional Quarterly Press, 1984.

Graham, Loren R. *Between Science and Values.* New York: Columbia University Press, 1981.

Grant, Gerald, and David Riesman. "An Ecology of Academic Reform," *Daedalus* 104 (Winter 1975): vol. 2: 166-191.

Grayson, Melvin, and Thomas R. Shepard, J. *The Disaster Lobby.* Chicago: Follet Publishing Co., 1973.

Green, James R. *The World of the Worker.* New York: Hill and Wang, 1980.

Greenberg, Bradley S., et al. *Life on Television: Content Analysis of U.S. TV Drama.* Norwood, N.J.: Ablex Publishing Corp., 1980.

Greenfield, Jeff. *The Real Campaign: How the Media Missed the Story of the 1980 Campaign.* New York: Summit Books, 1982.

Greer, Germaine. *The Female Eunuch.* New York: McGraw-Hill, 1970.

Gribbin, John. *In Search of Schrodinger's Cat: Quantum Physics and Reality.* New York: Bantam Books, 1984.

Gross, Ronald, and Paul Osterman, eds. *The New Professionals.* New York: Simon and Schuster, 1972.

Hadden, Jeffrey K., and Anson Shupe. *Televangelism: Power and Politics on God's Frontier.* New York: Henry Holt & Co., 1988.

Hadden, Jeffrey K., and Charles E. Swann. *Prime Time Preachers.* Reading, Mass.: Addison Wesley Publishing Co., 1981.

Halberstam, David. *The Best and the Brightest.* Greenwich, Conn.: Fawcett Publications, 1969.

——. *The Powers that Be.* New York: Alfred A. Knopf, 1979.

Hallin, Daniel C. *The Uncensored War: The Media and Vietnam.* New York: Oxford University Press, 1986.

Hammond, George Montgomery, J. *The Image Decade: Television Documentary: 1965-1975.* New York: Hastings House, 1981.

Harrington, Mona. *The Dream of Deliverance in American Politics.* New York: Alfred A. Knopf, 1986.

Harris, Louis. *The Anguish of Change.* New York: W.W. Norton, 1973.

Harris, Marvin. *America Now.* New York: Simon and Schuster, 1981.

Harris, Stephen E. *The Death of Capital.* New York: Pantheon Books, 1977.

Hayden, Tom. *Reunion: A Memoir.* New York: Random House, 1988.

Heisenberg, Werner. "The Representation of Nature in Contemporary Physics," *Daedalus* 87 (Spring 1958): 95-108.

Henry, William A. III. *Visions of America: How We Saw the 1984 Election.* Boston: The Atlantic Monthly Press, 1985.

Hiebert, Ray Eldin, and Carol Reuss, eds. *Impact of Mass Media.* White Plains, N.Y.: Longman, 1985.

Higgs, Robert. *Crisis and Leviathan.* New York: Oxford University Press, 1987.

Hill, Samuel S., and Dennis E. Owen. *The New Religious Political Right in America.* Nashville: Abingdon Press, 1982.

Hirsch, Fred. *Social Limits to Growth.* Cambridge: Harvard University Press, 1976.

Hodgson, Godfrey. *America in Our Time.* Garden City: Doubleday, 1976.

Hoffman, Abbie. *Revolution for the Hell of It.* New York: Dial Press, 1968.

Hole, Judith, and Ellen Levine. *Rebirth of Feminism.* New York: Quadrangle Books, 1971.

Holton, Gerald, and William Blanpied, eds. *Science and its Public: The Changing Relationship.* Boston: D. Reidel Publishing Co., 1976.

Holton, Gerald. "From the Endless Frontier to the Ideology of Limits." In *Limits to Scientific Inquiry*, edited by Gerald Holton and Robert S. Morison. New York: W.W. Norton Co., 1979.

Horowitz, Helen L. *Campus Life.* New York: Alfred A. Knopf, 1987.

Howard, Jane. *Please Touch.* New York: McGraw Hill Book Co., 1970.

Howitt, Dennis. *Mass Media and Social Problems.* New York: Pergamon Press, 1982.

Huntington, Samuel P. *American Politics: The Promise of Disharmony*. Cambridge: Harvard University Press, 1981.

Ignatieff, Michael. "Is Nothing Sacred?: The Ethics of Television," *Daedalus* 114 (Fall 1985): 57-78.

————. *The Needs of Strangers*. Boston: Viking, 1985.

Illich, Ivan. *DeSchooling Society*. New York: Harper & Row, 1970.

————. *Medical Nemesis*. New York: Penguin Books, 1976.

James, Marlise. *The People's Lawyers*. New York: Holt, Rinehart and Winston, 1973.

Jamieson, Kathleen Hall. *Packaging the President*. New York: Oxford University Press, 1984.

Johnson, Paul. *Modern Times*. New York: Harper and Row, 1983.

Jones, Charles O. *Clean Air*. Pittsburgh: University of Pittsburgh Press, 1975.

Jorstad, Erling. *The Politics of Moralism*. Minneapolis: Augsburg Publishing House, 1981.

Kalisch, Philip A., et al. *Images of Nurses on Television*. New York: Springer Publishing Co., 1983.

Kaplan, Marshall, and Peggy L. Cuciti. *The Great Society and Its Legacy*. Durham, N.C.: Duke University Press, 1986.

Karnow, Stanley. *Vietnam: A History*. New York: Viking Press, 1983.

Katz, Michael, et al., eds. *Earth's Answer*. New York: Harper & Row, 1977.

Kelman, Steven. "Regulation by the Numbers," *The Public Interest* 36 (Summer 1974): 83-102.

————. *Making Public Policy*. New York: Basic Books, 1987.

————. *Push Comes to Shove*. Boston: Houghton Mifflin Co., 1970.

Kerr, Clark, and Jerome M. Rosow, eds. *Work in America*. New York: Van Nostrand Reinhold, 1979.

Kerr, Clark. *The Uses of the University*. New York: Harper & Row, 1963.

Killian, Louis. *The Impossible Revolution: Black Power and the American Dream*. New York: Random House, 1968.

King, Anthony, ed. *The New American Political System*. Washington, D.C.: American Enterprise Institute, 1977.

King, Martin Luther, Jr. *Stride Toward Freedom*. New York: Harper & Row, 1958.

————. *Where Do We Go From Here?* New York: Harper & Row, 1967.

Klapper, Joseph. *The Effects of Mass Communications*. Glencoe, Ill.: The Free Press, 1961.

Klaw, Spencer. *The New Brahmins: Scientific Life in America.* New York: William Morris & Co., 1968.

Kluger, Richard. *Simple Justice: The History of Brown v. Board of Education and Black America's Struggle for Equality.* New York: Alfred A. Knopf, 1976.

Knowles, Louis L., and Kenneth Prewett, eds. *Institutional Racism in America.* Englewood Cliffs, N.J.: Prentice-Hall, 1969.

Krieghbaum, Hillier. *Science and the Mass Media.* New York: New York University Press, 1967.

Lang, Gladys Engel, and Kurt Lang. *Politics and Television Reviewed.* Beverly Hills: Iage Publications, 1984.

Lang, Kurt, and Gladys E. Lang. *Politics and Television.* Chicago: Quadrangle Books, 1968.

Langer, Suzanne K. *Feeling and Form.* New York: Charles Scribner's Sons, 1953.

Lasch, Christopher. *The Culture of Narcissism.* New York: W.W. Norton & Co., 1978.

————. *The Minimal Self.* New York: W.W. Norton & Co., 1984.

Lawless, Edward. *Technology and Social Shock.* New Brunswick, N.J.: Rutgers University Press, 1977.

Lefever, Ernest W., ed. *Will Capitalism Survive?* Washington, D.C.: Ethics and Public Policy Center, 1979.

Lester, Julius. *Look Out Whitey! Black Power's Gon' Get Your Mama!* New York: Grove Press, 1968.

Levine, Mark L., George C. McNamee, and Daniel Greenberg, eds. *The Tales of Hoffman.* New York: Bantam Books, 1970.

Levine, Robert A. *The Poor Ye Need Not Have with You.* Cambridge: The MIT Press, 1970.

Lewy, Guenter. *America in Vietnam.* New York: Oxford University Press, 1978.

Lichter, Robert, Stanley Rothman, and Linda Lichter. *The Media Elite: America's New Power Brokers.* Bethesda, Md.: Adler and Adler, 1986.

Linsky, Martin. *Impact: How the Press Affects Federal Policy Making.* New York: W.W. Norton & Co., 1986.

————. *Television and the Presidential Elections.* Lexington, Mass.: D.C. Heath & Co., 1983.

Lipset, Seymour M. *Rebellion in the University.* Chicago: The University of Chicago Press, 1971.

Lipset, Seymour M., and Sheldon S. Wolin, eds. *The Berkeley Student Revolt.* Garden City, N.Y.: Anchor Books, 1965.

Lipset, Seymour M., and William Schneider. *The Confidence Gap.* New York: The Free Press, 1983.

Lodge, George C. *The New American Ideology.* New York: New York University Press, 1986.

Lomax, Louis. *The Negro Revolt.* New York: Signet Books, 1963.

Lowe, Carl, ed. *Television and American Culture.* New York: The H.W. Wilson Co., 1981.

Lowery, Shearon, and Melvin L. DeFleur. *Milestones in Mass Communications Research.* New York: Longman, 1983.

Lund, Erik, et al. *A History of European Ideas.* Reading, Mass.: Addison Wesley, 1962.

MacLaine, Shirley. *It's All in the Playing.* New York: Bantam Books, 1987.

MacNeil, Robert. *The People Machine: The Influence of Television on American Politics.* New York: Harper and Row, 1968.

Malcolm X. *The Autobiography.* New York: Grove Press, 1966.

Mankiewicz, Frank, and Joel Swerdlow. *Remote Control.* New York: Times Books, 1978.

Mankiewicz, Frank. *U.S. v. Richard M. Nixon: The Final Crisis.* New York: Quadrangle Books, 1975.

Mann, Thomas E., and Norman J. Ornstein, eds. *The New Congress.* Washington, D.C.: American Enterprise Institute for Public Policy Research, 1981.

Mannheim, Karl. *Man and Society in an Age of Reconstruction.* New York: Harcourt Brace and World, 1940.

Mansbridge, Jane. *Why We Lost the ERA.* Chicago: University of Chicago Press, 1986.

Marable, Manning. *Black American Politics.* London: Verso Books, 1985.

Marc, David. *Demographic Vistas: Television in American Culture.* Philadelphia: University of Pennsylvania Press, 1984.

Matusow, Allen J. *The Unraveling of America.* New York: Harper & Row, 1984.

Maurice, Charles, and Charles W. Smithson. *The Doomsday Myth.* Stanford, Ca.: Hoover Institution Press, 1984.

Mayer, Martin. *Madison Avenue, USA.* New York: Harper & Row, 1958.

———. *Making News.* Garden City, N.Y.: Doubleday & Co., Inc. 1987.

Maynard, Joyce. *Looking Back: A Chronicle of Growing Up Old in the Sixties.* Garden City: Doubleday, 1973.

McGinniss, Joe. *The Selling of the President, 1968.* New York: Trident Press, 1969.

McLuhan, Marshal. "Interview," *Playboy* 16 (March 1969): 53-74.

———. *Understanding Media.* New York: Signet Books, 1965.

McRobie, George. *Small Is Possible.* New York: Harper & Row, 1981.

Meadows, Donella H., Dennis H. Meadows, Jorgen Randers, and William W. Behrens III. *The Limits to Growth.* New York: Universe Books, 1972.

Meier, August, and Elliott Rudwick, eds. *Black Protest in the Sixties.* Chicago: Quadrangle Books, 1970.

Messerer, Azary, "Is Television a National or an International Medium?" Unpublished manuscript.

Meyerwitz, Joshua. *No Sense of Place.* New York: Oxford University Press, 1985.

Mickelson, Sig. *The Electric Mirror: Politics in an Age of Television.* New York: Dodd, Mead & Co., 1972.

Milbrath, Lester W. *Environmentalists: Vanguard for a New Society.* Albany: State University of New York Press, 1984.

Miller, James. *Democracy in the Streets.* New York: Simon & Schuster, 1987.

Miller, Michael V., and Susan Gilmore. *Revolution at Berkeley.* New York: Dell Publishing Co., 1965.

Mishan, Ezra J. *The Costs of Economic Growth.* New York: Frederich A. Praeger, 1967.

Morgan, Richard E. *Disabling America.* New York: Basic Books, 1984.

Morris, Charles E. *A Time of Passion: America 1960-1980.* New York: Penguin Books, 1986.

Moynihan, Daniel P., ed. *On Understanding Poverty.* New York: Basic Books, 1968.

Moynihan, Daniel. *Maximum Feasible Misunderstanding.* New York: The Free Press, 1969.

Mumford, Lewis. *The Pentagon of Power.* New York: Harcourt, Brace, Jovanovich, 1970.

Murray, Charles. *Losing Ground.* New York: Basic Books, 1984.

Muse, Benjamin. *The American Negro Revolution.* New York: The Citadel Press, 1970.

National Academy of Engineering. *Hazards: Technology and Fairness.* Washington, D.C.: National Academy Press, 1986.

National Advisory Commission on Civil Disorders. *Report.* New York: Bantam, 1968.

Nelkin, Dorothy. *Selling Science*. New York: W.H. Freeman and Co., 1987.

Nelson, Michael, ed. *The Elections of 1984*. Washington, D.C.: Congressional Quarterly Press, 1985.

Neuhaus, Richard John, and Michael Cromartie, eds. *Piety and Politics: Evnagelicals and Fundamentalists Confront the World*. Washington, D.C.: Ethics and Public Policy Center, 1987.

New Age Catalogue. Compiled by the editors of *Body, Mind, Spirit* magazine. New York: Doubleday, 1988.

Newcomb, Horace, ed. *Television: The Critical View*. 2d ed. New York: Oxford University Press, 1979.

Newcomb, Horace. *TV: The Most Popular Art*. Garden City, N.Y.: Doubleday, 1974.

Nichols, Albert L., and Richard Zeckhauser. "Government Comes to the Workplace: An Assessment of OSHA," *The Public Interest* 49 (Fall 1977): 39-69.

Nielson Report on Television 1989. Northbrook, Illinois: A.C. Nielson Co., 1989.

Nisbet, Robert. *History of the Idea of Progress*. New York: Basic Books, 1980.

Novak, Michael, ed. *The Denigration of Capitalism*. Washington, D.C.: American Enterprise Institute, 1979.

O'Connor, John E., ed. *American History/American Television*. New York: Frederick Ungar, 1983.

O'Neill, William L. *Everyone Was Brave: The Rise and Fall of Feminism in America*. New York: Quadrangle Books, 1969.

O'Toole, James, ed. *Work and the Quality of Life*. Cambridge: MIT Press, 1974.

Oakley, Ann. *Subject Women*. New York: Pantheon Books, 1981.

Oates, Stephen B. *Let the Trumpet Sound: The Life of Martin Luther King, Jr*. New York: Harper & Row, 1982.

Oberland, Paul C., and Herman Estrin, eds. *The New Scientist*. Garden City: Anchor Books, 1962.

Ophuls, William. *Ecology and the Politics of Scarcity*. San Francisco: W.H. Freeman & Co., 1977.

Palmer, John L., and Isabel Sawhill, eds. *The Reagan Record*. Cambridge: Ballinger Publishing Co., 1984.

Patterson, James T. *America's Struggle against Poverty 1900-1980*. Cambridge: Harvard University Press, 1981.

Patterson, Thomas E. *The Mass Media Election*. New York: Praeger, 1980.

Plattner, Marc F. "The Welfare State versus the Redistributive State," *The Public Interest* 55 (Spring 1979): 28-48.

Polsby, Nelson W. *Consequences of Party Reform.* New York: Oxford University Press, 1983.

Popper, Karl R. *Postscript to the Logic of Scientific Discovery,* 3 volumes. Totowa, N.J.: Rowman and Littlefield, 1983.

————. *Objective Knowledge.* Oxford: Oxford University Press, 1972.

Porter, William E. *Assault on the Media: The Nixon Years.* Ann Arbor: The University of Michigan Press, 1976.

Postman, Neil. *Amusing Ourselves to Death.* Boston: Viking Press, 1985.

————. *Teaching as a Conserving Activity.* New York: Delacorte Press, 1979.

Price, Jonathan. *The Best Thing on TV: Commercials.* New York: Viking Press, 1978.

Rabi, I.I. "Faith in Science." In *The Science Reader,* edited by I.S. Gordon and S. Sorkin. New York: Simon and Schuster, 1959.

Ranney, Austin. *Channels of Power: The Impact of Television on American Politics.* New York: Basic Books, 1983.

————. *The American Election of 1984.* Durham, N.C.: Duke University Press, 1985.

Ravitch, Diane. *The Troubled Crusade: American Education, 1945-1980.* New York: Basic Books, 1983.

Reedy, George E. *Twilight of the Presidency.* New York: The World Publishing Co., 1970.

Reich, Charles A. *The Greening of America.* New York: Random House, 1970.

Reich, Robert B. *Tales of a New America.* New York: Times Books, 1987.

————. *The Next American Frontier.* New York: Times Books, 1983.

Ridgeway, James. *The Closed Corporation: American Universities in Crisis.* New York: Ballantine Books, 1969.

Rifkin, Jeremy, and Ted Howard. *The Emerging Order.* New York: G.P. Putnam's Sons, 1979.

Roberts, Joan I. *Beyond Intellectual Sexism.* New York: David McKay, 1976.

Robinson, Michael J. "Television and American Politics: 1956-1976," *The Public Interest* 48 (Summer 1977): 3-39.

Robinson, Michael J. and Margaret A. Sheehan. *Over the Wire and on TV: CBS and UPI in Campaign '80.* New York: Russell Sage Foundation, 1983.

Roseboom, Eugene H., and Alfred E. Eckes, Jr. *A History of Presidential Elections*. New York: Macmillan Publishing Co., 1979.

Rossman, Michael. *On Learning and Social Change*. New York: Vintage Books, 1972.

Roszak, Theodore. *Where the Wasteland Ends*. Garden City: Doubleday, 1972.

Rowen, Hobart. *The Free Enterprisers: Kennedy, Johnson and the Business Establishment*. New York: G.P. Putnam's Sons, 1984.

Rubin, Bernard, ed. *Grading the Media*. Lexington, Mass.: Lexington Books, 1985.

————. *Small Voices and Great Trumpets: Minorities and the Media*. New York: Praeger, 1980.

Rybczynski, Witold. *Taming the Tiger: The Struggle to Control Technology*. New York: Penguin Books, 1985.

Saldich, Anne Rawley. *Electronic Democracy*. New York: Praeger, 1979.

Schaefer, Anne Wilson. *Women's Reality*. Minneapolis: Winston Press, 1981.

Schell, Jonathan. *The Time of Illusion*. New York: Alfred A. Knopf, 1976.

Schram, Martin. *The Great American Video Game: Presidential Politics in the Television Age*. New York: William Morrow & Co., 1987.

Schram, Wilbur, Jack Lyle, and Edwin Parker. *Television in the Lives of Our Children*. Palo Alto, Ca.: Stanford University Press, 1961.

Schumacher, E.F. *Roots of Economic Growth*. Varanasi: Ghandian Institute of Studies, 1962.

Schwarz, John E. *America's Hidden Success*. New York: W.W. Norton, 1983.

Seabury, Paul, ed. *Universities in the Western World*. New York: The Free Press, 1975.

Searle, John. *The Campus War*. New York: World, 1971.

Sevareid, Eric. *Enterprise: The Making of Business in America*. New York: McGraw-Hill Book Company, 1983.

Seymour-Ure, Colin. *The Political Impact of Mass Media*. Beverly Hills: Sage Publications, 1974.

Shadegg, Stephen. *What Happened to Goldwater: The Inside Story of the 1964 Campaign*. New York: Holt Rinehart and Winston, 1965.

Shi, David. *The Simple Life*. New York: Oxford University Press, 1985.

Shin, Terry, ed. *Expository Science: Forms and Functions of Capitalization.* Dordrecht, Holland: D. Reidel Publishing Co., 1985.

Shupe, Anson, and William A. Stacey. *Born Again Politics and the Moral Majority.* New York: The Edwin Mellon Press, 1982.

Silverman, Sondra. *The Black Revolt and Democratic Politics.* Lexington, Mass.: D.C. Heath & Co., 1970.

Skolnick, Jerome H. *The Politics of Protest.* Washington, D.C.: U.S. Government Printing Office, 1969

Snorgrass, J. William, and Gloria T. Woody, comps. *Blacks and Media: A Selected, Annotated Bibliography, 1962-82.* Gainesville: University Press of Florida, 1985.

Spear, Joseph C. *Presidents and the Press.* Cambridge: The MIT Press, 1984.

Spender, Dale. *For the Record: The Making and Unmaking of Feminist Knowledge.* London: The Women's Press, 1985.

Stein, Ben. *The View from Sunset Boulevard.* New York: Basic Books, 1979.

Stein, Herbert. *Presidential Economics.* New York: Simon and Schuster, 1984.

Sundquist, James L., ed. *On Fighting Poverty.* New York: Basic Books, 1969.

Surgeon General's Scientific Advisory Committee on Television and Social Behavior. *Television and Growing Up: The Impact of Televised Violence.* Washington, D.C.: U.S. Government Printing Office, 1972.

Symposium on Civilization and Science: In Conflict or Collaboration? London: Associated Scientific Publishers, 1971.

Talbot, Michael. *Beyond the Quantum.* New York: Macmillan Publishing Co., 1986.

Tannenbaum, Percy H. *The Entertainment Functions of Television.* Hillsdale, N.J.: Lawrence Erlbaum Associates, 1980.

Tedesco, N.S. "Patterns of Prime Time." *Journal of Communication* 24 (Spring 1974): 119-124.

Terkel, Studs. *Working.* New York: Pantheon Books, 1972.

Theberge, Leonard J. *TV Coverage of the Oil Crises.* Washington, D.C.: The Media Institute, 1982.

Thernstrom, Stephen. *A History of the American People.* New York: Harcourt Brace Jovanovich, 1984.

Tolchin, Susan J., and Martin Tolchin. *Dismantling America: The Rush to Deregulate.* Boston: Houghton Mifflin Co., 1983.

Turner, Jonathan H., Royce Singleton, Jr., and David Musick. *Oppression: A Socio-History of Black-White Relations in America.* Chicago: Nelson-Hall, 1984.

Turner, Kathleen J. *London Johnson's Dual War: Vietnam and the Press.* Chicago: The University of Chicago Press, 1985.

Twin Cities Public Television. *Newton's Apple.* Los Angeles: General Communications Company of America, 1983.

U.S. Department of Health, Education and Welfare. *Work in America.* Springfield, Virginia: National Technical Information Service, U.S. Department of Commerce, 1972.

Viorst, Milton. *Fire in the Streets.* New York: Simon and Schuster, 1979.

Wattenberg, Ben J. *The Good News is the Bad News is Wrong.* New York: Simon and Schuster, 1984.

Watzlawick, Paul, et al. *Pragmatics of Human Communication.* New York: W.W. Norton Co., 1967.

Weidenbaum, Murray. *The Future of Business Regulation: Private Action and Public Demand.* New York: Amacom, 1979.

WGBH Boston. "NOVA." Reading, Mass.: Addison-Wesley, 1983.

White, Theodore H. *Breach of Faith: The Fall of Richard Nixon.* New York: Atheneum Press, 1975.

————. *The Making of the President, 1960.* New York: Pocket Books, 1961.

————. *The Making of the President, 1968.* New York: Atheneum Publishers, 1969.

Wilhoit, Francis M. *The Politics of Massive Resistance.* New York: George Braziller, 1973.

Williams, Juan. *Eyes on the Prize: America's Civil Rights Years, 1954-65.* New York: Viking Penguin, Inc., 1987.

Williams, Raymond. *Television.* New York: Schocken Books, 1975.

Williams, William Appleman, et al. *America in Vietnam, A Documentary History.* Garden City: Anchor Books, 1985.

Willie, Charles V. *Caste and Class Controversy.* Bayside, N.Y.: General Hall, Inc., 1979.

Wilson, Kenneth D., ed. *Prospects for Growth.* New York: Praeger, 1977.

Witcover, Jules. *The Resurrection of Richard Nixon.* New York: G.P. Putnam's Sons, 1970.

Wright, Robin. *The Day the Pigs Refused to be Driven to Market.* New York: Random House, 1972.

Yankelovich, Daniel. *New Rules.* New York: Random House, 1981.

————. *The New Morality.* New York: McGraw Hill, 1974.

Yates, Gayle G. *What Women Want.* Cambridge: Harvard University Press, 1975.

Index